The Lawyer's Guide to Internet Research

Kathy Biehl
and
Tara Calishain

The Scarecrow Press, Inc.
Lanham, Maryland, and London
2000

SCARECROW PRESS, INC.

Published in the United States of America
by Scarecrow Press, Inc.
4720 Boston Way, Lanham, Maryland 20706
http://www.scarecrowpress.com

4 Pleydell Gardens, Folkestone
Kent CT20 2DN, England

Copyright © 2000 by Kathy Biehl and Tara Calishain

All rights reserved. No part of this publication may be reproduced, stored in a retrieval system, or transmitted in any form or by any means, electronic, mechanical, photocopying, recording, or otherwise, without the prior permission of the publisher.

British Library Cataloguing in Publication Information Available

Library of Congress Cataloging-in-Publication Data

Biehl, Kathy, 1956–
　　The lawyer's guide to Internet research / Kathy Biehl and Tara
　　　Calishain.
　　　p. cm.
　　Includes bibliographical references and index.
　　ISBN 0-8108-3885-0 (pbk. : alk. paper)
　　1. Legal research—United States—Computer network resources. 2. Legal research—United States—Data processing. 3. Information storage and retrieval systems—Law—United States. 4. Internet (Computer network). I. Calishain, Tara. II. Title.

KF242.A1 L353 2000
025.06'34—dc21

00-041336

™
∞ The paper used in this publication meets the minimum requirements of American National Standard for Information Sciences—Permanence of Paper for Printed Library Materials, ANSI/NISO Z39.48–1992.
Manufactured in the United States of America.

Contents

Introduction	vii
How to Use This Book	viii
Acknowledgments	ix

1	**The Internet: The Law Library of the Future Is Here**	**1**
	What Is the Internet?	1
	What's Available on the Internet?	2
	The Components of an Online Law Library	2
	A Comparison of Library and Online Research	3
	A Comparison of Online Research and Fee-Based Computer Databases	4
	How Easy Is Online Research?	4
	A Few New Concepts	5
	A Word about Privacy	6

2	**Introduction to the Basic Tools**	**9**
	Browser Basics	9
	Mail Reader Basics	13
	Newsreader Basics	14
	Additional Tools	15

3	**Making the Most of Your Browser**	**19**
	Your Browser's Built-In Multimedia	20
	Plug-Ins and Helper Applications	22
	Managing Your Bookmarks	24
	Disk Cache Utilities	27
	Managing Information While Surfing	28

4	**Setting Up Your Online Library**	**29**
	Introduction to Internet Resources & Techniques	29
	Essential Bookmarks for Legal Research	32
	What to Do When an Address Doesn't Work	41
	Should You Use a Commercial Research Database?	42
5	**Locating Caselaw**	**47**
	Quick Reference List	47
	Searching for a Case	80
6	**Locating Statutes & Regulations**	**83**
	Quick Reference List	83
	Searching for a Statute	102
7	**Locating Court Information & Rules**	**105**
	Quick Reference List	105
8	**Locating Government Forms**	**147**
	Quick Reference List	148
9	**Locating Other Federal Resources**	**173**
	Judicial Branch	173
	Legislative Branch	174
	Executive Branch	177
	Agencies & Commissions	178
	General Federal Resources	185
10	**Locating Other State & Local Resources**	**191**
	Reaching Individual States	191
	Comprehensive State Sites	215
	Local Information	217
11	**Researching by Topic**	**219**
	How to Approach Topic Research	220
	Quick Reference List	221
12	**International Law Resources**	**239**
	Comprehensive Resources	239
	Regional Sites	244
13	**Law Libraries Online**	**249**
	A Catalog of Catalogs	249
	Physical Libraries with a Virtual Presence	250

	Virtual Libraries, Academic Style	254
	Virtual Libraries beyond the Ivory Tower	255
14	**Journals, Periodicals, & Legal News**	**257**
	Law Reviews	257
	Professional Journals	259
	Reviews & Journals: Where to Find Them	260
	Periodicals by E-Mail	261
	Legal News	262
15	**Locating Lawyers & Other Helpful People**	**271**
	You Have the Technology	272
	Mailing Lists	272
	Newsgroups	278
	Professional Associations on the Web	280
	Online Directories	281
	Locating & Investigating People Online	287
	Communicating Online	288
16	**General Research Resources**	**293**
	General Search Tools	293
	Reference Tools	296
	News & Information Sources	303

Glossary — 307

Appendix A–Where to Go When the Connection's Slow — 311
- Legal Reference Rooms — 311
- State Jurisdictions — 314
- General Reference Tools — 316
- Fun & Games — 317

Appendix B–Taking Care of Business — 321
- Continuing Legal Education — 321
- Law Office Technology — 323
- Get a Job — 324

Index — 326

About the Authors — 351

Introduction

Legal research has always been synonymous with going to the library. Books contain the cases, statutes, and interpretative materials that are the lifeblood of our profession. Legal reference sources are so numerous—not to mention so expensive—that no one lawyer owns more than a few essentials outright. (Even the books on our own shelves require such costly and constant maintenance that it feels like we're only renting them!) Sooner or later, every researcher heads for a library, whether it belongs to the firm or corporation, a university, the local federal district, or the county. But no matter how extensive the collection is, what you need is never completely within your control. You may have to fit into the library's schedule of operations, and even if you have twenty-four-hour library access, you can't always depend on the materials needed being available. Other people may be using them or, as happens with frustrating frequency, may have moved them to a place that no amount of looking uncovers.

The Internet is changing all this. It's a million times bigger than the largest library you could ever walk into. Just about any piece of information you could ever imagine needing is somewhere online. It no longer matters if someone else wants to use the same resources you do. The extraordinary nature of the Net allows many, many people to access the same information simultaneously, without inconveniencing anyone.

Because the Net's resources are so enormous, you'll make trouble for yourself if you approach them as you would a physical library—or, at least, approach them as I do. When I walk into a library, a hard-headed streak takes reign. I try to figure out the lay of the land without asking for help locating something. I'll follow my memory and instincts first, then look for posted signs. Only when I'm really stumped (or in a hurry) will I seek out a librarian. Follow my stubbornness on the Net and you'll end up overwhelmed. Because the data online expands every single day; little on the Web is the same—or sometimes even in the same place—as it was the last time you looked at it. Fortunately, there are lots of resources that act as clearinghouses of information and help you find your way through the mushrooming information. Luckily for us, this is particularly true in the area of law.

Don't let fear of technology keep you away from this emerging tool. You don't have to be a computer wizard to come online. If you can use a keyboard—even if your typing style is hunt and peck—and use a mouse, you can get around the Net. Really. You don't have to take a class or hire a consultant to teach you. This book will arm you with all the techniques you need to move your research online.

That's right: *move* your research online. Just about anything you do in a physical library you can accomplish online. The names of the sources will be different. Instead of statute books, reporters, and periodicals, you'll use Web pages, newsgroups, and mailing lists, while search engines, indexes, and links will take the place of digests, headnotes, and Key Numbers.

That's what this book will teach you: how to make the transition to the law library of the future. In this volume, I'll take each aspect of legal research and show how and where to accomplish it online. You won't have to alter the way you approach a research problem; you'll just change where you look for the answers.

This book will ease the transition for you. It zeroes in on the best sites, sources, and techniques for finding cases, statutes, regulations, legislative history, government forms, public records, other attorneys, experts, and anything else that normally comes up in the course of legal work. It identifies the government offices and agencies that accept online communication—not to mention filings—and catalogs comprehensive research sites, legal news sources, and general reference aids. You'll learn how to set up an online law library, master search engines and other Internet research tools, and get a painless crash course in using e-mail and newsgroups. You'll even get tips and shortcuts for maximizing use of your browser, whether it's Internet Explorer or Netscape Communicator.

How to Use This Book

I wrote this book from the standpoint of a practicing attorney, but it is equally suited for librarians, law students, paralegals, and anyone familiar with traditional legal research techniques. The book is structured for use as a desktop reference guide. Reading it from cover to cover (or at least, reading the explanatory sections in each chapter) will give you a well-grounded understanding of online legal research. My expectation, however, is that you will want a quick, specific answer when you open the book, so I have set it up with the goal of giving the solution to any research task at a glance.

If you are looking for a particular type of resource (an opinion, court rules, a government phone number, for example), flip to the appropriate chapter and scan the "Quick Reference List." This list, which appears in almost every chapter, arranges relevant Web sites by jurisdiction or topic.

For a quick overview of the Internet, read chapter 1, "The Internet: The Law Library of the Future Is Here"; for an overview of the programs you'll use and how they fit into legal research, head for chapters 2 and 3, "Introduction to the Basic Tools" and "Making the Most of Your Browser." For recommendations of good starting points for surfing, refer to chapter 4, "Setting Up Your Online Library." For tips on using search engines or tracking down a page with a bad address, look at the same chapter.

Acknowledgments

The following individuals and entities gave permission for publication of screen shots of their Web pages: Ch. 4, FindLaw, Inc., Hieros Gamos, Georgia State University College of Law, the Information Center of the Chicago-Kent College of Law of the Illinois Institute of Technology; Ch. 5, U.S. Court of Appeals for the Fifth Circuit, James Gottstein and the Alaska Legal Resource Center, Rutgers University School of Law-Camden, Fifth Court of Appeals, State of Texas; Ch. 6, the Libraries of the University of California, American Legal Sources Online, the Virginia General Assembly; Ch. 7, U.S. Court of Appeals for the District of Columbia Circuit (the consent of which should not be construed as endorsement of the book), U.S. District Court for the Eastern District of Missouri, U.S. Bankruptcy Court for the Eastern District of California, Wisconsin Court System; Ch. 8, Internal Revenue Service, the Federation of Tax Administrators, 'Lectric Law Library, Minnesota Secretary of State; Ch. 10, States of Alabama, Connecticut, Nebraska, Ohio, and Oregon, State of New Mexico General Services Department; Ch. 11, American Bankruptcy Institute, Stanford University Libraries, IBM Intellectual Property Network, Mark J. Astarita, Robert L. Sommers; Ch. 12, Hieros Gamos, Australasian Legal Institute, University of Texas Latin American Information Center, Delia Venables; Ch. 13, Hugh F. MacMillan Law Library of Emory University, Edward Bennett Williams Library of Georgetown University, Cornell Law School Legal Information Institute; Ch. 14, Richmond Journal of Law & Technology, National Law Journal, Lawyers Weekly, Inc., Boston, Mass.; Ch. 15, LawGuru.com, LegalEthics.com, 555-1212.com; Ch. 16, Yahoo!, Oingo, and RefDesk. All other images used are in the public domain.

This book would not have existed without the tenacity, faith, and determination of Tara Calishain. Her encyclopedic understanding of Internet resources and research techniques provided the foundation for this book, and I am grateful for her expertise.

I would also like to thank Shirley Lambert, Katie Regen, Kellie Hagan, and Christine Ambrose of Scarecrow Press, for their unflagging assistance and guidance in the development of this book.

In my own early days on the Web, Ben Hadad provided technical hand-holding and troubleshooting beyond the call of friendship. I appreciate the law-related

URLs that he and Tara forwarded to my e-mail box over the past three years. Art Snyder, Sharon Duckman, the *Texas Bar Journal*, and the "Circuits" section of the *New York Times* were other valuable sources of leads to resources.

My friends and family were generous with encouragement and assistance in all aspects of the completion of the manuscript. I am grateful to Edward R. Biehl, Julianne Biehl, and Carol Curro in particular for their support. And special thanks are in order to Frank M. Bland, who was there every step of the way.

Kathy Biehl
kbiehl@fortunaworks.com

1
The Internet: The Law Library of the Future Is Here

These days, you can't open a law journal or walk in to a seminar without being told how integral the Internet is to the future of the legal profession. There's only one problem with that message. The Internet's not a thing of the future. It's a tool of the present.

Only a few years ago it stretched the imagination to think of doing legal research without cracking a book—yet that's exactly what countless people do every day, all over the country and in many parts of the globe. They do it by turning on their computer and connecting to the Internet, which lets them tap in to resources they could find in a physical library, and a lot more to boot.

What Is the Internet?

The Internet is a complex network of networks, in which groups of computers are linked by telephone lines to other groups of computers all over the world. Even though it's come into the public eye only in the past few years, the Internet is not a new phenomenon at all. Its roots actually go back more than twenty-five years. It grew out of a U.S. Department of Defense research project that was initiated in the 1960s. Since then, academic, government, and research institutions developed ways of communicating by computer that gradually took the form we recognize as the Net.

When you dial in to the Internet, your modem connects your computer to your access provider's system, which in turn acts as a hub for contacting other computers. There are several forms that the contact can take; they depend on the nature of the information you're trying to access and the type of program you use to do it. We'll look at the most common types in chapter 2, "Introduction to the Basic Tools."

What's Available on the Internet?

Just about anything is available on the Net. You can find cases, statutes, and all the other primary legal sources you would look for in a library. You can read legislative history, comment on proposed regulations, and check the calendars of courts, legislatures, and agencies. You can get patent and trademark applications straight off the Web, along with a score of other forms promulgated by government agencies. To some extent you can look into public filings and flip through law review articles. You can glean all sorts of information about federal and state courts, legislatures, and governments—and a lesser amount about their counterparts in other countries. You can cull through university law libraries, pore over online directories of attorneys and experts, and ask colleagues for advice. You can catch the latest news, look words up in English and foreign language dictionaries... and even Shepardize citations.

There's plenty outside the legal arena, too. If a topic exists in the human psyche, odds are somebody, somewhere has built a page around it—toys, recipes, authors, musical stars, sitcoms, cartoons, movies, sports, sci-fi series, health resources, astrology, privacy issues, minority rights, kid shows from the 1950s, junk food, you name it. (Yes, there's pornography, too, but it's a drop in the ocean compared to the vastness of the rest of what's out on the Web. And it won't jump up and bite you, even if you stumble across some; it's not going to land in your e-mail box—though, alas, offers of it probably will.) You can play games, solve puzzles, consult oracles, send postcards and virtual flowers....

Are your eyes glazing over yet? I wasn't exaggerating: Just about everything is available on the Internet.

The Components of an Online Law Library

Using your own computer and the vast resources of the Net, you can re-create a law library online containing the following components:

- Federal and state court opinions
- Federal and state statutes, codes, and regulations, including the Code of Federal Regulations
- Legislative history
- Forms promulgated by federal agencies, Secretaries of State, and other government agencies
- Transactional document forms
- Topic-specific treatises
- Directories of attorneys and support service providers
- Nationwide phone and e-mail address books
- Dictionaries, thesauruses, and general reference books

Outside of the virtual stacks, the Net will help you expand your library with two additional rooms: a mailbox, for receiving correspondence and newsletters, and a reading room for periodicals, newspapers, and even broadcasts.

A Comparison of Library and Online Research

The building blocks really are the same. The rest of the Web may resemble a free-for-all, but the legal resources tend to be well organized. They have, for the most part, been structured by people who understand what's involved in legal research. How you go about using them, however, is a little different. Let's look at the methods one by one.

The Basics of Library Research

When you're researching an issue in the law library, what sorts of actions do you take? Here are my most common:

- Looking in an index for a specific statute or regulation
- Using key words to locate pertinent cases or statutes
- Checking the subsequent history of a case or a statute (otherwise known as Shepardizing and looking in the pocket parts)
- Using citations or headnotes to find subsequent law on point
- Taking notes or making photocopies

Let's see how they stack up against what you can do online.

The Basics of Online Research

Here are some of the steps involved in doing research online:

- Looking in an index for a specific statute or regulation
- Using key words to locate pertinent cases, statutes, other primary materials, or just about any resource whatsoever
- Checking the subsequent history of a case (Shepardizing)
- Using citations to a statute or case to find subsequent decisions on point
- Printing or saving copies of documents to disk

The parameters are remarkably similar. The basic difference is that online research doesn't use headnotes or pocket parts. (Yet.) On the other hand, it does employ the keyword search technique much more extensively than library research does.

A Comparison of Online Research and Fee-Based Computer Databases

Doing research online is also much like using computer databases such as LEXIS and Westlaw. Or rather, one aspect of it is. Keywords are the overlap. Both techniques require constructing queries out of words and phrases, which are compared against documents in the targeted database to pull up matches. To do this, both use Boolean logic, which employs symbols to connect, exclude, or define the proximity of keywords, or to expand them into wildcards. (We'll discuss Boolean logic in more depth in chapter 4 "Setting Up Your Online Library.") If you're familiar with either LEXIS or Westlaw, you already know that query writing often requires several tries, refining and restating a string of words to winnow out the irrelevant stuff that invariably comes up. The same is true with online keyword searches.

There are a few significant differences, though. In the two major computer research services, databases are set up according to jurisdictions, and sometimes you have to jump from one to the next depending on the courts you're interested in. With online research, you have a variety of choices of starting points, some of which permit searches across a wider spectrum of jurisdictions and types of materials. But the big difference is financial. Westlaw and LEXIS assess usage or subscription charges, while in most cases—unless you choose to use a specialized, fee-based service—online research involves just the cost of your Internet hook-up.

How Easy Is Online Research?

Let's break down research into tasks and arrange them in a hierarchy of difficulty. Most of the tasks—in fact, almost all—are easy. Here's a short list of them:

- Locating a statute, regulation, or case when you know the name and/or the jurisdiction
- Checking whether cases have been appealed or overturned
- Checking citations to cases
- Obtaining a copy of a government form
- Seeking advice from and swapping ideas with other professionals
- Locating hot spots of legal information on the Web
- Subscribing to online periodicals and information sources

In the next level of difficulty are locating statutes, cases, or regulations by keyword, and locating articles by topic. Both of these are slightly more complicated than the basic tasks listed above. We'll pay attention to keyword and topic researching in chapter 5, "Locating Caselaw," chapter 6, "Locating Statutes &Regulations," and chapter 11, "Researching by Topic."

Then there's the catch-all category of "it depends." For some resources, the question isn't the difficulty of finding them, but whether they exist online in the first place. Locating specific books and articles falls into this category. Whether you can find specific printed matter depends on whether it has been uploaded onto the Net yet. (Although many periodicals are on the Internet, many aren't, and even some that are provide only abstracts, not full texts, of articles. We'll explore this further in chapter 14, "Journals, Periodicals, & Legal News.")

A few things are simply not possible—yet. The biggest of them is searching case digests or annotations to statutes. Stay tuned, though. Change comes to the Internet with a rapidity that would make us all dizzy in real life. The fact that you can't do something now doesn't mean you won't be able to in six months or a year.

A Few New Concepts

Every area of life has its buzzwords, and the Internet is no exception. In fact, it's one of the more colorful examples of the phenomenon. Before you dive into online research, familiarity with a few new concepts is in order.

Surfing is spending time on the Web. Some people use the term to refer to looking at anything on the Net, but it makes most sense (as if any of these terms really do!) if you think of it as moving from one Web page to another.

Downloading refers to taking information off the Net (not just the Web) through your computer, by saving a file to disk or printing it.

Uploading or *posting* is doing the reverse: moving a copy of a file from your computer onto the Net.

A *virus* is a bug that sneaks onto your system and causes something to happen that you don't intend, usually by corrupting a program or data. You can't infect your system merely by looking at an e-mail message, newsgroup post, or, in most circumstances, a Web page. (Looking at graphics and HTML-coded text is perfectly harmless. We'll touch on this more in the browser security discussion in chapter 3, "Making the Most of Your Browser.") A virus can enter your system only by means of a program or macro, and not just a file. And you won't contract a virus merely by downloading a program from the Net, either. For a virus to wreak havoc on your computer, you have to actually run the tainted program, which can just as easily come from an infected disk as from the Net.

There are three main ways to minimize the risk of contracting a virus. First, be selective about the types of sites from which you download programs. If a major institution—an academic library, a government entity, or a software company—is behind a site, it's going to be more trustworthy than a personal home page put up by someone about whom you know nothing. In other words, risk is minimal with the major legal resources online.

Second, do not open any e-mail attachment unless you know what it is, know the sender, and are certain that person intended to send the attachment to you. The newer generation of viruses use e-mail attachments as their means of gaining entry to systems. Finally, buy a program that scans for viruses—and use it. This includes regularly updating the program by downloading the latest virus recognition files from the manufacturer's Web site. (Chapter 3 recommends a few popular applications.)

For a complete picture of the jargon we'll be using throughout this book, turn to the Glossary at the back.

A Word about Privacy

A serious analysis of the privacy issues raised by Internet technology warrants a volume in itself. My point in raising them is to discourage you from assuming that anything you do or say online is private. It isn't, necessarily. I am not referring to somebody breaking into the data on your computer. That's a different concern, which can be safeguarded against by requiring passwords and other security measures. What I want to alert you to involves information that has left your computer and gone out on to the Net.

Some of this information you send intentionally, through e-mail, newsgroup posts, and comment forms on Web pages. You have no guarantee that any message will be read only by the designated recipient. Any of these transmissions can be intercepted by a hacker with sufficient dedication. Even if a message arrives undisturbed (which I'd venture to say most do), the recipient might send it on to all sorts of people you never expected to see it; because the process is fast as lightning, people forward e-mail much more frequently than anyone would ever bother with paper correspondence. Your message could also end up in unintended hands if any other person has access to the recipient's e-mail.

Client Confidentiality & E-Mail

The potential implications for the attorney-client privilege should be obvious. It's a topic every practice should examine. For an exhaustive analysis (and a calming viewpoint) that may assist the process, see David Hricik's article "Lawyers Worry Too Much About Transmitting Client Confidences by Internet E-Mail," 11 *Georgetown J. Leg. Ethics* 459 (Nov. 3, 1999).

One solution is not putting anything confidential in an electronic transmission. (In other words, limit e-mail to matters that you could ethically discuss in front of a third party.) Personally, I treat e-mail as I do leaving messages on an answering machine: Unless I know that only my client has access to the e-mail address to which I'm sending a message, I do not mention anything confidential.

Encrypting client e-mail is another option. Encryption requires generating two keys, one public and one private. You trade public keys with the people with whom you wanted to exchange encrypted correspondence. When you want to send a message, you use the recipient's public key to encrypt it. When someone sends you a message encrypted with your public key, you use your private key to decipher it. Netscape and Internet Explorer's security features will generate keys, as well as a digital signature (a means of identification that is associated only with the specific computer on which it is issued). You can also use a software program called PGP, for Pretty Good Privacy. It's available from **http://www.pgp.com/** for Windows, Macintosh, and Linux platforms.

A more practical and realistic alternative is to discuss concerns about confidential communication with your clients thoroughly, reference the discussion in your fee agreement or engagement letter, and have them give specific consent to your contacting them by e-mail.

The Invasion of Your E-Mailbox

One more warning about posting to newsgroups: It will expose you to a torrent of unsolicited commercial e-mail. E-mail addresses are picked up in bulk from Usenet and other public forum postings and sold for mass e-mailings. Some people thwart the onslaught by altering the "reply-to" address that their newsreader automatically includes when sending messages. I've seen this done by sticking an extra word in the address (for example, adding "dont" to "panix.com"), or by replacing the @ sign with "[AT]." When an address like that gets picked up, the solicitation will be misdirected from your mailbox and bounced back to the sender. If you take this route, be sure to put something in the message explaining what has to be changed for legitimate correspondents to reach you.

You may also want to instruct your mail reader to filter out the inevitable solicitations; we'll talk about how to do that in chapter 15, "Locating Lawyers & Other Helpful People."

What Your Surfing Says About You

The information you send out on to the Net doesn't just come from your keyboard. When you surf, you leave virtual tracks that reveal a lot more than fingerprints. They say what kind of computer and browser you have, what access provider computer you're coming through, what page you just visited, and even what city you're in. The name for this information is a cookie. When a page asks you whether you want a cookie, it's not offering you a sweet treat, but a statement of the identifying details it has picked up about you. When your browser accepts a cookie, it is stored on your hard drive, where the originating site may read and update it on later visits.

Not all cookies are objectionable. You might want to accept them from sites you frequent that require a user name and password, for example. The problem arises when cookies end up on your system without your conscious awareness.

There are several options for maintaining privacy. You can set your browser to reject all cookies automatically or to notify you before accepting any. It's also possible (not to mention advisable) to find and delete existing cookies that are on your machine. For details on how to perform all these tasks, visit **http://www.cookiecentral.com/faq**.

As a further safeguard, install an application that blocks banner ads and cookies that they might surreptitiously plant on your system, such as Guard Dog, **http://www.mcafee.com**, Norton Internet Security, **http://www.symantec.com**, or WebWasher, **http://www7.trans-it.net/**. If nothing else, eliminating the ads will make pages load more quickly in your browser.

For the greatest privacy, begin your surfing at a site that cloaks your identity. Anonymizer.com, **http://www.anonymizer.com/**, will do this for free, if you're willing to endure a delay at each succeeding page you visit. The Anonymizer also offers a faster-loading service by subscription, as well as a number of other services to clean up your tracks. Take the Who Are You? link to see eye-opening samples of what the site can pick up about you.

Online research tasks require specific, easy-to-use software tools that retrieve, display, and exchange information. The next chapter will introduce the basic applications, as well as a few less common ones that still surface occasionally. To jump directly into legal research starting points, turn to chapter 4, "Setting Up Your Online Library," or to the chapter that addresses your specific research need.

2
Introduction to the Basic Tools

Most activity on the Internet falls into three major categories: visiting Web pages, exchanging e-mail, and reading or participating in newsgroups. A variety of programs exist for each of these, although it's possible to do all three with both Netscape Navigator and Internet Explorer. We'll take a general look at tools for these activities one at a time, then discuss a few less common tools that you will eventually encounter.

Browser Basics

A *browser* is a program that displays documents from the World Wide Web. These documents go by various names, like home pages, Web pages, and Websites, and they all mean the same thing. Instead of turning the leaves of a book, you use the browser to go from one Web page to another. (That's why it's called a browser.) In simplest form, the browser takes a request for a page, finds the underlying files, and interprets the code in them to arrange text and graphics on your screen.

Decoding Hypertext

Without the browser's interpretation, the underlying files would contain just a sequence of text interspersed with pointed brackets containing commands, which are also known as source code. This code is called *Hypertext Mark-up Language*, or *HTML*. It tells the browser what the page is supposed to look like—where to center or italicize text and place paragraph and line breaks, for example, what font sizes to use, and what graphic files go where. (You can see this source code for any Web page by using the View from the menu bar of either Netscape or Internet Explorer.) It also embeds instructions that can be activated to tell the browser to go to a different page. These commands cause designated text to be displayed in a different color. When you click on this text, the targeted page is retrieved. You'll see the term "link" used to refer to both the connected pages and the differently colored text.

Navigating the Web

The browser's process begins with a *Uniform Resource Locator*, or *URL*, which you can think of as a Web page's address. This sequence of letters tells the browser where the file is located on the Internet. If the file is a Web page, the URL will begin with "http," which stands for hypertext transfer protocol. (For now, don't worry about the other possible types of files. We'll get to them later in this chapter.)

Let's take apart an imaginary URL and decipher the components:

http://www.legalresearch.com/~federal/cases.html

The first four letters tell the browser that this is a hypertext file. The abbreviations between the double slashes and the first single slash give the domain name, which you can think of as the Web equivalent of a street address. The domain name indicates what server (or computer) to contact to find the requested files. Everything after the domain name gives increasing specificity as to the location. The letters between the single slashes indicate the directory, within the domain, where the file is stored. The letters after the final slash give the file name. In plain English, our imaginary URL instructs the browser to get the hypertext file called "cases.html" from the federal directory in the domain "www.legalresearch.com."

There are several ways to give your browser the URL you want to view. Type the URL in the box labeled Location (or Address) on the icon bar. Selecting File from the menu bar and pressing Open Page will bring up another location box, which you can also get to by typing CTRL+O. These methods work for both Netscape and Internet Explorer.

Three other methods send a browser to a page without your entering the URL:

- Clicking on a link in a Web page.
- Using the Back and Forward icons on the browser button bar. When you move from one Web page to another, your browser retains the URLs, in the sequence of your visits. The Back button takes you to the pages you viewed before the one that's on the screen; Forward goes to the ones you viewed later. If one of the buttons is not lit, you've hit the end of the line in that direction.
- Selecting a bookmark.

Bookmarking without Paper

A browser will save a URL, so you can go back to a page any number of research sessions later. For a change, Web lingo has adopted a familiar term for this that means about what it does in the three-dimensional world. When you're reading printed material and you want to save your place, you put in a bookmark. Bookmarking is easy; you can do it in two motions, and you don't even have to memorize the sequence. When you find a Web page you want to remember, you tell the browser to make the URL into a bookmark.

> *In Netscape, click the Bookmark icon on the button bar and select Add Bookmark from the menu. In Internet Explorer, look for Favorites instead of Bookmarks; otherwise, the method is the same. Or you can just hit CTRL+D. Your browser will add the URL of the current page to the end of your bookmark list.*

It doesn't take many bookmarks for the list to become unwieldy. Some people don't find them worth the bother. My co-author Tara discourages bookmarking a page if you can reach it within four keystrokes. I, on the other hand, like them; they fit in with my approach. (I'm used to digging through stacks of paper on my desk to find things, a situation that no other attorney on this planet has ever encountered, I'm sure.) There's no question but that they're a matter of taste. This book will show you how to use them to set up your online library, and I recommend that you try out bookmarks first, before jettisoning the concept. Software programs do exist to help you manage them, as we'll discuss in chapter 3, "Making the Most of Your Browser." Still, a browser can go a long way by itself to maximize their usefulness.

Organizing Bookmarks

I group my bookmarks under broad category headings, such as Humor, Film, Music, and, of course, Law. When the number of bookmarks under a heading start getting out of hand—as they will quickly with Law—I'll rearrange the entries under subheadings. Mine are idiosyncratic; the Law ones include Forms, Judicial, Periodicals, Statutes, Schools, and Topic. I haven't worried about grammatical parallelism or following library categories or even having them make sense to anyone else but me. You shouldn't, either; use whatever names create a quick association in your mind. The point is being able to find things quickly.

To create subheadings, take the same steps that you use to create a heading. Rearrange the bookmarks' order by dragging them to the appropriate subheadings. If a subheading becomes too large, you can use the same method to split it into even narrower subheadings. I did this when the Library subheading in my Law folder grew to more than ten entries; my solution was to set up a Schools subdivision to segregate the academic law libraries.

> To organize your bookmarks in Netscape, go to the Bookmark menu and select Edit Bookmarks. Under File take the option titled New Folder, which brings up a Bookmark Properties window where you type in the name you want to use for the heading. (In Explorer, do the same thing by editing Favorites.) When you exit the window, a folder by that name will be in the bookmark list. To move bookmarks into that folder, click on a name, drag it to the folder, and release the mouse. When you're finished, close the folder by clicking on the minus sign to the left of it. This will turn the icon into a plus sign. To see what's in a closed folder, click on the plus sign. The symbols are self-evident: plus means closed; minus means open.

Taking the time to organize bookmarks, as you enter them, will save you lots of time and aggravation in the long run. But to be honest, I'm not very good at practicing what I preach. Invariably I'll bookmark a cluster of pages with every intention of getting around to filing them, soon. When I finally tire of scrolling through screen after screen of page names, some of which can be pretty cryptic, I'll find the time to move all the stuff at the bottom of the list into the proper folders.

After Browsing, Then What?

You can do more with a Web page than read it and use it as a springboard to other sites. To save it on your hard drive (or on a diskette, if you prefer), choose the File option from the browser menu, then click Save As. In the window that pops up enter the file name and indicate in which directory you want it to be saved. Keep in mind that Web pages will be saved with HTML codes intact. If you try to read a saved file in a word processing program or the Notepad, you will end up wading through a mass of brackets and commands. To get around the code, try one of two techniques:

- Use the browser to read the saved file, which will appear as if it were being read from the Web. (Open the file by selecting Open Page from the File menu and typing in the directory and name.)
- Or forget about saving the page in the first place—mail it to yourself as a document, which will arrive in your e-mail box free of codes. Choose Send Page from the File menu; then press the Attach icon on the button bar and, from the resulting menu, pick Web page. (In Internet Explorer, select File, then Send, then Page By Email.) A window will pop up containing the current

page's URL, which you may change. Enter your address on the mail form and send it.

To print the page, press the Print icon, or click File on the menu bar and select Print from the pull-down menu. If you've loaded a page that uses frames, be sure to place the cursor in the frame you wish to print. (Some pages—mostly state and federal agencies—require a special form reader for printing. These pages will always let you know when one is needed—and they'll offer you the option of downloading the reader on the spot.) And if you want to download a program from a site, the page will contain a highlighted download link that you can click to set the process in motion.

Mail Reader Basics

A *mail reader* is a program that lets you send and receive messages electronically. The messages are called e-mail, and they're stored and displayed in, no surprise here, mailboxes. A reader starts out with at least three basic mailboxes or folders: in, out, and trash (to which you transfer messages to be deleted). Most readers, like Eudora Pro and Netscape Messenger, will also let you create any number of additional ones. (Mine, for example, has four for different types of correspondence related to this book.)

There's one more concept you should know about that a mail reader takes from paper-based correspondence: a *signature* or *sig*. This is a saved file that the mail reader automatically puts at the end of your messages. It contains whatever you type into it. It's common for a sig to display the sender's name, e-mail address, and Web page URL. Some people include their work affiliation, street address, and phone number. It's common to add a personal touch by including a favorite quote. (If you do this, change it periodically or frequent readers are going to ignore your sig altogether.) You can always disable the function—or change the contents—if a sig is inappropriate for a particular message.

How Mail Fits Into Research

To appreciate e-mail's usefulness in research, you have stop thinking of it as just an electronic version of the U.S. mail (a.k.a snail mail). You can use e-mail, of course, for communicating with colleagues and clients. It's also a vehicle for receiving newsletters and magazines in electronic form. You subscribe to these just as you would a print periodical (except that electronic newsletters rarely charge a fee), and they're automatically sent to your in box until you say you don't want them anymore.

Because of the immediacy of the Net, though, an information exchange is possible with e-mail that you'd never dream of with paper-based correspondence. This exchange takes place by means of mailing lists, which allow subscribers to communicate with each other by sending a message to one central address, from which it is disseminated to the entire list. Mailing lists exist on a zillion topics, many of which relate to law or legal research. After you subscribe, you can send out a cry for help on any topic related to the list and, if it's active or well populated, receive answers back within minutes.

Chapter 15, "Locating Lawyers & Other Helpful People," will explore the possibilities and workings of e-mail, electronic newsletters, and mailing lists.

Newsreader Basics

Here Internet terminology starts to remove words from their meanings in the three-dimensional world. A *newsreader* has nothing to do with newspapers or what we normally think of as news. It is a program for displaying information that has been posted in online discussion forums called *newsgroups*. Tens of thousands of these groups exist on every conceivable topic (including some that strain credulity). Participants use them to trade information, gossip, and opinions, and there's also a sizable contingent that just plain rants and raves at everything and anything. In chapter 15, "Locating Lawyers & Other Helpful People," we'll talk about tracking down newsgroups on law-related topics. For now, however, we'll focus on form rather than content.

> *If a newsreader did not come with your Internet service provider's set-up package, there are cheap, easy options for getting a program. Netscape and Internet Explorer include newsreader applications. Freeware (no-charge) programs are also available, such as Free Agent (for PC), http://www.forteinc.com/agent/, or Yet Another NewsWatcher (for Mac), http://www.macupdate.com/info/36052.html.*

Let's go over the basic concepts. *Subscribing* is the term for selecting the groups you want your newsreader to handle. When you pick a specific newsgroup from your list, the reader displays a list of messages, called *articles*, that have been posted to that particular group. Each list entry contains the writer's user name, the date, and a subject line, which is supposed to give some indication of the content. Articles with the same subject line or topic are said to follow a *thread*. After you read an article, you have several options. You can make it go away by doing nothing to it; if you just return to the menu, the article will be deleted when you exit the newsreader. You can follow the article by posting a response to the entire group or reply privately to the writer. You can *archive* (or save) an article, or e-mail it to someone. And, of course, you can also send, or post, an article to a newsgroup on a topic of your own choosing—the group will let you know if you've strayed out of bounds.

Additional Tools

There is more to the Internet than the World Wide Web, e-mail, and newsgroups. Long before the Web existed, a number of other avenues flourished for locating, presenting, and accessing files and information online. They weren't particularly flashy, but they worked.

They still do, albeit in limited fashion. Sooner or later you'll run in to them, so you should have an idea of how they function. Even though their popularity is on the decline in general, FTP (and, to a lesser extent, Gopher) sites still exist for a good many legal documents, and Telnet remains a means of access to many library catalogs. Let's look at each in turn.

FTP

FTP (File Transfer Protocol) is a means of moving files back and forth between individual computers and online archives. This is how all the component files of a Web page get from the designer's computer to the directory of a domain server, where any browser can pick them up for reading. Its importance in research, however, involves transfers in the other direction. FTP allows you to access archives and download files from them.

If you know the URL, you can use a program called an FTP client to connect to a site. (Some client programs come with contact information for a number of large sites already entered.) Once you've logged in to a site, finding anything useful is haphazard; scrolling through directories with one-word headings and inscrutable file names can be worse than looking for a needle in a haystack. Often the only way to identify something is downloading and running it.

An FTP search tool does exist, called Archie, but there's no practical reason to use it in legal research. You can get to what you'll need from the World Wide Web. Many FTP sites have gateways from the Web into their archives. More importantly, Web search tools are going to include FTP sites in their results. If a Web page contains a link to an FTP site, the link will work the same as any other—clicking on it will pull the site up into your browser. And if you do happen to have an FTP URL, you can reach it with your browser by typing it in the Location box. The URL will begin with "ftp" instead of "http," but otherwise the process is the same.

Gopher

Gopher is a vanishing species—at least, the virtual kind is. It was developed at the University of Minnesota (whose mascot is guess what kind of buck-toothed critter), long before the advent of Netscape, Explorer, and current Internet protocols, for a simple environment of an operating system called UNIX. It uses a simple, linear menu, without visual or multimedia punch—which explains in part why it's been eclipsed by the razzle-dazzle of the Web.

If you come across an address for a Gopher site, you can access it directly from the Web. Type the Gopher URL into your browser. The URL will begin with "gopher" rather than "http."

Gopher started out as the major way to burrow through the Net. Some government entities still maintain Gopher sites, but the trend is to discontinue them. Most Gopher sites have transferred their holdings to Web pages; to be honest, a lot are just lying dormant, filled with outdated files.

Gopher menus don't strain your brain or your patience. You can figure out how to use one at a glance. Clicking on a menu choice brings up at most another menu; within a click or two, a document has filled your screen. Because of the simplicity, and the lack of memory-hogging graphics, Gopher menus and files load quickly.

Telnet

Unlike FTP and Gopher, Telnet does not pop documents into a browser screen. It logs you in to another computer and gives you access to the remote system, as if your computer were plugged in to it with cables. Effectively, your monitor turns in to a terminal, and a primitive looking one at that. What you see on the screen is just text, not graphics. You don't use a mouse, but type in word commands.

In your research, you'll going to find Telnet sites primarily for library catalogs. In most instances you will get in to Telnet by clicking on a Web page link, which will automatically launch the program. You can also access a Telnet site by running your Telnet program.

> *Don't know whether you have a Telnet program on your system? You probably do. If you use Windows 95, 98, or NT, your operating system came with one called HyperTerminal. Many Internet access providers include a Telnet program in the bundle of applications they provide. If you don't have an application, you can get one for Windows called EWAN at* ***http://www.lysator.liu.se/~zander/ewan.html****.*

If you launch Telnet by clicking a link, the correct information will automatically be entered to access the appropriate host computer. If you go through your own Telnet program instead of a Web page, it's a little more complicated. You're going to be asked for the host name or Internet protocol (IP) address (depending on the program) of the computer you're contacting. The host name is a series of words separated by periods, such as martini.eecs.umich.edu 3000; the IP address is a string of numbers separated by periods, such as 111.1121.243.31 3000. In each example, the number after the string—in this case, 3000—is the port number. (Obviously, you'll need to have this information about a site in order to Telnet to it. Fortunately, most Web sites that list libraries with Telnet access will also give you the information you'll need to connect, if they don't provide a link directly to it.) You'll get a message when you're connected, which may take a few minutes.

Once you Telnet into a system, don't worry about needing a guide. Telnet menus give very clear, concise lists of the commands you'll use.

The programs discussed in this chapter will gain you access to the online legal research world. Of them, the tool you will most consistently use is the browser. The next chapter explores auxiliary applications that expand the range of what a browser can do.

3
Making the Most of Your Browser

As powerful as a browser is, it can't interpret every single type of file that somebody thinks of programming into a Web page. For functions like displaying animation or broadcasting sound, it teams up with programs called plug-ins and helper applications. It also works with other support programs called utilities, which maximize one aspect or another of the browser.

Though they all expand your browser's capabilities, these programs work in different ways. A plug-in is added directly to your browser on installation and operates automatically as an extension of the browser. A helper application is an external program that your browser has to find and launch. When your browser encounters a file it can't read, it displays a dialog box asking you to identify the helper application that runs the file. From then on, your browser associates that file type with that particular application. A utility, in contrast, runs outside of your browser, although it may make handling some aspect of the browser easier.

> There is a dizzying array of browser choices out there, and we don't know which ones you're using. You could be using Netscape Navigator or Microsoft Internet Explorer, which are the two most popular choices right now. You could be using Opera, which is a smaller browser that's gained some popularity. You might be surfing using WebTV. You may even be getting on the Internet using your cellular phone!
>
> Guiding you through the options generated by all the browsers would be a book in itself. Most everything in this chapter will work with Internet Explorer or Netscape Navigator (and if they won't, we'll let you know). If you choose to use another browser, you may have to check its help file to see how it treats the plug-ins and helper applications mentioned here.
>
> Want a full list of the browsers available? Check out *http://www.internetbrowserwatch.internet.com/*.

In this chapter, we'll begin with the multimedia capabilities that are built in to your browser. After that, we'll look at the plug-ins and helper applications that you are most likely to encounter on Web pages to which your legal research takes you. Finally, we'll end the chapter with a few utilities that help manage information in the browser.

Your Browser's Built-In Multimedia

Let's look first at what your browser's components can do on their own.

Graphics

Your browser can view several graphics files: Graphics Interchange Format (GIF), Joint Photographic Experts Group (JPEG or JPG), and XBM. The first two are what you'll find in most pages. PNG (Portable Network Graphics) is a new format that's gaining a lot of followers. You can learn more about it at **http://www.cdrom.com/pub/png/png.html**.

> *Here's a quick way to determine the format of a graphic file: Right click on the image (Mac users click and hold the mouse button). Look for View Image in the list of options. The file name is next to it, and the three letters after the dot (those three letters are called the extension) identify the format.*

Sound

Accessing your browser's sound capabilities depends on your platform. If you're using a Mac or a Mac clone, you've got all you need, because your computer came with built-in multimedia capabilities, including 16-bit stereo sound. If you're using Windows, you'll need to have a sound card and speakers hooked up. For the most part, your browser can play AIFF, AU, MIDI, and WAV sound files—assuming your sound card is compatible with MIDI. (Unless you're using a really old computer, you're okay.) The reason for the distinction is that MIDI works differently from other sound files. It's not a recording, but a sequence of digital instructions, and as a result usually much smaller than other sound files. If you're not sure, the documentation for your sound card will say whether it supports MIDI.

Browser Security

The days when a browser rendered only HTML documents are long gone. Nowadays, your browser can handle programs written in JavaScript and Java. Microsoft's Internet Explorer also includes ActiveX functionality.

Theoretically all these programs are totally secure and you don't have to worry about leaving them enabled on your browser. In reality, researchers are constantly finding bugs that might compromise your computer's security when you use one of these technologies. Often patches are available for these bugs almost immediately, but they pop up so often it's hard to keep up.

You may already have a firewall or some other security measures enabled. If you don't, here are some things you can do to ensure your system remains secure:

- Install anti-virus software and update it on a regular basis. Norton AntiVirus (**http://www.symantec.com**), for example, protects against some malicious Java applets in addition to viruses. McAfee VirusScan (**http://www.mcafee.com/anti-virus/**) is another popular package.
- Consider deactivating technologies that you don't need. In Netscape Navigator, you can go to Edit-Preferences, and choose Advanced from the menu on the left. You'll see checkboxes for JavaScript and Java. If you unclick these boxes you've disabled JavaScript and Java. (A lot of Web pages don't function without JavaScript enabled, though. If you're trying to use a page and it doesn't work, enable JavaScript, reload the page, and try to use it again.) For Internet Explorer, you can set a "security zone" on high for as much protection as possible, or you can tweak the individual settings to enable JavaScript, cookies, Java, etc. We advise against tweaking the settings unless you really know what you're doing.
- Don't download files off the Internet unless you're sure they're safe. (Some file download sites certify that their programs have been scanned with an anti-virus program.) And of course, if you get any unsolicited attachments in your e-mail delete them immediately.

Moving Images

We remember the days when moving images were in QuickTime or AVI format, and that was it. They were huge and we had to wait hours for them to download, but we liked it that way! We had to walk three hours, backwards, in the snow... sorry, we got sidetracked there for a second. Let's talk moving pictures.

In the beginning, there were moving pictures that required massive downloads before you so much as saw as single frame. Now you can view moving images through what's called streaming media. Streaming media means simply that the media plays as it downloads—you don't have to wait for the download to end before you start seeing pictures or hearing sound.

Many moving images nowadays are available using the Windows Media Player format or the RealMedia format. We'll discuss those in a moment.

If you have Windows, your browser will play AVI files without any tinkering. If you use a Mac, you may need a plug-in for AVI files. One that does the trick is MacZilla, which you can get for $10 from **http://www.maczilla.com**. Besides AVI files, it'll also play QuickTime and MPEG movies and AIFF, AU, MP2, MIDI, and WAV sounds.

Regardless of your platform, you'll need to install the latest version of QuickTime for your browser to display files in that format properly. You can get it (for both Mac and Windows) from **http://www.apple.com/quicktime/**.

> Movie files may be fun—but they're also enormous! They can run from one megabyte to more than twenty. Most pages will warn you when you're about to download something that large. Just remember: the bigger the size, the longer the download time.

Once you've gotten your browser up to speed on handling all its basic multimedia, you're only about halfway there. Plug-ins and helper applications will supercharge your browsing experience—and as you'll discover, a couple of these programs are absolutely required.

Plug-Ins and Helper Applications

A myriad of plug-ins have been developed to expand a browser's capabilities. We will highlight the ones that you are going to encounter most often. To keep abreast with new plug-ins and helper applications as they become available, visit Netscape's page at **http://www.netscape.com/plugins/index.html**. Other reliable fishing holes are TUCOWS, **http://www.tucows.com** (which uses cows to rate software) and Plug-In Plaza, **http://browserwatch.internet.com/plug-in.html**.

Adobe Acrobat Reader

This program is the essential aid to legal research. It's what you're going to need to download—and sometimes, even to read—forms and documents from a staggering number of sites listed in this book. Just about every government agency uses it, and it's also popular with libraries and private firms' sites. The reason for such a widespread appeal is that it displays files in their original design and layout. An IRS form, for example, looks exactly like what you'd pick up at the local office, without any HTML or other codes distorting its appearance. It doesn't matter what program or format a document was originally produced in; Acrobat creates a Portable Document Format (PDF) file from it, which it can then read.

> *You're going to be seeing more and more PDF documents floating around the Web as time goes by. It is becoming an increasingly popular format for electronic books.*

You can download the Adobe Acrobat Reader for free from **http://www.adobe.com/products/acrobat/readermain.html**. If you don't get around to it beforehand, the first time you get to a site that uses PDF files, you'll most likely be able to obtain the Reader there. Most pages that use it link to Adobe's Acrobat page for downloading.

RealPlayer

RealAudio was a pioneer in facilitating streaming audio, or playing sound files as they load on your computer. Now you can listen to streaming audio files and watch streaming video with RealPlayer. Sites all over the Web have adopted it, and you'll need it to run news broadcasts (on NPR, ABC, and C-SPAN, for example), congressional floor debates, and recordings that catch your eye. You can also use it to watch live "Webcasts" of oral arguments, speeches, sports events, and even rock concerts. If you're accessing the Internet through a dial-up telephone line, the quality of the audio and video you get won't be very good, but it will be watchable. Those of you with broadband access to the Internet (using a T1 line, cable modem, DSL, or other very fast service) are in for a treat!

At this writing RealPlayer comes in two flavors: RealPlayer 7 Basic and RealPlayer 7 Plus. The Basic version is free. The Plus version costs $29.99 and includes better audio and video quality. RealPlayer requires an IBM-compatible Pentium or Macintosh PowerPC, as well as a 14.4K connection for audio and a 28.8K connection for video transmission. You can download either version from **http://www.real.com/player/index.html**.

Windows Media Player

The Windows Media Player (brought to you by Microsoft) plays streaming media in several different formats, including: WMA (the Windows Media Player format), MP3 (sound), WAV (sound), AVI (moving images), and MPEG (also moving images). There are versions for Windows and Macintosh. You can get the player at **http://www.microsoft.com/windows/mediaplayer/en/default.asp** (it's free), then sample diverse content at **http://www.windowsmedia.com**.

Shockwave

You're less likely to come across Shockwave doing serious research, but sooner or later you will need it to view a page, whether it's a Web magazine, a game, or a postcard. This program plays animation (including sound effects, and sometimes interactive) that's been embedded in home pages.

There are two types of Shockwave. Shockwave Flash is for basic display purposes—menus that move around and make noises and the like. Regular Shockwave is for more interactive browser content, such as science demonstrations and video games.

Download it for free from **http://v2.shockwave.com/bin/v2/download/fs.jsp?id=shockwave**. From there you'll be able to check out the arcade, games, cartoons, music, and more. Of course, you won't get a lot of work done this way, but all work and no play. . . .

> We might be erroneously giving you the impression that Shockwave is only for fun and games. It isn't—you can do some impressive demonstrations and teaching with it. Check out CNN's World Time page at ***http://www.cnn.com/WEATHER/worldtime/***, where Shockwave allows you to get information about time zones and local times all over the world.

Once you've put these plug-ins and helper applications in place, your browser is really powered up. You are ready to surf the Web, generate huge amounts of information, and pull together some terrific, on-target research!

But wait a minute. If you're going to generate information, you're going to have to organize it, aren't you? And one of the primary things you're going to organize is your bookmarks.

Managing Your Bookmarks

As you expand your collection of online resources, you will invariably create a huge collection of bookmarks. At some point the collection will evolve from a useful set of pointers to resources to a morass of unmanageable information. Browsers can do only a limited amount with organizing bookmarks. You need a bookmark manager.

Initially when we got involved with Internet research and bookmark managers were just becoming popular, they were all software-based. That is to say, they were all programs that you downloaded to your hard drive and used. These days, however, you can either use software-based bookmark managers or online bookmark managers.

Online bookmark managers? Yes. These are Web sites and services that allow you to log on and access your bookmarks, sort them, and track changes to them.

Which type should you use? It depends. Having your bookmarks on your hard drive means that you don't have to be as concerned about your privacy being violated. You don't have to be worried about somebody else's hard drive getting wiped out—just your own. (You are doing regular backups, right?) You don't have to worry about remembering a user name and a password. If you use one computer, all the time, you may want to stick to bookmark managing software.

But what if you travel a lot? What if you use several different computers? What if you work on one computer at work and one computer at home? Then you might want to consider an online bookmark manager. You don't have to keep all your bookmark software up to date. You don't have to make sure you have your bookmarks with you when you're using a different computer. You don't have to find things online when you're away from your bookmarks. As long as you can access the Web, you can get to your bookmarks.

Let's examine some options for online bookmark management, and then look at ways you can manage your bookmarks with software.

Online Bookmark Management

At this writing there are dozens of online bookmark managers. If you want a good list visit **http://www.webwizards.net/useful/wbbm.htm**. We'll give you an overview of a few.

Backflip
http://www.backflip.com/
Backflip is one of the newer bookmark managers. It allows you to integrate a small bookmark into your Web browser, and painlessly bookmark sites as you come across them. Backflip also claims to automatically organize your pages so you can come back to them later. You can also search all the pages that you've already added to the site.

MySpider.com
http://www.myspider.com/
Like Backflip, MySpider gives you a bookmark to put on your browser bar. When you find content you want to save to a personal bookmark folder, you click the button and MySpider indexes it. Later, within MySpider, you can edit the content you've indexed, add notes, and search your bookmarks and those of other users (though you can choose to make your personal notes on bookmarks private). You can also check and see which other users have archived the same sites as you, to see if they might have other items of interest.

Oneview
http://www.oneview.com/
Oneview not only has bookmark management; it has have private communities that allow you to share information about hot new spots and links. If you're part of a large legal research firm or law library, this sounds like it could be a lot of fun! You can also make your own index structure, like you do when you use Windows Explorer.

Bookmark Software

If you want your bookmarks to stay on your hard drive, consider one of these bookmark managing software packages (and again, we're just scratching the surface here). For more packages, check out Tucows, **http://www.tucows.com**.

Powermarks
http://www.kaylon.com/power.html
Powermarks allows you to maintain your bookmark list independently of any browser you use. You can also bookmark a page with only a URL and have Powermarks retrieve the title and other information from the page itself. Powermarks can also automatically notify you of changed pages and export bookmarks into several different formats—handy when you need to share them with people. Powermarks is available for Windows 95, 98, and NT.

URL Manager Pro
http://www.url-manager.com/
URL Manager Pro is the top of the line of bookmark utilities specifically for Macintosh. Working within your browser, it has special features like storing not just a current page's URL, but all hypertext links contained in it. It will also catalog and sort bookmarks for FTP and Gopher sites, newsgroups, and e-mail addresses, and lets you add custom bookmark menus (set up in the categories and hierarchies you designate) to the Navigator tool bar. URL Manager Pro runs for $30.

Webspector
http://www.illumix.com/webspector.htm
Webspector is not a traditional bookmark manager that organizes bookmarks for you. Instead, what it does is keep you informed of changes to pages. Here's how it works: you enter a list of Web pages you want to keep track of. (You can enter pages into different "folders" and only check one folder at a time, which is handy if you're tracking several different folders and you have lots of bookmarks.) Periodically (you can program certain times or activate it manually) Webspector will go out and download copies of the pages you've specified, then highlight the page changes. Since copies of the pages are downloaded to your hard drive, checking page changes in this manner becomes incredibly fast. (Webspector also has its own built-in browser so you don't have to launch a new application to view the downloaded pages.) If you have lots of bookmarks that you don't visit often but would like to keep current, you'll want to give Webspector a try. It comes in several versions (for PC only), which monitor different numbers of pages and cost between $49 and $99.

Managing the Clipboard

You've probably never thought about where information goes between the moment you highlight and copy it and when you paste it someplace else. It's stored in a part of your system called the clipboard. The clipboard has limited capabilities; it can hold only one piece of information at a time, and overwrites whatever's in it each time you copy something. If you want to save several bits of information, in one place or in separate documents, use a clipboard replacement program. One that works for Windows is ClipMate, which hangs on to hundreds of items at once and lets you recombine and glue them any way you want. It costs $25 with a diskette or $20 if you download the software from **http://www.thornsoft.com**.

Disk Cache Utilities

URLs aren't the only thing you accumulate as you browse the Web. You gather fragments of Web information, too, in a kind of holding pen for your browser that's called the *disk cache*. It's what makes pages load so quickly when you use the Back and Forward buttons, because the data comes from the cache, rather than having to be downloaded from scratch each time. Your browser accesses the cache automatically when you're online. It's possible to look at the cache when you're offline, too, by using an explorer program. This type of utility lets you look at the last Web pages you've visited, even after you've exited your browser. Here are two that work with Windows.

CacheX

CacheX lets you explore your browser's cache with an Explorer-type interface. If you double-click on an entry, your browser displays it. A single-user license runs $20 and there are versions available for Netscape and Internet Explorer. You can download it from **http://www.mwso.com/**.

UnMozify

This heavy-hitter does more than list the files in your cache. It organizes the information by domain and allows you to look at archives based on domain and date ranges. It will search for keywords in the documents' text as well as their URLs. After you've selected files, UnMozify launches your browser and gives you a menu of what you can browse. It sells for about $30 and comes in a 30-day trial version, available from **http://www.evolve.co.uk/unmozify/**. Despite the name—taken from the Netscape mascot "Mozilla"—UnMozify comes in an Internet Explorer and a Netscape version.

Managing Information While Surfing

While you surf, you're going to accumulate lots of bits and pieces you'd like to hold on to—from citations and case names to phone numbers and addresses. To keep track of these tidbits, try an information manager like InfoSelect. It keeps a list of records and folders at the side of the screen, so you can get at everything easily. It includes a calendar that will remind you of specified events. The latest version, for Windows, includes bookmark management, extensive search capabilities, and a label printing utility. A variation is also available for Palm Pilot. You can get either from **http://www.miclog.com**; the Windows version is about $100, while the Palm Pilot version costs around $70. Mac users have a powerful alternative, Consultant, which also has sophisticated capabilities for managing calendar and address book entries (including dialing the phone for you). Consultant sells for $49.99; test drive it at **http://www.chronosnet.com/**.

Now you know how to beef up your browser so that it can run all the different files you're going to come across in Web pages. You'll want to get the plug-ins, regardless; Acrobat's a must, and you will run into RealMedia and Shockwave with enough regularity to make installing them worthwhile. Applications like bookmark managers, clipboard expanders, and disk cache utilities are a matter of personal preference. Though these programs may make your tasks easier, you'll certainly be able to accomplish research without them. What we've looked at is just the tip of the iceberg; drop by TUCOWS (**http://www.tucows.com**) every now and then to see what new gizmos are available to soup up your surfing.

4
Setting Up Your Online Library

Imagine how convenient it would be if you had a personalized shelf in the library, where you could tuck away copies of all the reference books you use most frequently. With a Web browser, you can turn your computer into your own private research cubicle, stocked with everything you might possibly want or need—without running the risk that irritated colleagues will hunt you down and accuse you of hoarding (or worse, raid your precious stash). By bookmarking, you can set aside handy resources for yourself. As if in a Lewis Carroll book, everything you've taken off the shelf is still right where you got it, ready for the next researcher. (For an explanation of bookmarking, refer to chapter 2, "Introduction to the Basic Tools.")

In this chapter, we'll begin assembling your online holdings. We'll select a few resources that belong in any virtual law library, no matter what your area of practice or interest may be. They're so fundamental and helpful that I have given them the name "Essential Bookmarks."

Instead of jumping straight into legal resources, though, we'll lay some groundwork first, by examining the categories of resources on the World Wide Web and the techniques they use.

Introduction to Internet Resources & Techniques

The bytes of information available on the Web are starting to rival the number of grains of sand on a beach. The big difference is that sand is finite (if unmeasurable) in quantity, while Web pages are anything but. They're growing constantly at an exponential rate that would put fruit flies to shame.

The legal arena is no exception. When I stepped online in 1995, legal resources with any substance were few and far between. Even as recently as 1998, full text versions of opinions and statutes were so hit-and-miss that I never bothered looking for them. The explosion of materials since then has reversed my attitude. Now I always go to my computer first, and head for the physical books only as a last resort.

Blazing a path through this virtual maze is surprisingly easy. I don't have to figure out where something is, and neither do you. The Web is teeming with ample, extensively connected search resources that will do the looking for us. All we have to do is define what we want. What I especially like about the process is that I no longer have to read the minds of legal indexers, who have a maddening way of filing things under obscure and inexplicable headings. In comparison, the Net's search resources are refreshingly straightforward. What you see (and ask for) is what you get.

Search resources fall into three major categories:

- *Search engines,* which comb an index of Web pages or titles for occurrences of a specified phrase. Newsgroup posts or locations of FTP and Gopher sites may also fall into an index's database. These databases are usually put together without review or screening.
- *Edited search engines,* which operate in the same way, except that they review sites for content before adding them to their database. Some general ones prohibit offensive listings; others, such as legal search engines, limit the collections to a specific topic.
- *Hierarchical indexes,* which contain lists of subject headings and subtopics arranged in increasingly specific order, much like a series of nested boxes. More and more, these indexes also allow keyword searching.

The distinctions among these three types are growing increasingly blurry. It's common for legal reference sites to incorporate both an index and at least one edited search engine. A hybrid phenomenon has developed among high-traffic general engines and indexes, which have refashioned themselves as Web portals. A more accurate term would be home bases, since portals offer a blinding array of services and resources (news, entertainment, shopping, Web-based e-mail accounts) to encourage visitors to use the site for their every online need. Regardless of a site's form, the techniques for locating resources remain the same.

How to Phrase a Search: Using Boolean Operators

Don't be thrown by the name; Boolean operators are not characters out of some obscure sci-fi story. If you've ever run a search on LEXIS or Westlaw, you've used them, whether you knew it or not.

Boolean operators are the symbols that define the parameters of a database search. You type them in between words, or between groups of words, to tell the computer what to look for (and what to leave out). You don't have to memorize them, although it's easy enough to pick up a few key ones. Many search engines display a list, alongside their query forms, of which operators they recognize; if they aren't immediately apparent, look for a link to "advanced search options."

To get you started, I've provided an explanation of common operators in table 4.1. Keep in mind that Boolean operators may vary subtly from engine to engine. When we look at specific engines in the next section, I'll alert you to unusual variations. When all else fails, look for an engine's search instructions.

Table 4.1: Examples of Boolean Operators and Their Use

Description	Operator	Example
To include words *(find pages with all, in any sequence or proximity)*	+ AND	invention+developer+bond Miranda AND waiver
To exclude words *(find [x] but not [y])*	- NOT	forfeiture-drug fraud NOT consumer
To group words *(find this sequence only)*	""	"search and seizure"
To include alternatives *(find either / or)*	OR	debt OR claim
To include variants or wildcards *(find everything beginning [x])*	* $	commerc* eviden$

Searching Is Easy

Whether you will want to try a search engine or an index for a particular problem depends on personal preference and how much you already know about what you're looking for. The resources are equally easy to use. Regardless of type, they are self-explanatory and designed for you to dive right in, without having to plow through elaborate instructions first.

With a search engine, simply look for the rectangular box. Type your request into this search form and click the button, usually to the right, labeled with some variant of the command "send." On your first visit to an engine, take a moment to scan the page. Hyperlinks and labeled buttons will show what sorts of options, help tips, and other aids are there. Be on the lookout for any special search term requirements specific to that engine; these may appear directly on the page, or there may be a link to them.

With an index, look over the list of subject headings and click on the relevant one. It will usually bring up a subindex with more narrowly focused headings. The process of eyeballing and clicking will eventually end with an alphabetical list of pages that fall under the last subheading. Click on a name to display the desired page.

> *If you've used Westlaw or LEXIS, you've already learned this tip the hard way: Phrase a search as specifically as possible. The more narrowly you target your search, the more likely what it brings up will even remotely address your needs. Glancing over the list of results (rather than jumping to a bunch of pages) is usually enough to tell whether it is overloaded with irrelevance. When that happens, just rephrase the search and run it again.*

Essential Bookmarks for Legal Research

Begin compiling your online library with the following research starting points. From these sites, you can access just about anything you need. All of them have a stable, reliable online presence, since they're associated with institutions that have been around for a while, at least in Net years. Each has a distinctive focus and personality; experiment to see which matches yours. One of them is bound to appeal to you for general, regular use, but eventually, every single one will come in handy.

I'm recommending that you launch your library with all of the following:

- *Searchable indexes.* A couple of solid indexes are the cornerstone of an online library. For most research I prefer them to search engines, because I'd rather look through a list of headings than try to guess the exact keywords that appear in the document I'm seeking. Your attitude may be different, so experiment.
- *Search engines.* Since these compare key words against documents, they're especially useful in polar opposite situations: when you're trying to find a specific agency or organization, and when you're trawling for discussions of a concept.
- *Government resources you frequently use.* If your practice puts you in regular contact with an agency or a clerk's office, its page belongs in your online library. Odds are every one you're dealing with has a Web page. A surprising number of federal and state agencies, departments, and courts have a virtual presence; increasingly, so do their city and county counterparts. If you find a page for an office you call, write to, file with, or appear before even as little as four times a year, make and file a bookmark. My bookmarks include the IRS, U.S. Copyright Office, and the Texas Secretary of State. Now my computer gives me forms I often need and local information I never seem to

remember, such as filing fees and holidays. If you want to follow suit, go to chapter 7 for court pages, chapter 8 for government form sites, chapter 9 for federal entities, and chapter 10 for state and local governments.
- *Legal research news sources.* Mailing lists and online law journals will keep you abreast of developments in both the profession and legal research on the Internet.

> *As soon as you add a bookmark, take the time to move it right then to a logical place in your bookmark list. The more you research on the Web, the longer and more unmanageable your bookmark list will become—if you don't organize it regularly. Rather than piling up a long list of URLs in random sequence, you'll save yourself a lot of time in the long run by making this tip a habit.*
>
> *After adding a bookmark, click on it and drag it to the appropriate folder; when you release the mouse button, the bookmark will drop into place. Use the File menu in Netscape's Bookmarks window to create folders, add separators, and create your own names for sites with opaque titles. (In IE, use Organize Favorites.)*

General Searchable Indexes

All of the sites discussed in this section contain these primary materials:

- U.S. Supreme Court, Circuit Court of Appeals, district, and bankruptcy court decisions
- Federal statutes, codes, and regulations
- Law reviews and journals.

In each description below I've highlighted additional resources, beyond these basics, under the heading "Special Features." Visit each site and see which ones best suit your own personal style.

FindLaw
http://www.findlaw.com/
If I could have only one legal research site, FindLaw would be my choice. Updated daily, it's an unbeatable all-round reference tool. Although FindLaw has embraced the giveaway clutter of a Web portal, its structure is still sparse and clean enough to make for easy and efficient navigation. You can search the entire index from the main page. Choose one of the fourteen subject headings and run a search through just it, or scroll down through a quick reference list of the sites under it. (And the URL is so simple to remember that I always just type it into my browser, rather than pull it up from the bookmark list.)

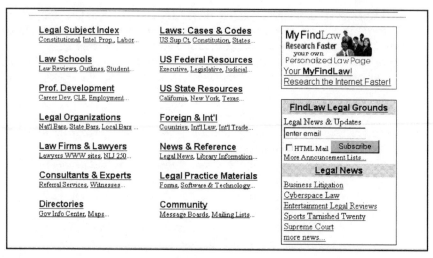

Figure 4.1: FindLaw's top level index.

The instructions for this searchable index (see figure 4.1) are easy to digest. On your first visit, click "Options," next to the search form, and get acquainted with the search variants FindLaw recognizes. It supports the Boolean operators AND, OR, NOT, and NEAR. How FindLaw handles wildcard searches is sophisticated; besides looking for pages containing words with a prefix (which is specified with an asterisk), it responds to two asterisks by finding pages containing words based on the same stem. (To put this in English: FindLaw will search a verb for all tenses, even if the spelling changes.) For example, if you search for fly**, FindLaw returns items with fly, flying, and even flown.

Special Features: In addition to the basic resources, FindLaw offers:

- Supreme Court decisions since 1893 (which you can browse or search by citation, party name, or full text)
- Voluminous state resources, including caselaw, statutes, court and agency sites, and municipal codes
- Full-text searching of journals online, abstracts by e-mail, and access to *A Uniform System of Citation* (the "Bluebook")
- The LawCrawler search engine (about which more in the next section)
- Online Continuing Legal Education (CLE) courses.

Hieros Gamos
http://www.hg.org/hg.html
The name means harmonizing things that seem to be opposites, such as electronic and written information. To live up to such an ambitious name, this site has compiled staggering resources that encompass 200 areas of practice and, it claims, every government in the world.

Reminiscent of a tabbed file folder, HG's distinctive frame sits atop every page and offers immediate access to both the search engine and the top level subject headings from the index. (See figure 4.2.) As you venture deeper into Hieros Gamos, the levels remain neatly and legibly laid out, with clickable bars and buttons and lots of welcome white space.

Special features: In addition to the basic resources, Heiros Gamos provides:

- Downloadable guides for doing business in more than twenty countries and a handful of states
- A topic index of seventy areas of practice, broken into 130 subtopics
- Access to the Securities Exchange Commission's searchable database of public filings
- A searchable database of vendors, court reporters, expert witnesses, translators, process servers, private investigators, document management services, and marketing, financial, and employment consultants
- German, French, Italian, and Spanish language versions
- Online CLE
- Free ClicknSearch software, which will launch your browser and run an Internet search based on highlighted text in any document on your computer.

Figure 4.2: Hieros Gamos.

Meta-Index for U.S. Legal Research
http://gsulaw.gsu.edu/metaindex/

Georgia State University School of Law offers one-stop access to the searchable legal indexes on the Web. Rather than just shipping you off to an index by hyperlink, it launches your search for you. Not only does the Meta-Index have a separate search form for each index, but it also has filled in each form with an example request, which it calls a default search. You can run this search to preview a particular index's workings. Just select the maximum number of results (from five to 300, depending on the database) and click the button labeled "Search." I selected forty as the maximum number of hits in the search request shown in figure 4.3.

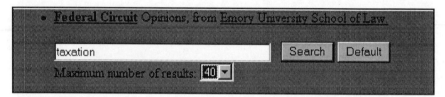

Figure 4.3: A default search request in GSU's Meta-Index for U.S. Legal Research.

Because this page is merely a clearinghouse, it doesn't have one uniform set of advanced search options. Everything it does depends on the ground rules of the index that it is contacting for you. If a particular index does have special options, the Meta-Index gives a link to them, right next to the search form.

Special features: In addition to federal decisions and legislation, Meta-Index for U.S. Legal Research provides links to:

- Pending legislation (searchable by full text and bill number) and the *Congressional Record*
- The Legal Domain Network archives of law-related Usenet groups.

The Meta-Index also sends notice, on request, of changes to the site.

Yahoo! Law
http://dir.yahoo.com/Law/

Chapter 16, "General Research Resources," will explore the general scope of this enormously popular index. The traits that make Yahoo! so appealing for all-purpose nosing around also make it a must for legal research. Think of Yahoo! Law as one of those people—we've all run into one—who knows everybody. This colleague has the Rolodex of the gods, and flipping through it is wonderfully easy. You can tell what to do with one glance at the Law page. You can launch a search through all of Yahoo! or just the Law section of the index. (Press Help, in the upper right corner, for a concise explanation of how the index works, as well as search and syntax tips.) With one click, you can travel to a law-related club or to any law-related events taking place on Yahoo! that day. You can also browse a list of more than forty subtopics, including some that other indexes do not address (such as lawyer jokes, or lesbian, gay, and bisexual resources). Yahoo! even tells you the number of items under each heading. When you click on a heading, you can run a search through it or browse an alphabetical list of everything under it.

Legal Search Engines

You'll need a search engine with a broad scope and quick response time. Either LawCrawler or LawRunner will do the trick. Experiment with each and bookmark the one that works better for you. (My choice is LawCrawler, because more often than not, I'm already at FindLaw when I want to run a search.)

LawCrawler
http://lawcrawler.findlaw.com/

You can reach this search engine within one click from FindLaw; look for it in the pull-down menu next to any search box. Still, LawCrawler is useful enough to warrant special mention for its own merits. Powered by AltaVista's search engine, LawCrawler (shown in figure 4.5) sends your search request through the database that you select from a pull-down menu. Straightforward and uncomplicated, it recognizes the Boolean operators AND, OR, NEAR, and NOT.

LawCrawler offers four additional options for searching:

- Federal departments, statutes and regulations, as well as decisions by the Supreme Court and Circuit Courts of Appeals
- California state and federal databases and sites
- State government servers outside California
- Legal sites outside the United States.

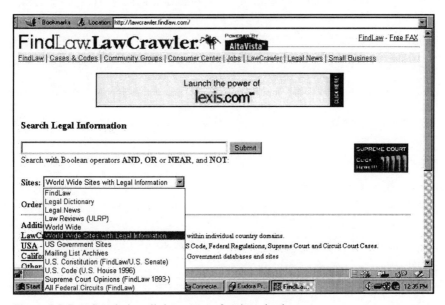

Figure 4.5: LawCrawler's pull-down menu for site selection.

LawRunner
http://www.lawrunner.com/

Although this engine also piggybacks on AltaVista, it offers a wider range of fine-tuning than does LawCrawler. You can direct a search to sites within a single geographic jurisdiction, from all fifty states to more than 230 worldwide. Within a jurisdiction, a pull-down menu lets you narrow the targeted sites even further, by type. Syntax options run from the simple (AND, OR, NEAR, and AND NOT) to the elaborate. LawRunner is a feature of the Internet Legal Resource Guide, which is discussed in appendix A, "Where to Go When the Connection's Slow."

Other Resources

In this section we'll pick up a grab-bag of resources that have one important trait in common: They've laid critical groundwork for you. We'll look at a shortcut to U.S. government sites, indexes of mailing lists, an important journal, and a source for step-by-step Internet instruction.

The Federal Web Locator
http://www.infoctr.edu/fwl/

On this page (see figure 4.6), the Center for Information Law and Policy strives to link every Web site related to the U.S. federal government. It gives you two avenues of navigation. Click Federal Quick Jumps to access an alphabet soup directory, which will take you straight to any organization's home page. For a more

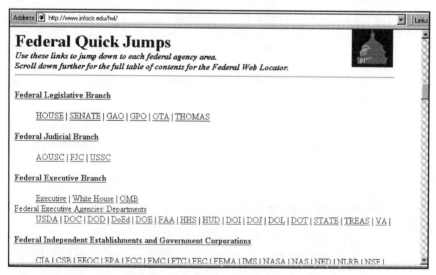

Figure 4.6: Quick Jumps from the Federal Web Locator.

leisurely approach, scroll down the table of contents. To learn what's recently arrived, scan the latest links. The site is hosted by the Information Center at the Chicago-Kent College of Law, Illinois Institute of Technology.

LAW*link*
http://www.abanet.org/lawlink/home.html

The American Bar Association's Legal Research Jumpstation arranges its extensive links on one long scroll-down page. On your first visit, I'd recommend taking the time to browse through the headings, to get a feel for how the ABA has assigned topics. The basics are all there, but not necessarily where you'd expect. Statutes and codes, for example, are not under the legislative branch, but under general federal government resources, and while that heading says it includes agencies, four appear instead at the bottom of the page, under miscellaneous sites. On the plus side, once you find the appropriate heading, all the links are neatly listed beneath it, in one convenient place, without your having to jump around.

Whether you choose to save this site as a bookmark or not, the ABA offers two valuable features worth your attention:

- Site-tation will send you a periodic grab-bag of online legal URLs and listservs, randomly selected by the ABA's staff. (Initially distributions were weekly, but since late 1999 they have been as infrequent as once a month.) I always find something useful in the listings, and often something unexpected, as well. If nothing else, this service will give you a good idea of the directions into which online resources are expanding.
- The abanet.org discussion groups catalog, at **http://www.abanet.org/discussions/**, offers avenues to hook up with fellow lawyers to pass information and pose questions about an array of practice areas. I'll be explaining this phenomenon at greater length in chapter 15, "Locating Lawyers & Other Helpful People." For now, set aside fifteen minutes to browse through the list of groups and sign up for everything remotely interesting. You can always unsubscribe if something turns out not to meet your needs.

Law Lists
http://www.lib.uchicago.edu/~llou/lawlists/info.html

It took a librarian to tackle the unruly mass of legal mailing lists and newsgroups that run rampant across the Internet. Her name is Lyonette Louis-Jacques, of the University of Chicago Law School, and this site is where she's cataloged them. They are listed alphabetically, with descriptions of their focus and instructions on how to subscribe. The site discloses the date through which the list is current and offers a search feature. We'll pay more attention to these lists in chapter 15, "Locating Lawyers & Other Helpful People." Look through the mailing lists for your usual practice areas, and sign up to try out a couple.

LLRX
http://www.llrx.com/
Focusing on legal research, management, and technology, this online publication is a boon to Web novices and veterans alike. It's not alone in its field, by any means; we'll examine many other periodicals in chapter 14, "Journals, Periodicals, & Legal News." LLRX (formerly Law Library Resource Xchange), however, is especially effective. Its articles and columns are practical and to the point, from a round-up of rules of court online to a comparison of search engines. Other features include commentary on congressional activity and a survey of Web pages in the news. The searchable site also maintains a formidable index of research and library-related links. On request, LLRX will notify you by e-mail when new articles have appeared.

Whether you bookmark LLRX or not, be sure to sign up for Tara's free, weekly research newsletter LLRXBuzz. Her e-mail discusses new sites, services, and developments that either involve online legal research or interest lawyers.

The Virtual Chase
http://www.virtualchase.com/index.shtml
The site, maintained by Genie Tyburski, Web Research Applications Specialist for Ballard Spahr Andrews & Ingersoll LLP, presents only links to resources that meet stringent quality standards. It organizes recommendations into clearly written guides and teaching webs, and points as well to Tyburski's prolific articles and teaching tools. The searchable, multichapter Annotated Guide to Resources for Legal Professionals compiles starting points, topic research sites, resources for litigation, industry, and insurance, and a variety of other aids. Guides are also available for Internet research strategies and locating online company information or government resources. For a tutorial, walk through the outline from her seminar Internet Research for Legal Professionals.

Citations & Headnotes

Looking up citations and headnotes is a mainstay of legal research, and only recently possible online. Shepard's Citations, updated daily, are part of the LEXIS-NEXIS service at **http://www.lexis.com**. Though LEXIS claims to be Shepard's exclusive online home, query boxes for the citator are also up at **http://www.shepards.com** and **http://www.bender.com/bender/open/**. West Group's KeyCite Citation Research Service, at **http://www.keycite.com**, tracks case citations, headnotes, and Key Numbers. All services charge a fee; check the sites for details.

What to Do When an Address Doesn't Work

Sooner or later, you will have trouble reaching a site. It can happen whether you're typing in an address from this book or pressing a link on a Web page. The failure doesn't necessarily mean that the resource has disappeared. The site may have moved to a different domain, restructured its directories, or renamed the file. When you come across a broken link, a few quick steps will tell you whether the resource still exists.

1. Look at the error message
If it says "404: Not Found" (or some variation), your browser can't locate the file. Go to the next step.

If the message says that it cannot connect with the server or that the domain does not have a valid DNS entry, make sure you are still connected to the Internet (unless you're on a network, in which case check the connection only if you suspect that the entire network may be down). If you have not been disconnected, it's possible that the site's server is temporarily down. Then again, the site could be gone; this type of message, unfortunately, can indicate several things. If you can wait, try again in a few hours. Otherwise, proceed to the next step.

2. Shorten the URL
Remove the file name from the URL. Do this by putting the cursor at the end of the URL and deleting everything after the last slash mark. For example, take:

http://www.state.ct.us/sots/Forms/forms.htm

and shorten it to:

http://www.state.ct.us/sots/Forms/

The shortened URL should reach a directory (or a page) called Forms, where you should look for a sign of the resource you want. If nothing comes up, or there's neither a reference to the resource nor a search engine, move on to the next step.

This technique will not work if the file name consists of only the domain name, such as http://www.findlaw.com. For a URL in that format, go to the fourth step.

3. Shorten the URL again.
Take out everything between the last sets of slashes, like this:

http://www.state.ct.us/sots/

The shortened URL should get you to the "sots" subdirectory or page. Again, if a page comes up in your browser, look for a reference to the resource or for a search engine. If nothing comes up, shorten the URL again:

http://www.state.ct.us/

This should bring up the top page, assuming the site has not moved or gone down. If the site still contains the resource, there should be some way to locate it, either through an index, a search engine, or a site map. If the shortest address does not work, go to the last step.

4. Run a search for the resource
It may be that the page has moved to a different address or merged with another site. My approach is to run a search with LawCrawler. If that come up blank (not uncommon, because sometimes sites change their names), I'll scan the appropriate index at FindLaw, **http://www.findlaw.com**. If neither technique turns up anything, I'll give up on the URL and look for the resource elsewhere.

Should You Use a Commercial Research Database?

Up to now I've been focusing on freely available information. It should come as no surprise that there are plenty of places for you to spend your money on the Web, too. This is especially true in the legal area. I've already pointed out a few sites that charge for access to a specialized database. A number of comprehensive ones specifically target legal research—offering not just a full range of library resources but sometimes services, as well.

Whether it's worth springing for one depends very much on your situation and needs. A service may well be the answer to your prayers. It also might provide fancy frills that you don't really need, along with information that you can get at no cost elsewhere. In evaluating online services, I take the same approach that I do when a publisher's sales rep pitches a practice area guide and update service. How often am I going to use the information? If rarely, what are my other options for getting it? Do they cost more, or less, in either time or money?

Let's look at factors that may be helpful in your decision about whether to sign up for a service. After that, I'll identify some comprehensive and specialized commercial databases for your consideration.

Advantages

"You get what you pay for," they always say, and the statement is as true on the Internet as it is in the rest of life. The legal research arena does offer more of a free lunch than do general Web resources, because of the number of institutions that have taken it upon themselves to collect and upload law libraries. Even in the legal area, though, times still arise when what you can get for free just doesn't meet your need. When that happens, a fee-based service may be attractive.

The main reason is gaining access to the pagination of the official text, headnotes, and Key Numbers of opinions, and the absolute latest versions of statutes and codes. If you need to locate a volume and page citation and Shepardize the case, you will have to pay to do that online. The latest cases and statutes are available for free, but, as chapter 7 will point out, verifying statutory text may take some doing.

Many, but not all, commercial services offer these benefits, at least in part (except for Key Numbers, which are proprietary to West Group). Before signing up for a commercial service, check the fine print. If you're paying for cases and statutes, you'll want assurances that the texts are in fact official issue and as current as possible.

Disadvantages

The main one is the cost. Commercial sites usually require monthly subscriptions, which run from the moderate to quite steep. Though single-use pricing is increasingly available (LEXIS and WestDoc, for example, offer it), it doesn't take many visits to run up a heady tab.

As far as primary sources are concerned—case law, legislation, and regulations—much of what comprehensive commercial research sites provide is available for free elsewhere online. The main difference is, again, giving you access to the official texts and citation systems..

The bottom line depends on your needs. Fee-based databases are great for litigators who need the official pagination of opinions they want to cite in briefs (and don't have time or access to a library to verify citations). For anyone else, it all depends on your level of comfort with the Internet. If you're a newcomer to the Net, these comprehensive pay sites are a way to ease into online research. They do provide a bit more hand-holding and offer a sense of community. If you already have your surfing legs, though, you may well find that the comprehensive pay databases duplicate your own capabilities. If you use the Web only occasionally, for times when you just can't run to a physical library, the cost of a commercial service may not be worth it at all.

Comprehensive Fee-Based Databases

Here is a sampling of the bigger, better known fee-based legal research databases. Keep in mind that charges may have changed since publication.

LEXIS-NEXIS
http://www.lexis.com/
One of the pioneers of computerized legal research, LEXIS offers a variety of plans for online access. The flat-rate libraries consist of primary legal materials from a selected state (or states) or resources for a selected practice area. The fixed monthly rate varies according to firm size and library; quotes are available from the site. Nonsubscribers may Shepardize citations, print federal and state decisions, statutes, and administrative materials, law review articles, and practice-area aids for a per document fee ($4-$9) charged to a credit card.

Westlaw
http://www.westlaw.com
The other leading computer research pioneer, Westlaw, offers its extensive databases of primary materials, practice aids, and treatises online as well. Customized subscription options are available for firms, government offices, and corporations. The WestlawPRO product allows small firms and sole practitioners to select products based on jurisdiction or practice areas. Nonsubscribers may obtain a free password for fourteen days.

Loislaw.com
http://www.pita.com/
You may already be familiar with the electronic publisher Law Office Information Systems (LOIS) because of its CD-ROM products. Loislaw.com maintains comprehensive libraries for federal and state jurisdictions, though the scopes vary. Court rules, jury instructions, and attorney general's opinions are often in the mix, and some of the archives go back further than other providers; North Carolina case law, for example, stretches back to 1778. Cases and statutes are available within twenty-four to seventy-two hours of receipt, and the databases duplicate the official versions. As a result, some opinions do contain headnotes, if the releasing court issues them as part of the official decision. Loislaw.com permits searching across jurisdictions and has developed a GlobalCite feature for verifying citation history. All subscriptions include LawWatch, which performs continuous, user-defined searches of the database and news feeds, then e-mails the results. Subscription plans run from approximately $50 a month to more than $1,600 annually, depending on the library selected. Visitors may try out the service for ten days at no charge.

V.
http://www.versuslaw.com/
V. is a searchable caselaw database, offering full text state appellate opinions, federal appellate opinions (some as early as 1930), and post-1900 Supreme Court cases. If you know a case's name and jurisdiction and/or citation, the COD service will save you the bother of searching and send you a copy of the decision, by fax

($12.50) or e-mail ($7). Although V. has no citator feature, the FAQ explains how to approximate one by running citations through the search engine. V. has three subscription options: $14.95 for twenty-four hours, $6.95 a month, and $83.40 a year. Encrypted credit card payment is accepted for all three; the two longer options may be arranged over the phone, as well.

LawResearch
http://www.lawresearch.com/home.htm
LawResearch boasts that it has the largest law library online, containing more than 200,000 worldwide resources. It puts up a small fraction of them on an unlimited access demonstration page; slightly more are available with a free trial account, which lasts till the end of the month after you set it up. Even its free offerings can overwhelm: extensive Web navigation tools, organized alphabetically and also by categories; browsable legal indexes; a search engine for financial industry data; and a monthly newsletter spotlighting sites for law and international resources, topic research, state directories, and more. An annual membership runs $99, while quarterly stints go for $28. Membership includes some Web advertising, but its main benefit seems to be expanded library access, which isn't described in any detail other than number of resources. LawResearch's copyright restrictions, by the way, specifically prohibit downloading or saving the directory pages.

> An alternative to subscribing to a comprehensive database is buying a program that puts legal search capabilities in place on your computer, such as Net Lizard, *http://www.netlizard.com/lizard/lexloci.html*. This research sidekick allows you to search a collection of URLs of more than 15,000 sites. The range is comprehensive—federal and state courts, legislation, and agencies; international laws, governments, courts, and organizations; tax, litigation, and business forms; ethics opinions; law journals; and more. It will store information for offline viewing, to enable quoting a statute or opinion in a brief. The program sells for $69.95 and requires Windows 95/98/NT. (There's not a version for the Mac.) It works with versions 3.0 and above of Netscape and Internet Explorer, as well as with Lycos Neoplanet and Opera. You can download a demo from the site

Your online library is off to a solid start with the resources we've examined in this chapter. Here's a weird wager for you: You could get by with never bookmarking another legal reference page beyond the ones I recommend as Essential Bookmarks. They are not the be-all and end-all of what's on the Web, by any means. In fact, you may well find other ones that you like better. (Spend some time in Appendix A to get a fuller idea of the competition in legal research starting points.)

But you've been outfitted with sturdy, reliable workhorses— maybe they're not particularly exciting, but they will come through for you time and again. And when you're doing research, you don't want dazzle; you want answers. Fast.

The next step is augmenting the broad resources you've collected with some targeted ones. The next chapter will narrow the focus to caselaw. It will outfit you with a list of sites that contain federal and state decisions, then demonstrate techniques for locating opinions using the search tools you've bookmarked.

5
Locating Caselaw

The common reasons to look for caselaw boil down to three main categories:

- You need a specific case and you know something about it—the name, the court, the gist of the holding.
- You need case law on a particular point.
- You have a leading case and you need to know whether any later opinions have followed or varied from it.

You can accomplish all three on the Web, and you don't even have to tinker much with the way you approach caselaw research. Here's how to do them:

- Need a specific case? Run a search using the name of the case as your keyword. If you don't know the name, build the search request from as much as you do know—a range of dates, the court, keywords important to the subject matter or holding.
- Need a case on point? Run a search using keywords in the holding, just as you would with LEXIS or Westlaw.
- Need subsequent citations to a leading case? Instead of running citations or headnotes, use the case name as the keyword in a search.

The end of the chapter will walk you through examples of each. First, though, let me point you toward the online substitutes for Reporters.

Quick Reference List

I've compiled the major Websites for case searches in one handy list, broken down into jurisdictions. Each category starts with the highest court and proceeds downward. Some of these pages are much more than archives of opinions. They also teem with court rules, filing requirements, and practical information about pending litigation. (We'll discuss all those extras at greater length in chapter 7, "Locating Court Information & Rules.") Be sure to bookmark the ones for the jurisdictions in which you routinely appear.

Caveat: None of the free sites have opinions marked with the West Reporter volume and pagination. So far only two, Rutgers University's New Jersey courts database and the Oklahoma Supreme Court home page, provide a search function that even addresses official citations. To obtain the proper citation for a published opinion, you will need to consult a source with West's information, whether an online subscription database or library containing the actual books. The same is true of Shepard's Citators, which are available on a pay-as-you-go basis at LEXIS-NEXIS, http://www.lexis.com.

Federal Case Websites

A pair of sites offers different approaches to federal decisions. American Law Sources On-Line is the more efficient option for broad-brush research, since it will search all appeals decisions in one fell swoop. The Meta-Index for U.S. Legal Research is a quick alternative when you want to search one jurisdiction.

American Law Sources On-Line
http://www.lawsource.com/also/usa.cgi?us1
The site's acronym (ALSO) plays into a phrase common in legal citation: *see also*. Supreme Court decisions back to 1893 are just the start of this site's bounty. (Search by citation, party name, or keyword, or browse by years or U.S. volume.) You can browse or search Courts of Appeals decisions, from everything that's online to a specific circuit selected from a pull-down menu. (This database includes bankruptcy appellate decisions.) A few special courts are also searchable, such as the Court of Appeals for the Armed Forces, Court of Federal Claims, Court of Appeals for Veterans Claims, Tax Court, and Air Force Court of Criminal Appeals. Decisions of the Court of International Trade and the Judicial Panel on Multidistrict Litigation are only browsable. Two noteworthy features lurk in the introduction page's fine print: The site disclose the date of its latest revision and follows *A Uniform System of Citation*.

Meta-Index for U.S. Legal Research
http://gsulaw.gsu.edu/metaindex/
From this one page (which is recommended as an Essential Bookmark in chapter 4, "Setting Up Your Online Library"), you can search databases of Supreme Court and Circuit Courts of Appeals cases. Each jurisdiction or database has its own query form. The caselaw databases consist of FindLaw's Supreme Court

holdings, the FLITE database at FedWorld (which will be discussed in the next section), and each Circuit Court of Appeal.

> *BriefServe.com,* ***http://www.briefserve.com/home.asp****, has a searchable, commercial database of briefs and appendixes from cases before the U.S. Supreme Court since 1984 and selected appeals before the Circuit Courts of Appeals and California Supreme Court. The site is adding all Circuit Court decisions since 1981, as well as appellate cases in New York and Pennsylvania.*

U.S. Supreme Court

Several sites compile decisions of the U.S. Supreme Court, which posts only bench and slip opinions at its official site. The easiest to use is FindLaw, which is listed first and is the most complete. Project Hermes, at Cornell University's Legal Information Institute, is the official repository of decisions the Court has issued in the past decade. The recent focus limits the site's usefulness, but the Court affiliation may appeal to you. More valuable, to my thinking, is the site's searchable database of orders in pending cases—and its free service that distributes syllabi of opinions as they are issued.

You will, sooner or later, come across references to the U.S. Air Force's FLITE (Federal Legal Information Through Electronics) database of Supreme Court decisions. The archive only covers 1937-75, and the opinions are posted in all capitals, which makes them hard to read. I'd just as soon stick with FindLaw. Try out the FLITE database at **http://www.fedworld.gov/supcourt/index.htm**.

FindLaw: Supreme Court Opinions
http://www.findlaw.com/casecode/supreme.html
Every reported decision since 1893 is accessible through this index, which offers just about every imaginable avenue of approach. You can browse decisions by volume or year, or search by citation, party name, or keywords. The Supreme Court Resources include the Court's calendar and rules, news reports, and Real-Audio recordings of oral arguments. You can subscribe here to receive free summaries of recent opinions by e-mail.

The Legal Information Institute Supreme Court Collection
http://supct.law.cornell.edu/supct/
Since May 1990 the U.S. Supreme Court has been distributing its opinions electronically under the name of Project Hermes. Initially two universities housed the project online; this collection is the surviving database. Cornell has converted most of the archive through 1997 into HTML documents and categorized them by

topic, year, and party name. Since 1997, the Supreme Court has been releasing its opinions in Adobe Acrobat format. It's possible to search for keywords in case names or summaries. You can read opinions online or download them in PDF files (which require Adobe Acrobat Reader for viewing). The site warns that the database may be incomplete; check the errata and items under construction link if you can't find a case or question what you do find.

The collection includes 600 pre-1990 decisions that the LLI considers the most important in the court's history. These can be found by party name, topic, or author of the opinion.

Two site features are noteworthy: access to court order lists and free delivery of the latest opinions. The order database covers irregular orders and regular Monday morning order lists, which announce disposition of petitions for writs of certiorari, as well as administrative matters. Search by party names, date range, or docket number.

For Supreme Court opinions hot off the press, subscribe to the listserv, which sends out the official syllabi of court decisions (prepared by the Reporter of Decisions) the day they are issued. To receive the full text of any decision, all you have to do is request it by reply e-mail. Both the syllabi and the decisions are free. To subscribe, send e-mail **listserv@listserv.law.cornell.edu**. The body of message should contain only the words: subscribe liibulletin [your name].

U.S. Supreme Court
http://www.supremecourtus.gov
On the day that decisions are announced, the Court posts bench and slip opinions at its official site, which was launched in April 2000. Decisions begin with the October 1999 term. The site points to bench opinions from the 1992 term on.

USSCPlus
http://www.usscplus.com
A commercial site, UCCSPlus permits limited, no-charge access to portions of its database, which covers Supreme Court decisions since 1922 and leading cases since 1793. Free online viewing is available for decisions of the current term and the 1,000 decisions the court has most frequently cited. You may download an individual opinion for a nominal charge; the text is in Adobe Acrobat format and includes a list of cases that cite the downloaded decision. You may also subscribe to online access to the complete database (in increments of a day, month, or year), or purchase it on CD-ROM. Whether you subscribe to the service or not, the site offers free e-mail notification of new Supreme Court decisions, which summarizes and links to the opinions' full text.

Federal Circuit Courts of Appeal

Only two of the following pages are actually maintained by the court in question; most find a home instead at a university law library working in cooperation with a particular court. Regardless of their affiliation, these sites provide only recent decisions, which rarely predate 1990.

Reported opinions from all but one circuit are also available from FindLaw, **http://www.findlaw.com**. (For the Federal Circuit, FindLaw posts a query box that searches a database at Georgetown University Law School.) Under each circuit heading below I have included the scope and search options of FindLaw's database. Although they begin in differing months and years, depending on the court, the FindLaw pages are consistently up to date; choose the Recent Cases option for the latest cases, which may include the current week's releases. I have listed the FindLaw site first when its holdings or search options are superior to court-affiliated page.

> *The Appellate Bulletin Board System of the Administrative Office of the U.S. Courts permits downloading slip opinions and docket information from all of the Circuit Courts of Appeals, for a per-minute fee, from **http://pacer.psc.uscourts.gov/pubaccess.html**.*

All Circuits
http://www4.law.cornell.edu/cgi-bin/empower?DB=USCA-BATCH2
This search engine, at Cornell University's Legal Information Institute, combs databases of all the circuits' decisions at once. Though its reach is wide, it's simple to use. Simply type keywords (the more, the better) in the query box and press Enter. Each entry in the search results gives the case's court, docket number, and name; results are ranked by how closely they match the keywords. If the results are short, proceed to browsing opinions. Otherwise, you can focus the search by marking documents that look interesting and pressing Improve. The scope of each database varies from court to court; most go back no further than 1995.

First Circuit
http://www.law.emory.edu/1circuit/
The Hugh F. MacMillan Law Library at Emory University School of Law stores decisions since November 1995 by year and month. It also offers browsable alphabetical plaintiff/defendant tables and supports full text search by keywords. You may read the decisions online, or download them; download formats vary from Rich Text Format (RTF) for older cases and WordPerfect 5.1 for newer.

The First Circuit site at FindLaw, **http://www.findlaw.com/casecode/courts/1st.html**, allows browsing, by month of issue, of opinions since November 1995. Individual query boxes permit searching by docket number, party name, and keyword.

Second Circuit
http://law.touro.edu/2ndcircuit/
Knowing the year of a decision is necessary to locate reported decisions at this site, which is a project of Touro Law Center. From 1995 on, the site arranges its reported decisions by year. Selecting a year leads to folders for each of its months. Click a folder to view a list of the decisions that were issued in that month. Cases before 1995 are lumped together in one folder (and one enormous list); the site does not disclose how far back its pre-1995 holdings go. Options for sorting each list are first party, docket number, and date of posting. From this site you may jump to Web pages for the district courts in the Second Circuit, as well as the other Circuit Courts of Appeals. You may also search the U.S. Code or use a handful of search engines, all of which are general and not geared to law.

FindLaw's site, **http://www.findlaw.com/casecode/courts/2nd.html**, allows browsing, by month of issue, of opinions since January 1995. Individual query boxes permit searching by docket number, party name, and keyword.

Third Circuit
http://www.findlaw.com/casecode/courts/3rd.html
For the most locating options, visit FindLaw, which allows browsing, by month of issue, of reported opinions since May 1994. Individual query boxes permit searching by docket number, party name, and keyword.

An alternate Third Circuit site is maintained by the Villanova University School of Law at **http://vls.law.vill.edu/Locator/3/index.htm.** This site lists decisions by month and year (back to 1995) and alphabetically by party name. It also supports full text search of the opinions by keyword. Introductory material states that 1994 decisions, beginning with May, appear in the database, but they are not listed in the browsing options. The site does not explain whether they are included in full text searches.

Fourth Circuit
http://www.law.emory.edu/4circuit
This site also follows Emory University School of Law's First Circuit page structure, and no surprise; it's another project of the school's Hugh F. MacMillan Law Library. Decisions since January 1995 are browsable by month and alphabetically by party name, or searchable by keyword.

FindLaw's site, **http://www.findlaw.com/casecode/courts/4th.html**, allows browsing, by month of issue, of opinions since January 1995. Individual query boxes permit searching by docket number, party name, and keyword.

Fifth Circuit
http://www.ca5.uscourts.gov/
A searchable archive of reported decisions since 1985 is only the beginning of the practice aids stuffed into the Fifth Circuit's page (see figure 5.1). The ISYS:Web

search engine is itself a change of pace. It has something for everybody—one search form recognizes plain English, another responds to commands like Boolean and proximity operators, and a third gives a menu of clickable buttons to set the query parameters. It's also possible to locate decisions by date of release, docket number, and exact name. The database is constantly updated, as newly published opinions are posted twice daily (at 12:30 p.m. and 5 p.m. Central Time). To receive these opinions by e-mail as they are released, subscribe to the Circuit's free opinion mailing list. We'll return to the Fifth Circuit's site for its treasure trove of promulgated forms in chapter 8, "Locating Government Forms."

FindLaw's site, **http://www.findlaw.com/casecode/courts/5th.html**, allows browsing, by month of issue, of opinions since only July 1997. Individual query boxes permit searching by docket number, party name, and keyword.

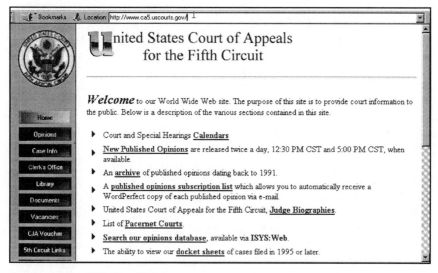

Figure 5.1: The Fifth Circuit's site.

Sixth Circuit
http://pacer.ca6.uscourts.gov/opinions/main.php
The largest database of Sixth Circuit decisions is on the Court's own Website. The archive begins with 1994 cases and is as current as the most recently released opinions. To reach the latter, press the Today's Opinions button. For other cases, there are two search options. Opinion Search looks for cases by any combination of opinion number, case number, case title (which does not need to be complete), or date range of publication. Word Search uses keywords to locate decisions. The database includes Bankruptcy Appellate Panel decisions after June 1997. Files are available in Adobe Acrobat format.

FindLaw's site, **http://www.findlaw.com/casecode/courts/6th.html,** allows browsing, by month of issue, of opinions since January 1995. Individual query boxes permit searching by docket number, party name, and keyword.

Emory University School of Law also maintains Sixth Circuit decisions at **http://www.law.emory.edu/6circuit/.** The page follows the structure set for the First and Fourth Circuits. Decisions from January 1995 to June 1999 are browsable by month and alphabetically by party name, or searchable by keyword.

Seventh Circuit
http://www.kentlaw.edu/7circuit/
The database runs from January 1993 to the latest opinions, but methods of accessing a case depends on its year of issue. Browsing by docket number is the only option for 1993 and 1994 decisions. From 1995 on, cases are browsable alphabetically by month and, in some instances, by first or second party name. For decisions starting in May 1995, a full text search engine is available that uses keywords. This site is maintained by the Chicago-Kent Center for Law and Computers at Chicago-Kent College of Law, Illinois Institute of Technology.

FindLaw's site, **http://www.findlaw.com/casecode/courts/7th.html,** allows browsing, by month of issue, of opinions since June 1995. Individual query boxes permit searching by docket number, party name, and keyword.

Eighth Circuit/Eighth Circuit Bankruptcy Appellate Panel
http://www.wulaw.wustl.edu/8th.cir/
Washington University School of Law is the force behind this page, which houses both the Eighth Circuit Court of Appeals and its Bankruptcy Appellate Panel (BAP). The two entities have separate index pages, which have similar structures and data: recent opinions, calendars, rules and publications, and information about the judges and library. Opinions are posted as they are issued, at 10:05 a.m. every weekday. The Circuit index contains both reported and unreported opinions since December 1995, while BAP opinions appear to go back to only 1997. (The format is PDF; the site allows downloading the Adobe Acrobat Reader.) Both databases are searchable by keyword or release date; search options for the Circuit court also include party name or cause number. Court forms (in PDF format) are available from the Circuit Court index, as are the text of pleadings and orders in pending FCC cases. Both indexes have a form for electronically requesting docket sheets.

FindLaw's site, **http://www.findlaw.com/casecode/courts/8th.html,** allows browsing, by month of issue, of opinions since November 1995. Individual query boxes permit searching by docket number, party name, and keyword.

Ninth Circuit
http://www.findlaw.com/casecode/courts/9th.html
FindLaw indexes Ninth Circuit opinions from 1990-1995 alphabetically and allows browsing, by month of issue, of reported opinions since 1996. Individual

query boxes permit searching by docket number, party name, and keyword. FindLaw also e-mails abstracts of slip opinions as they are released; register at the site for this free service.

Subscribers to JuriSearch, **http://www.unilegal.com/**, may read Ninth Circuit opinions the day after their release.

Tenth Circuit
The Tenth Circuit's reported decisions are split between two school-sponsored sites. For opinions from August 1995 to October 1997, visit the Emory University School of Law project at **http://www.law.emory.edu/10circuit/**. Decisions are browsable by month and alphabetically by party name, or searchable by keyword. From October 1997 on, go to WashLaw Web (of Washburn University School of Law) at **http://www.washlaw.edu/searchlaw.html#10th Circuit**. A keyword search is necessary to retrieve cases.

FindLaw, **http://www.findlaw.com/casecode/courts/10th.html**, allows browsing, by month of issue, of opinions since November 1995. Individual query boxes permit searching by docket number, party name, and keyword.

Tenth Circuit cases are also accessible, for a fee, through an electronic bulletin board called the Appellate Bulletin Board System. The Circuit posts instructions for registering at **http://www.ck10.uscourts.gov/circuit/abbs.html**.

Eleventh Circuit
http://www.law.emory.edu/11circuit/
This Emory University School of Law project is set up just like its other opinion banks. Reported decisions since November 1994 are browsable by month and alphabetically by party name, or searchable by keyword. Files are downloadable in RTF or WordPerfect 5.1, depending on the case's age.

FindLaw, **http://www.findlaw.com/casecode/courts/11th.html**, allows browsing, by month of issue, of opinions since December 1994. Individual query boxes permit searching by docket number, party name, and keyword.

The Eleventh Circuit posts monthly collections of opinions (starting in October 1998) in ZIP format at **http://www.ca11.uscourts.gov/opinions.htm**. Download the current log to see what's online. To read any of these files after downloading, you will have to decompress or unzip them. If you do not have a decompression utility, you can download a decompression tool called PCDEZIP from *PC Magazine* from this page, too.

Alabama's Legal Information Center, **http://www.alalinc.net**, includes Eleventh Circuit opinions in its database, which is available by subscription only.

D. C. Circuit
http://www.ll.georgetown.edu/Fed-Ct/cadc.html
The Edward Bennett Williams Law Library of the Georgetown University Law Center indexes decisions since March 1995 alphabetically by month and year. The site is updated each weeknight.

FindLaw's site, **http://www.findlaw.com/casecode/courts/dc.html**, allows browsing, by month of issue, of opinions since February 1995. (Thought its database is slightly older than that of the law center's site, I've given the school's priority because of its daily updating.) Individual query boxes permit searching by docket number, party name, and keyword.

Federal Circuit
http://www.law.emory.edu/fedcircuit/
This is another page maintained by the Hugh F. MacMillan Library of the Emory University School of Law. Decisions since August 1995 are listed by month and alphabetically by party, or you can search the database by keyword. Download formats are Rich Text Format or WordPerfect 5.1, depending on the case's age.

The Edward Bennett Williams Law Library of the Georgetown University Law Center, at **http://www.ll.georgetown.edu/Fed-Ct/cafed.html**, indexes decisions since August 1995 alphabetically by month and year. The site is updated each weeknight. To search this site by keyword, use the query box at Find-Law, **http://www.findlaw.com/casecode/courts/fed.html**.

Federal District Courts

At this level you may well have to hit the books, use LEXIS or Westlaw, or call the court to get a copy of an opinion. While the number of courts uploading their rulings has doubled in the past two years, Internet availability of reported district court opinions remains minimal, sporadic, and, above all, recent.

In this section I am providing only a list of courts and their URLS, along with a brief description of the scope of decisions posted. (For the full range of each court's online offerings, see chapter 7, "Locating Court Information & Rules.") If you are interested in a court that is not listed, it is worth checking whether the jurisdiction has begun posting opinions since the publication of this book. Look first at FindLaw's index, **http://www.findlaw.com/10fedgov/judicial/district_courts.html**, then search for the court on LawCrawler. You'll find it in FindLaw's pull-down menu box or at **http://lawcrawler.findlaw.com**.

District Courts
Alabama, Northern District (selected recent opinions) at **http://www.alnd.uscourts.gov/**
Alaska (selected recent opinions), at **http://www.akd.uscourts.gov/**
California, Central District (recent opinions) at **http://www.cacd.uscourts.gov/**
District of Columbia (recent rulings only of judges who elect to publish online) at **http://www.dcd.uscourts.gov**
Idaho (bankruptcy and civil, about a year's worth) at **http://www.id.uscourts.gov/opinions.htm**

Illinois, Central District (last 60 days only) at **http://www.ilcd.uscourts.gov/**
Illinois, Northern District (must know judge or case number) at **http://www.ilnd.uscourts.gov/**
Indiana, Southern District (recent only, by judge) at **http://www.insd.uscourts.gov/**
Iowa, Northern District (selected recent opinions) at **http://www.iand.uscourts.gov/**
Iowa, Southern District (selected recent opinions) at **http://www.iasd.uscourts.gov/**
Kentucky, Western District (selected important opinions, in WordPerfect 7 format only; searchable by number, date, judge, keyword), at **http://www.kywd.uscourts.gov/**
Maine (must know judge's name) at **http://www.med.uscourts.gov/**
Maryland (since September 1998) at **http://www.mdd.uscourts.gov**
Massachusetts (selected recent ones) at **http://www.mad.uscourts.gov/**
Michigan, Eastern District (selected current opinions) at **http://www.mied.uscourts.gov/**
Michigan, Western District (recent, high profile opinions and orders) at **http://www.miwd.uscourts.gov**
Mississippi, Northern District (since August 1994) at **http://sunset.backbone.olemiss.edu/~llibcoll/ndms/**
New Jersey (since October 1998; searchable by keyword) at **http://lawlibrary.rutgers.edu/fed/search.html**
New Mexico (password required) at **https://www.nmcourt.fed.us/indexatty.htm.srch**
New York, Eastern District (recent only), at **http://www.nyed.uscourts.gov/**
New York, Southern District (selected recent rulings only of judges who elect to publish online; must know judge or case number) at **http://www.nysd.uscourts.gov/courtweb/**
North Carolina Middle District (selected only) at **http://www.ncmd.uscourts.gov**
North Dakota (extensive search options) at **http://www.ndd.uscourts.gov/**
Oregon (recent only) at **http://ord.uscourts.gov/**
Pennsylvania, Eastern District (since June 1, 1997, keyword searchable) at **http://www.paed.uscourts.gov/**
South Carolina (since May 1994; index includes case summaries) at **http://www.law.sc.edu/dsc/dsc.htm**
South Dakota (since 1998; 1996-1997 listed but missing; state bar site) at **http://www.sdbar.org/opinions/dsdindex.htm**
Texas, Eastern District (decisions since August 1996 in Norplant litigation, plus frequently requested opinions) at **http://www.txed.uscourts.gov**
Texas, Southern District (selected recent) at **http://www.txs.uscourts.gov/**
Texas, Western District (selected recent) at **http://www.txwd.uscourts.gov**

Bankruptcy Courts

All bankruptcy courts (opinions only of participating judges; indexed by name, date, state and judge; searchable by keyword, phrase, document or subject) at **http://www.abiworld.org/chambers/newchambers.html**

Alabama, Southern District at **http://www.alsb.uscourts.gov/default.htm**

California, Central District (recent; by judge) at **http://www.cacb.uscourts.gov/**

California, Northern District (indexed by judge; searchable by keyword) at **http://www.canb.uscourts.gov/**

California, Southern District (since 1998, indexed alphabetically by judge) at **http://www.casb.uscourts.gov/html/opinions.htm**

Colorado (very recent only) at **http://www.cob.uscourts.gov/bindex.htm**

Illinois, Southern District (previous two weeks) at **http://www.ilsb.uscourts.gov/**

Iowa, Northern District (searchable by date, judge, keyword; summaries available) at **http://www.ianb.uscourts.gov/index.html**

Kentucky, Eastern District (since 1991 for Judges Lee and Howard; mid-1999 for Judge Scott) at **http://www.kyeb.uscourts.gov/**

Kentucky, Western District (selected only) at **http://www.kywd.uscourts.gov/**

Maryland (scope not disclosed) at **http://www.mdb.uscourts.gov/**

Minnesota (since 1990; indexed by judge; keyword searchable) at **http://www.mnb.uscourts.gov**

Missouri, Eastern District at **http://www.moeb.uscourts.gov/**

New Hampshire (current year) at **http://www.nhb.uscourts.gov/**

New Jersey (selected recent) at **http://njuscourts.org**

New Mexico (password required) at **http://www.nmcourt.fed.us/bkdocs/**

New York, Northern District (posted by date and division; searchable by keyword and case number) at **http://www.nynb.uscourts.gov/**

North Carolina, Western District (opinions of past thirty days) at **http://www.ncbankruptcy.org/opinions/opinions.html**

Pennsylvania, Eastern District (recent) at **http://www.paeb.uscourts.gov**

Pennsylvania, Middle District (since 1980; unofficial site) at **http://www.uslawcenter.com/usmiddle/**

Rhode Island at **http://www.rib.uscourts.gov/**

South Carolina (indexed by judge) at **http://www.scb.uscourts.gov/**

South Dakota (since 1987, indexed alphabetically and by topic) at **http://www.sdb.uscourts.gov**

Texas, Western District (searchable) at **http://www.txwb.uscourts.gov/**

Utah (since January 1979) at **http://www.utb.uscourts.gov/**

Vermont (since 1985) at **http://www.vtb.uscourts.gov/**

Virginia, Eastern District (selected; no-cost registration required for access) at **http://vaeb.uscourts.gov/index.html**

Wyoming (searchable only) at **http://www.wyb.uscourts.gov/Default.htm**

Other Federal Courts

Several federal courts with specialized jurisdictions now offer their recent opinions online.

Air Force Court of Criminal Appeals
https://afcca.law.af.mil/
The court indexes recent published opinions by release date, starting with the most recent, and lists the year's unpublished memorandum opinions by month of release.

Armed Services Board of Contract Appeals
http://www.law.gwu.edu/ASBCA/
Decisions since March 1996 are indexed by date and searchable by keyword. The format is MS Word. If you do not have that program, use the site's links to download a viewer.

Court of Appeals for the Armed Forces
http://www.armfor.uscourts.gov/
Using this site requires knowing a decision's name and year of issue. Beginning with the 1997 term (from October 1, 1997), opinions are posted, in HTML, in an order that appears to be by release date.

Court of Federal Claims
http://www.law.gwu.edu/fedcl
The court posts its opinions since 1997, which are indexed by year and searchable by keyword. George Washington University Law is the sponsor of this page. The identical material is also available from the Contract Law Division of the Office of General Counsel of the United States Department of Commerce at http://www.contracts.ogc.doc.gov/fedcl/.

Court of International Trade
http://www.uscit.gov/
The court indexes slip opinions by release date, beginning with the most recent. Cases are in Adobe Acrobat format.

Tax Court
http://www.ustaxcourt.gov
The Tax Court's site makes available the day's opinions, as well as decisions issued since January 1, 1999. The search engine's options include release date, case name, and keyword. Cases are downloadable in Adobe Acrobat format; you may download the Reader from the site.

State Cases

Recent decisions are available in some form online from the highest courts of almost all the states, with courts of appeals opinions lagging somewhat behind. Many of these sites target only slip opinions that are hot off the press, before they appear in the advance sheets. Some will even send notice of opinions to your e-mail box as they are released. Looking for the recent decisions is the only reason to use these state resources, in fact. Few of the databases in this section venture as far back as 1990; most are only two to three years old. Extensive research projects will require a trip to the library or subscribing to a commercial database.

The list begins with two all-encompassing sites. (Don't forget that FindLaw, **http://www.findlaw.com/11stategov/index.html,** and ALSO, **http://www.lawsource.com/also/#[United States],** are one-stop starting points for all the states as well.) After them, resources for individual states appear in alphabetical order. I have given the URL for the first page of a site when the location of the decisions database is obvious or easy to find. Otherwise, I have listed the exact URL for the caselaw index or search page.

StateLaw—State Government and Legislative Info
http://www.washlaw.edu/uslaw/statelaw.html
This comprehensive index of resources, courtesy of the Washburn University School of Law, is one easy place to check whether a state's caselaw is online. Simply click on a name to see what it has on the Internet. In some instances, WashLaw's state summary pages include a query box to search a decision database at another site. To reach this resource from WashLaw's opening page, scroll down the index to the heading Search State Law Full-Text.

U.S. States
http://www.law.emory.edu/LAW/refdesk/country/us/state/
Emory University School of Law's list works just like Washburn's. Choose a state from the alphabetical list. If its cases are online, the next page will have a link to them. This index also includes a multistate option. I find the links less useful here than at WashLaw, because they tend to be only names, without any elaboration on the nature of the resources at the linked site.

Alalinc (Alabama Legal Information Center)
http://www.alalinc.net
Alalinc provides electronic access, by annual subscription, to a searchable database containing reported decisions of all of the state's appellate courts. An enhanced subscription package includes both the database and Internet service.

Alabama Supreme Court Decisions
http://www.wallacejordan.com/decision.htm
The firm of Wallace, Jordan, Ratliff & Brandt, L.L.C. maintains this searchable database of opinions since April 1998. For browsing, decisions are grouped by calendar quarter and year. The site also sends e-mail updates announcing and

describing opinions released the previous week. The top of the page contains instructions for subscribing to this free service.

Alaska
The latest Supreme Court slip opinions are available from the Alaska Court System at **http://www.alaska.net/~akctlib/sp.htm**. The system posts Court of Appeals slip opinions at **http://www.alaska.net/~akctlib/ap.htm**. Both types of opinions remain online only until they are published in the *Pacific Reporter*. For the past three months' memorandum decisions of the Court of Appeals, visit **http://www.alaska.net/~akctlib/moj.htm**.

Alaska Legal Resource Center
http://www.touchngo.com/lglcntr/index.htm
This public interest page (see figure 5.2) indexes Supreme Court opinions by year and subject, while it lists Court of Appeals criminal opinions by release date. Recent Supreme Court opinions are also listed by release date, often accompanied by a capsule description. The databases for both courts, which go back to 1991, are searchable by keyword. The law offices of James B. Gottstein provides the content for the site.

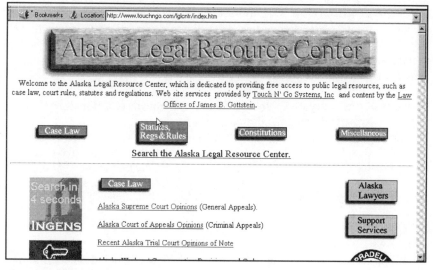

Figure 5.2: The Alaska Legal Resource Center.

Arizona Supreme Court Opinions
http://www.supreme.state.az.us/opin/
The Supreme Court posts opinions in reverse chronological order here. The archive starts with December 23, 1997. There is not a search engine specifically tailored to the decisions; use the site's general engine instead.

Arizona Court of Appeals
http://www.state.az.us/co/
The court's two divisions take differing approaches to releasing recent opinions on the Internet. Division One indexes its rulings by subject matter. Under each heading, cases appear in reverse date order, accompanied by a statement of the question involved in the appeal. For Division Two decisions, take the link from this site's index page, or surf directly to **http://www.apltwo.ct.state.az.us**. Division Two indexes posted decisions by release date and retains them for at least 180 days.

Older decisions of both appeals courts appear on FindLaw, **http://www.findlaw.com/11stategov/az/azca.html**. The archive starts in August 1997 for Division One and in July 1998 for Division Two. Both are searchable by docket number and case name. Supreme Court decisions since 1997 are also available here.

Arkansas Courts
http://courts.state.ar.us/opinions/opmain.htm
The Arkansas Judiciary site indexes opinions of the Supreme Court and the Court of Appeals by term. The database goes back to the Spring Term of 1996. (To search cases back to September 1994, use the search engine at WashLaw's Arkansas page, **http://www.washlaw.edu/uslaw/uslal_co.html#Arkansas**.) The site includes a full text search engine, as well as two unusual features: The first is a list of opinions that have been corrected since their original posting, with an explanation of the changes. Also, a table of parallel cites gives the corresponding S.W. 2d. volume for recent Arkansas and Arkansas 2d. cases.

Opinions of the Supreme Court and Courts of Appeals (California)
http://www.courtinfo.ca.gov/opinions
Come here to obtain decisions as they are handed down. This site posts Supreme Court and Court of Appeals slip opinions from the previous 100 days. It also allows no-charge downloading of slip opinions from the previous sixty hours, in Word 97 and Adobe Acrobat formats. Supreme Court opinions are posted immediately after filing; appeals decisions come online within hours of filing.

Cal Law
http://www.callaw.com/index.shtml
A subscription to this wide-ranging legal information site includes access to the published decisions issued by the Supreme Court and the Courts of Appeals in the previous six months. A free 30-day trial subscription is available. This site is now an affiliate of American Lawyer Media and Law.com.

JuriSearch
http://www.unilegal.com/
This subscription service provides a searchable database of all California cases since 1934 (back to Cal. 2d and Cal.App.2d). The Daily Opinion feature posts the

previous day's decisions of the Supreme Court and Courts of Appeals (as well as the U.S. Supreme Court and Ninth Circuit Court of Appeals). JuriSearch also offers a free 30-day trial membership.

Colorado Supreme Court
http://www.cobar.org/coappcts/scndx.htm
Here's where the Colorado Bar Association posts opinions issued since October 1996. The browsable index includes only opinions since November 1998. Accessing the full database and search engine requires membership in the state bar and a password. Bar members may also sign up for a free opinions listserv, which delivers case captions and summaries of Supreme Court and Court of Appeals decisions promptly after release.

Colorado Court of Appeals
http://www.cobar.org/coappcts/ctappndx.htm
The Colorado Bar Association, working with the Court of Appeals BBS, posts appeals decisions issued since October 1996. Again, the browsable index of cases goes back to only November 1998, and access to the full, searchable database is open only to state bar members.

Supreme Court of Delaware
http://courts.state.de.us/supreme/ordsops/list.htm
The court posts opinions and final orders, three days after issuance. Indexed for browsing by release date, they remain on the site for thirty days. Afterwards, all the opinions from the month are posted in a compressed or zipped file, which requires a decompression utility for viewing. Compressed opinions date back to November 1998. FindLaw indexes Supreme Court opinions since October 1998 at **http://www.findlaw.com/11stategov/de/deca.html**. An engine allows searching by case name or docket number.

District of Columbia Court of Appeals
http://www.dcbar.org/dcca/opinions.html
The District of Columbia Bar hosts appellate opinions since September 1999, indexed by month, in Adobe Acrobat and WordPerfect 6.1 formats.

Supreme Court of Florida Opinions
http://www.law.ufl.edu/opinions/supreme/
This site, which is maintained by the University of Florida Levin College of Law, indexes opinions by year and month, starting with September 1995. The search function is not a full-fledged engine, but requires that you select a year to access cases. More routes to locating cases exist at FindLaw, **http://www.findlaw.com/11stategov/fl/flca.html** which indexes the cases by month and year and allows searching by case name or docket number.

Supreme Court of Florida Slip Opinions
http://www.flcourts.org/
When the Supreme Court releases opinions each Thursday, it also posts them here, in three formats: Adobe Acrobat, ZIP, and EXE (a self-extracting file type, whose contents can be read in a word processing program). Opinions are available online the day of issue, usually by 2 p.m. Eastern time. The site archives a few months' uploads.

Florida Courts—Florida Law Online
http://www.gate.net/~wyman/flo.html
This privately maintained site, courtesy of attorney James Wyman, permits browsing Supreme Court opinions since September 1995, or searching them by case name. It permits the same type of browsing of Second District Court of Appeals opinions since March 3, 1998, which may be searched by keyword. The site links to the Fourth District Court of Appeals' bare-bones list of decisions from the previous two months, indexed by date, which you can access directly at **http://www.flcourts.org/4dca/opdate.html**.

Supreme Court of Georgia
http://www2.state.ga.us/Courts/Supreme/sc_opidx.htm
At its official site, the court posts summaries of published decisions since January 1996. Knowing the date of a decision is necessary to find it, because the index takes the form of actual calendar pages. Click on a date to see the cases that were decided that day, which are arranged under subject matter headings.

Daily Report Online (Georgia)
http://www.dailyreportonline.com/
E-mail notification of newly issued Georgia appellate decisions comes with a paid subscription to the online services of this newspaper, an affiliate of American Lawyer Media and Law.com. A free 30-day trial membership is available.

Hawaii Appellate Court Opinions
http://www.hsba.org/index/court/CASELAW.HTM
The Hawaii State Bar Association offers several avenues of attack on opinions issued by the Supreme Court and the Intermediate Court of Appeals since 1989. Besides an alphabetical index and a search engine, it provides a subject matter index.

Hawaii Appellate Court Orders and Opinions
http://www.state.hi.us/jud/ctops.htm
The Hawaii Supreme Court Law Library posts slip opinions since January 1998 of the Supreme Court and the Intermediate Court of Appeals. Browse decisions by date, or search by keyword or case name. The same range of opinions is also available at FindLaw's Hawaii page at **http://www.findlaw.com/11stategov/hi/hica.html**. They are indexed by date and are searchable by case name or docket number.

Idaho Judicial Branch
http://www.state.id.us/judicial/apellate.htm
The Idaho Judiciary posts opinions of the Supreme Court and Court of Appeals the day they're released and retains them for ninety days. The site separates Supreme Court cases into the categories of civil, criminal, and agency appeals, while the Courts of Appeals listings split between civil and criminal. The database is searchable by keyword. For decisions of both courts back to November 1998, use FindLaw's Idaho page at **http://www.findlaw.com/11stategov/id/idca.html**, where you can search by case name or docket number.

Illinois Judicial Decisions Online
http://www.state.il.us/court/
The Office of the Reporter of Decisions posts Supreme Court opinions filed since May 23, 1996, and Appellate Court opinions since September 1, 1996. All opinions are indexed by year of release, while the Appellate Court's are further broken down by district. The Recent Uploads section contains compressed files of all opinions that were released on the listed date. The site discloses modifications that the courts have made to opinions since they were posted. It also supports searching the opinions by keyword.

At FindLaw, **http://www.findlaw.com/11stategov/il/ilca.html**, you can browse a comparable database by month and date of release, or search by case name or docket number. (Here, Third District Court Appellate Court decisions begin in 1997.)

Illinois Court Reports
http://www.prairienet.org/fordiroq/law/
Besides linking to the Illinois courts' site (including separate links to each index, as well as to the search engine), this privately maintained page sends out e-mail notification of new opinions. Subscribe, at no charge, at the site.

Indiana Supreme Court and Court of Appeals Opinions
http://www.findlaw.com/11stategov/in/inca.html
FindLaw indexes opinions since 1998 by date and permits searching by case name or docket number.

1996 Indiana Judicial Decisions
http://www.law.indiana.edu/law/incourts/incourts.html
1995 Judicial Decisions
http://www.law.indiana.edu/law/incourts/1995/1995.html
The Indiana University Law School-Bloomington provides Supreme Court, Court of Appeals, and Tax Court opinions for 1995 and 1996 only. They are searchable by subject matter and keyword, and browsable by party, date, and month.

Indiana Judicial Opinions
http://www.ai.org/judiciary/opinions/
Look under headings for the Supreme Court, Court of Appeals, and Tax Court for the day's opinions, if any. Under Judicial Opinions Archive, you may browse opinions from a selected court. The site, part of the Access Indiana Information Network, does not disclose the scope of the caselaw database or whether it works with the Network's general search engine.

Iowa Judicial Branch
http://www.judicial.state.ia.us/decisions/
Use the Recent Decisions links to view the latest week's slip opinions issued by the Supreme Court and Court of Appeals. The Archive links permit browsing the decisions of the selected court, which are indexed by week of release and accompanied by summaries. The search engine finds cases from either court by case number, title (or fragment), parties, or keyword. The Supreme Court database begins with May 1998, while Court of Appeals' is slightly older, going back to January 1998.

Kansas Supreme Court/Kansas Court of Appeals Opinions
http://www.kscourts.org/kscases/
Opinions since October 25, 1996, are searchable by keyword and browsable by case name, docket number, and date of release. The site, which is updated every Friday morning, is a joint effort of the Kansas Court and the law libraries of Washburn University and the University of Kansas.

Much the same database is available at FindLaw's Kansas page, **http://www.findlaw.com/11stategov/ks/ksca.html**. There are two differences: The appeals decisions begin one month later, in November 1996, and, unlike the other FindLaw pages for state caselaw, this one lacks a search function.

Supreme Court of Kentucky
http://www.aoc.state.ky.us/supreme/
The slip opinion index gives the docket number, case name, and date of issuance for the decisions, which are from the previous few months only and listed roughly chronologically. There is no search engine.

To search by case name or docket number, go to FindLaw, **http://www.findlaw.com/11stategov/ky/ky.html**. You can browse a handful of decisions as well, which are listed by case number.

Supreme Court of Louisiana Home Page
http://www.lasc.org/
The terminology may be one of a kind, but the method of indexing cases here is similar to many other sites, minus the convenience of a search engine. To reach the index, select Court Documents from the top page. The index groups decisions

by year under documents called news releases. Choose a year (beginning in 1996) and then browse news releases by date until you hit the one pertaining to the opinion you want. Clicking on the case number brings up a window to save the file to disk or view it in Adobe Acrobat Reader.

Maine Supreme Court Judicial Opinions
http://www.courts.state.me.us/mescopin.home.html
Opinions since January 1, 1997, are listed by release date; scroll to the bottom for the most recent. They're available in a generic text format and PDF.

Cleaves Law Library posts published opinions and unpublished memoranda of decisions since July 1996 at **http://www.cleaves.org/supreme.htm**. The index groups cases by year and month; there is no search function. The page is updated frequently and announces the date and number of the latest court rulings.

At FindLaw, **http://www.findlaw.com/11stategov/me/meca.html**, you may search published decisions since 1997 by case name or docket number, or browse them by year and month of release.

Maryland Appellate Court Opinions
http://www.courts.state.md.us/opinions.html
This site contains reported opinions of the Court of Appeals and Court of Special Appeals since 1995. To search the database by keyword, scroll to the bottom of the page, where a link will take you to a query box. Otherwise, making good use of the page requires knowing something about the case you are seeking. A form at the top of the page requires you to select a court, a year, and a method of sorting the results (which may be by docket number, term, complete case name, party name, date of filing, or judge).

The same database is browsable by date and searchable by docket number or case name at FindLaw, **http://www.findlaw.com/11stategov/md/mdca.html**.

Massachusetts Supreme Court and Court of Appeals Opinions
http://www.lweekly.com/sjc.htm
The print newspaper *Massachusetts Lawyers Weekly* makes its searchable judicial archives available online to nonsubscribers. (The URL takes you to the Supreme Court page; look for links to Appeals Court Opinions at both sides of the screen.) The database of Supreme Judicial Court and Court of Appeals decisions begins in 1997. The top page for each court spotlights the latest opinions, as well as all opinions from the current month. Accompanying each case name is a list of keywords indicating the subject matter. Other recent opinions are browsable by month of issue. A newspaper subscription is necessary to read summaries of unpublished decisions and receive e-mail notification of slip opinions.

FindLaw, **http://www.findlaw.com/11stategov/ma/maca.html**, covers Supreme Judicial Court decisions since July 1998 and Court of Appeals decisions since February 1998. Cases are indexed by month and year of release and are searchable by docket number or case name.

Social Law Library (Massachusetts)
http://www.socialaw.com/
An unusually extensive database is available only to members of the Social Law Library, a 200-year-old Boston research institution. Members may search Supreme Judicial Court decisions since 1930 and Appeals Court decisions since 1972 (both current to within about six months) and browse the latest slip opinions from each court. Selected Superior Court slip opinions are also available. The Library sends e-mail notification of appellate slip opinions as they are issued; register at the site for the service.

Michigan Institute of Continuing Legal Education
http://www.icle.org/michlaw/
Come here for Supreme Court opinions since October 1995 and Court of Appeals decisions beginning August 1996. You can search either database by keyword or party name, or have decisions listed by practice area. You may also browse recent decisions chronologically, starting with the latest.

FindLaw's database, **http://www.findlaw.com/11stategov/mi/mica.html**, begins with the same dates (October 1995 for Supreme Court, August 1996 for Court of Appeals). Browse by month and year, or search by docket number and case name.

Michigan Court Opinions
http://www.michbar.org/opinions/content.html
The State Bar of Michigan gives three means of access to Supreme Court and Court of Appeals opinions since 1998. Use the pull-down menu to browse them by month and year of issue. Enter the defendant's name in the query box, choose a year, and press search. You may also take the link to the most recent posted decision, the date of which is given. (The menu and query box for Court of Appeals decisions are lumped together with the U.S. Sixth Circuit Court of Appeals, just above the Supreme Court box.)

Michigan Supreme Court and Court of Appeals Opinions
http://www.michlaw.com/
This site follows the same format as *Massachusetts Lawyers Weekly*. The print newspaper *Michigan Lawyers Weekly* makes its searchable judicial archives available to nonsubscribers. The database of Supreme Court decisions begins in October 1996, while Court of Appeals rulings start in June of the same year. The top page for each court spotlights the latest opinions, as well as all opinions from the current month. Accompanying each case name is a list of keywords indicating the subject matter. Other recent opinions are browsable by month of issue. A newspaper subscription is necessary to receive e-mail notification of slip opinions.

Washtenaw County Trial Opinions (Michigan)
http://www.co.washtenaw.mi.us/excite/AT-opinionsquery.html
The Washtenaw County Trial Court has a searchable online archive of selected trial opinions on dispositive motions and other matters it deems of interest.

Minnesota State Court System
http://www.courts.state.mn.us/
The latest Supreme Court opinions are posted here each Thursday, while the latest appeals opinions go up each Tuesday, both days at 1 p.m. You may browse individual decisions or download a week's set in a self-extracting compressed file, which will read in your choice of Rich Text Format or Word 97 formats. The archive consists of Supreme Court opinions and orders, as well as published, unpublished, and order opinions of the Court of Appeals since May 1996. The entire archive is searchable, or you may browse the holdings of either court by release date, docket number, or first party name. To reach the archive you will need to scroll through the current opinions page for either court. Look for a link to previous weeks' opinions, which will take you to the archive page.

FindLaw, **http://www.findlaw.com/11stategov/mn/mnca.html**, has the same scope of cases. They are indexed by month and year and searchable by docket number and case name.

Minnesota Finance and Commerce Appellate Courts Division
http://www.finance-commerce.com/court/acehome.htm
This publication has uploaded opinions of the Supreme Court, Court of Appeals, Tax Court, Office of Administrative Hearings, Worker's Compensation Court, and the Attorney General since February 1996. Indexing is by date of the issue in which the opinion originally appeared.

Mississippi Supreme Court
http://www.mslawyer.com/mssc/
Despite the name, one site umbrellas both the Supreme Court and Court of Appeals. The Decisions button leads to a search page, which requires a two-step process. You must first mark boxes in the left frame to specify criteria by which you wish to search (for example, case name, appellant or appellee name, date range, keyword). When you press the Load Criteria button, a query form comes up containing boxes customized to your specifications. (A simpler, alternative keyword search engine is also available.) You may browse chronological and alphabetical indexes, as well as the courts' hand down lists. The site does not disclose the extent of the database; in an earlier format, it extended to 1996.

The current month's opinions and hand down lists dating back to 1996 are also available for browsing at the Mississippi Lawyers WWW Domain, **http://www.mslawyer.com/mssc/case.html**. You must be a member to search the database. The Subscription Options link explains the organization's myriad membership levels, all of which are annual.

Missouri Public Opinions
http://www.osca.state.mo.us/Courts/PubOpinions.nsf/
Part of the Missouri Judiciary site, this index is the entryway to extremely recent decisions of the Supreme Court and Courts of Appeals. You may access all appellate opinions as a group; the Eastern, Southern, and Western Appellate Districts each have a page of their own as well. Opinions, of the past few months only, are listed by release date; there is also a search engine.

For cases since March 1997, use FindLaw, **http://www.findlaw.com/11stategov/mo/moca.html**. Decisions are indexed by month and year and browsable by docket number and case name.

Missouri Supreme Court and Court of Appeals Decisions
http://www.missourilaw.com/
This site follows the same format as *Massachusetts Lawyers Weekly*. The print newspaper *Missouri Lawyers Weekly* makes its searchable judicial archives available to nonsubscribers. The database of Supreme Court decisions begins in January 1999, while Court of Appeals rulings start in August of the same year. The top page for each court spotlights the latest opinions, as well as all opinions from the current month. Accompanying each case name is a list of keywords indicating the subject matter. Other recent opinions are browsable by month of issue. A newspaper subscription is necessary to receive e-mail notification of slip opinions.

Montana Supreme Court Opinions
http://www.lawlibrary.state.mt.us/
The State Law Library posts opinions since January 1997 by month of release, then lists them by case number. The search engine supports free-text queries, which means you may type in natural language (even a full question), without worrying about form.

The same scope of cases is accessible through FindLaw, **http://www.findlaw.com/11stategov/mt/mtca.html**, which indexes by month and year and allows searching by docket number or case name.

Nebraska Opinions of the Courts
http://court.nol.org/opinions/opinindex.htm
The Nebraska Judicial Branch posts slip opinions issued by the Supreme Court and the Court of Appeals within the previous ninety days. The site is updated within hours of each release. (The Supreme Court files opinions at 8 a.m. Central Time on Fridays, while the Court of Appeals files by the same time on Tuesdays.) You may browse opinions by court and week of filing, or use the search engine.

FindLaw's database has an older scope, going back to 1997 for both courts, at **http://www.findlaw.com/11stategov/ne/neca.html**. Decisions are browsable by month and year and searchable by docket number or case name.

Nevada Supreme Court Advance Opinions
http://www.leg.state.nv.us/scd/OpinionListPage.html
The Office of the Clerk posts opinions here for ninety days after release. Official versions are available, on request, by fax.

For decisions as far back as November 1998, visit FindLaw, **http://www.findlaw.com/11stategov/nv/nvca.html**, which is browsable by date and searchable by docket number or case name.

New Hampshire Supreme Court Opinions
http://www.state.nh.us/courts/supreme.htm
The New Hampshire Judicial Branch posts slip opinions by month for the current year, and otherwise by year, starting with November 1995. To search this group of decisions by docket number or case name, go to FindLaw, **http://www.findlaw.com/11stategov/nh/nhca.html**.

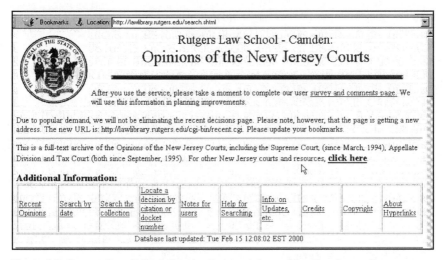

Figure 5.3: Rutgers Law School-Camden hosts opinions of the New Jersey Courts.

Opinions of the New Jersey Courts
http://lawlibrary.rutgers.edu/search.shtml
Rutgers Law School-Camden archives decisions of the Supreme Court since March 1994, and of the Appeals and Tax Courts since September 1995. Besides searching by keyword, you may locate decisions by docket number or reporter citation in *New Jersey Reports* (N.J.), *New Jersey Superior Court Reports* (N.J. Super.), or *New Jersey Tax Reports* (N.J. Tax). The Recent Decisions option leads to summaries of opinions from the past few weeks, as well as links to the full text of decisions. Figure 5.3 shows the opinions index page.

New Mexico 1999 Supreme Court and Court of Appeals Opinions
http://www.technet.nm.net/cgi-bin/noauth/prod/download/download.cgi/download/n/opinion
New Mexico Technet lists the entire year's slip opinions in an order that is neither discernible nor explained. The site may be useful if you know a case name.

To browse decisions of both courts since 1998, go to FindLaw, **http://www.findlaw.com/11stategov/nm/nmca.html**, where you can also search by docket number or case name.

Decisions of the New York Court of Appeals
http://www.law.cornell.edu:80/ny/ctap/
This site is part of the Legal Information Institute at Cornell University School of Law. Decisions from January 1990 onward are accessible by date and case name, topic, or keyword search. Summaries of decisions issued in the current year are posted by date. The site offers an analysis of new decisions by e-mail within a week or so after their release. To subscribe to liibulletin-ny, send an e-mail message to **listserv@listserv.law.cornell.edu**. The body of the message should contain only the words: subscribe liibulletin-ny [your name].

New York Courts
http://www.nycourts.com/
The *New York Law Journal* stores decisions from the past six months of the New York Court of Appeals, the Appellate Division (First through Fourth Departments), and the Supreme Courts of Bronx, Kings, Queens, Nassau, New York, Richmond, Suffolk, and Westchester Counties. The Supreme Court decisions do not purport to be exhaustive, but consist only of cases as reported by the law journal. After selecting a court (the site does not permit searching all of them at once), you may search by keyword and practice area or browse by date. The Quick Decision Service sends free, daily e-mail summaries of decisions, the full text of which may be ordered by phone and received by fax twenty-four hours a day. Sign up for the service by filling out the form at **http://www.nyqds.com/subscribe/**.

Housing Court Decisions (New York)
http://tenant.net/Court/Hcourt/
This specialty site, the work of attorneys Colleen McGuire, Linda Rzesniowiecki, and Robert E. Sokolski, offers legal and factual synopses of Housing Court decisions since 1995, which are searchable by keyword.

New York State Court of Claims
http://www.nyscourtofclaims.state.ny.us
Only unpublished decisions are available here. The searchable database consists of opinions issued in 1995, while only decisions from 1997 and 1998 are available for browsing.

North Carolina Court Opinions
http://www.aoc.state.nc.us/www/public/html/opinions.htm
Because opinions are available only in zipped WordPerfect format, this site is unwieldy to use. The North Carolina Courts post slip opinions of the Supreme Court (since February 1997) and of the Court of Appeals (since January 1997), indexed by file date, case name, and subject.

For opinions as far back as November 1994, go to the Insider's browsable archives at **http://www.nando.net/insider/supreme/supco.html** and **http://www.nando.net/insider/appeals/appeals.html**. To locate cases from 1994 to the present by docket number or case name, use the North Carolina page at FindLaw, http://www.findlaw.com/11stategov/nc/ncca.html.

North Carolina Supreme Court and Court of Appeals Decisions
http://www.nclawyersweekly.com/
To search by keyword for recent cases, visit *North Carolina Lawyers Weekly*'s site, which follows the same format as *Massachusetts Lawyers Weekly*. The print newspaper makes its searchable judicial archives available to nonsubscribers. The database of Supreme Court decisions begins in February 1999, while Court of Appeals rulings start in August of the same year. The top page for each court spotlights the latest opinions, as well as all opinions from the current month. Other recent opinions are browsable by month of issue. A newspaper subscription is necessary to receive e-mail notification of slip opinions.

North Dakota Supreme Court
http://www.court.state.nd.us/Court/Opinions.htm
Opinions from mid-1993 are indexed alphabetically and by month of release, topic, citation, justice, and trial judge. Decisions from 1996 to the present are browsable by year and month of release. The entire span of cases is searchable by keyword. You can register here for free e-mail notification of new opinions.

Supreme Court of Ohio
http://www.sconet.state.oh.us/rod/Opinions/List.asp
Keyword searches are the means of access to the decisions database on the Supreme Court's site. The page does not disclose the scope of the database, which previously went back to 1992. Documents are available only in MS Word format. It is possible to download a free Word Viewer from the site, which provides a link to Microsoft for that purpose.

Ohio Supreme Court Opinions
http://www.lawyersweekly.com/ohsc.htm
This site follows the same format as *Massachusetts Lawyers Weekly*. The print newspaper *Ohio Lawyers Weekly* makes its archive of decisions since 1997 available online to nonsubscribers The top page spotlights the latest opinions, as well

as all opinions from the current month. Accompanying each case name is a list of keywords indicating the subject matter. Other recent opinions are browsable by month of issue. A newspaper subscription is necessary to read summaries of unpublished decisions and receive e-mail notification of slip opinions.

The Oklahoma Supreme Court Network
http://www.oscn.net/
The Oklahoma courts are light years ahead of the rest of the nation, in terms of uploading caselaw. The searchable archive here is the most extensive at any free, much less official state site. The database goes back to 1955 for the Supreme Court, 1968 for the Court of Civil Appeals (which is that court's entire body of published caselaw), and 1943 for the Court of Criminal Appeals. Use the query box at the top of the page to search for cases by keywords or official Reporter citations; select the Search Engine option in the left column to run a search through the network's entire legal database, which includes legislation, federal caselaw, and court rules. Press New Decisions to browse opinions from the past thirty days.

The same scope of cases and searching parameters are available at the Court of Criminal Appeals' official site, OCCA Online, at **http://www.occa.state.ok.us/**.

Oregon Judicial Department
http://159.121.112.45/
From the top index you can jump to your choice of Supreme Court, Court of Appeals, and Tax Court decisions since 1998 (the first two courts start at the first of the year; the Tax Court's pick up in May). All are updated roughly weekly, and the top page for each court gives the date of the latest posting. There is a link on all the pages, including the top index, to a search engine.

For earlier Tax Court decisions, beginning in 1997, go to FindLaw, **http://www.findlaw.com/11stategov/or/orca.html**. This site is searchable only by docket number and case name. Indexing is by month and year; Supreme Court and Court of Appeals cases are also here, from 1998 on.

The Supreme Court of Pennsylvania
http://www.aopc.org/OpPosting/index/SupremeOpindex.cfm
Supreme, Superior, and Commonwealth Court opinions are posted by month of release. Supreme and Commonwealth Court opinions begin with January 1997, while the Superior Court database picks up in December of that year. There is no search engine. To reach the two lower courts, scroll to Current Month's Postings, then select General Information.

Rhode Island Court Resources
http://www.ribar.com/Courts/courts.html
The Rhode Island Bar Association's site permits browsing or full-text keyword searches of Supreme Court cases since September 30, 1997. Cases are also indexed by month of release for browsing.

Opinions of the Supreme Court of South Carolina
http://www.law.sc.edu/opinions/opinions.htm
The University of South Carolina Law Center posts Supreme Court decisions since 1996 by date and party name. Its database also allows simple keyword searching; the query box is at the bottom of the page.

State of South Carolina Administrative Law Judge Division
http://www.law.sc.edu/alj/alj.htm
Scroll to Recent Decisions to browse administrative law opinions released in the previous four weeks. To locate older cases, you can browse by the agency from which the appeal was taken. The search engine currently works only within one agency at a time and lacks the capability of searching the entire archive at once. The scope of the archive varies from agency to agency; most of it begins in November 1996, but some cases are as old as 1994.

South Dakota Supreme Court Opinions
http://www.sdbar.org/opinions/index.htm
The State Bar of South Dakota posts opinions since 1996 by year and month of release. You'll have to browse the index here, or use the engine at FindLaw, http://www.findlaw.com/11stategov/sd/sdca.html, where you can search by docket number or case name.

Tennessee Courts Opinions Directory
http://www.tsc.state.tn.us/opinions/opinopts.htm
Here at the courts' Website you'll find Supreme Court, Court of Appeals, and Court of Criminal Appeals opinions posted since the third quarter of 1995, and selected Workers Compensation Panel rulings since 1996. All dates refer to when the files were posted to the Web, and not when the decisions were rendered.

TBALink Opinion-Flash
http://www.tba.org/op-flash.html
This service of the Tennessee Bar Association delivers the latest appellate decisions and Supreme Court rules and orders by e-mail. Archives of mailings are available online, starting with 1995. Searching the archives requires a subscription to TBALink

Texas Supreme Court Opinions
http://www.supreme.courts.state.tx.us/scopn.htm
The Supreme Court has indexed its decisions since October 1997 by date of release. Instead of putting a search engine on the site, the page's programmers recommend using the browser's find function (CTRL+F). The earliest cases are available only in compressed PKZIP format, which requires a decompression utility for reading. Beginning in February 1998, archived cases are also available in WordPerfect 5.1 format.

Texas Court of Criminal Appeals
http://www.cca.courts.state.tx.us/
The Court of Criminal Appeals uploads opinions (in compressed WordPerfect 7 format) to this site as they are released each Wednesday. If you don't have WordPerfect, look for the link to download the Corel WordPerfect viewer. You can browse cases and hand down lists by date, going back to July 15, 1998.

Court of Appeals, Fourth Judicial District of Texas
http://www.4thcoa.courts.state.tx.us/opinions.htm
The Fourth Judicial District offers its opinions in both zipped and HTML formats. Starting with July 1998, the opinions are browsable by month. The site is updated weekly, as opinions are released.

Court of Appeals, Fifth Judicial District of Texas
http://courtstuff.com/5th/index.html
This page allows you to run full-text searches of the district's more than 9,000 decisions, both published and unpublished. Click Opinions to see what's been decided within the past month (the page is updated almost daily). If your browser supports Java, as versions 4.0 and up of both Netscape and Explorer do, press the Recent icon to access uncommonly sophisticated search and sorting options for the current month's rulings. The court offers an extensive array of free electronic notifications, which will alert you to opinions as they issue. When you register for the service, you can specify whether you want to receive notice of all opinions, all civil or criminal opinions, or all published opinions (among other options). Select the vNotices! icon for an explanation of services and registering, which you can do by filling out the form at the site. The icons appear in figure 5.4.

Utah's Appellate Courts
http://courtlink.utcourts.gov/opinions/index.htm
This one site umbrellas both the Supreme Court and the Court of Appeals. Decisions are indexed in the same way for both: alphabetically or chronologically. Posted Supreme Court decisions begin on September 20, 1996, while the Court of Appeals archive starts in 1997. The Supreme Court issues opinions at 10 a.m. Tuesdays and 1 p.m. Fridays; the Court of Appeals releases its rulings at 10 a.m. Thursdays (all times Pacific). The cases appear to be promptly posted to the Web site.

You can search the same range of opinions by docket number or case name at FindLaw, **http://www.findlaw.com/11stategov/ut/utca.html**.

Vermont Supreme Court Opinions
http://dol.state.vt.us/www_root/000000/html/supct.html
This rudimentary site, courtesy of the Vermont Department of Libraries, allows you to browse a list of current decisions (about two years back), arranged by date

of entry, or search a Gopher index by keywords. For Supreme Court decisions as old as 1997, go to FindLaw, **http://www.findlaw.com/11stategov/vt/vtca.html**, where you can search by docket number or case name.

The Department of Libraries uses the same format for three archives of administrative agency decisions. Opinions of the Environmental Board (since 1994) and Environmental Court (1995 and from 1999) are at **http://dol.state.vt.us/WWW_ROOT/000000/HTML/_ENV.HTML**. Beginning with 1995, Labor Relations Board decisions are at **http://dol.state.vt.us/GOPHER_ROOT1/000000/labor_rel_bd/vlrb.HTML**. For workers compensation decisions since 1995, go to **http://dol.state.vt.us/GOPHER_ROOT1/000000/labor_rel_bd/vlrb.HTML**.

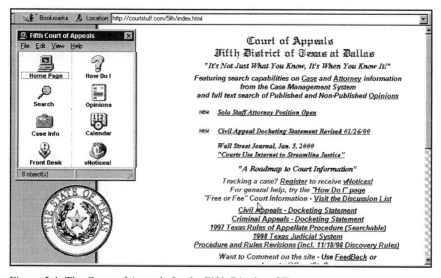

Figure 5.4: The Court of Appeals for the Fifth District of Texas.

Virginia's Judicial System
http://www.courts.state.va.us/opin.htm
Here you can read synopses of the latest Supreme Court opinions, and view Supreme Court and Court of Appeals published decisions back to mid-1995. Unpublished opinions of the Court of Appeals are also available, for the same time period. The search engine combs cases only from the past eighteen months. Cases are posted in two formats, text and a word processor. (In February 1998, the latter format switched from WordPerfect to Word.) Even if you have to locate a viewer to read it, use the word processor format, because only it contains the court's footnotes.

Virginia Supreme Court and Court of Appeals Decisions
http://www.virginialaw.com/
Following the same format as *Massachusetts Lawyers Weekly*, the print newspaper *Virginia Lawyers Weekly* makes its searchable judicial archives available online to nonsubscribers. The Supreme Court database begins in January 1998, while Court of Appeals decisions start with February 1997. The top page for each court spotlights the latest opinions, as well as all opinions from the current month. Other recent opinions are browsable by month of issue. A newspaper subscription is necessary to receive e-mail notification of slip opinions.

Washington State Courts
http://www.courts.wa.gov/opinpage/home.htm
The courts maintain this keyword searchable database of Supreme and Appellate Court slip opinions of the previous ninety days. The Appellate offerings include unpublished decisions. You can browse both courts' opinions of the past four months at **http://www.cdlaw.com/cases.htm**. For older cases, you'll need to go to FindLaw, **http://www.findlaw.com/11stategov/wa/waca.html**, which archives opinions of both courts (included unpublished appellate decisions) since December 1998. Browse by date or search by docket number or case name.

West Virginia Supreme Court of Appeals
http://www.state.wv.us/wvsca/opinions.htm
The Supreme Court has posted its decisions since the fall of 1991. You can browse them by season (fall or spring) and year. Slip opinion summaries are also available. There is also a search engine, which the site warns will access only recent cases that have been converted to HTML. The warning may be outdated, however, because I randomly selected cases from the earliest year and found they had HTML extensions. A quirk of the site is that it does not automatically open HTML files in your browser, but requires you to download them first. Beginning with spring 1998, files are available in both HTML and Adobe Acrobat formats. For efficiency and simplicity, opt for the PDF version.

Decisions of the West Virginia Court of Claims
http://www.legis.state.wv.us/coc/decisions/dectoc.html
Here you may browse Court of Claims decisions by volume or search by keywords. The archive is unusually extensive, going back to July 1985.

Wisconsin Supreme Court Opinions
http://www.courts.state.wi.us/WCS/sc_opinion_search.html
The Supreme Court's own site offers two methods of searching its database of decisions since September 1995. Besides specifying keywords and concepts, you may limit a request to fields in the database, such as docket number, date range, party name, and disposition (the last of which you choose from a pop-up menu).

Wisconsin Court of Appeals Opinions
http://www.courts.state.wi.us/WCS/ca_opinion_search.html
The Court of Appeals' site follows the lead of the Supreme Court. The database is slightly older, going back to June 1995. The search parameters are more varied, allowing you to specify trial court judge or county and appeals district.

WISBAR Legal Resources—Case Law (Wisconsin)
http://www.wisbar.org/legalres/
This page also gives access to opinions of the Supreme Court and Court of Appeals. Updating may lag a couple of weeks behind releases from the courts. The archives (indexed by date, docket number, and party name) begin in 1995, as do those on the official court sites. Each court's database on the WISBAR page has its own search engine. To get into a database, look for the pop-up menu about a third of the way down the main page. Click the arrow to the right of the box, and the first selections displayed should be Wisconsin Supreme Court, Wisconsin Supreme Court Pending Cases, and Wisconsin Court of Appeals.

This site also stockpiles administrative rulings; look for the heading just below the pop-up menu that takes you to the courts. Use keywords or dates to search Labor and Industry Review Commission unemployment, workers compensation, and equal rights decisions since September 1999. Wisconsin Employment Relations Committee decisions and grievance awards, starting in 1999, are searchable by decision number, date, employer, and examiner or arbitrator.

Wyoming Supreme Court Opinions
http://courts.state.wy.us/newopn.htm
The court posts opinions since 1996 here by month of release. An engine at the bottom of the page supports full text searching.

Territories and Protectorates

Browse decisions of the Supreme Court of Guam since 1996 at **http://www.justice.gov.gu/supreme/OPNSpage.htm**. The Commonwealth of the Northern Mariana Islands has posted Supreme Court decisions since 1993 and Superior Court opinions since 1989 at **http://www.cnmilaw.org/**; they are listed by date and are not supported by a search engine. Caselaw is not yet online from American Samoa, Puerto Rico, or the Virgin Islands; when any of these jurisdictions do come onto the Internet, ALSO has a place for them in its index at http://www.lawsource.com/also/#[United States].

Commercial Web Sites with Comprehensive Caselaw

Federal and state decisions are available at the following comprehensive commercial sites, though the years of coverage may vary.

LEXIS-NEXIS
http://www.lexis.com/
Subscribers may access the entire LEXIS-NEXIS database online here. Nonsubscribers may obtain copies of opinions for a per-document fee of $9, charged to a credit card.

Loislaw.com
http://www.pita.com/
Loislaw.com has compiled U.S. Supreme Court opinions since 1899, Circuit Court of Appeals opinions from 1971, and state appellate decisions from varying years. Access is pricey (currently topping out at around $1,600 annually), but the site does offer a ten-day trial period and low monthly rates to single-state subscribers.

V.
http://www.versuslaw.com
The electronic library of VersusLaw, Inc., has opinions of the U.S. Supreme Court, the Circuit Courts of Appeals, and appeals courts of all the states. D.C. Supreme Court decisions date back to 1900, while the rest go back to about 1950. V. charges for unlimited access on either a monthly or annual basis and offers a two-week trial run for free. I have found this site useful for preliminary research. It's helped me quickly get my hands on opinions from other jurisdictions and cut out what might have been a couple of hours of looking in a library. To get the correct citations, though, I have still had to make a library run, because the opinions that V. provides do not follow the official pagination system.

WestDoc
http://westdoc.com/
The company that brings you the nation's caselaw in print now serves it up, case by case, online, for a per-case charge (currently a mere $8). To pull up a decision, you need to know the parties, the citation, or the docket number. WestDoc would be a cost-effective way to get a hold of the official pagination for opinions that you have located elsewhere online.

Westlaw
http://westlaw.com
Subscribers may access the complete Westlaw database online here. Nonsubscribers may obtain a free password for fourteen days.

Searching for a Case

I'll run a couple of sample searches to help you get the hang of it. When you launch a search of your own, use table 5.1 for tips on phrasing searches.

Table 5.1: Tips for Caselaw Searches

If You Want to	Run a Search Using
Find a known case	the name of the case as keywords OR any combination of: • the name of the court as keywords • the subject matter in keywords • the holding in keywords • a range of dates for the decision
Find cases on point	keywords describing the subject matter or holding
Find subsequent citations to a known case	the case name as keywords, and limiting the search to dates after the decision came down

Sample Search for a Specific Case

Let's say I want to read the opinion in *Roe v. Wade*. To demonstrate one way to find it, I went to FindLaw's Supreme Court Opinions index at **http://www.findlaw.com/casecode/supreme.html**. I scrolled down to the Party Name search box and entered the party names, separated by a space:

Roe Wade

It worked: The search results brought up *Roe v. Wade*, 410 U.S. 113 (1973).

What if instead I want recent decisions that have cited a case? Let's take *Roby v. Corporation of Lloyd's*. I know it's a 1992 Second Circuit opinion, which means it's not recent enough to be online itself.

To look for later citations, I started at the Legal Information Institute's search engine for all federal appellate courts, **http://www4.law.cornell.edu/cgi-bin/fx?DB=Circuits**. In the query box I typed:

Roby AND Lloyd's

This turned up an error message because of the apostrophe. I decided to try a wildcard for the defendant's name. Since this search engine uses a period instead of the more common asterisk, I entered:

Roby AND Lloyd.

These keywords brought up the URLs for twenty cases, along with a list of lines in each that contained a keyword. To look at the opinions, all I had to do was click a link and read, then come back to the search results and click on the next.

The results page also offered the option of refining the search by marking up to eight suggested terms. I selected "london." and "underwrit." (which would pick up such variations as underwriter and underwriting), the results dropped to twelve URLs. Again, the page offered the opportunity to refine the search further by marking up to eight more suggested terms. I did not pursue this, since my goal was viewing all mentions of the case with which I'd started.

Sample Search for a Case on Point

Let's say I'm embroiled in a consumer fraud suit in Dallas and I'd like to know what the local state Appeals Court has had to say lately about the Texas Consumer Fraud—Deceptive Trade Practices Act. To find decisions from the past year or so, I went to the Texas Court of Appeals for the Fifth District's site at **http://courtstuff.com/5th/index.html**. I clicked the option to search the full text of the court's decisions. The keywords:

> consumer and deceptive

brought up a page with summaries of and links to ten decisions. A link at the bottom took me to the next ten decisions, which led to ten more, which led to ten more, which led to . . . my deciding that adding a date constraint to the search might be a good idea. I clicked my browser's Back button and refined the search to:

> consumer and deceptive and 1999

Voila! This brought up just what I needed: links to eleven opinions that the court handed down in 1999 on the statute.

You've just cleared the first big hurdle in moving your research online. If you can locate a case on the Web, you can find anything. You'll soon see that the techniques (and often the resources) are much the same, no matter what you are seeking. Case in point? Statutes. The next chapter will show how to find statutes and regulations at both the federal and state levels.

6
Locating Statutes & Regulations

Tracking down a statute is one of the most straightforward things you can do in legal research. At the very worst, you have to thumb through headings in an index until you find one containing a pertinent citation. In the best scenario, you head for a book and open it to the statute. In between, you start with a title or a code, skim tables of contents or popular names tables, and zero in on your target. All of which—it should come as no surprise by now—you can do on the Internet.

The range depends on the jurisdiction, of course. The federal government is leading the way in this regard. With a lot of help from its librarian friends, it has whipped all the federal codes, rules, and regulations into Web-shape—coded, indexed, uploaded, and linked to search engines.

State statutes are a different story. Legislation of some sort is now online for every state. (Louisiana, the last holdout, began uploading its statutes in the spring of 2000.) In some cases, though, only the latest statutes are available. As with everything on the Internet, however, the situation is in constant flux. It's only a matter of time till full libraries are available for all fifty states and the District of Columbia.

This chapter will point out the federal and state statutes and regulations that are online. At the end, I'll run two sample searches: one to locate a statute when you know its name, and one to locate a controlling law.

Quick Reference List

Here, for handy reference, is a list of online collections of statutes and regulations, split again into federal and state categories. When you visit one for statutes that comes up frequently in your practice, remember: Bookmark it!

Federal Statutes

A handful of stable sites maintain easily accessible collections of the entire U.S. Code. I'm listing several so you can see which best fits the way you work. If you have trouble getting through to one, try another. If you're looking for federal rules, turn to chapter 7, "Locating Court Information & Rules," for short-cuts (unless you want to practice combing through the online code for rules, which you can do at any site in this section with a search engine). For legislative history, go to chapter 9, "Locating Other Federal Resources."

In each instance, be sure to check how recent the posted statutes are. To be certain that you have the latest version, use the method recommended by legal reference author and librarian Diana Botluk in her April 3, 2000, article for LLRX.com, "Strategies for Online Legal Research: Determining the Best Way to Get What You Need." First, look in the U.S. Code Classification Tables at **http://uscode.house.gov/ucct.htm** to see if a public law has affected the statute. If one has, retrieve the public law from THOMAS, **http://thomas.loc.gov/**, or GPO Access, **http://www.access.gpo.gov/nara/nara005.html**, and compare the texts.

American Law Sources On-Line
http://www.lawsource.com/also/usa.cgi?usl

Halfway down this page you'll find tidy search forms, with pull-down menus, for searching the U.S. Code, statutes at large, and bills. Keep scrolling and you'll hit ALSO's link-heavy Popular Name Table. You can also search the Code of Federal Regulations and the Federal Register; only the first has a browse function.

U.S. Code—Legal Information Institute
http://www.law.cornell.edu/uscode/

The entire code is here, in the most current version available from the U.S. House of Representatives. Cornell's Legal Information Institute gives you five avenues to a statute. You can browse a listing of the titles or search any one of them. You can browse the Table of Popular Names. You can go straight to a statute, via a form, if you know the title and section number. You can also run a keyword search of the entire code, though your search will go more quickly if you limit it to a title. Once a section of the Code is on screen, the page will let you know whether any amendments have been enacted since the effective date. This update information comes from the House of Representatives's server and THOMAS, the Library of Congress's legislative server.

Search the United States Code
http://uscode.house.gov/usc.htm

The House of Representative's Office of Law Revision Counsel gives a choice of search forms. One combs the entire code by keyword and allows you to limit the scope by filling boxes with such fields as title, subtitle, chapter, subchapter, section, and rule number. A second offers four ways to process a query. It will search by concept, relate your query to words that occur in the database, suggest words with similar spellings, or verify the existence and popularity of a word in the database. The third, at the bottom of the page, locates cross references to a specified title and section number. For help with any of them, look at the FAQ ("Frequently Asked Questions") at **http://uscode.house.gov/uschelp.htm**.

Public Laws—The Libraries of Purdue GPO Access
http://thorplus.lib.purdue.edu:8100/gpo/GPOAccess.cgi
You can run a full text search, using keywords and Boolean operators, of the Public Laws of the 104th-106th Congresses. You'll have to scroll down the menu box to locate them. You will also find the Code of Federal Regulations and the Federal Register here.

Much the same information is available on other gateways to the General Printing Office (GPO) database. Not all of these go back as far as Purdue's, though. The University of California GPO Gate, for example, begins with the 105th, but it has a flair that makes it worth a visit—it allows focusing a search on words in the titles of the laws. Try it at **http://www.gpo.ucop.edu:80/search/publaw.html**.

For the current session's public laws, another option is THOMAS, the legal server of the Library of Congress, **http://thomas.loc.gov/**. Here you can find public laws by law number or keyword. For an extensive look at THOMAS, flip to chapter 9, "Locating Other Federal Resources."

U.S. Constitution
http://www.law.emory.edu/FEDERAL/usconst.html
Thank Emory University School of Law for uploading the Constitution, complete with search engine. The Constitution also appears at FindLaw, **http://www.findlaw.com/casecode/constitution**, with hypertext annotations to U.S. Supreme Court decisions, prepared by the U.S. Senate's Congressional Research Library. Cornell's Legal Information Institute posts the Constitution unadorned at **http://www.law.cornell.edu:80/constitution/constitution.overview.html**.

Federal Regulations

Two sites affiliated with the Government Printing Office maintain the Code of Federal Regulations and the Federal Register.

Code of Federal Regulations—National Archives and Record Administration
http://www.access.gpo.gov/nara/cfr/cfr-table-search.html
This site is a joint project of the National Archives and Records Administration's Office of the Federal Register and the Government Printing Office, which are uploading the Code in increments. More than two-thirds of the titles from 1999 are here, in some form, while their 1997 and 1998 versions are almost complete. Check

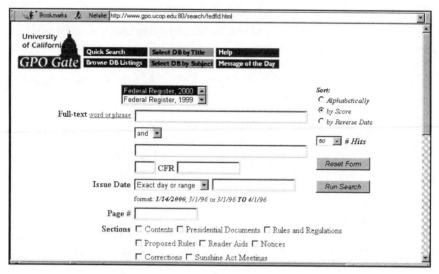

Figure 6.1: Search the Federal Register through the Libraries of the University of California's GPO Gate.

the chart at the bottom of the page to see how up-to-date each title is. The database is searchable; it's a good idea to read the section about the CFR first.

The Federal Register—University of California GPO Gate
http://www.gpo.ucop.edu:80/search/fedfld.html
This searchable database of the 1998-1999 Federal Register gives you lots of options (see figure 6.1). You can look for keywords in the full text or the title. You can enter the citation, issue date (exact or a range), or the page number. You can also limit your request to specific sections of the publication, such as proposed rules or notices.

Don't forget: you can search either database through the ALSO page described at the top of the chapter, just under the heading Federal Statutes.

Comprehensive State Sites

The Web is teeming with sites that will launch you to every state statute online. A word of warning is in order, though. Many of the pages that follow have nice, long alphabetical hyperlink listings of every single state. Don't jump to any conclusions about what these links lead to, though. The fact that a state's name is in a directory is no guarantee that all of its statutes and regulations are on the Net—yet. As I keep stressing, though, the situation constantly changes. If your state's entire catalog of statutes and regulations isn't online now, it will be eventually.

American Law Sources On-Line
http://www.lawsource.com/also/usa.htm
This one takes you to everything. Names of the states are arranged alphabetically in orderly columns. Click on a name and you'll land on a page with search forms and browsable links to any statutory resource that jurisdiction has uploaded, down to municipal codes. Figure 6.2 shows ALSO's page for Delaware.

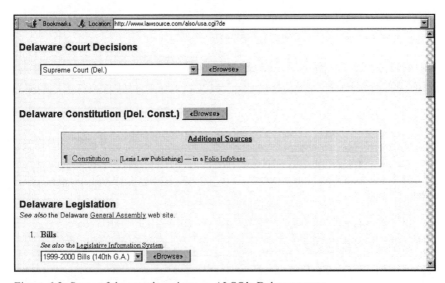

Figure 6.2: Some of the search options on ALSO's Delaware page.

Constitutions, Statutes & Codes—Legal Information Institute
http://www.law.cornell.edu:80/statutes.html
This site has three helpful categories of links. First, it has locators for a slew of uniform laws as they are enacted in individual states (the Uniform Commercial Code, Probate Code, and Code of Evidence, as well as uniform laws pertaining to matrimony, family, health, business, and finance). Second, it has a browsable topical index of more than thirty areas of law, arranged alphabetically; clicking on one will take you to a subindex of online state statutes on the topic. Third, it has an alphabetical listing of all the states; clicking on one will take you to a page of links to that state's legislative resources.

Full-Text State Statutes & Legislation on the Internet
http://www.prairienet.org/~scruffy/f.htm
This privately compiled page strives to link to constitutions, statutes, legislation, and session laws. It gives brief descriptions of each site's contents and, when appropriate, tips for accessing.

StateLaw—State Government & Legislative Info
http://www.washlaw.edu/uslaw/statelaw.html
Use the form to run a keyword search, or click on a state's name to access a well-organized list of its online resources. The index indicates when a search engine is available for a state's statutes. Thank the Washburn Law School for the thoroughness of this site.

Substantive Law on the World Wide Web
http://www.mother.com/~randy/law.html
California attorney Randy B. Singer maintains an alphabetical list of links to state law sites, which strives to be all-inclusive. The index includes federal statutes and decisions, as well as links to resources by legal topic.

U.S. States
http://www.law.emory.edu/LAW/refdesk/country/us/state/
A feature of Emory Law Library Electronic Reference Desk, this easily navigable site begins with a simple index of state names. Since it separates resources on each state's page by subject headings, you can tell at a glance which statutes are among them.

Individual State Sites

As recently as two years ago, looking for state laws online was like sticking your hand into a grab bag. Now the Web has statutes for every state. While a few make only the latest legislation available, most of the state pages post the full range of statutes and codes. For jurisdictions that don't, other institutions have stepped in to pick up the slack. For each site in the list below, I'll specify exactly what laws it contains and will point out anything else it offers in the way of legislative information.

Alabama Legislative Information System
http://www.legislature.state.al.us/Search/SearchText.htm
The Alabama's Legislature search engine sifts through the 1975 code, the 1901 constitution, and documents from the latest legislative session. Visit **http://www.legislature.state.al.us/CodeofAlabama/1975/coatoc.htm** to browse the code by title.

Alaska State Legislature Textual Infobases
http://www.legis.state.ak.us/
This browsable index contains statutes as far back as 1983; look for the link to ALECSYS Infobases. The state's constitution and bill tracking information are also available.

Arizona Legislative Information System Online
http://www.azleg.state.az.us/
Search current statute and bills by keyword or browse floor calendars, committee agendas, and session laws since 1995. Portions of the Arizona Administrative Code are also online, but at a different location. The Secretary of State posts the titles and chapters from Supplements 96-1 through 99-2, with a browsable table of contents, at **http://www.sosaz.com/Rules_and_Regulations.htm**. According to the fine print, the office will make other portions available as they are updated.

Arkansas Code
http://www.arkleg.state.ar.us/data/ar_code.asp?
The Arkansas Code is available for searching in two formats: basic HTML, for older browsers, and a Java-enabled version, which will work with either Netscape or Internet Explorer 4.0 and above. (The introduction page warns that the search engine may not consistently work with the AOL browser. If you use that one, you may prefer to try browsing the code.) Both formats use frames. Once you choose a version, click the Arkansas Code icon to browse the code by title. To view the most recently enacted legislation, go back to the introductory page you started from and press Return to the Main Page. The link will take you to the index for the Arkansas General Assembly.

California Law
http://www.leginfo.ca.gov/calaw.html
Run keyword searches of all or selected codes, or click the home page button to access information about bills from the 1993-94 Session to the present.
    You can also search the code at FindLaw, **http://california.findlaw.com/CA01_codes/index.html**

Colorado State Legislature - Revised Statutes
http://www.leg.state.co.us/inetcrs.nsf/revstat?OpenView
Browse the statutes by title, or search them by keyword or section number.

State of Connecticut Website
http://www.state.ct.us/
Follow the legislative link to reach daily journals of each house's activities and a searchable index of bills. These appear on the General Assembly page. At the bottom, select Statutes to search bills by keyword back to 1993.
    You may also browse and search the 1997 and 1999 statutes at **http://www.cslnet.ctstateu.edu/statutes/index.htm**.

Delaware Code On-Line
http://www.state.de.us/research/dor/code.htm
The Division of Research points to the Delaware Code Annotated at a page of state resources offered at no-charge by Lexis Law Publishing, where you may search or

browse the code. It's current through the 1998 Regular Session. Lexis Law Publishing has placed the statutes in a Folio Infobase. An in-depth explanation of this sophisticated set-up appears on the Montana Code site later in this section.

From the Division of Research page, you can also jump to the Legislative Information System to track bills from the 138th-140th General Assemblies. To read or search the Register of Regulations, surf to **http://www.state.de.us/research/dor/current.htm**.

District of Columbia Code
http://www.lexislawpublishing.com/resources/
As with Delaware, the D.C. code is among the Lexis Law Publishing's free state legal resources. The document, which supports browsing or searching, contains the General and Permanent Laws as of April 27, 1999.

Online Sunshine: The Official Guide to the State of Florida Legislature
http://www.leg.state.fl.us/
This page posts daily calendars and journals, not to mention summaries of legislation, searchable indexes of bills, and sponsoring legislators, for both the house and senate. The Statutes and Constitution button on the top page leads to a search engine that covers statutes back to 1993.

Official Code of Georgia
http://www.ganet.state.ga.us/services/ocode/ocgsearch.htm
The code database, current through the 1999 General Assembly, is searchable by keyword and code number.

Hawaii Revised Statutes
http://www.capitol.hawaii.gov/site1/docs/docs.asp?press1=docs
The search engine (at the bottom) covers the 1999 Revised Statutes, which are also listed by volume for browsing. The tips for phrasing search queries are uncommonly extensive.

Idaho Statutes
http://www.idwr.state.id.us/legislat/idstat.html
Use this site to search Idaho statutes by keyword, or retrieve them by section number. To run a search, select Verity Search under Constitutions and Statutes; otherwise, press the link to the statutes.

Illinois Compiled Statutes
http://www.legis.state.il.us/ilcs/chapterlist.html
The Illinois Legislative Reference Bureau maintains this database of the compiled statutes, which includes legislation at least through August 1998. (Acts from the 1999 spring legislative session were slated for updating at this writing.) To search or browse more recent law, press either of the hyperlinks to Public Acts.

Indiana Code
http://www.state.in.us/legislative/ic/code/
Here you will find the code, indexed by title and searchable by keyword. You may browse the code by title online, or download an entire title in zipped PDF. The help section explains how to extract the files.

Iowa Code
http://www2.legis.state.ia.us/Code.html
Retrieve the 1995, 1997, and 1999 codes here by chapter and section. Each code has a search engine, although the one for the 1999 code was not working as of this writing. Follow the Iowa General Assembly Home link for calendars, journals, bills, and their history.

Information Network of Kansas Legislative Services
http://www.ink.org/public/legislative/main.html
Scroll down the page to find the link to the statutes. Enter a statute number to obtain its text, or type keywords into the query box to search the statute database, which is current through the 1998 Legislative Session. To search the annotated statutes, you need to register for the Information Network's premium services and obtain a user name. There's full public access, however, to legislative calendars, bills, and session laws.

Kentucky Revised Statutes
http://www.lrc.state.ky.us/statrev/frontpg.htm
Access the statutes by title and chapter or the table of contents, or search by keywords. You'll need the Adobe Acrobat Reader to view the documents here. Although this is a government site, it draws a distinction between official and certified versions of the statutes. What's on the site is not certified; the only versions that the Kentucky Legislative Research Commission has certified are printed editions.

Louisiana Constitution, Codes & Revised Statutes
http://www.legis.state.la.us/tsrs/search.htm
The codes, constitution, and revised statutes are available at the legislature's new search engine.
    The Administrative Code is available, and searchable, at the Office of the State Register, **http://www.state.la.us/osr/osr.htm**. The other online option for statutes is joining the Louisiana Legislative Subscriber System; see **http://senate.legis.state.la.us/Systems&Services/** for rates and instructions.

Constitutions, Statutes & Session Laws of Maine
http://janus.state.me.us/legis/ros/meconlaw.htm
The statutes online are current through the 119th Maine Legislature, First Regular Session. You may browse them by title, or search by title, section number, or keyword. Session laws go back to December 1996. You may browse them by

chapter or subject. Keyword searches are possible for the 1997 and 1999 session laws. The session law search engine is not on the session laws index page, but on the URL listed above.

Maryland General Assembly
http://mlis.state.md.us/

The statutory database here is not complete. It encompasses only legislation that was enacted in the 1996-2000 regular sessions (the last of which includes laws from 1999). To search the database, select Search from the index at the top of the page. Below the query box, you can mark which years and types of documents you want to include in the search. To see which statutes were amended in a session, go back to the main page. This information appears under Bill Indexes for the latest session, and otherwise under Prior Session Information. In either instance, pressing Statutes will take you to a pop-up menu with names of the sections that were modified.

General Laws of Massachusetts
http://www.state.ma.us/legis/laws/mgl/

This page contains the General Laws prior to July 1, 1998. Retrieve them by chapter or section number, or browse the full text, which is divided into five parts. The query box for the search engine is at the bottom of the page. To browse or search the 1998 session laws, go to **http://www.state.ma.us/legis/laws/seslaw98/**; for 1999 enactments, see **http://www.state.ma.us/legis/laws/seslaw99/**.

Michigan Compiled Laws Online
http://MichiganLegislature.org/law/Default.asp

All laws in force through PA 81 of 2000 are accessible here in a myriad of ways. Under the chapter index, you may browse the laws or perform simple keyword searches. The basic search page will retrieve a statute by chapter, section or statute number, session, or popular name. The advance search page permits using a number of uncommon options, such as popular names, catchlines, long titles, or conditions on a law's effectiveness (such as being repealed at a future date, or not applying under certain circumstances). Accessible from either page, the full text search function recognizes basic Boolean operators for proximity and root words. (Yet another alternative will search the constitution alone.) The help documentation is also uncommonly extensive, explaining not just the scope of the database and its search engines, but also the structure of Michigan's laws. Register at no charge as a user to obtain a "personal filing cabinet" at the site, which will store your searches and bookmarked pages. You'll be able to access them any time you log on.

Minnesota State Legislature
http://www.leg.state.mn.us/

Both houses maintain pages here, with full text of bills, legislation tracking, journals, committee and session schedules, and publications. You may browse the table of contents for the current (1999) statutes, or search by keyword, section, or chapter. Session laws since 1994 are indexed by year and also have a search engine.

Administrative rules appear at **http://www.revisor.leg.state.mn.us/arule/**. The Office of Revisor of Statutes is responsible for the site, which contains the most current compilation of the rules. You may retrieve a rule by the agency or department name or the number of the chapter or rule. It's also possible to pull up an entire chapter or search the database by keyword.

Mississippi Code
http://www.sos.state.ms.us/policy_admin/mscode/index.html
The Secretary of State offers two search routes into the unannotated code. Besides a keyword search, it will look for statutes by title, chapter, or section.

The code of 1972, as amended through the 1998 legislative session, and current session's bills are available by subscription at **http://www.mscode.com/**. The site permits browsing selected sections of the code at no charge; the choices, while haphazard, do include a significant chunk of the Civil Practice and Procedure Code. Annual fees run $249 ($149 for government or nonprofit access).

Missouri Revised Civil Statutes
http://www.moga.state.mo.us/homestat.htm
Search by keyword, retrieve sections by exact number, or browse the revised statutes by title. Click the General Assembly link at the bottom of the page to track bills in progress.

The Code of State Regulations, which is updated monthly, appears at **http://mosl.sos.state.mo.us/csr/csr.htm**. Press a title to see the divisions and chapters under it. Viewing a chapter requires the Adobe Acrobat Reader, which is available at the site. For recent issues of the Missouri Register, jump to **http://mosl.sos.state.mo.us/moreg/moreg.htm**.

Montana State Documents Online
http://statedocs.msl.state.mt.us/cgi-bin/om_isapi.dll?clientID=14003
Choose MCA-Oct. 1999 to access the Montana Code Annotated, current through the 1999 session. (MCA-Sept. 1997 leads to the previous version of the code.) Click the buttons above the query box to run a search, browse the table of contents, or read the entire code page by page. Use the hyperlinked table of contents to browse the code by title. For full text browsing of the latest bills, return to the index and select 1999 Bills and Resolutions. This site uses a Folio Infobase, which is a single file that stores and indexes vast quantities of text and multimedia information for rapid retrieval. Select What Is An Infobase? for an in-depth explanation, as well as a table of Boolean operators.

Nebraska Statutes
http://www.unicam.state.ne.us/statutes.htm
After clicking on the photo of the statute book, you may find and read sections by browsing the titles and chapters (press the + next to Statutes to display the table of contents). Enter a query in the box to run a full text search. The Uniform Commercial Code was not yet in the database as of this writing. Look for a search engine for bills, amendments, resolutions, and slip laws on the legislative documents page at **http://www.unicam.state.ne.us/Bills.htm#introduced bill.** Bills are in PDF, which requires the Adobe Acrobat Reader for viewing.

The Secretary of State has posted sections of the Administrative Code, indexed by agency name, at **http://www.nol.org/home/SOS/Rules/rrdisc.htm**. You'll need the Adobe Acrobat Reader to view these as well.

Nevada Law
http://www.leg.state.nv.us/law1.htm
Browse or search the 1999 Revised Statutes, Administrative Code, or Nevada Register. The statutes also have a table of contents, while the code has an index.

New Hampshire Revised Statutes
http://199.192.9.6/rsa/
New Hampshire State Government Online provides the revised statutes, including acts of the General Court's 1998 Session (through September 1998). Scroll down the page to browse by title, or search by simple keyword. To learn whether a statute was changed in the 1999 Session, take the link to List of Sections Affected and check the Revised Statutes Annotated table. You can also track down changes by the number of the bill number or the affected chapter. To determine whether legislation is pending that would affect the statute, go to the Bills Status Database.

New Jersey State Legislature
http://www.njleg.state.nj.us:80/
From this index you can search or browse the permanent statutes (in a Folio Infobase, similar to Delaware's and Montana's), chapter laws back to 1996, and bills. Bills are searchable by number, sponsor, committee, subject, or synopsis keyword. You can also read regularly updated legislative calendars and digests. The site use three formats for its documents: Adobe Acrobat, Envoy, and HTML. Envoy works much like Adobe Acrobat, duplicating the appearance of the official document. The Adobe Acrobat Reader and Envoy viewer software are both downloadable from the site. Current statutes are available in all three, but older chapter laws and bills require the Envoy viewer.

New Mexico Legislature Legislative Archives
http://legis.state.nm.us/archives.html
The Statutes link will take you to a page of no-charge Lexis Law Publishing state resources, which include the 1978 compilation of the New Mexico unannotated

statutes and the Administrative Code, current through September 30, 1999. They're in a Folio Infobase, much like the ones for the Delaware, Montana, and New Jersey codes. You may browse either the statutes or codes by their tables of contents or run a keyword search. The state's archives include Legislative Concordances from 1997 through the 1999 Special Session and arguments for and against constitutional amendments in 1997 and 1998. To retrieve current legislation, use the New Mexico Legislature's searchable bill finder at **http://legis.state.nm.us/scripts/firstbillfinderform.asp**.

New York State Laws
http://assembly.state.ny.us/ALIS/laws.html
Consolidated and unconsolidated laws are indexed by subject. The chapters of 1999 are retrievable only by chapter number. There is no search engine for the laws and chapters at this site, which permits searching only for bills in progress. Follow the links to the New York State Assembly pages to search pending legislation.

To run a keyword search of enacted laws, head instead to FindLaw, **http://www.findlaw.com/11stategov/ny/nycl.html**.

North Carolina General Statutes
http://www.ncga.state.nc.us/statutes/statutes.html
Before proceeding to the bottom of the page to browse or search the statutes, read the fine print carefully to verify the scope of the database. If updating 1999 session enactments is still in progress, consult the index of General Statutes and Session Laws that were affected in the 1999 session.

North Dakota Century Code
http://www.state.nd.us/lr/index.html
To use this site efficiently, it's best to know the title of a statute. There is no way to search the entire code, or any title, from this page. Instead, you must download the code, a title at a time, and view it in the Adobe Acrobat Reader (version 4.0 is required). Once you have launched the reader, scroll through the title by section or chapter or use the viewer's search function to locate the statute you're seeking.

Ohio's Laws, Rules & Constitutions
http://www.state.oh.us/ohio/ohiolaws.htm
This one index is a convenient starting point for the Revised Code, session laws, and the Administrative Code. Under Laws, you may browse or search session laws enacted in each General Assembly since 1995. Neither the Revised Code nor the Administrative Code is actually part of this site, which instead points to outside pages. Under Ohio Revised Code are links to two outside pages that offer it in slightly varying forms. Both were prepared in cooperation with the Ohio General Assembly and Department of Administrative Services.

At **http://orc.avv.com/**, which is maintained by A.V.V., Inc., each code section comes with its House and General Assembly bill number, as well as its effective date. The default URL for the site will split your screen into two frames. The right frame has a search engine for the code (which you may limit to a specific title and chapter); the left gives access via a browsable table of contents. A no-frames version is also available; just click the link to it. The site does not disclose the date of this version of the statutes.

Anderson Publishing Company posts the code at **http://onlinedocs.andersonpublishing.com/**. Here you may browse and search only in a frames-based format, because the code is in a Folio Infobase, much like what is used for the Delaware, Montana, New Jersey, and New Mexico codes. Don't hesitate to consult the help documentation, which is extensive and contains a long list of supported Boolean operators. The Administrative Code is here as well. It's also in a Folio Infobase and comes with ample use tips.

Oklahoma Public Legal Research System Statutes Search
http://oklegal.onenet.net/statutes.basic.html
Search the 1995-1998 statutes here; choose a year from the pull-down menu first. An alternative search engine appears at the Supreme Court Network's site, **http://www.oscn.state.ok.us/**. Check the second paragraph of the fine print for a link to the scope of the database, which is still under construction. As of this writing, the administrative code was not available online.

Oregon Bills & Laws
http://www.leg.state.or.us/billsset.htm
At the Oregon Legislature's site you may browse or search the 1999 revised statutes and bills from regular sessions from 1995 on.

The Pennsylvania Code Online
http://www.pacode.com/
The site contains the code effective as of April 15, 2000. Browse it by title or search by keyword. You may direct a search to the entire code or a specific title, selected from a browsable menu. Selected consolidated and unconsolidated statutes are available at **http://members.aol.com/StatutesPA/Index.html**, the privately maintained page of the Martin Law Offices. Look for the table at the bottom. To research pending legislation, use the search engines and indexes at the General Assembly's Electronic Bill Room, **http://www.legis.state.pa.us/WU01/LI/BI/billroom.htm**.

Rhode Island General Assembly
http://www.rilin.state.ri.us/gen_assembly/genmenu.html
Look for the link to the searchable statutes (Rhode Island General Laws) toward the bottom of the page. You may view or search public laws from the 1994 session

through the current one, the last of which is listed under 2000 Legislative Session Information.

South Carolina Code of Laws
http://www.lpitr.state.sc.us/code/statmast.htm
Browse or search the full text of the code, which is current through the end of the 1999 Extra Session. The Code of Regulations is also here, effective as of October 22, 1999. For this you may browse the table of contents by chapter, search the code, or download a chapter in either HTML or Word 97 formats.

South Dakota Codified Laws
http://www.lexislawpublishing.com/resources/
Lexis Law Publishing provides the South Dakota Codified Laws free of charge, current through the 1999 legislative session. Browse them by title, or search by keyword. They're in a Folio Infobase, similar to the ones for the Delaware, Montana, New Jersey, New Mexico, and Ohio codes.

Tennessee Code Unannotated
http://www.lexislawpublishing.com/resources/
The Tennessee Code is current through the 1999 Regular and Extraordinary Sessions. Like the South Carolina laws, it is one of Lexis Law Publishing's no-cost, browsable, searchable offerings.

For the Public and Private Acts of the 101st General Assembly, go to **http://www.state.tn.us/sos/acts/acts.htm**. This Website fulfills the Secretary of State's statutory obligation to publish the acts, which otherwise would have to take the form of printed pamphlets. The acts are indexed by number and require the Adobe Acrobat Reader for downloading and viewing.

The Secretary of State's official compilation of the state's Rules and Regulations, current through October 31, 1999, appears in Adobe Acrobat format at **http://www.state.tn.us/sos/rules/rules.htm**. Select an agency for browsing, then a chapter for downloading. The fine print warns that the rules for some agencies may still be in the process of being constructed; you won't know if anything is missing until you surf down to the chapter level.

Texas Statutes
http://www.capitol.state.tx.us/statutes/statutes.html
Browse the table of contents, or download an entire code or the uncodified civil statutes in zipped ASCII files, which require a decompression utility for opening and viewing. The search engine will perform a Boolean search or look for concepts that are related to your keywords. A pop-up menu allows you to search the entire statutory database, or specify one code or the general civil statutes. When I have been uncertain about a statute's location, I have found it easier and more efficient to run a couple of successive searches, rather than search the entire database and

then wade through pages of results. The legislation on the site is complete through the 75th Regular Session in 1997. The 1999 changes had not been uploaded at this writing. For pending bills and calendars, search the Texas Legislature Online at **http://www.capitol.state.tx.us/tlo/billnbr.htm**. Another option for searching the statutes and codes appears at FindLaw, **http://www.findlaw.com/11stategov/tx/txst.html**.

The Texas Administrative Code is posted at **http://www.sos.state.tx.us/tac/**. Locating a rule requires surfing through successive levels, from the title down to the rule. (To begin your descent, start with the link to the Viewer.) The site is adding a search engine and rule summaries, which will be available only on a subscription basis.

Utah Code
http://www.le.state.ut.us/~code/code.htm
Full-text, zipped, WordPerfect 6, 7, and 8 versions of the code are here, title by title. The search engine will handle keywords, names, and full questions. For bills from the 1997-99 General Sessions, rules of the legislature and a digest of current legislation, click the link to the Legislature home page.

The Utah Administrative Code, effective as of August 1, 1999, is online at **http://www.rules.state.ut.us/publicat/code.htm**. As you browse the table of contents, notice that each title comes in two formats. Choose HTML to view the title index online, from which you can surf to specific sections. If you prefer to download the entire title, it will reach your computer as a zipped archive of WordPerfect 5.1 files. The site states that a utility called PKUNZIP 2.04g is necessary to extract the files and conveniently provides a link for downloading it. If you'd like to download several titles (or the whole code), using the related FTP site is a more efficient plan of action. Don't dismiss this option without looking at the FTP page, which gives extremely detailed instructions. It's at **http://www.rules.state.ut.us/publinfo/ftpinst.htm**.

State of Vermont
http://www.leg.state.vt.us/statutes/statutes.htm
Search the statutes by keyword, browse them by title, or download them by title in zipped word processor format. (The site no longer specifies the format, which was previously WordPerfect 6.1.) The Home icon at the top left leads to the Vermont Legislature's welcome page. Take the Legislative Bill Tracking System link to access session information as far back as 1987, or Text of Bills and Other Legislative Documents to get bills, calendars, and journals since 1993.

Legislative Information System—Virginia General Assembly
http://leg1.state.va.us/
Browse or search the Code of Virginia, the Administrative Code, and current session legislation at the General Assembly's Legislative Information System,

Locating Statutes & Regulations   99

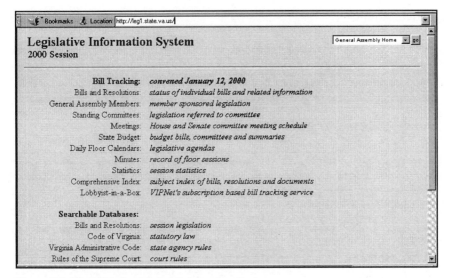

Figure 6.3: Virginia's Legislative Information System.

shown in figure 6.3. The page also posts meeting schedules and a variety of bill tracking aids for sessions as far back as 1994.

Washington State Legislative Information
http://www.leg.wa.gov/wsladm/ses.htm
From this index select RCW to browse the Revised Code of Washington (current as of January 12, 2000) by chapter and section. WAC leads to the browsable Administrative Code, effective May 24, 2000. The search function will simultaneously comb through both codes and bills from the last pair of sessions. Check the RCW Sections Affected Table for a rundown of statutes that were modified in the 1999 session.

West Virginia Code
http://www.legis.state.wv.us/Code/toc.html
Run keyword searches of the code, current through 1999, by section, article, or chapter. The page also allows searching the list of 1999 enrolled bills, which have not yet been incorporated into the code.

Wisconsin Statutes & Codes
http://www.legis.state.wi.us/rsb/Statutes.html
The 1997-98 code is current through May 1, 2000. It's unofficial text, even though this is a government site, because only printed versions are official. Each chapter is posted in a separate discrete Adobe Acrobat file. The Adobe Acrobat Reader is downloadable from the site. A Folio Infobase search engine is available, which

requires a browser that can handle frames and run JavaScript (both are true of versions 4.0 and above of both Netscape Navigator and Internet Explorer).

The Administrative Code and Register are available in two formats at **http://www.legis.state.wi.us/rsb/code/**. Choose the Folio version as long as you're searching, but switch to Adobe Acrobat for downloading. That format will duplicate the pages' appearance in the printed codes.

The Wyoming State Legislature
http://legisweb.state.wy.us/
Search the 1999 statutes by keyword or chapter title. (To find the search engine, you need to follow the links all the way down to the index page for the current statutes.) Each title is also available in zipped files that will self-extract into WordPerfect 5.1 documents; the Compressed Format page explains how. The site also makes available the 1996-98 versions of the statutes. The Session Information link contains an explanation of what the legislature has in process.

Wyoming Rules and Regulations are indexed at **http://soswy.state.wy.us/cgi-win/sscgi_1.exe**. Select the agencies, program, and type of rules. You may also place date restrictions on your retrieval request.

Municipal Codes

A surprising number of municipal codes are online. One way to find them is through state government sites, which are examined in chapter 10, "Locating Other State & Local Resources." If a state site links to city and county Websites, it sometimes provides pointers to municipal codes, as well. Five compilation sites offer alternative starting points.

Municipal Code Corporation
http://www.municode.com/
The MCC, a nearly fifty-year-old business, posts a massive number of online codes from forty states. With more than 200 entries, Florida is the most heavily represented; Texas and North Carolina come in a distant second and third, respectively. It's possible to run a search query across some of the codes. Take the link to Multiple Document Query Request for the search engine and a scroll-down menu of codes available for this feature.

Municipal Codes Online
http://www.spl.org/govpubs/municode.html
The Seattle Public Library has compiled this list, by state, of city and county codes on the Web. Covering some thirty states, it is not merely a repeat of the information provided by the Municipal Code Corporation; the California listings are particularly extensive. In addition to its own index, the site links to the databases of six

municipal code publishers (including MCC). Two are of limited usefulness: FIEN Group nfoweb sprinkles a handful of codes into a long list of the Infobases it houses, while Sterling Codifiers has only four codes. The remaining three publishers have distinctive advantages, which are discussed below.

Book Publishing Company Library of Codes of Ordinances
http://www.bpcnet.com/codes.htm
Codes from twenty-three states are here. California cities have the greatest representation; most states have less than ten, and many have only one or two. Each code contains links to statutory reference and ordinance disposition tables, which are in PDF.

American Legal Publishing
http://www.amlegal.com/alpeg004.htm
This site permits simultaneous searching of its entire database of codes, which comes from eighteen states. Illinois, Indiana, Ohio, and Pennsylvania have more representation here than at the other sites.

General Code Publishers
http://www.generalcode.com/webcode2.html
This publisher posts codes from sixteen states, most of which have only one or two cities in the database. The dramatic exceptions are New Jersey, New York, and Pennsylvania, which have more than twenty, forty, and twenty-five, respectively.

Commercial Databases with Comprehensive Statutes

Federal and state statutes are available by subscription at several comprehensive sites.

LEXIS-NEXIS
http:/www.lexis.com/
Subscribers may access the entire LEXIS-NEXIS database online here. Nonsubscribers may retrieve statutes for a per-document fee.

Loislaw.com
http://www.pita.com/
The Internet-All service includes federal and state statutes and regulations, with the exception of administrative regulations for Delaware, Hawaii, Maine, Mississippi, New Hampshire, Rhode Island, Vermont, and Wyoming.

WestDoc
http://westdoc.com/
This Westlaw service provides copies of statutes electronically for a per-document charge. Knowing the title or citation is necessary for retrieval.

Westlaw
http://westlaw.com
Subscribers may access the complete Westlaw database online here. Nonsubscribers may obtain a free password for fourteen days.

Searching for a Statute

Two concepts contain everything you need to locate a statute: If you know the statute's name, use it in a keyword search. Otherwise, use key concepts to phrase your search.

Sample Search for a Specific Statute

Let's say I'm setting up organizational minutes for a corporation that wants to adopt a Section 1244 plan for its stock. The minute book needs to include a copy of the corresponding section of the Internal Revenue Code. Here's one way I can get it:

I'll start with the U.S. database at Cornell, **http://www.law.cornell.edu/uscode/**. Rather than search the entire code, which could eat up a lot of time, I'll scan the Table of Contents to get the title number of the tax code (which I can never remember), then run a search of only that title. It's Title 26, Internal Revenue Code, halfway down the list. I could run a keyword search using the section number, but there's an easier option on the page. Just above the Table of Contents I'll enter the title and section numbers in the search form with the heading "Find US Code Materials by Title and Section." One click later, the statute's on my screen.

Sample Search for a Controlling Statute

Suppose a client wants to know what the residency requirement is for filing a divorce petition in California. I'd head over to California Law at **http://www.leginfo.ca.gov/calaw.html** and check the box next to Family Code. In the search form I'd type:

(divorce OR dissol*) AND petition AND residenc*

and press the Search button. This query tells the search engine to look for documents that contain three elements: either the word "divorce" or words that being "dissol" (such as dissolve and dissolution), the word "petition," and words that begin with "residenc*" (which would cover residence and residency). My query would bring up nine documents, with no description except for code sections. Nine are not that many to sift through, so I'd click and browse until I located the right section. As luck would have it, the answer's in the fourth result, Section 2320.

With cases and statutes under your belt, you've tackled the meatiest part of virtual legal research. Your online horizons are just beginning to open, though. Now you're ready to explore some territory that may not have been in your physical law library. The next chapter will save you and your staff countless phone calls. We'll look at the spectrum of court information available at the click of a mouse. This information is far more than addresses and phone numbers. Judicial Web pages are gaining popularity as low-maintenance distribution points for rules, calendars, pleadings, and other officially sanctioned forms. And for a change, you don't have to stand in line to get what you need.

7
Locating Court Information & Rules

Across the nation, courts are uploading everything from fee schedules, phone numbers, and addresses to rules and form pleadings. In the process, they're simplifying life for everyone, as workers spend less time fielding routine questions, and we spend less time standing in line, waiting on hold, and wading through endless voice mail menus.

Court information is actually easier to ferret out than caselaw, because you always start out with the most critical piece of information: the name of the court. That's all you need to find out whether the information you want is online.

Quick Reference List

Here is a master list of contact and information sites for courts throughout the United States, arranged by jurisdiction. Each category starts with the highest court and proceeds downward. I've noted where you can find court rules, filing requirements, and other helpful information. As always, bookmark the ones for the courts in which you routinely appear. If you don't find a court on this list, run a search for it, because new pages come online constantly.

All Courts

If you appear before courts in several jurisdictions, you may find it handy to have a single virtual springboard to all of them.

Courts.Net
http://www.courts.net
This site has links to most of the state and federal courts online throughout the nation. (All bankruptcy and a few federal district courts are missing.) If you intend

to bookmark a court site, however, be forewarned: When you follow links at Courts.Net, the site design keeps its frame and URL in place and obscures the address of the court page you are viewing. Two quick ways around this are to open a new browser window to view the page or right click on the link, copy the location, and paste the address into your browser. (In Internet Explorer, the option is called Copy Shortcut.) If these tips are too much bother, locate the page instead through the state and federal judicial indexes at FindLaw—or the next resource.

Court Web Sites, Opinions, Court Rules
http://www.nocall.org/courtbbs.htm
The Northern California Association of Law Libraries has compiled this master list of federal and state court Websites, opinion databases, and court resources.

> *Court Link, a fee-based provider of dial-up access to federal and state court records, is launching a Web service for U.S. District and Bankruptcy Courts and Courts of Appeals docket information at **http://www.courtlink.com/main/index.html**.*

Federal Courts

Use the comprehensive sites below to access rules or courts across the spectrum of the federal judiciary. For specific rules, head to the following, which support browsing and keyword searching:

- Federal Rules of Appellate Procedure with local rules for the Fifth Circuit, at **http://www.ca5.uscourts.gov/docs/frap-iop.htm**
- Federal Rules of Bankruptcy Procedure, at **http://www2.law.cornell.edu/cgi-bin/foliocgi.exe/frb?**
- Federal Rules of Civil Procedure, at **http://www.law.cornell.edu/rules/frcp/overview.htm**
- Federal Rules of Criminal Procedure, at **http://www2.law.cornell.edu/cgi-bin/foliocgi.exe/frcrm?** or **http://www.law.ukans.edu/research/frcrimI.htm**
- Federal Rules of Evidence, at **http://www.law.cornell.edu/rules/fre/overview.html**
- Supreme Court Rules, at **http://www.law.cornell.edu/rules/supct/**.

American Law Sources On-Line U.S. Federal Government
http://www.lawsource.com/also/usa.cgi?us1
Two-thirds of the way down this massive posting are query forms for the Supreme Court Rules, Rules of the Courts of Appeals, the Rules of Bankruptcy Appellate Panels, the Rules of Civil Procedure, Evidence, Bankruptcy Procedure and Crimi-

nal Procedure, and the Tax Court Rules of Practice and Procedure. Most are searchable; some are only browsable. The forms let you know which is which.

United States Federal Judiciary
http://www.uscourts.gov/
The Administrative Office of the U.S. Courts maintains this compendium of general information about the judicial branch. Look under About the Courts, then Federal Rulemaking for the Federal Rules of Appellate, Civil, and Criminal Procedure, the Federal Rules of Evidence, and official bankruptcy forms.

At the top of the Publications and Directories links is the Directory of Electronic Public Access Services, which explains (and gives contact information for) bulletin boards, electronic filing, docketing systems, accessing records, and obtaining case information by voice mail. These services include the Supreme Court Clerk's Automated Response System, which giving case status information via automated phone response; the Appellate Bulletin Board System, which provides electronic access to oral argument calendars, dockets, and local rules; Public Access to Electronic Records, a district and bankruptcy information retrieval system (see "District Courts" and "Bankruptcy Courts" later in this chapter); and the U.S. Party/Case Index, which is a searchable national index of appellate, district and bankruptcy cases. To jump straight to the Directory, point your browser to **http://pacer.psc.uscourts.gov/pubaccess.html**.

U.S. Supreme Court

Practical information about the Supreme Court is available from Cornell University's Legal Information Institute and the Court itself.

Supreme Court
http://www.supremecourtus.gov
The Supreme Court posts its rules, as well as calendars and schedules for the current term, case handling guides, bar admission requirements, and latest opinions.

Legal Information Institute/Project Hermes
http://supct.law.cornell.edu/supct/
This page contains the Court's current calendar and schedule of oral arguments.

Supreme Court Rules
http://www.law.cornell.edu/rules/supct/overview.html
Browse the table of contents or run a full text search of the rules here.

Circuit Courts of Appeals

Almost three-fourths of the Courts of Appeals have ventured online. Packed with practical and useful information, each of the following is the very embodiment of public service.

First Circuit
http://www.ca1.uscourts.gov/
The First Circuit's site features a searchable database of published and unpublished opinions (posted the day of issuance), local rules, and access to PACER and the U.S. Party/Case Index.

Fifth Circuit
http://www.ca5.uscourts.gov/
This page, which also has a searchable opinion database, allows access to docket sheets by case number or party name. It posts instructions for oral argument, including an explanation of signal procedures in the courtroom and lounge, and a checklist of requirements for briefs and record excerpts. Other downloadable documents include local rules, forms for appearance of counsel, and sample briefs and petitions. The Fifth Circuit Library subpage contains pattern jury instructions and Virtual Library links to legal sites in Louisiana, Mississippi, and Texas. The circuit's main page links to sites to district courts in its jurisdiction. A free service delivers the full text of opinions by e-mail as they are released.

More information about the Fifth Circuit (including contact information for the judges) is at the Tarlton Law Library at the University of Texas School of Law, **http://www.law.utexas.edu/us5th/us5th.html**.

Sixth Circuit
http://www.ca6.uscourts.gov/
The Sixth Circuit posts its local rules, oral argument calendar, notices, and journals of filings and orders. A transcript purchase order form, preargument statements, admission and appearance forms, and checklist for briefs are among the available forms. The site archives opinions issued since 1994, links to all other federal court pages, and offers access to PACER.

Seventh Circuit
http://www.ca7.uscourts.gov/
General practice aids include the local rules and internal operating procedures, misconduct complaint rules, standards for professional conduct, and a practitioner's handbook. Docket sheets and recent opinions are retrievable by case number or party name. The circuit posts a filing checklist and type requirements for briefs, a sample brief, disclosure statement forms, an admission application, and pattern criminal jury instructions. Many documents are in PDF format, and the Adobe

Acrobat Reader is available from the site. The page links to federal public defenders' newsletters and an index of pages for the circuit's courts and library (which is online at **http://www.lb7.uscourts.gov/**).

Eighth Circuit
http://www.ca8.uscourts.gov/index.html
Docket sheets are retrievable by using PACER. The court's local rules, practitioner's handbook, internal operating procedures, and model jury instructions (civil and criminal) are available in PDF. Unpublished opinions and appeal information, such as a briefing checklist and admission and appearance forms, are also PDF. (The Adobe Acrobat Reader is available for downloading from the Appeal Information page.)

Ninth Circuit
http://www.ca9.uscourts.gov/
The Federal Rules of Appellate Procedure, Bankruptcy Appellate Rules, and local rules are highlighted on the top page of the circuit's Website. Status information is available here for pending en banc cases. The site provides the court calendar, court locations, and a variety of forms, such as a motion for admission, entry of judgment, notice of appeal, and petitions. Every document on the site (not merely every form) must be downloaded in PDF; the Adobe Acrobat Reader is available.

Ninth Circuit—Office of the Circuit Executive
http://www.ce9.uscourts.gov/
The Circuit Executive's page includes a primer on the workings of federal courts in general and the Ninth Circuit in particular, as well as links to federal court home pages. The available publications are extensive, among them the circuit's local rules, capital punishment handbook, misconduct rules and forms, gender fairness resource guide, manuals on jury trial procedure, and model jury instructions. They can be hard to find, though. If you don't see a pointer on the top page to a document you want, you'll have to wade through news releases and meeting minutes in the Document Library to locate it. Courthouse history links are a novel feature.

Ninth Circuit—Appellate Counsellor
http://www.appellate-counsellor.com/9thcir.html
This site links to the Federal Rules of Appellate Procedure and the Ninth Circuit's own rules. In addition to judicial profiles, the host (a commercial outfit called Calvin House) has tucked in practice tips about timely filing and the record on appeals, and an article about the Circuit's track record on appeals to the U.S. Supreme Court. The site sponsors a mailing list for Ninth Circuit practitioners.

Tenth Circuit
http://www.ck10.uscourts.gov/
Here you will find the court and Bankruptcy Appellate Panel calendar, attorney admissions information, and links to district court pages in the Circuit. In addition

to the Federal Rules of Appellate Procedure, the circuit posts local rules for itself and the Bankruptcy Appellate Panel. The local practitioner's guide and forms are in Word and Adobe Acrobat formats (with a download link for the Adobe Acrobat Reader). A unique touch is providing travel guides to the major cities in the circuit.

Eleventh Circuit
http://www.ca11.uscourts.gov/opinions.htm
The Eleventh Circuit's local rules and internal operating procedures are downloadable in compressed ZIP files. (If you don't already have a decompression utility, from here you can download one called PCDEZIP. Its program screen is more streamlined than the commonly used PKUNZIP, with significantly fewer instructions on booting up; apart from the list of commands, though, the two programs work much the same.)

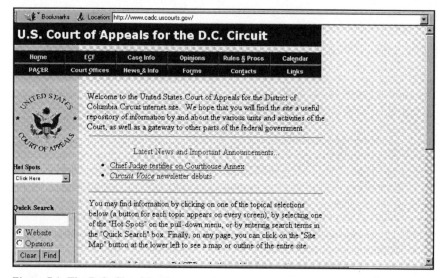

Figure 7.1: The D.C. Circuit's site.

District of Columbia Circuit
http://www.cadc.uscourts.gov/
With a few tidy buttons, the D.C. Circuit presents a vast amount of practical information, from local rules, Handbook of Practice and Internal Procedures, and oral argument guidelines, to calendaring and oral argument forms, to nearby eateries (including the courthouse's cafeteria menu). Pending case information is available through PACER, the Appellate Bulletin Board Service, the Appellate Voice Information System, each of which the site explains. Opinions since September 1997 are online as well. If you can't figure out what category something's tucked away under, the entire database is searchable by keyword. Figure 7.1 shows the top page.

Federal Circuit
http://www.fedcir.gov/
The Federal Circuit posts its rules, internal operating procedures, argument calendar, case disposition sheet, and a form for admission to its bar. Look under Court Information for directions to the court by foot, subway, taxi, and car. Recent precedential opinions are available, listed by date of decision.

Other Federal Appeals Courts

U.S. Court of Appeals for the Armed Forces
http://www.armfor.uscourts.gov/
In addition to explaining the appeals process, the site makes the court's rules of practice and procedure available in Microsoft Word format. Other practical postings include the hearing calendar for the current term, library information, judges' biographies, and a downloadable application for admission to practice. The Daily Journal, which reports all actions (such as filings and orders, but not opinions released), is available from May 1998.

Federal District Courts

Many of the district court sites contain information on registering for Public Access to Court Electronic Records (PACER). This system works much like online banking, except with a per-minute access fee. PACER allows registered users to connect their modem to a court computer and receive docket and case information. A list of PACER access numbers for U.S. district courts is at **http://pacer.psc.uscourts.gov/**. A few courts now offer entry to their PACER system directly from their Websites; this feature sometimes goes by the name WebPACER or PACERNet. A few courts use an online system called RACER.

Alabama, Middle District
http://www.almd.uscourts.gov/
This district posts its local rules, guidelines to civil discovery, standing orders in criminal and civil cases (including standards for professional conduct), and magistrate judge procedures. There is a link to the bankruptcy court's site.

Alabama, Northern District
http://www.alnd.uscourts.gov/
Local rules and trial guidelines are online. Judges post their special requirements, as well as selected opinions and orders, on their individual pages. Links are in place for adding a calendar, forms, and a docket information retrieval system called WEBDOCK.

Alabama, Southern District
http://www.als.uscourts.gov/
The local rules are available in PDF. There's a link for downloading the Adobe Acrobat Reader.

Alaska
http://www.akd.uscourts.gov/
This site umbrellas both the district and bankruptcy courts for Alaska. A U.S. Probation and Pretrial Services page is under construction. The district court posts calendars only a day ahead. Federal, local, and admiralty rules are available for downloading, as are model jury instructions. The court accepts docket sheet requests by e-mail. Magistrate's Rules are at the Alaska Legal Resource Center, http://www.touchngo.com/lglcntr/usdc/usdcak.HTM. In addition to judges' calendars, the bankruptcy court site has five types of rules (federal civil procedure and bankruptcy, Bankruptcy Appellate Panel, and local bankruptcy and district rules). The form downloads cover locally sanctioned notices, motions, plans, and certificates, as well as a variety of federal applications, schedules, and statements.

Arizona
http://www.azd.uscourts.gov/
Local rules, fee schedules, holiday closures, and postjudgment interest rates are posted at this searchable site, which offers Web access to PACER. Forms are available for attorney admission, subpoenas, notices, summonses, and other miscellaneous litigation matters.

Arkansas, Eastern District
http://www.are.uscourts.gov/default.html
Docket information is retrievable by case number or keyword. The service was free at time of publication but the site advises that the situation may change. A variety of civil, criminal, prisoner, and miscellaneous forms are available, in addition to instructions and forms for attorney enrollment. Visitors may view the local rules and pattern jury instructions online or download the latter in WordPerfect format.

Arkansas, Western District
http://www.arwd.uscourts.gov/
The site posts a list of pending cases; for other docket information, use the court's e-mail PACER system. A few complaints are posted under Documents, as are the local rules and a calendar of federal holidays. Miscellaneous civil forms (summonses, a notice of lawsuit, a transcript order form) are available for downloading.

California, Central District
http://www.cacd.uscourts.gov/
In addition to local rules, this court posts general filing information for both civil and criminal cases, a bill of costs handbook, and guides to filing appeals and sealed documents. Resources include postindictment arraignment calendars, each judge's

special requirements, court rosters and duty schedules, and a variety of forms for attorney admissions, litigation, and magistrate proceedings. Recent opinions and orders are on the site.

California, Eastern District
http://www.caed.uscourts.gov/
Local rules and calendars by judge dominate the resources at this nascent site.

California, Northern District
http://www.cand.uscourts.gov
This district posts local rules, calendars for each judge, and directions and maps to the courts. Downloadable forms include an admission form, ADR agreement, civil cover sheets, complaints, and notices, criminal subpoenas and warrants, prisoner petitions and applications, and trial exhibit labels. Judges' orders, jury instructions, and voir dire questions are available.

California, Southern District
http://www.casd.uscourts.gov/
Local rules, filing procedures (including a general manual), and each judge's calendar lead off the resources. A variety of civil and criminal forms are available. Docket information is accessible through PACER.

Colorado
http://www.co.uscourts.gov/dindex.htm
This court posts local rules, fees, PACER information, and individual judge's requirements. Links are in place to add calendars, filing procedures, and forms.

Connecticut
http://www.ctd.uscourts.gov/
Links are in place for local rules, forms, and opinions.

District of Columbia
http://www.dcd.uscourts.gov
Along with the local rules, the D.C. district court posts the Federal Rules of Civil, Criminal, and Appellate Procedure. Other resources include Treasury Bill rates, daily and weekly court schedules, fees, and a PACER guide. A large selection of litigation and admissions forms are available as PDF files; a link allows downloading the Adobe Acrobat Reader. Some opinions are on the site, which links to Supreme Court and D.C. Circuit opinions.

Florida, Middle District
http://www.flmd.uscourts.gov/
The district posts local rules, fees, attorney admission information (including forms), and a guide to services and procedures. Contact information and a map are available for each district. Docket information is available through PACER.

Florida, Southern District
http://www.netside.net/usdcfls/
This court posts civil case filing requirements, local rules, and an attorney admission application. Pending case information is available through PACER.

Georgia, Middle District
http://www.gamd.uscourts.gov/
Local rules and fees are under Court Information. Attorney admission documents and a few subpoenas, summonses, and miscellaneous forms are available. PACER information is on the site.

Georgia, Northern District
http://www.gand.uscourts.gov
Local civil, criminal, and bankruptcy rules are on the site. Downloads include an attorney admission form and a handful of criminal and civil forms. Docket information is available through PACER.

Georgia, Southern District
http://www.gasd.uscourts.gov/
This rudimentary site offers contact information and log-in to PACER. It links to the bankruptcy court and the U.S. Probation and Pretrial Services office.

Hawaii
http://www.hid.uscourts.gov
The court posts its daily calendar and local rules for admiralty, bankruptcy, civil, and criminal cases. For docket information, use PACER.

Idaho
http://www.id.uscourts.gov/
Arbitration, bankruptcy, district, and mediation local rules are available, along with the Federal Rules of Evidence; Federal Rules of Appellate, Bankruptcy, Civil, and Criminal Procedure; and Ninth Circuit Rules of Bankruptcy Appellate Procedure. Docket information for civil, criminal, and bankruptcy cases is retrievable by case number, party or attorney name, or keyword; PACER access is also available. The site posts calendars for both the bankruptcy and district courts, as well as a variety of pleading forms.

Illinois, Central District
http://www.ilcd.uscourts.gov/
Local rules and a variety of forms for each division of the district are available. For docket information, use PACER. Some recent opinions are posted, by judge.

Illinois, Northern District
http://www.ilnd.uscourts.gov
The district clerk's office posts its drop box guidelines. Elsewhere on the site are daily calendars for the coming week, Federal Rules of Civil and Criminal Procedure and Evidence, and pattern criminal jury instructions. There are forms for attorney admission and civil motions, notices, and subpoenas. The searchable CourtWeb system allows locating information on recent rulings. An associated free service is the Watch List, which sends e-mail notification of changes in cases selected by the user. Other pending case information is available through PACER.

Illinois, Southern District
http://www.ilsd.uscourts.gov/
Local rules and a handful of district-wide forms are available in PDF; there's a link to download the Adobe Acrobat Reader. The district posts general case filing requirements and the fee schedule. For docket information, use PACER.

Indiana, Northern District
http://www.innd.uscourts.gov/
This district posts local rules, sentencing guidelines, the holiday schedule, and PACER information. A link is in place for forms.

Indiana, Southern District
http://www.insd.uscourts.gov/
The court information includes the current trial calendar. Individual judges have posted their trial practice and courtroom procedures, case management plans, and recent opinions. Look under Resources for the local rules, Attorney's Handbook, Video Evidence Presentation System Guide, and the Seventh Circuit Standards for Professional Conduct. A handful of litigation forms lurk under the same heading. Docket information is retrievable online by case number or party name.

Iowa, Northern District
http://www.iand.uscourts.gov/
This district posts local rules, individual judge's courtroom procedures, and an electronic access reference manual. Also available are civil and criminal model jury instructions, as well as each judge's preferences for voir dire, jury instructions, orders, and conferences. Unusual postings include verdicts (by case name and judge) and the judges' conflict of interest lists. Attorney admission and general litigation forms are on the site, which also posts selected recent opinions by judge.

Iowa, Southern District
http://www.iasd.uscourts.gov
In addition to the local rules and the judges' calendars, this district posts civil and criminal model jury instructions. Downloadable forms consist primarily of cover sheets, notices, waivers, and an attorney admission petition. Selected recent opinions are available; for docket information, use PACER.

Kentucky, Western District
http://www.kywd.uscourts.gov/
Calendars and maps are posted for the four district courts, while docket information is available through WebPACER (at no cost, currently). The district posts local bankruptcy, civil, and criminal rules and offers a search engine for selected judicial opinions. A few forms are available, mostly pertaining to attorney admission. Registered users may access the district's electronic filing system through the site.

Louisiana, Eastern District
http://www.laed.uscourts.gov/
Local rules, filing fees, and the schedule of motion hearing dates are available. The site posts forms for attorney admission, receiving electronic notices, closed records request, subpoenas, summonses, and waiver of service. Docket information is accessible through WebPACER.

Louisiana, Middle District
http://www.lamd.uscourts.gov
There's not much at this site, besides local rules (under Forms), hours, fee schedules, attorney admission forms, and a sprinkling of civil documents. For docket information, use PACER.

Louisiana, Western District
http://www.lawd.uscourts.gov/
When construction finishes, Louisiana's Western District will be at this URL.

Maine
http://www.med.uscourts.gov/
Here the District of Maine disseminates its local rules, as well as criminal pattern jury instructions, a criminal voir dire checklist, postjudgment interest rates, and fee schedules. The available forms are primarily notices and subpoenas. Opinions are posted by judge. For docket information, use PACER.

Maryland
http://www.mdd.uscourts.gov/
The court posts local rules, guidelines for filing pleadings, discovery and attorneys' fees, fee schedules, admission forms, and sample orders. Opinions are available dating back to mid-1998. Docket information is accessible through PACER.

Massachusetts
http://www.mad.uscourts.gov/
Resources include the local rules of civil procedure, fees, courthouse directions, and forms for judgment and first execution. A handful of recent opinions are posted. The site links to the bankruptcy and state courts, as well as the First Circuit. PACER access is available for docket information.

Michigan, Western District
http://www.miwd.uscourts.gov/
Both the district and bankruptcy courts are at this address. In addition to local rules and fees, the district court posts standard civil jury instructions and lists of arbitrators, mediators, pro bono attorneys, and certified voluntary facilitative mediators. Forms consist of a civil cover sheet and a blank summons; orders and opinions are available for a handful of high profile cases. Docket information is accessible through WebPACER.

Mississippi, Northern District
http://www.msnd.uscourts.gov/
The site has expanded beyond its former focus on rules and contact information for the district's four divisions. The miscellaneous civil and criminal forms include summonses and subpoenas. Practice aids include the local rules and a timetable for civil cases. A handful of recent opinions are on the site.

Mississippi, Southern District
http://www.mssd.uscourts.gov
Come here for local rules, fee and holiday schedules, and forms for bonds, certificates, notices, and subpoenas.

Missouri, Eastern District
http://www.moed.uscourts.gov/
Resources (shown in figure 7.2) include the local and disciplinary rules, judges' requirements, a list of alternative dispute resolution neutrals, evidence presentation system instruction manuals, and the drop box policy. A variety of civil and criminal

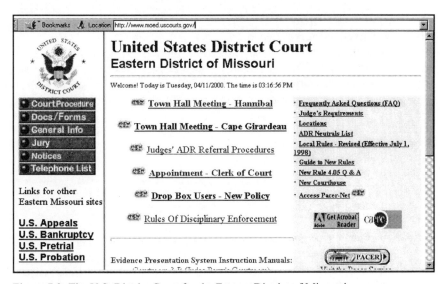

Figure 7.2: The U.S. District Court for the Eastern District of Missouri.

forms are available for download. For docket information, access PACER from the site. The page links to the bankruptcy and circuit courts, as well as sites for the district's pretrial and probation services.

Missouri, Western District
http://www.law.umkc.edu/fdcwm/index.html
This address is home to both the district and bankruptcy courts. The district court posts its local rules, model jury instructions, and manuals for general and electronic filing procedures. Standard litigation forms are available, along with an admission application. Docket information is retrievable by case number (or type) or party name; it's also possible to generate a report of cases filed. (At this writing, these search functions were hidden at the bottom of the Document Filing System page under Electronic Case Filing.)

Nebraska
http://www.ned.uscourts.gov/
Local rules and a variety of litigation forms are downloadable as PDF files. Besides contact information and fee schedules, the site offers e-mail announcements from the district. Docket information is available through PACER.

New Mexico
http://www.nmcourt.fed.us/dcdocs/
Subscribe to the Advanced Court Engineering (ACE) System for online filing and access to the court's master calendar, pending case information, opinion database, and e-mail alert service. No password is required to view local rules and a wide variety of litigation forms.

New York, Eastern District
http://www.nyed.uscourts.gov/
In addition to local rules, this district discloses motion practices and schedules. Litigation forms, under Court Information, include complaints, notices, orders, and summonses. Docket information is available through PACER; the site also offers an electronic filing system, which requires registration. A handful of recent decisions are on the site.

New York, Northern District
http://www.nynd.uscourts.gov/
Resources include local rules, litigation forms, a postjudgment interest table, and travel directions. Docket information is accessible through PACER. The site also posts the Federal Public Defender's Office newsletter.

New York, Southern District
http://www.nysd.uscourts.gov/
This district makes available its local rules, as well as extensive litigation and attorney admission forms, postjudgment rates, travel information, and fee sched-

ules. Use CourtWeb to retrieve information about rulings; sign up for Watch List to receive free e-mail notification of developments in cases you designate. Other docket information is accessible through PACER.

North Carolina, Eastern District
http://www.nced.uscourts.gov/
When construction finishes, the Eastern District will be online at this address.

North Carolina, Middle District
http://www.ncmd.uscourts.gov
Local civil, criminal, and bankruptcy rules are posted here, along with selected published opinions. The court calendar is updated nightly. Docket information is available through WebPACER.

North Carolina, Western District
http://208.141.47.221/
Fees, holidays, and court calendars are available. Document information is accessible through WebPACER.

North Dakota
http://www.ndd.uscourts.gov/
The district posts local rules, the fee schedule, and the court calendar, which is updated nightly. Opinions are available, but the site does not disclose the scope of the database.

Ohio, Northern District
http://www.ohnd.uscourts.gov/
Civil, criminal, and bankruptcy local rules are available to the public. Authorized attorneys may access the court's electronic filing system here. The site posts the court's latest memoranda and orders at the top of the welcoming page.

Oregon
http://ord.uscourts.gov/
Local rules on the site cover admiralty, bankruptcy, and civil cases. Only a few litigation forms are available, including attorney admission documents. Trial court guidelines and a handful of recent opinions are also posted. You can register for and access the court's electronic filing system.

Pennsylvania, Eastern District
http://www.paed.uscourts.gov/
Local civil, criminal, and bankruptcy rules are here. Also available is the Clerk's Office Procedural Handbook, which contains fees, forms, and procedures for filing cases, pretrial, and motion practice. The site posts multidistrict and breast implant litigation documents as they are released, and archives opinions since June 1997.

Pennsylvania, Middle District
http://www.pamd.uscourts.gov/
This district posts its local rules, fee schedule, and the Code of Professional Conduct. Downloadable forms cover attorney admission and prisoner or pro se filings. A link is in place for opinions. Docket information is accessible through WebPACER.

Pennsylvania, Western District
http://www.pawd.uscourts.gov/
The clerk has posted local rules, fees, attorney admission information, the Attorney Handbook, and the rules and practices of individual judges. Downloadable forms include notices, subpoenas, and writs. Through the links you can reach all the circuit courts of appeals and all the federal rules.

Puerto Rico
http://www.prd.uscourts.gov/
The site offers local rules, postjudgment interest rates, and a good-sized library of litigation forms geared to foreclosure and collections. Docket information is available through PACER.

South Carolina
http://www.scd.uscourts.gov/
The district posts local civil and criminal rules, along with an information manual. Also available are an extensive filing guide, the court calendar, a list of certified mediators, and an outline of postjudgment procedures. The form library is extensive and includes attorney admission, ADR tracking, and an application to be a mediator. The site archives published opinions dating back to 1994. Docket information is accessible through PACER.

South Dakota
http://www.sdd.uscourts.gov
The district posts local rules and postjudgment interest rates. Access to civil and criminal docket information is available through an online version of PACER called RACER. This site links to the district's bankruptcy court.

Texas, Eastern District
http://www.txed.uscourts.gov/
Besides local rules and PACER information, this site posts opinions and orders in ongoing major litigation, such as cases involving Norplant. Forms are available for subpoenas, a summons, and a complaint.

Texas, Northern District
http://www.txnd.uscourts.gov/
This site provides PACER access, plus a variety of filing guides on topics such as bankruptcy, bill of costs, using drop boxes, general civil suits, and notices of

appeal. The local rules disclose judge-specific practices. Available publications include the current Attorney Handbook (and forms), Criminal Justice Act Panel Attorney Handbooks, and clerk's office forms.

Texas, Southern District
http://www.txs.uscourts.gov/
Umbrellaing the district and bankruptcy court, this site posts local rules for both, postjudgment interest rates, filing fees, required forms for litigation and attorney admission, and approved Alternative Dispute Resolution neutrals. Some judges have uploaded their calendars and practice manuals. Docket information is available through PACER; a few recent opinions are accessible through the Attorneys and Litigants page.

Texas, Western District
http://www.txwd.uscourts.gov
Local rules, attorney admission forms, and a handful of litigation documents are the meat of this site. Selected recent opinions are posted here as well. Docket information is available through PACER.

Utah
http://www.utd.uscourts.gov/
Here you'll find local rules, lots of filing and alternative dispute resolution forms, fee schedules, postjudgment interest rates, calendars, and court locations. You can download rules and forms in PDF or WordPerfect format. The site offers an instruction manual for the electronic evidence presentation system, forms for attorney admission and discipline, and decisions in a few high-profile cases. Docket information is available through PACER-NET.

Virginia, Eastern District
http://www.vaed.uscourts.gov/
When construction finishes, the Eastern District of Virginia will be online at this address.

Washington, Eastern District
http://www.waed.uscourts.gov/
Here you may access the local rules, court calendars, and information about attorney admission, filing, fees, and postjudgment interest rates. A small number of litigation forms (such as summonses and a subpoena) are available for download. The recent opinion postings are sparse. For docket information, use PACER.

Wisconsin, Eastern District
http://www.wied.uscourts.gov/
This court posts its local rules and fee schedule. Attorney admission forms and a few civil and criminal documents (such as subpoenas) are available. Docket information is accessible through WebPACER.

Wisconsin, Western District
http://www.wiw.uscourts.gov/
This site covers the district and bankruptcy courts, as well as U.S. Probation and Pretrial Services (which offers little more than contact information.) The district court posts its calendar, local rules, and a couple of recent opinions. Docket information is available through PACER. Download forms for attorney admission, subpoenas, appeals, transcripts, and case handling procedures.

Wisconsin, Eastern & Western District
http://www.wisbar.org/rules/index.html#fed
The local rules for these two districts are downloadable from this site.

Wyoming
http://www.ck10.uscourts.gov/wyoming/district
Local civil and criminal rules are here, along with civil, criminal, and prisoner forms. Docket information is available through PACER.

Bankruptcy Courts

Given the ceaseless flood of litigants that a bankruptcy court has to process, the growing Web presence of this segment of the lower federal judiciary makes perfect sense. Posting standard information online fits hand in glove with an efficient use of resources.

As with the federal district court sites, many bankruptcy court pages contain information on registering for Public Access to Court Electronic Records (PACER). A list of PACER access numbers for bankruptcy courts is at **http://www.uscourts.gov**. Some courts allow entry to PACER directly through their Websites; this feature sometimes goes by the name WebPACER or PACERNet. A few courts use an online system called RACER.

Many of the bankruptcy courts will send notice electronically to creditors on request. The umbrella site for the program, known as Electronic Bankruptcy Noticing, appears at **http://www.ebnuscourts.com/**.

Alabama, Middle District
http://www.almb.uscourts.gov/
The site offers the judges' dockets and a calendar for the entire year.

Alabama, Southern District
http://www.alsb.uscourts.gov/default.htm
Local rules, calendars, the fee schedule, and a list of cases discharged, by month, provide the bulk of the resources. A search engine allows access to opinions of the district, but the site does not disclose the scope of the database.

Alaska
http://www.akb.uscourts.gov/

Along with its local rules and judges' calendars, this court posts the federal bankruptcy, civil procedure, and bankruptcy appellate rules. Downloadable documents include standard bankruptcy schedules and pleadings. An electronic service for creditors' notices is available from the site.

Arizona
http://www.azb.uscourts.gov

The court offers local rules, miscellaneous bankruptcy forms (such as address changes and proof of claim), and an application for the Electronic Case Filing system.

California, Central District
http://www.cacb.uscourts.gov/

This site has local rules, filing information and forms, court locations, and a desk reference manual. Additional helpful material includes a list of mediators and individual judges' forms and instructions. The site provides the Federal Bankruptcy Code and Rules of Bankruptcy Procedure. A few recent opinions are available, by judge. Docket information is accessible through WebPACER.

California, Eastern District
http://www.caeb.uscourts.gov

In addition to judges' and meeting calendars, this district offers official forms, local rules, the bankruptcy code, and the Ninth Circuit Bankruptcy Appellate Panel rules. A PACER password and user ID are necessary to access the court's Electronic Case Information system. The opening page is shown in figure 7.3, which appears on the following page.

California, Northern District
http://www.canb.uscourts.gov/

The district posts the bankruptcy and civil local rules, procedures of the division and individual judges, §341 meeting and judges' calendars, and official and local case forms. Decisions are posted by judge. Docket information is accessible through PACERNet.

California, Southern District
http://www.casb.uscourts.gov/

This district has set up its Website as a virtual courthouse, complete with front counter, file room, courtrooms, and bulletin board for notices—and photographs of each area's counterpart in the "real" courthouse. Registered users of the electronic filing system may file pleadings directly at the front counter, which provides registration information and a procedures manual, as well as local rules and court forms. Docket information is accessible on the site through PACER. The file room page offers both an online file reservation system (which will notify you when the clerk's office has retrieved a requested file for viewing) and step-by-step instructions and forms for obtaining a closed file. Visit the library for local rules, guidelines of the U.S. Trustees, and recent published opinions of this court. In the courtrooms are calendars, the code of conduct, and an online hearing date request form. This may well be the only court Web page that uses QuickTime, which is necessary to take the virtual courthouse tour. The top page has a link for downloading the free application.

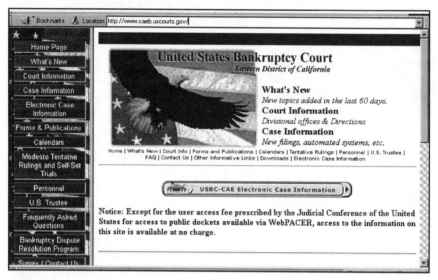

Figure 7.3: The welcoming page for the bankruptcy court for the Eastern District of California.

Colorado
http://www.cob.uscourts.gov/bindex.htm
Besides local rules, this site provides fees, official forms, the district's procedures, and judges' guidelines. The calendar, divided by judge, is updated weekly. A few opinions are posted on the site. Docket information is accessible through PACER.

Florida, Middle District
http://www.flmb.uscourts.gov/

Here you'll find local rules, postjudgment interest rates, fee schedules, and judges' guidelines. A proof of claim form is available. An electronic filing system is being launched. Docket information is accessible through PACER.

Georgia, Middle District
http://www.gamb.uscourts.gov
This district posts its reference manual, fee schedules, and filing checklists, as well as its local rules. Other resources include court and §341 meeting calendars, the bankruptcy code, all the federal rules, and a few recent opinions. Docket information is available through PACER. Creditors may request e-mail noticing.

Georgia, Northern District
http://www.ganb.uscourts.gov/
Practice aids include the local rules, district procedures, a directory of trustees, and a smattering of pleading forms. The research links point to the federal bankruptcy code and rules of procedure, the district court and Eleventh Circuit sites, and a spectrum of gateways, libraries, and associations. The court accepts electronically filed pleadings through the Electronic Case Files Initiative. Docket information is accessible through the Website for cases that are part of the electronic filing system. Using PACER is necessary to obtain information about earlier cases.

Georgia, Southern District
http://www.gas.uscourts.gov/usbc/usbc.html
Notices and contact information are posted at this site.

Idaho
http://www.id.uscourts.gov/doc.htm
This site posts the court calendar, local rules, Federal Rules of Bankruptcy Procedure, Ninth Circuit Rules of Bankruptcy Appellate Procedure, and official pleading forms. Docket information is retrievable by case number, party or attorney name, or keyword; PACER access is also available. The case number is necessary to print a creditors' list for a mailing matrix.

Illinois, Northern District
http://www.ilnb.uscourts.gov
Here you'll find local rules (which cover mediation, too), national and local pleading forms, and judges' calendars. For docket information, use PACER.

Illinois, Southern District
http://www.ilsb.uscourts.gov/
The Southern District of Illinois offers local rules, filing fees, an administrative guide, available hearing dates for objections to claims, and a smattering of forms (including variants of the proof of claim for two courts). The site posts opinions that have been submitted for publication in the previous two weeks. Docket information is available through PACER.

Indiana, Northern District
http://www.innb.uscourts.gov/
Resources include calendars for the court and §341 meetings, a list of cases discharged since 1998, a trustees' directory, holidays, and fees. The site posts the

local rules, the Seventh Circuit's Standards for Professional Conduct, a court information manual, and official pleading forms. Docket information is accessible through WebPACER.

Iowa, Northern District
http://www.ianb.uscourts.gov/
Iowa's Northern District posts local rules, each judge's calendar, fees, matrix requirements, and official pleading forms. It provides a search engine for retrieving recent opinions of the court. The court information index has hot links to the Southern District and Eighth Circuit Court of Appeals' Websites. Docket information is accessible through WebPACER.

Kentucky, Eastern District
http://www.kyeb.uscourts.gov/
Monthly calendars, special Chapter 13 procedures, filing requirements, post-judgment interest rates, explanations of courtroom technology, and fees are among the general resources here. The site provides local rules and forms, as well as selected opinions by judge (some of which date back to 1991). Docket information is accessible through PACERNet.

Kentucky, Western District
http://www.kywd.uscourts.gov/
This is an umbrella site for the district and bankruptcy courts. The local rules are available, along with court calendars, fees, and some opinions. The court accepts electronic filing of documents from registered users with an ID and password. Docket information is accessible through WebPACER.

Louisiana, Western District
http://www.lawb.uscourts.gov
Calendars are posted by judge and city. The local rules, a guide to practice, and the Federal Rules of Civil Procedure are available.

District of Maine
http://www.meb.uscourts.gov/
The court posts local rules, format requirements for the creditor matrix, a glossary, holidays, and fees. Forms are extensive and include petitions and schedules. For case information, use PACER.

Maryland
http://www.mdb.uscourts.gov/
The clerk uploads the hearing and motion calendars, local rules, local and official pleading forms, mailing matrix guidelines, and a schedule of fees. The site provides an online form for attorney change of address. There is an opinion database (with

search engine), but the site does not disclose the scope. Docket information is available through PACER.

Massachusetts
http://www.mab.uscourts.gov/
The clerk's office posts filing and mailing matrix requirements, as well as notices of intended sales, and conducts online auctions of the inventory of liquidating debtors. The local rules and the First Circuit Bankruptcy Appellate Panel rules are available; the site also links to the federal code and related statutes. Docket information is accessible through WebPACER.

Michigan, Western District
http://www.miwb.uscourts.gov/
Resources include the local rules, fee schedules, court calendar, and contact information for trustees. Docket information is available through PACER.

Minnesota
http://www.mnb.uscourts.gov/
This court offers local rules and forms, a searchable calendar, and manuals for the electronic records system. Registered users may file documents electronically at the site. The judges have posted opinions that date back to 1990. Docket information is retrievable by case or social security number or party name; PACER is also available.

Missouri, Eastern District
http://www.moeb.uscourts.gov/
This slickly designed site offers the usual fees and office information, scads of downloadable case forms, §341 meeting information, and access to the Electronic Bankruptcy Noticing program, which distributes notices to creditors by e-mail. Related documents are available from the noticing page. The site accepts changes of address by e-mail. Docket information is accessible through PACER.

Missouri, Western District
http://www.law.umkc.edu/fdcwm/index.html
In addition to providing the local rules, this site allows retrieving case information by number, type, or party name.

Nevada
http://www.nvb.uscourts.gov/
Resources include the judges' daily hearing calendars, local rules, the Nevada Revised Statutes, the Ninth Circuit Bankruptcy Appellate Panel Rules, standard forms, and fees. Docket information is retrievable by a variety of criteria through an electronic system called RACER.

New Hampshire
http://www.nhb.uscourts.gov/
The local rules contain links for downloading each referenced local form. The court posts its fee schedule, filing and mailing matrix requirements, a directory of trustees, calendars, and postjudgment interest rates. Docket information is available through PACER. The judges post opinions issued in the current year.

New Jersey
http://njuscourts.org
The site posts local rules and a list of mediators. A handful of published opinions is available by judge. Docket information is accessible through a public access imaging system, which requires downloading a free, self-extracting program for a TIFF viewer.

New Mexico
http://www.nmcourt.fed.us/bkdocs/
Downloads include the Bankruptcy Appellate Panel rules, creditor mailing lists, and a few official forms. An account is required to access opinions, the electronic filing system, or §341 meeting information, and to receive e-mail notification of case activity.

New York, Northern District
http://www.nynb.uscourts.gov/
The district posts division calendars, motion and §341 hearing dates, the clerk's practice and procedure manual, and official forms. Other resources include the local rules, Bankruptcy Appellate Panel Rules, and recent opinions. The court participates in electronic noticing to creditors.

New York, Southern District
http://www.nysb.uscourts.gov/
The local rules, a register of mediators, and a few forms are available here. The court accepts electronic filing and posts a manual and registration forms for the system. Docket information is retrievable by case or social security number or party name.

North Carolina, Eastern District
http://www.nceb.uscourts.gov/
Calendars are available for each judge, §341 meetings, and the year. The site posts the local rules, auction notices, the postjudgment interest rate, and filing fees. A credit matrix program is available for download. Docket information is accessible through WebRACER, which is replacing PACER.

North Carolina, Middle District
http://www.ncmb.uscourts.gov/
This site posts court calendars, hearing and §341 meeting dates, fees, local rules and guide, a trustees' directory, and official forms. Docket information is retrievable through WebPACER.

North Carolina, Western District
http://www.ncwb.uscourts.gov/
The court provides local rules and procedures, weekly and monthly calendars, and official forms. The site has jumps to the U.S. Bankruptcy Code, Federal Rules of Bankruptcy Procedure, and excerpts from U.S.C. Title 28 and the North Carolina General Statutes. Docket information and the claims register are retrievable by case name or number, while accessing a creditors' matrix requires the case number. An electronic filing system is being instituted. A link is in place for opinions issued in the previous month. Electronic noticing is available to creditors.

North Dakota
http://www.ndb.uscourts.gov/
Calendars, local rules and procedures, a trustees' directory, and official forms are available here. Docket information is accessible through WebPACER.

Ohio, Northern District
http://www.ohnb.uscourts.gov/
Downloads include local rules, judges' requirements, the Sixth Circuit Bankruptcy Appellate Panel Rules and manual, and the fee schedule. Docket information is available through PACER.

Pennsylvania, Eastern District
http://www.paeb.uscourts.gov
The clerk posts a schedule of fees, §341 meeting locations, hearing calendars for each judge, and the local rules and forms. A few recent opinions are archived. Docket information is available through PACER.

Pennsylvania, Middle District
http://www.uslawcenter.com/usmiddle/
Bankruptcy practice orders and forms for the Northern Tier are at this unofficial site, which is hosted by USLawcenter. There is an e-mail address directory for the Middle District Bankruptcy Bar Association, as well as a search engine for digests of the association's mailing list.

Rhode Island
http://www.rib.uscourts.gov/
This site posts a fee schedule, trustees' directory, Treasury Bill rates, a daily hearings calendar, and notices of intended sales. Practice aids include the local

rules, Bankruptcy Appellate Panel Rules, and local and standard forms. There is a search engine for the unclaimed funds database. The court offers electronic noticing to creditors. Docket information is accessible at the site through PACER.

South Carolina
http://www.scb.uscourts.gov/
The site posts calendars for hearings, §341 meetings, passive notice scheduling, and §362 scheduling. Also available are local rules, an attorney desk reference manual, miscellaneous and local forms, and selected opinions. Docket information is accessible at the site through WebPACER.

South Dakota
http://www.sdb.uscourts.gov/
In addition to local rules and court calendars, this site offers practice pointers discussing notice and service requirements, as well as conversion or dismissal. A few dozen pleading forms are available, which require the PaperPort Viewer. (There's a download link for it on the forms page.) The site archives decisions since 1997. Docket information is accessible at the site through WebPACER, which replaces a free case look-up system.

Tennessee, Eastern District
http://www.tneb.uscourts.gov/
This site posts court and §341 meeting calendars, creditor matrix requirements, a partial fee schedule, a directory of trustees, and local rules. The court participates in electronic noticing to creditors. Docket information is available through PACER.

Tennessee, Middle District
http://www.tnmb.uscourts.gov/
In addition to local rules and court calendars, this site offers access to docket information by party name or case or adversary number. If you have trouble locating the search engine, look for the phrase "Enter databases" on the top page.

Tennessee, Western District
http://www.tnwb.uscourts.gov/
The site offers calendars, local rules and forms, and a partial fee schedule. A link is in place for opinions. The court participates in electronic noticing to creditors. For docket information, use PACER.

Texas, Northern District
http://www.txnb.uscourts.gov/
Take the Site Contents link for an overview of the resources, which include judges' calendars; national and local forms; local rules; and filing, mediation, and operating procedures.

Texas, Southern District
http://www.txsd.uscourts.gov
Resources include local rules, judges' calendars, and forms for proceedings under all chapters. Docket information is available through PACER.

Texas, Western District
http://www.txwb.uscourts.gov/
This district posts its fee schedule, filing requirements and forms, hearing and §341 meeting calendars, and local rules. The creditor's and debtor's FAQs are available in Spanish. The court is implementing an electronic case management and filing system and will send creditors' notices by e-mail. There is a search engine for opinions, but the site does not disclose the scope of the database.

Utah
http://www.utb.uscourts.gov/
This site provides local rules, postjudgment interest rates, and recent opinions. Docket information is available through WebPACER.

Vermont
http://www.vtb.uscourts.gov/
This site includes calendars for hearings and creditors meetings, general orders, draft local rules, and opinions since 1985.

Virginia, Eastern District
http://vaeb.uscourts.gov/
This page has local rules, the fee schedule, and an extensive menu of standard and local forms, downloadable in PDF. Docket information is retrievable by name or case, adversary, social security, or tax ID number. Registered users of the electronic filing system may access it here. Registration with the site is necessary to view the opinions database and receive e-mail notices from designated courts.

Virginia, Western District
http://www.vawb.uscourts.gov/courtweb/enter1.html
Local rules, filing fees and instructions, monthly court calendars, and national and local forms are available. The court is evaluating a system for online docket information.

Washington, Eastern District
http://www.waeb.uscourts.gov/
The district posts courts and §341 meeting calendars, postjudgment interest rates, master mailing lists, local forms, and opinions since 1998. The clerk accepts online requests for copies, archival retrievals, and file searches. Docket information is retrievable from the site through RACER.

Washington, Western District
http://www.wawb.uscourts.gov/
This site offers motion and creditors meeting calendars, local bankruptcy and district court rules, standard and local forms, and Tacoma County Courthouse security restrictions. Docket information is available through PACER.

Wisconsin, Eastern & Western Districts
http://www.wisbar.org/rules/
The Wisconsin Bar Association has the local rules for both bankruptcy courts.

Wisconsin, Western District
http://www.wiw.uscourts.gov/bankruptcy/
Local rules and filing guidelines lurk among the Court Documents. The site posts date assignments for creditors' meetings. Forms include petitions, schedules, and proof of claim. One or two recent opinions may also be available. The judiciary Internet links encompass virtually every federal court online.

Wyoming
http://www.wyb.uscourts.gov/Default.htm
This site posts local rules, fees schedules, and a trustees' directory. A search engine exists for opinions, but the site does not disclose the scope of the database. Docket information is retrievable through RACER. The site links to the Administrative Office of the U.S. Courts homepage for official forms.

State Courts

Almost all of the states have some sort of judicial presence online. Most of the pages are under the auspices of the highest court in the state, but in some jurisdictions, such as Texas, appellate courts have established their own individual sites as well.

Alabama Administrative Office of Courts
http://www.alacourt.org/
This is home to the Alabama Unified Judicial System. Resources include the Supreme Court Rules, Attorney General and Judicial Inquiry Commission opinions, standardized appellate, trial, and other court forms, child support guidelines, and the Canons of Judicial Ethics. Docket information is retrievable online after you install a free application called WebPrint for Java.

Alaska Court System
http://www.alaska.net/~akctlib/akct.htm
This site contains directories for the court system and mediators, oral argument calendars for the Supreme Court and Court of Appeals, trial court calendars, and

the current rules of court. It offers forms for appeals and trial courts, a guide to appearing before the Supreme Court, and opinions of the Supreme Court, Court of Appeals, and trial court. Library resources include statutes, codes, and municipal ordinances, and rules of evidence and civil, criminal, probate, and appellate procedure.

Alaska Appellate Courts Case Management System
http://www.appellate.courts.state.ak.us/
This site allows retrieving information about a pending appeal by case or trial court number or party name. It links to the Alaska Legal Resource Center page for appellate opinions, rules, and forms, as well as the oral argument schedules of the Supreme Court and Court of Appeals.

Arizona Judicial Department
http://www.supreme.state.az.us/
Here you can access the Arizona Rules of Court, Civil, Criminal, and Appellate Procedure, and Evidence. The page umbrellas a variety of divisions, such as Adult Services, Certification and Licensing, and Court Services, which includes the Domestic Relations Unit. The Water Cases link discusses general stream adjudication issues before the Supreme Court. Opinions are available from the Supreme Court and both appeals divisions. The site links to both Appeals Courts as well. Out of the ordinary resources include a child support calculator.

Arizona Courts
http://www.apltwo.ct.state.az.us/othercrt.html
Division Two of the Court of Appeals maintains this cover page of links to the Supreme Court and various superior and lower courts throughout the state.

Arkansas Judiciary Home Page
http://courts.state.ar.us/index.html
This umbrella site offers court forms, rules, and administrative orders. It posts approved Continuing Legal Education courses, child support guidelines, and the House Style Guide. Search engines are available for licensed attorneys and the Arkansas Code, as well as Supreme Court and Court of Appeals opinions. The Supreme Court and Court of Appeals maintain sparse individual pages.

California Courts
http://www.courtinfo.ca.gov/
Come here to reach Web pages for the Supreme Court, Courts of Appeal, and trial courts. The searchable site has calendars for all appellate courts, rules of court, Judicial Council forms, and appellate slip opinions issued in the previous 100 days. (There is also an opinion archive, but it does not disclose the scope of the database, except to warn that it includes superseded decisions.)

Colorado State Courts
http://www.courts.state.co.us/
This site encompasses the Colorado Judicial Branch, which covers all appellate, district, and county courts except Denver. The Second Judicial District (under Trial Courts) links to the Denver County Court, and the welcoming page has a jump to the Denver Probate Court. Resources include a map showing the districts and counties of the courts, fees, and approved forms (with links to other sources). The Supreme Court posts case announcements, adopted rule changes, and oral argument schedules, while the Court of Appeals offers case announcements. The Supreme Court Library points to appellate and Attorney General opinions, statutes, and court rules.

Connecticut Judicial Branch
http://www.jud.state.ct.us/
The Supreme Court posts its calendar and summaries of cases scheduled for argument. Superior Court resources include fees, short calendars, assignment lists, and search engines for docket information for civil and family cases. Official forms are available for civil, criminal, administrative, family, grievance, housing, juvenile, appellate, and probate proceedings. The information geared to lay people is extensive.

Supreme Court of Delaware
http://courts.state.de.us/supreme/
This court offers its rules and forms, as well as the Delaware Appellate Handbook. The argument list and recent orders and decisions round out the practice aids.

District of Columbia Court of Appeals
http://www.dcca.state.dc.us/
This official page directs visitors to the District of Columbia bar site, http://www.dcbar.org/, which houses resources for both the Court of Appeals and Superior Court. For the Court of Appeals, appellate forms, calendars, and opinions since January 1999 are available, and links are in place for local rules and guidelines. The Superior Court pages provide explanations and directories of the services and divisions.

Florida State Courts
http://www.flcourts.org/
Supreme Court oral argument calendars, the Code of Judicial Conduct, and the Supreme Court Protocol & Jurisdiction manual are here. The site broadcasts live oral arguments in the morning; RealPlayer is required. There's a download link, as well as a broadcast schedule. Recent opinions are available from the Supreme Court, the Second and Fourth Courts of Appeal, and the Judicial Ethics Advisory Committee. Family law rules and forms are also online. The site points to pages for the District Courts of Appeal, Circuit Courts, and County Courts.

Locating Court Information & Rules 135

Supreme Court of Georgia
http://www.state.ga.us/Courts/Supreme/
Georgia offers a court calendar, with summaries of pending cases; descriptions of recent grants of certiorari; rules of procedure for the Supreme Court and Court of Appeals; and local operating rules and procedures of the judicial circuits. Supreme Court opinion summaries date back to 1996; a search engine covers reported appellate decisions, but the site does not indicate the scope of the database. The site links to a few lower court pages.

Hawaii State Judiciary
http://www.hawaii.gov/jud/
Besides the rules of court, this site has fee schedules and official forms for District Court, Family Court fees, and Circuit Court forms. The availability of official forms for other levels varies by district. There is an archive of slip opinions since January 1998 of Supreme Court and Intermediate Court of Appeals. Docket information is retrievable through a system called Ho'ohiki, which will load a Java applet onto your computer to run it.

Idaho State Judiciary
http://www.state.id.us/judicial/judicial.html
Synopses are available of cases set for hearing before the Supreme Court and the Court of Appeals; recent opinions of both courts are retrievable through category indexes or a search engine. Rules online include civil procedure, evidence, criminal, misdemeanor criminal, infraction, juvenile, administrative, and appellate. The site maintains rosters of civil and child custody mediators, domestic assault/battery evaluators, and court interpreters.

Fourth Judicial Circuit of Illinois
http://www.effingham.net/4thcircuit/
This site contains local rules, directories of clerks, judges, probation offices, and state's attorneys, and a breakdown of judicial assignments.

Nineteenth Judicial Circuit of Illinois
http://www.19thcircuitcourt.state.il.us/
In addition to local rules, the Nineteenth Judicial Circuit posts court schedules, calendars, and courtroom assignments for all divisions, as well as for the federal bankruptcy court, U.S. Trustees hearings, and Industrial Commission worker's compensation hearings. The site contains a list of certified mediators, explanatory brochures for services and programs (such as adult probation and civil case mediation), and a variety of court publications, including explanations of probate and small claims court.

Supreme Court of Indiana
http://www.ai.org/judiciary/supreme/
Besides explanatory essays and contact information, this site has the court calendar and documents from a handful of cases in which the media has expressed interest. The Webcast feature permits viewing of a hearing. Either RealVideo or IP/TV is required; the site offers download links for both.

The Court of Appeals of Indiana
http://www.ai.org/judiciary/appeals/
This page offers only biographies and a chronological listing of judges, a breakdown of the districts, and a background essay.

Iowa Judicial District
http://www.judicial.state.ia.us/
The Judicial Branch posts oral argument schedules for the Supreme Court and the Court of Appeals, as well as calendars for the Supreme Court, Court of Appeals, and district courts. The site archives Supreme Court and Court of Appeals decisions since 1998, which have a search engine. Other resources are a civil petition cover sheet, court rules (on the Iowa Legislature's site), local rules by district, child support guidelines, and information about attorney regulation, including the standards for professional conduct.

Kansas Judicial Branch
http://www.kscourts.org/
Supreme Court rules are here, including attorney discipline, CLE requirements, child support guidelines, and judicial conduct. The welcoming page is an umbrella to a host of programs and offices, such as Child Support Enforcement and Dispute Resolution. Mediator resources include rules, an application packet, and a calendar of approved training opportunities.

The site also points to pages for the Supreme Court, Court of Appeals, and district and municipal courts. They contain Supreme Court and Court of Appeals dockets for the current and next month, as well as decisions of both courts since October 25, 1996. Individual district court pages have their local rules; some also offer forms, online docket information retrieval, and an electronic filing system.

Kentucky Court of Justice
http://www.aoc.state.ky.us/
This site offers the local rules of practice, domestic violence protocols, and emergency protective orders for each county. Local circuit and district rules are also accessible from the Supreme Court page, which contains the oral argument calendar, rules and procedures, and unpublished versions of recent opinions. Official court forms are available for appeals, civil and criminal actions, hospital/disability cases, and probate matters. The format is PDF, and the site has a link for down-

loading the Adobe Acrobat Reader. The Circuit Court page contains a roster of certified court-ordered domestic violence treatment providers. The Administrative Office of the Courts posts its policies and procedures and rules for its video project.

Louisiana Judicial Information
http://www.state.la.us/state/judicial.htm
Jump from this index to pages for the Supreme Court of Louisiana, the Orleans Parish Civil District Court, the Fifteenth District Family Court, the Clerks of Court for Lafayette, St. Landry, and St. Tammany Parishes. (Federal courts and a variety of research resources are also linked.)

The Supreme Court page contains rules of court, the docket, and opinions (also called News Releases) since February 28, 1996. (The opinion format is PDF, and the page has a link for downloading the Adobe Acrobat Reader.) The local rules, interest rate, and trial and appeals forms are available from the Orleans Parish Civil District Court. The Fifteenth District Family Court offers its calendar, rules, and forms (most of which involve mediation or mental evaluation).

State of Maine Judicial Branch
http://www.courts.state.me.us/
In addition to fee schedules and staff directories, this site has Supreme Judicial Court opinions since 1997, in PDF. The Adobe Acrobat Reader is available from the opinion page.

Maryland Judiciary
http://www.courts.state.md.us/
Fee schedules are here for all levels of courts. Appellate opinions since 1995 are available in PDF or WordPerfect formats. The site also has links to the ADR and Attorney Grievance Commissions, local bar associations, and the Maryland Electronic Capitol, which we will explore in chapter 10, "Locating Other State & Local Resources."

Massachusetts Court System
http://www.state.ma.us/courts/courts.htm
Child support guidelines are accessible from the welcoming page, which is home to the Supreme Judicial Court, the Appeals Court, and trial court pages. The Supreme Court posts model jury instructions on homicide and an explanation of retrieving opinions on its electronic bulletin board system. The appeals and trial court pages primarily contain explanatory essays and press releases.

Michigan's One Court of Justice
http://www.supremecourt.state.mi.us/
The Supreme Court, Court of Appeals, and trial courts make this site their home. The Supreme Court page archives public information releases and the *Michigan*

Supreme Court Report. Look under the Clerk's Office for court rules (which include discipline and judicial conduct) and the oral argument schedule. The Court of Appeals Clerk's Office posts a form for requesting special accommodations for appearances before the court.

Minnesota State Court System
http://www.courts.state.mn.us/
Civil, criminal, and juvenile court rules are here, along with rules for admission to the bar, guardians ad litem, and frivolous litigation. The site archives opinions of the Supreme Court and Court of Appeals since 1996; a separate page spotlights the most recent week's decisions. The Alternative Dispute Resolution button leads to rosters of civil and family law mediators. A clickable map of the state offers access to information about each judicial district. The page links to the Minnesota Board of Continuing Legal Education (which provides rules and a list of approved courses) and the Lawyers Professional Responsibility Board and Office (which contains the Rules of Professional Conduct, Rules on Lawyers Professional Responsibility, board opinions, and lists of disbarred or suspended lawyers and approved financial institutions for trust accounts). Other pointers go to the Client Security Board (which posts its rules) and the Tax Court. That court has a search engine for its opinion database; links are in place to add forms, rules, and procedures.

Mississippi Supreme Court
http://www.mssc.state.ms.us/
Besides calendars for the Supreme Court, Court of Appeals, and Judicial College, this site has Clerk's Office appeal procedures and searchable databases of court rules, bar rolls, and appellate opinions and hand down lists.

Mississippi Supreme Court
http://www.mslawyer.com/mssc/
Part of the Mississippi Lawyers World Wide Web Domain, this unofficial site contains the Supreme Court docket, the Judicial College calendar (including the Court Administrator's Handbook), court rules, appellate opinions, and the Clerk's Office fee schedule.

Missouri Judiciary
http://www.osca.state.mo.us/
This site is home to the Supreme Court, Court of Appeals, and circuit courts. The Supreme Court posts its oral argument dockets (which includes case summaries), rules, order, and recent opinions. Each district of the Court of Appeals has a discrete page. Common resources include oral argument dockets, local rules, and recent opinions and orders. The Eastern District also offers an appellate guide. Circuit Court information consists primarily of staff directories and contact infor-

mation. CaseNet allows online access to docket information from participating courts. (Each Court of Appeals district indicates that it has implemented the program.)

Montana Supreme Court Opinions
http://www.lawlibrary.state.mt.us/dscgi/ds.py/View/Collection-36
This state library page, which archives opinions since 1997, also contains the Supreme Court calendar and Municipal Court Rules of Appeal.

Nevada Eighth Judicial District Court
http://www.co.clark.nv.us/distcrt/courthome.htm
Located in Las Vegas, this court offers an online query system for retrieving civil, criminal, domestic, and probate docket and calendar information. Court forms are available for arbitration, discovery, and probate.

New Hampshire Judicial Branch
http://www.state.nh.us/courts/home.htm
The Supreme, Superior, and Probate Courts post information here. The Supreme Court page contains its oral argument calendars, orders, and slip opinions since November 1995. The Superior Court has zipped domestic relations forms and rosters of guardians ad litem, marital neutral evaluators, and Rule 170 mediators, while the Probate Court provides administrative orders, procedure bulletins, and zipped files of forms. Each court page explains how to subscribe to the Judicial Branch's listserv.

The New Jersey Judiciary
http://www.judiciary.state.nj.us/
The calendar page contains Superior Court motion days and civil motion calendars for judges in the Somerset/Hunterdon/Warren Vicinage (which also posts decisions on motions). Links are in place to add Supreme and Appellate Court calendars. The site houses appellate opinions issued in the previous week. Look in the Legal Resource Room for civil and criminal jury charges; guidelines for child support, case captioning, and sentencing; Rules of Court and of Professional Conduct; the Manual of Style for Legal Citation; and standards of appellate review.

New Mexico State Judiciary
http://www.nmcourts.com/
The Case Lookup feature permits online retrieval of docket information for district and magistrate court cases. (To search cases in Bernalillo County Metropolitan Court, go to **http://www.technet.nm.net/menu/metro-ct.htm**. Calendar information for that court appears at **http://www.metrocourt.nmcjnet.org/**.) Judicial and local district rules are on the Supreme Court Law Library page, which also contains slip opinions and civil and criminal forms approved by the Court. Family law forms

are accessible from the top page of the judiciary site. The page for the First Judicial District Courts contains hearing schedules, local rules, fees, and forms for child support, domestic violence, meditation, and litigation. The Second Judicial District Courts page is little more than directories and explanatory information, while the Fifth Judicial District Courts does offer local rules. The Supreme Court is instituting an electronic filing system.

New York State Unified Court System
http://www.courts.state.ny.us/

The rules link leads to an index of amendments, but careful browsing will uncover the Mandatory CLE Program rules and those of the Courts of Appeal, Appellate Division, Fourth Department. To find the local rules for a particular court, select its name from the pop-up menu on the main page. The site has a search engine and allows access to the state's roster of attorneys and future scheduled court appearances in cases in thirteen counties.

The law library for the Appellate Division, Fourth Department, has slip opinions. State and local bar association links are on the system's top page, which also points to MCLE information and forms.

North Carolina Courts
http://www.aoc.state.nc.us/

The Supreme Court, Court of Appeals, and trial courts are accessible here. From the top page you can reach the Rules of Appellate Procedure, General Rules of Practice for Superior and District Courts, State Bar Rules, and the Judicial Code of Conduct. The main site also contains Superior Court rotation calendars and query forms for the impaired driver calendar, law enforcement officer court appearance schedule, and District and Superior Court criminal and infraction calendar. The availability of trial calendars depends on the court; check the trial court sites directly. The forms library covers criminal, civil, juvenile, small claims, mediated settlement conference, and estate matters. All are PDF, and the Adobe Acrobat Reader is available for downloading.

The Supreme Court posts full and summary docket sheets, oral argument calendars, and lists of petitions that have been granted or denied. Supreme Court opinions are accessible since 1997, while the Court of Appeals opinion database starts in 1996. Both courts participate in an electronic filing system, which requires registration for a user name and password. The trial court link leads to a clickable map of the state's counties and a searchable criminal calendar for all 100 counties.

North Dakota Supreme Court
http://www.court.state.nd.us

The day's schedule leads off the top of the North Dakota Supreme Court's site. The month's calendar is also available. The entire database of state court rules is searchable, or you can browse them by section (such as appellate, criminal, or civil procedure, continuing legal education, or lawyer discipline). The site contains a directory of attorneys, appellate practice tips, and civil procedure forms (under Guides). Opinions are searchable since 1993 and browsable since 1996. The Court offers free e-mail notification when new opinions and notices are posted to the site.

Supreme Court of Ohio
http://www.sconet.state.oh.us/navigat.htm
The Supreme Court posts rules of court and attorney registration rules. Hearings are occasionally broadcast on the site in live streaming video. There is a search engine for Supreme Court opinions, but the site does not disclose the scope of the database. (Opinions are in MS Word format; if that is not your word processor, use the link to download the Word viewer.) Some opinions are available for the First, Third, Fifth, Sixth, Eighth, and Ninth District Courts of Appeals

The Oklahoma Supreme Court Network
http://www.oscn.net/
The search engine allows access to court rules (including Supreme, Criminal Appeals, Tax Review, Workers Compensation, CLE, and district court), ethics rules, Attorney General opinions, state statutes, state and federal opinions, civil and criminal jury instructions, and dispositions of writs of certiorari. The query form on the top page will convert citations between the National Reporter and Public Domain systems. Docket information is retrievable for cases before the Supreme Court, Courts of Civil or Criminal Appeals, Court of Tax Review, and eight county civil and criminal courts. Forms are available for appeals, worker's compensation, and child support cases.

The Oklahoma Court of Criminal Appeals
http://www.occa.state.ok.us/
This court posts its rules, uniform jury instructions, and approved forms. Docket information is retrievable by case number or name. The opinion database goes back to 1938.

Oregon Judicial Department
http://www.state.or.us/agencies.ns/19800/index.html
This index of courts leads to staff directories.

Pennsylvania's Unified Judicial System
http://www.aopc.org/
From this page you may reach resources for the Supreme, Commonwealth, and Common Pleas Courts, as well as a few special courts. Civil, landlord-tenant, and private criminal complaint forms are available from the main page. The Supreme Court posts the current and next year's calendars, argument and download lists,

filing fees, and rules. The Superior Court has a calendar of its sessions for the current year and opinions since December 1997. The Commonwealth Court uploads its calendar, while the Common Pleas Courts have their local rules online. Pennsylvania Local Court Rules are under Special Courts. From there, jump to the few local court sites.

Rhode Island Judiciary
http://www.courts.state.ri.us/
This is an umbrella site for the Supreme, Superior, District, Family, and Worker's Compensation Court, as well as the Traffic Tribunal. The Supreme Court posts its hearing calendar, recent opinions and orders, and rules for admission to the bar (including an application). The Superior Court makes filing fees and recent opinions available, while the Family Court offers filing fees and explanations of its programs. The remaining courts use their pages only for an overview of their operations.

South Carolina Judicial
http://www.state.sc.us/judicial/
The page links to a database of Supreme Court opinions at the University of South Carolina Law Center. The Administrative Law Judge Division posts its rules and decisions by agency, beginning in the mid-1990s.

Tennessee Supreme Court
http://www.tsc.state.tn.us/
In addition to court rules and certiorari lists, the Supreme Court has archived its opinions, as well as those of the Court of Appeals, Court of Criminal Appeals, and workers compensation board. All but one of the opinion postings begin in the third quarter of 1995; workers comp cases start in 1996. Judicial ethics opinions and Board of Professional Responsibility formal ethics opinions are also available. Postings include documents in pending death penalty cases, the ADR Newsletter, and a schedule of mediation training courses.

Texas Judiciary Online
http://www.courts.state.tx.us/
Under Court Rules are Texas Judicial System Procedures, Rules, and Revisions, as well as the Rules of Appellate and Civil Procedure, Evidence, and Judicial Administration. This page also points to state statutes, codes, regulations, Supreme Court opinions since 1997, Court of Criminal Appeals opinions from the current year, and Judicial Ethics Advisory Opinions. On the top page, civil and criminal case information is retrievable by a number of criteria, such as appellate or trial court case number, trial court name, and style.

The Supreme Court posts its filing fees and submission calendar, along with its opinions and procedures, rules, and revisions. The Court of Criminal Appeals (which you can reach directly at **http://www.cca.courts.state.tx.us/**) uploads its rules and revisions, hand downs for the year, opinions, summaries of issues presented by petitions granted in the current week, and the Court Reporters' Uniform Format Manual.

The judiciary server links to home pages of each Court of Appeals. The First Court posts court schedules, docketing statement forms, and a few months' worth of opinions. It points to the page of the Fourteenth Court, which, despite the gap in numbering, is in the same city (which is Houston). The Fourteenth Court has its submission schedule for the current and next month, docketing statement forms, fees, ADR procedures, standards for appellate practice, and a search engine for docket information and the court's opinions since September 1999.

At the Second you'll find docketing statements, the current proceeding sheet, local rules, and an original proceeding worksheet. The Third has the submission docket, proceeding sheets, fees, docketing statements, and a guide to practice. The Fourth offers local rules, the submission calendar, docketing statements, and opinions since 1998.

The Fifth Court of Appeals maintains a separate Website at **http://www.courtstuff.com/5th/index.html**. Visitors may browse the submission calendar and search current case information (including attorneys) and published and unpublished opinions. This court also offers a free e-mail service that alerts subscribers to case changes, calendar due dates, case filings, and new opinions.

The Sixth Judicial Court's bare-bones page has contact information, judge's biographies, and filing requirements only (because this court has not promulgated local rules). For cases before the Seventh Court, docket information is retrievable by party name, appellate or trial court number, or trial court county. This site also posts practice aids, which include docking statement forms.

The Eighth Judicial District makes a wealth of practice aids available: case and events calendars, local rules, Rules Pertaining to Video Conferencing, Texas Rules of Appellate Procedure, the submission and disposition lists, standards of appellate practice, and form docketing statements. This site even offers Southwest Airlines' flight schedule and search engines for retrieving current case information and opinions of the Supreme Court and Court of Criminal Appeals. Oral arguments are broadcast at the site; RealPlayer is required for viewing and is available for download.

The Ninth, Eleventh, Twelfth, and Thirteenth Courts of Appeals have a search engine for current case information. Local rules and docketing statement forms are at the Tenth Court's site.

Utah State Courts
http://courtlink.utcourts.gov/
All Utah courts are online at this site, but the appellate level offers the most practice-oriented resources. Oral argument calendars are here for the Supreme

Court and Court of Appeals, along with law and motion calendars for the latter. The site has all the court rules, as well as opinions of the Supreme Court since 1996 and of the Court of Appeals since 1997. Certiorari petition dispositions are available dating back to May 1998. Contact and explanatory information is posted for the district, juvenile, and justice courts. Scanned copies of judgments from the past thirty days may be downloaded in daily batches; viewing them requires either version 4.0 or higher of Internet Explorer or a plug-in called WebSeries Viewer, which you can obtain free of charge at the site. Other resources include rosters of mediators and arbitrators, judicial ethics opinions, and the uniform fine/bail schedule.

Vermont Judiciary
http://www.state.vt.us/courts/
Calendars are available for the state's courts at all levels (except the Chittenden, Franklin, and Rutland Superior Courts) and the Judicial Conduct, Professional Conduct, and Professional Responsibilities Boards. Court calendars are also posted by attorney. The site has amendments to court rules, the Supreme Court's docketing statement form, and a pointer to the Vermont Department of Libraries's searchable database of Supreme Court opinions. Legal resource links include the state bar association, the Vermont Code, and the Vermont Automated Library System, which has Supreme Court and Professional Conduct Board decisions.

Virginia's Judicial System
http://www.courts.state.va.us/
The top page lists certified mediators and Spanish language interpreters and qualified guardians ad litem for adults. It also offers approved forms for the Circuit Court and the Judicial Inquiry and Review Commission. The Supreme Court posts its session calendar, list of appeals granted (with case information for each), summaries of cases set for argument, argument dockets, and synopses of its latest decisions. Published and unpublished opinions are available for the Supreme Court, Court of Appeals, Judicial Ethics Advisory Committee, and Workers Compensation Commission. Use the Judicial System site to reach home pages of the Circuit Courts, General District Courts, and Juvenile and Domestic Relations Courts, which offer varying resources.

Washington State Courts
http://www.courts.wa.gov/
Besides state and local court rules, this site posts instructions for the state's fee-based electronic case information retrieval system, a list of provisionally certified professional guardians, and downloadable forms for divorce, custody, protection against domestic violence, and criminal sentencing. Supreme Court and Court of Appeals opinions are here for ninety days after release; archived judicial ethics opinions are current through June 1999.

West Virginia Supreme Court of Appeals
http://www.state.wv.us/wvsca/
Come here for the court calendar and docket, trial court rules, habeas corpus forms, and opinions dating back to 1991. The page links to the Board of Law Examiners and the Judicial Investigation Commission, which posts the Rules of Judicial Disciplinary Procedure, Code of Judicial Conduct, synopses of advisory opinions, and a complaint form. To search the court rules, use the legislature's query form at **http://www.legis.state.wv.us/Code/toc.html#allrul**.

Wisconsin Court System
http://www.courts.state.wi.us/
This site has similar resources for the Supreme Court and Court of Appeals: oral argument schedules, internal operating procedures, memos of opinions scheduled for release, the text of opinions released that day, and search engines for decisions since 1995. (Figure 7.4 shows the top of the site.) The Supreme Court also posts its calendar, disposition tables, pending cases, and rules.

Circuit Court documents include the local rules, fees, and forms for general, criminal, civil, traffic, small claims, family, and probate matters. The Circuit Court Automation Program enables online retrieval of docket information in all but Outagamie and Walworth Counties; some of the participating counties use the system only for selected types of cases.

Figure 7.4: The top page for the Wisconsin courts' Website.

WISBAR Legal Resources
http://www.wisbar.org/legalres/ (Wisconsin)
Each county's circuit court rules and the Trial Court Administration Rules are downloadable in PDF. The site links to the Supreme Court Rules of Professional Conduct, browsable by chapter.

The Wyoming Judiciary
http://courts.state.wy.us/
Rules are the most extensive resources here. They cover appellate, civil, criminal procedure, evidence, small claims, teen cases, and professional conduct. Also among them are the bar disciplinary code and the Code of Judicial Conduct. The site additionally offers the oral argument schedule, a notice of appeal checklist, bar admission rules and procedures, and a searchable database of Supreme Court opinions since 1996. Look under Law Library for links to statutes, administrative rules, and the bar association.

Miscellaneous Lower Courts

A surprising number of trial, municipal, and justice courts are online. Rather than bury you in an avalanche of URLs, I'm going to give the address of one staggering directory. At **http://www.ncsc.dni.us/COURT/SITES/Courts.htm** the National Center for State Courts has links to more than 150 state, federal, and miscellaneous court sites, which contain a hodge-podge of county, justice, municipal, and family courts throughout the country, cataloged by state. If the court you want is not on the NCSC list, check the state court resources at FindLaw, **http://www.findlaw.com**.

Courts aren't the only government bodies that have embraced the ease of spreading routine information through the Internet. Many federal and state agencies have adopted the same notion. Most of them have taken this idea of convenience a step further and turned the Web into a distribution point for their forms. The phenomenon is so widespread that it's changed my work habits. When I need a government publication, I don't head for a book anymore. I use a phone line—the one hooked up to the modem.

8
Locating Government Forms

Keeping all the right forms in stock is one of the necessary evils of an office practice. The task is easy to manage when the forms are ones that you and your staff can generate. A number of the documents I've prepared for my clients are subject to statutory requirements for which there is no prescribed form; in many situations it's enough if a document tracks statutory language, which means you can have it keyed into a computer and printed out on demand. Sometimes, though, a government office requires you to use the actual forms it has prepared. Getting ahold of them involves, at the very least, a trip out of the office. In the rare case of a government entity that will mail them to you—as, for example, the U.S. Copyright Office will—more often than not you have to leave your order on voice mail and wait weeks for the precious papers to arrive. If you work in a large firm or legal department, you're probably happily unaware that this is going on around you. If your office is small, you know all too well what I'm talking about.

Once a form comes up in my practice, I stockpile it. Still, supplies have an annoying way of running out without anyone noticing, and usually right before I need one on the fly. The solution used to be sending a runner to the country clerk or the IRS or some other government office downtown—until I started logging on.

I can't think of a government-generated form I've needed in the past three years that I haven't been able to find on the Web. From Subchapter S elections to an array of applications—copyright registrations, federal and state trademarks, assumed name certificates, federal employer identification numbers, state sales tax licenses—everything has gone from my computer screen to my desk in a matter of minutes. The time savings in this one area alone has more than compensated for my Internet service provider's monthly access charge.

Lately I've also been coming across that first type of document I mentioned at the outset—the one that doesn't have to be on or in a specific form, but merely meet statutory requirements. Downloading a file onto your disk is almost always quicker than having someone type a document from scratch. In the "General State & Common Law Forms" section at the end of the chapter, I'll point out some places where you can save a lot of time doing just that.

> *The addresses in this chapter should take you directly to the forms pages referenced. If you cannot access a resource, it may be that the site has restructured its directories and moved the forms to a different address. Flip back to chapter 4, "Setting Up Your Online Library," for tips on tracking down a page that has moved.*

Quick Reference List

Here's a short list of Web sites for a myriad of common forms. If you need something that's not on the list, you know the drill by now: run a search for it. (If it's a court form, go back to the Quick Reference List in chapter 7, "Locating Court Information & Rules.")

To read and print most of these forms, you're going to need Adobe Acrobat Reader. If you haven't already downloaded and installed it, you can get it from most of the sites that require it. Or you can point your browser directly to **http://www.adobe.com/products/acrobat/readstep.html** and pick the one designed for your operating system.

One final thing: downloading is idiot-proof. Really. All these sites have browsable indexes, usually very short ones. To begin a download, all you do is click on a document's name. A pop-up screen will tell you what to do next.

Federal Forms

In this section you'll find everything from commonplace tax forms to highly specialized applications for patents, broadcasting licenses, and the like. If you or your clients have business before an agency other than those listed below, don't assume it hasn't posted its official forms electronically. Check out its Web page anyway; you'll probably be pleasantly surprised. (Go to chapter 9, "Locating Other Federal Resources," for agency URLs and research starting points.)

Administrative Office of the U.S. Courts
http://www.uscourts.gov/bankform/index.html
Official bankruptcy pleadings and forms are available for downloading in PDF. There's a link for obtaining the Adobe Acrobat Reader.

Federal Communications Commission
http://www.fcc.gov/formpage.html
What's here is extremely technical, but that's the nature of the Federal Communication Commission. It posts applications for licenses and construction permits and a host of other forms and reports, some of which are set up for electronic filing. The download index indicates whether a file's format is PDF, Lotus, Excel, Word-

Perfect (5.1 or 6), Word 97, or ASCII. Most are PDF. The Adobe Acrobat Reader is available from the site.

> ### Alphabet Soup Is Not Just a D.C. Specialty
>
> What's with all the three-letter anagrams? They're not that hard to crack (and no, they're not obscure government agencies). They are simply file extensions, which means they come *after* the dot in a file name. The letters are codes (often, abbreviations) for the type of file—that is, they identify the format of the file. When you find one you want to download from the Web, the extension lets you know the type of program you'll need to read it.
>
> Think "graphic" when you see GIF (Graphics Interchange Format). PCL is Hewlett Packard's Printer Control Language. PDF stands for Portable Document File, but all you need to remember is that the Adobe Acrobat Reader is necessary to view or print it. PostScript or PS describes a page to a printer, in either letter (8 1/2x11 inches) or ledger (11x17) output sizes. SGML is Standard General Markup Language that meets federal and international specifications for identifying a document's structure and contents. TXT (Text) and RTF (Rich Text Format) are two types of text-based formats, readable by most word processors, including WordPerfect and Microsoft Word. ZIP means the file has been compressed to save space; to read it, you will have to put it through PKUNZIP or another decompression program first.

Freddie Mac
http://www.freddiemac.com/
Uniform Mortgage Instruments for single-family homes are available here, tailored to each state. The site also posts the agency's multifamily guide and standard forms for notes, security instruments, guarantees, ground lease mortgage provisions, and Illinois land trust documents. Everything requires the Adobe Acrobat Reader, which is available from the site.

Immigration & Naturalization Service
http://www.ins.usdoj.gov/graphics/formsfee/forms/index.htm
All INS forms (in PDF) and the Adobe Acrobat Reader are available from this page. For each document the chart gives both the filing fee and where to file it.

Internal Revenue Service
http://www.irs.ustreas.gov/forms_pubs/index.html
Coming up with the right tax form can be like looking for a needle in a haystack. With its Web site, called the Digital Daily, the IRS has actually made the process

easier. (And hipper, too—look at the retro icons at the bottom of the page, which figure 8.1 shows.) Select Search for a Form or Publication to locate a form by keyword or partial name. The Forms and Instructions link will take you to a complete index of forms, easily browsable and available in multiple formats: PCL, PDF, Postscript, and Standard Generalized Markup Language (SGML). To download a publication in any of those formats, select the Publications and Notices link on the top index page. Selected publications are also available for viewing, under the link Publications Online. Use the Prior Year Tax Forms link to get tax forms from earlier years (1992-1998.) You can even retrieve state tax forms from this site; just take the link by that name.

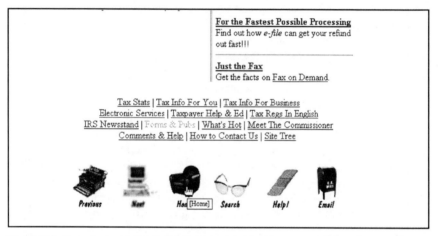

Figure 8.1: Retro icons on the IRS's forms and publications page. The computer image (which leads to the next page in a sequence) is fuzzy because it is inactive here.

For information about filing tax returns electronically, consult **http://www.irs.ustreas.gov/elec_svs/partners.html**. To bypass the top page and go directly to the complete index of IRS forms, enter the URL **http://www.irs.ustreas.gov/forms_pubs/forms.html**. If you encounter download delays, try retrieving what you need from the IRS FTP server, which you'll find under Expert Interface. Or hop over to **http://www.fedworld.gov/taxsear.htm**, the FedWorld Tax Form Search.

A couple of words of warning about the search engine at the IRS site: First, if you're looking for a form or publication, do not use the first query box you see after selecting the Search icon. (Even if you enter the exact form number or title, this box will outfit you with tens of results, none of which will be what you want.) Instead, take the link below it to Search for a Form or Publication to Download. Second, popular names are not the best approach to navigate this file system. You'll do better if you can remember any part of the form's title, and best of all with the form number. I found this out when looking for what's commonly called a Subchapter S election. The keywords "Subchapter S" turned up no matching documents. The actual form number, "2553," didn't fare any better. Determined to locate the form, I picked some keywords out of the actual title, "Election by a Small Business Corporation." "Election" by itself didn't work, but "small business corporation" did; so did the entire title—on one occasion. Another time, the last two entries generated no results. The moral of this story: Experiment—and if that doesn't work, use the search engine at FedWorld.

One more hint: Do not put a phrase within parentheses. The engine will read them as part of the words and turn up nothing.

For information about the IRS's free electronic newsletters, visit the Tax Information for Business Page, **http://www.irs.ustreas.gov/prod/bus_info/**. The Digital Dispatch discusses IRS announcements, new tax forms and publications, and Web site additions. IRS Local News Net tailors its content to the recipient's geographic area.

National Labor Relations Board
http://www.nlrb.gov/forms.html
Three charge forms and a petition are at the site. The format is PDF, and the Adobe Acrobat Reader is available.

Securities Exchange Commission
Small Business Forms & Associated Regulations
http://www.sec.gov/smbus/forms/formssb.htm
The SEC now posts forms for exempt stock offerings, Securities Act registration statements, Exchange Act registration and reporting, and Electronic Data Gathering, Analysis, and Retrieval (EDGAR) submissions. The site also provides all the applicable regulations. Because each form must be tailored to the situation, the format is HTML.

Social Security Administration
http://www.ssa.gov/online/forms.html
The Social Security Administration posts its most frequently requested forms, in Postscript and PDF formats. An application for a social security card is not likely to come up for the average client, but the documents pertaining to a hearing before an administrative law judge might. Some documents appear in Spanish, as well. There's a link to the Adobe home page, for downloading the reader.

U.S. Copyright Office Forms
http://www.loc.gov/copyright/forms/
Forms for all the classes of registration (and their instructions) are indexed here, in PDF, along with detailed printing directions and a download link for Adobe Acrobat Reader. Note that you must print these documents on both sides of the

page, to replicate the appearance of the Copyright Office's forms. If you don't know which form you need, select Registration to download the office's explanatory circulars, which are grouped by category of artistic work.

U.S. Patent and Trademark Office Forms
http://www.uspto.gov/web/forms/
This lengthy page offers patent forms, Patent Cooperation Treaty related forms, and trademark applications and related documents. Adobe Acrobat Reader is necessary; you can download it from the site.

Veterans Administration Forms
http://www.va.gov/forms/default.asp
Benefits, medical, and damage claim forms are here, along with an application for 10-point veteran preference, a request for locating military service records, and direct-deposit authorization for benefits. Almost all come in PDF, GIF, and MS Word formats. The PDF files require Adobe Acrobat Reader, which you can download here. Internal VA forms (such as vouchers and letterheads) are also available, in Word and PDF. This site includes a search engine, a rarity for forms pages.

State Business Organization & Trademark Forms

Most states have promulgated official forms for statutory filings of all sorts—from the creation of fictitious entities to the registration of trademarks, in particular. Secretaries of state across the country, not to mention a handful of private organizations, have done us the favor of uploading their forms for quick, no-charge access. You'll find something available from every state except South Carolina.

In each listing below, I have included a paragraph at the end surveying other business-related forms that are available online in the jurisdiction. These include business and professional licenses, financial institution forms and reports, and securities registrations and applications.

Alabama Secretary of State
http://www.sos.state.al.us/downloads/dl1.cfm
Five divisions make forms and publications electronically available here. Use the pull-down menu to select a division; you can also specify type of file (data, form, or publication). The first and last divisions have the most widespread appeal. The Corporations Division offers all the basic corporate (including nonprofit), limited partnership, limited liability company (LLC), and limited liability partnership (LLP) creation and dissolution documents, as well as forms to change corporate name and registered agent. Under UCC, you can download the entire Uniform Commercial Code filing guide. Elections Divisions downloads include election

results, ballot access petitions, PAC and candidate reporting forms, and an array of filing guidelines. Choose Home Inspectors for applications and bond, insurance, and net worth forms; Sports Agents contains comparable forms for registering as an athletic agent. Files are in PDF, Excel, or ZIP formats; from this top page you can download viewers for the first two and the decompression utility WinZIP. Real Estate Commission forms and applications are posted at **http://www.arec.state.al.us/forms.htm**. For State Oil and Gas Board forms in Rich Text Format, go to **http://www.ogb.state.al.us/**.

Alaska Division of Banking, Securities & Corporations Forms
http://www.dced.state.ak.us/bsc/bsc.htm
Head for the three mustard colored columns at the bottom of the page. Under the Securities Section, you'll find the spectrum of forms related to standard and Regulation D registrations, private offerings and other exemptions, mutual funds, broker-dealers, agents, federal covered advisers, state investment advisers, and investment adviser representatives. The Corporations Section posts cradle-to-grave forms for every imaginable business organization—corporations, nonprofits, limited partnerships, LLCs and LLPs, domestic and foreign. Miscellaneous corporate forms (mostly pertaining to registered agents and changes in officers) are also online, along with trademark applications, and assignments. Everything requires the Adobe Acrobat Reader, which is available from each download page. For liquor license renewals, go to the Alcoholic Beverage Control Board site at **http://www.revenue.state.ak.us/abc/abc.htm**.

Arizona Corporate Filing Section Filing Checklists & Forms
http://www.cc.state.az.us/corp/filings/forms/
All the necessary papers are here to create, change, or shut down corporations (including nonprofit) and LLCs, as well as a variety of documents related to foreign entities. All are in Adobe Acrobat format; the reader is available at the site. They are also on the Corporation Commission's site at **http://www.cc.state.az.us/corp/index.htm**. The Commission's Securities Division posts a wealth of broker-dealer, investment advisor, securities registration and related forms at **http://www.ccsd.cc.state.az.us/forms/**. Insurance license applications and a variety of report forms are at the Department of Insurance site, **http://www.state.az.us/id/licensing/licensing.htm**. For real estate licensing forms, go to **http://www.re.state.az.us/**. The Department of Liquor Licenses and Controls posts applications at **http://www.azll.com/license.htm**.

Arkansas Business Department Corporation Forms
http://www.sosweb.state.ar.us/business.html
This collection is especially large. It provides creation and dissolution forms for corporations (including nonprofit), general or limited partnerships, LLCs, LLPs, and limited liability limited partnership (LLLPs), and qualification forms for the same array of foreign businesses. It also offers forms geared to home builder and

home inspector registration, notary public, trademark registration, and franchise taxes. The site offers an online filing system for articles of incorporation. To use it, you must register first with the Information Network of Arkansas, which costs $50 a year.

The State Bank Department posts a myriad of application, reporting, and miscellaneous forms at **http://www.state.ar.us/bank/banking1.html**. For broker-dealer, investment advisor, check issuer, loan broker, or mortgage loan company forms, visit the Securities Department at **http://www.state.ar.us/arsec/forms.html**.

California Secretary of State Corporate Forms, Samples & Fees
http://www.ss.ca.gov/business/corp/corp_formsfees.htm
Highlighted text in the filing fees table indicates the forms that are available for downloading. They consist largely of all the basic filings required of business, nonprofit, and foreign corporations. Franchise tax and name reservation forms are also here. For domestic partnership declaration or termination forms, go to **http://www.ss.ca.gov/business/sf/sf_dp.htm**. UCC filing forms are at **http://www.ss.ca.gov/business/ucc/ucc_download.htm**.

Colorado Secretary of State Commercial Recordings Forms Index
http://www.sos.state.co.us/pubs.html
This list is huge. It has documents to create, fine-tune, and dissolve corporations, nonprofits, limited partnerships, and LLCs. Trademark-related applications are here, too, inexplicably listed under the heading Name Reservation. Uniform Commercial Code forms (UCC-1, 2, 3, and 11) are available, as well as documentation for LLPs, limited liability limited partnerships, and limited partnership associations. Everything is in Adobe Acrobat format, and there's a link to download the reader.

Connecticut Secretary of the State Forms
http://www.sots.state.ct.us/
Choose Commercial Recording Forms to download all the basic applications for domestic and foreign corporations and LLCs, UCC-1 and UCC-3 forms, and applications to register, assign, and transfer trademarks. Election Service Division postings include registration and absentee ballot applications (also in Spanish) and a handful of campaign finance documents. A few notary public forms and State Board of Accountancy applications are also available, under the appropriate headings. Connecticut uses the Adobe Acrobat format and gives a link for downloading the Reader.

An array of environmental permit applications is on the Department of Environmental Protection site at **http://dep.state.ct.us/pao/download.htm**. The Department of Banking posts applications from the Banking Examination, Consumer Credit, Legal, and Securities and Business Investment Divisions at **http://www.state.ct.us/dob/pages/dobforms.htm**. The Office of the Comptroller posts its forms in two formats at **http://www.osc.state.ct.us/agencies/forms/**. You can download the entire form collection in a self-extracting file, or select individual forms in PDF.

Delaware Division of Corporation Forms
http://www.state.de.us/corp/forms.htm
Delaware limits its postings primarily to documents that will create a domestic entity (stock, nonstock or close corporation, limited partnership, LLC, LLP, or business trust) or qualify a foreign corporation to do business in the state. The page offers the option of downloading the entire collection at once. The format is PDF, and the Adobe Acrobat Reader is available.

The State Bank Commission posts applications for nondepository licenses (such as lenders, check cashers or sellers, mortgage brokers) at **http://www.state.de.us/bank/applyfor.htm**. A handful of miscellaneous securities forms are available from the Attorney General's Securities Division at **http://www.state.de.us/securities/pdf.htm**.

District of Columbia Business Regulation Administration
Corporations Division Business Forms
http://www.dcra.org/
The division indexes formation, amendment, and dissolution documents by type of business entity: corporation, nonprofit, LLC, LLP, and limited partnership, with separate headings for domestic and foreign versions of each. Guidelines for a number of topics (mergers, for example) lurk among the listings. These forms are posted only in HTML format. If you print from the page, the document may not come out in a condition that you could file. Achieving that might require saving the file to disk, then opening it and correcting the spacing in a word processing program. The department is in the process of revising the online forms, but does not say whether converting everything to print-friendly PDF is part of the project.

From this page you can also get the corporate annual report and the LLP biennial report, both of which require the Adobe Acrobat Reader.

For business license applications (from ambulance to vendor, Class B), go to **http://www.dcra.org/blicapp.shtm**. Click on a letter in the alphabetical index to see which packages are available online. The files are also in Adobe Acrobat format and give a link for downloading the reader. The Office of Banking and Financial Institutions posts applications for a few licenses (check cashing and mortgage lending and brokering) at **http://www.obfi.dcgov.org/**.

Florida Department of State Forms Download
http://www.dos.state.fl.us/doc/form_download.html
Like D.C., Florida's site arranges documents by business, which includes corporations (nonprofit, too), general and limited partnerships, LLPs, LLLPs, and LLCs. Besides the usual creation, amendment, and dissolution papers, forms are also available for mergers, resignation of officers, directors or registered agents, or change of registered agent. Look for name reservation and registered agent desig-

nation under Florida Miscellaneous Filing Forms at the bottom of the index. Just above them are a variety of trademark and fictitious name applications, as well as UCC-1 and 3. All of them require the Adobe Acrobat Reader, which you may download here.

At **http://www.dos.state.fl.us/fgils/index.html** the Comptroller's Office Division of Securities and Finance posts applications and other forms related to money transmitting, mortgage brokering and lending, consumer finance companies, retail installment sales, collection agencies, and securities agents and offerings. For banking applications, visit the Banking Division's page at **http://www.dbf.state.fl.us/banking.html**. The Division of Elections has candidate and campaign forms at **http://election.dos.state.fl.us/forms/index.shtml**. A host of Division of Business and Professional Regulation forms are online at **http://www.state.fl.us/dbpr/index.shtml**.

Georgia Secretary of State
http://www.sos.state.ga.us/

PDF documents are scattered throughout the Georgia site. The ones under Corporations aren't plentiful, but they include a trademark application, transmittal information forms, and applications for a certificate of authority for a variety of foreign entities. The Web site accepts online requests for name reservations, annual registrations, status certificates (also called certificates of good standing), and certified copies. A welcome feature is the online corporate database, through which you can find information about Georgia corporations, such as their registered agent, officer, or entity status.

The Securities section offers forms for dealer's and securities salesman bonds, the spectrum of registration and exemption filings, and regulation forms for charitable organizations and cemeteries. The Examining Board links include a CPA certificate application. Surf to **http://www.state.ga.us/index/forms.html** for forms required or accepted by the Department of Banking and Finance, Environmental Facilities Authority, Merit System, Department of Natural Resources, Department of Revenue, and State Board of Worker's Compensation.

Hawaii Business Registration Division Forms
http://www.hawaii.gov/dbedt/bac/forms.html

This is a wide-ranging collection. Besides basic business applications and trademark registration forms, the site offers documents to create, register, or dissolve a variety of entities, from general or limited partnerships and LLPs to corporations (including nonprofit) and LLCs. Domestic and foreign versions are included, as are name registration applications. Among the employment forms are three extraordinary touches of convenience. After you pick up the paperwork to launch a business, you can also obtain some federal forms it might need: an IRS application for federal employee identification number (SS-4), the election by a small business corporation for Subchapter S status (2553), and the Immigration and Naturalization Service employment eligibility verification (I-9). All the files require the Adobe

Acrobat Reader, which you may download here.

The Department of Commerce and Consumer Affairs Division of Financial Institutions posts a handful of applications, reports, and complaint forms at **http://www.state.hi.us/dcca/divisions/dfi/forms02.html**. For real estate licensing forms, visit **http://www.state.hi.us/hirec/**.

Idaho Secretary of State's Office
Corporation Division Forms
http://www.idsos.state.id.us/corp/corindex.htm

This site allows downloading of assumed name certificates and all the usual creation and dissolution documents for corporations, limited partnerships, LLCs, LLPs, and unincorporated nonprofit associations. Everything is PDF, and you may download Adobe Acrobat from the site. You can also jump from here directly to the Idaho statute that controls each type of business organization represented.

The Department of Insurance posts agent licensing forms at **http://www.doi.state.id.us/**. Start at the Bureau of Occupational Licenses for individual board pages, many of which offer applications online. Real Estate Commission licensure and complaint forms are at **http://www.state.id.us/irec/apps.htm**.

Illinois Department of Business Services
http://www.sos.state.il.us/depts/bus_serv/forms.html

The PDF documents are divided into nonprofit, domestic, and foreign corporations, LLCs, limited partnerships, LLPs, and trademarks. The Adobe Acrobat Reader is available from each subpage.

Indiana Secretary of State Forms
http://www.ai.org/sos/forms/forms.html

Much more than the basic corporate formation and dissolution forms are here. The offerings include articles of merger, certificate of acceptance for professional corporations, change of registered agent or office, trademark registration or renewal, corporate reports, notary public applications, and a variety of securities complaint forms. As usual, everything is in Adobe Acrobat format, but with a convenient twist: almost all the documents have been set up so that you can fill them out in your browser while you are online. A few of the complaint forms even support online filing.

The Department of Insurance posts a wide variety of application, license, report, and complaint forms for both companies and agents at **http://www.state.in.us/idoi/**. Many of the Professional Licensing Agency boards provide their forms at **http://www.state.in.us/pla/index.html**.

Iowa Corporation and UCC Forms
http://www.sos.state.ia.us/business/corpforms.html

A variety of corporate, limited partnership, and LLC creation and amendment forms are here, along with a scattershot of other documents. Besides trademark registration and assignment applications, you'll find registration papers for several types of businesses (such as athletic agent or travel agency) and for agricultural liens under the UCC. Adobe Acrobat is the format, and the reader is available for download.

Division of Banking applications and forms for bank and finance bureaus are at **http://www.idob.state.ia.us/**. For Real Estate Commission forms, go to **http://www.state.ia.us/government/com/prof/realesta/formsindx.htm**.

Kansas Secretary of State
Corporations and Business Services Corporation Forms
http://www.ink.org/public/sos/corpdown.html

This is another enormous archive, indexed alphabetically by document title. Creation, amendment, and dissolution paperwork for an array of organizations (corporations, business trusts, LLCs, and limited partnerships among them) are just some of the PDF files you may download or view here. Annual report forms for the same array of organizations are available, and also for professional fund raisers. Applications for trademarks or professional solicitors are on the site as well, along with warehouseman's bonds. Adobe Acrobat Reader is available from the site.

Real Estate Commission licensing forms are available at **http://www.ink.org/public/krec/**.

Kentucky Business Service Forms
http://www.sos.state.ky.us/BUSSER/BUSFIL/FORMS.HTM

This page is not as complete as many. The corporate and LLC forms concentrate on foreign entities, with only a few addressing domestic needs. (Those tend to involve name reservations, addresses, or registered agents.) Limited partnerships, registered LLPs, and foreign business trusts rate a few applications. Assumed name certificates, renewals, and withdrawals are also available. Take the Trademark link at the bottom of the page to obtain forms for registration, renewal, or assignment. All the documents are PDF, and the Adobe Acrobat Reader is available from both the Business Service Forms and the Trademark pages.

Many of the agencies under the Division for Occupations and Professions (which is part of the Department for Administration, Finance and Administration Cabinet) post their applications online. Start at the agency listing at **http://www.state.ky.us/agencies/finance/occupations/**. The Division of Financial Institutions offers a few downloadable documents pertaining to credit unions at **http://www.dfi.state.ky.us/**. Alcoholic Beverage Control license applications are at **http://www.state.ky.us/agencies/abc/licensin.htm**. These require software called OneForm, which the site makes available at no charge.

Louisiana Secretary of State Commercial Division Corporations Forms
http://www.sec.state.la.us/comm/corp-index.htm

This bare-bones page posts an alphabetical index of available forms. They include some creation and withdrawal forms for corporations, LLCs, LLPs, and partnerships, registration applications for a variety of foreign businesses, and trademark registrations and assignments. All require Adobe Acrobat Reader, which you can download here. Below the index, the division explains the procedure and fees for other types of filings.

Maine Corporations Division Forms and Fees
http://www.state.me.us/sos/cec/corp/formfees.htm
Almost every business form that Maine accepts for filing is downloadable from this site. Articles of merger or consolidation, director resignations, and statements of cancellation of shares are among the uncommonly extensive listings, which include trademark registrations, amendments, renewals, and assignments. Next to each entry the division has posted the applicable filing fee. The files require Adobe Acrobat; the reader is available from the site.

The Financial Institutions Bureau posts banking applications and related forms at **http://www.cis.state.mi.us/fib/formindx.htm**.

Maryland Corporate Charter Forms
http://www.dat.state.md.us/sdatweb/charter.html
This site contains a lot of explanatory information, such as drafting guides, but little in the way of forms. You'll find forms to register a trade name, foreign limited partnership, or foreign LLC, change a registered agent's address, or qualify a foreign corporation. The format is PDF and Adobe Acrobat Reader is available.

Massachusetts Secretary of State Corporations Division
http://www.state.ma.us/sec/cor/coridx.htm
This is a pretty complete list of statutory filings for business, nonprofit, professional, and foreign corporations. (No forms for limited partnerships are available here, but only information.) An annual report of voluntary associations and trusts, applications to register, renew, and assign trademarks, and tax disclosure reports fill out the page. Everything requires the Adobe Acrobat Reader, which is downloadable from each subpage. A variety of other state forms, such as license applications, homestead declarations, and agency complaints, are indexed at **http://www.state.ma.us/dld.htm**. Insurance and investor complaints and an application and agreement for child support services are among the handful at http://www.state.ma.us/app.htm.

Michigan Corporation Division On-line Information
http://www.commerce.state.mi.us/corp/divisions/corp_div/corp-home.htm
Every imaginable filing is here for corporations, LLCs, and limited partnerships, but for LLPs, only the application to register is available. The site also offers applications to register or renew trademarks or insignia. PDF is the format, and the Adobe Acrobat Reader is available from each subpage.

Minnesota Secretary of State Business Services Forms
http://www.sos.state.mn.us/business/forms.html
Minnesota's downloads focus on forms to create or annually register business and nonprofit corporations, cooperatives, LLCs, LLPs, and limited partnerships. A variety of partnership statements are available, as are forms to qualify foreign business organizations. Assumed name and trademark filings are also on the site, which appears in figure 8.2. Everything is PDF, and you can download the reader here. Uniform Commercial Code forms are under UCC and Authentication, at http://www.sos.state.mn.us/uccd/forms.html.

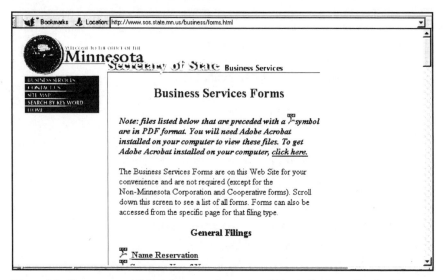

Figure 8.2: The top page of the Minnesota Secretary of State's Business Service Forms.

Mississippi Secretary of State Forms
http://www.sos.state.ms.us/forms/omni_instruct.html
Mississippi veers from the norm by requiring a special browser plug-in called OmniForm Internet Filler to view, much less download, any form. A special bar code font is also necessary. The site provides both, as well as instructions for downloading and installing them. Once you do, you will have access to the gamut of business organization forms, as well as applications and reports required for campaign finance, charities, lobbyists, and a host of securities industry personnel. A notary application is also available, along with UCC-1, 1F, 3, and 3F statements.

Real estate appraiser license applications, in .PDF, are at **http://www.mab.state.ms.us/licensing.htm**.

Missouri Secretary of State Forms
http://mosl.sos.state.mo.us/sosforms.html
Cradle-to-grave forms are available for corporations (including nonprofits), limited

partnerships, LLCs, and LLPs. Nothing more than an index, the page includes applications for a notary public commission, franchise tax reports, and extension requests, and registration forms for both fictitious names and athletic agents. The format is PDF, and the reader is available.

Montana Secretary of State Appendix of Forms
http://www.state.mt.us/sos/Business_Services/business_services.html
The spectrum of organizational forms, listed alphabetically by business type, are downloadable here in PDF. (As usual, Adobe Acrobat Reader is available at the site.) They cover corporations, nonprofit, LLCs, LLPs, and limited partnerships, both domestic and foreign. Forms for trademarks and tax clearance certificates, as well as UCC-1 and 3 statements, are also here.

The Division of Professional & Occupational Licensing makes a number of license applications available at **http://vhsp.dphhs.state.mt.us/com_r1.htm**. A master business license application is at the One Stop Business Licensing site at **http://www.state.mt.us/onestop/**.

Nebraska Secretary of State
Corporate and Business Forms
http://www.nol.org/home/SOS/corps/corpform.htm
The domestic entity forms are primarily changes of registered agent or office or certificates of revival or renewal; there is also an application for registration of an LLP, as well as a slew of LLC forms. Applications exist to qualify and maintain foreign corporations, nonprofits, and LLCs, or to register or assign trade names or marks. The office promises that more are on the way. The format is PDF, and the reader is available.

For UCC filings, go to **http://www.nol.org/home/SOS/htm/services.htm**. From that page you may access a UCC financing statement and arrange to transmit UCC filings electronically.

Nevada Secretary of State
Commercial Recordings Division Corporate Forms
http://sos.state.nv.us/comm_rec/index.htm
Creating a business is the thrust of this page. Nevada's Secretary of State has limited its postings, so far, to organizational or qualifying papers for corporations (including nonprofit and foreign), LLCs, limited partnerships, and business trusts. The site includes filing instructions, fee schedules, and a list of persons or corporations willing to serve as resident agents. Everything comes in either PDF or ZIP format. Adobe Acrobat Reader is available.

Securities representative licensing applications, as well as forms to claim exemption from securities registration, are available at the Securities Division's page, **http://www.sos.state.nv.us/securities/licensing/index.htm**. Some professional licensing boards (such as accountancy) make their applications available at their respective sites. The Department of Business & Industry maintains a document directory at **http://www.state.nv.us/b&i/docindex.htm**. Apart from miscellaneous Insurance and Real Estate Division forms, most of the postings are publications by its divisions.

New Hampshire Department of State
http://www.state.nh.us/sos/corporate/index.htm
Creation, amendment, merger, and dissolution forms are here for corporations, LLCs, LLPs, limited partnerships, investment trusts, nonprofit corporations, and cooperative associations. (The last four appear under Miscellaneous.) The library also includes trademark and trade name papers. Each form listing discloses the filing fee. All the documents require the Adobe Acrobat Reader, which is available from the site.

The Real Estate Commission posts license applications and renewal requests at **http://www.state.nh.us/nhrec/**.

State of New Jersey Department of State
Division of Commercial Recording Online Business Forms
http://www.state.nj.us/treasury/revenue/dcr/geninfo/corpman.html
Three major categories of PDF forms are available: corporate, notary public, and trademark. The page groups the first category into tidy subheadings: formation documents, foreign authorizations, changes of registered agent or office, amendments, mergers and consolidations, dissolutions, alternate names, and name reservations. The notary public section contains just the application. The trademark forms cover registering, renewing, assigning, amending, and canceling a mark. The site supports Adobe Acrobat Reader downloading.

For Real Estate Commission forms (including subdivided land sale documentation), go to **http://www.naic.org/nj/realcom.htm**. Insurance producer licensing applications are at **http://www.naic.org/nj/inslic.htm**.

New Mexico Public Regulation Commission Forms and Instructions
http://www.nmprc.state.nm.us/forms.htm
Download PDF forms to create domestic corporations, nonprofits, and LLCs or to qualify foreign entities. Tax reports are also available for corporations and nonprofits. Adobe Acrobat Reader is available from the site. Partnership, trademark, and notary public forms are available through the Secretary of State at **http://www.sos.state.nm.us/**. Lobbyist, political committee, and candidate forms and reports are at the same site.

The Real Estate Commission offers a handful of applications at **http://www.state.nm.us/nmrec/**. Securities Division registration and licensing forms are at **http://www.rld.state.nm.us/sec/forms/forms.htm**. Many of the Regulation and Licensing Department's boards and commissions (such as accountancy and dental) post their applications online; check the index at **http://www.**

rld.state.nm.us/b&c/index.htm. The Financial Institutions Division offers a variety of applications and forms for banks, credit unions, mortgage companies, collection agencies, and endowed care cemeteries at http://www.rld.state.nm.us/fid/forms/formsinfo.htm.

NYS Department of State
Division of Corporations, State Records and Uniform Commercial Code
http://www.dos.state.ny.us/corp/corpwww.html
This site maintains separate pages for corporations, miscellaneous state records, and Uniform Commercial Code filings.

There's more here than initially meets the eye. Look under Filing Fees, Forms and Publications for the corporation forms. They cover organizing, merging, and dissolving a variety of entities (from business corporations and nonprofit to LLCs, LLPs, and limited partnerships), as well as applying for an assumed name, qualifying a foreign entity, and making the required biennial statement disclosures. In the miscellaneous arena, you'll find trade and service mark application and renewal forms, as well as games of chance registration documents. The Uniform Commercial Code page posts UCC-1, 3, and 11 forms. Everything's PDF, and each subpage permits downloading Adobe Acrobat Reader.

North Carolina Secretary of State Corporations Division Forms
http://www.secretary.state.nc.us/corporations/
Take the Download Forms link to find an application to reserve a corporate name; formation, merger, and dissolution documents for corporations (including nonprofit), limited partnerships, and LLCs; and applications for a certificate of authority for foreign corporations and LLCs. Annual report forms are toward the bottom of the page. All files require Microsoft Word 6 (or later) or the Adobe Acrobat Reader; the site allows free downloading of the latter.

Return to the Secretary of State's home page (the link's at the very bottom) and scroll down to the index. A motherlode of documents lurks in this lineup. Under Athlete Agents, Lobbyist Registration, Notary Public, and Securities Division you will find the appropriate application or registration forms. (The same are on the way for Solicitation Licensing.) The Business Licensing Information Office link leads to a wealth of state and federal tax, labor, industrial, and other forms for starting a business. Trademark forms include affidavits of use and counterfeit complaints. All these documents require Adobe Acrobat; the reader is available from the index page, as well as each subpage.

North Dakota Secretary of State Business Information/Registration Forms
http://www.state.nd.us/sec/
Choose Business Information, then Forms to reach the chart of forms available for download. The chart has been set up to cover everything that will eventually be on the site. Only documents marked with a star are actually present. As of this writing,

that amounted to a scant handful: partnership fictitious name certificates, trade name registrations, and foreign qualification applications for a few business types. It's worth checking the site for other forms, though. An extensive library was under construction elsewhere on the Secretary of State's page.

Notary public, trade and fictitious name, contractor, and lobbyist forms are at the Secretary of State's Administrative/Licensing page, **http://www.state.nd.us/ sec/administrativelicencing.htm**.The Office of Securities Commissioner has uploaded registration and personal representative forms at **http://www.state.nd.us/ securities/forms.html**. The Department of Banking and Financial Institutions posts money broker, collection agency, bank facility, check selling, and consumer finance applications at **http://www.state.nd.us/bank/**. The Office of the Attorney General's Licensing Section has applications for tobacco, alcohol, and a variety of amusement licenses at **http://expedition.bismarck.ag.state.nd.us/ndag/buslic/ bli.html**.

Ohio Secretary of State
http://www.state.oh.us/sos/formlist.asp
This site indexes forms alphabetically by title. If you don't feel like browsing the lengthy list, locate a form quickly by entering a keyword in the search engine's query box. The index includes documents to create, modify, merge, and dissolve most common business organizations (and a few not so common, such as business or real estate investment trusts). Forms are also available to register fictitious names, trademarks, and trade names. For each document the site gives the address and fee for filing. Files come in two formats: Excel 97 and PDF; the Adobe Acrobat Reader is available at the site.

The Commerce Department Division of Financial Institutions posts bank, savings and loan, and credit union applications and forms at **http:// www.com.state.oh.us/dfi/dfiform.htm**. The Division of Industrial Compliance offers Board of Building Appeals hearing forms and Board of Building Standards applications at **http://www.com.state.oh.us/dic/dicform.htm**, along with a number of Bureau of Construction Compliance documents. The Division of Real Estate and Professional Licensing has appraiser and real estate sales and licensing applications (including a residential property disclosure form) at **http://www.com.state.oh.us/ real/realform.htm**.

Oklahoma Forms
http://www.state.ok.us/~sos/forms/forms.htm
The gamut of creation-to-dissolution forms are here for corporations (including nonprofit), limited partnerships, LLCs, and LLPs. Documents to register or withdraw the foreign counterparts of the same entities are available as well. Other registration forms pertain to trade names, trademarks, charitable organizations, professional fund raisers, notaries public, and agricultural liens. The sizable offerings are indexed by entity type. Everything is PDF, and the Adobe Acrobat Reader may be downloaded here.

The Securities Commission posts registration and representative certification forms at **http://www.securities.state.ok.us/**. The Banking Department has applications and forms for bank, credit unions, and all the other institutions it regulates, at **http://www.state.ok.us/~osbd/**. (If you have trouble accessing the downloads page, hold your cursor over the downloads button—but don't click—until a menu of institutions appears on the screen. Make your choice from that menu.)

Oregon Secretary of State
Corporation Division's Business Registry Forms
http://www.sos.state.or.us/corporation/bizreg/BRForms/brforms.htm
Oregon breaks its offerings into twelve categories; click on the appropriate one at the top of the page to jump to what you need. Categories include assumed names; trademark registrations, assignments, and cancellations; and formation, amendment, merger, and withdrawal documents for the major business organizations (business, professional, and nonprofit corporations; limited partnerships; LLCs; and LLPs), as well as for a few specialized creatures like business trusts, cooperative corporations, and district improvements. PDF is the format of choice, and you can get the reader from the site.

Many Oregon licensing boards make their application forms available online. Find each board's Website in the alphabetical agency index at **http://www.state.or.us/agencies.htm**.

Pennsylvania Corporation Bureau Filing Forms
http://www.dos.state.pa.us/corp/forms.htm
This enormous index begins with creation, amendment, and dissolution forms for business, nonprofit and cooperative corporations, limited partnerships, LLCs, and LLPs. Forms are also available for registering, domesticating, and canceling foreign versions of the same entities. Trademark or insignia registrations, renewals, assignments, and reports are here, followed by UCC financing statements and a variety of miscellaneous forms. The document format is PDF, and you can download the reader here.

A number of professional licensing boards post their applications. Consult the index of business and health-related agencies at **http://www.dos.state.pa.us/bpoa/bpoaboards.htm**. For charitable organization registration forms, go to **http://www.dos.state.pa.us/charity/index.htm**. The Department of Health has order forms for birth and death records at **http://www.health.state.pa.us/hpa/apply_bd.htm**. The Securities Commission offers offering and representative registration forms at **http://www.psc.state.pa.us/**.

Rhode Island Corporate Forms and Fees
http://www.state.ri.us/corpforms.htm
The pull-down menu requires you to select the business entity for which you are seeking a form. The options are domestic or foreign corporations (including

nonprofit), limited partnerships, LLCs, or LLPs. Each type has a separate page, with a list of available documents, respective filing fees, and formats. (Everything comes in both Adobe Acrobat and self-executable, zipped Word.) The documents cover the full range of an organization's existence, from creation to dissolution, and include annual reports, name reservations, and changing the registered agent or office. The miscellaneous forms are sparse, being only designations of registered agents for nonresidents.

For probate forms, go to the State Archives and Public Records Administration at **http://www.state.ri.us/probateforms.htm**.

South Dakota Corporation Forms
http://www.state.sd.us/state/executive/sos/Corpadmn.htm
A short hodge-podge of documents is available here, arranged in no discernible order, and pertaining to the spectrum of domestic and foreign organizations. The report forms include farm qualifications and annual reports. Files are in Adobe Acrobat, and the reader is available from the site.

For a complete list of online forms available from South Dakota agencies, use the index and search tools at **http://www.state.sd.us/forms/forms.cfm**.

Tennessee Business Forms Menu
http://www.state.tn.us/sos/forms.htm
Formation, amendment, dissolution, termination, and foreign qualification documents are here for nonprofits, corporations, limited partnerships, LLPs, and LLCs. Name reservation and registration, assumed names, and a variety of documents pertaining to registered agents and offices are also available. You may access files by entity type or by SS number. As usual, everything's in PDF. You can download Adobe Acrobat Reader here.

Texas Business Organization Forms
http://www.sos.state.tx.us/function/forms/formidx.html
The Secretary of State's Corporation Division has posted the forms necessary to create domestic entities or qualify foreign ones to do business in the state. Amendment, name reservations, and dissolution applications are also included. Head to the bottom of the page for trademark forms. To browse the complete listing, select Index of Forms. The archive contains everything that the Secretary of State has promulgated and duplicates its paperbound filing guide. The format is PDF (some are also available in Word); the Adobe Acrobat Reader is available.

Some banking applications and documents related to cemeteries, sales of checks, and currency exchange are available from the Department of Banking at **http://www.banking.state.tx.us/**. The Securities Board posts a handful of miscellaneous forms (none involving registrations or exemptions) at **http://www.ssb.state.tx.us/forms/forms.html**.

Utah Division of Corporations and Commercial Code
http://www.commerce.state.ut.us/corporat/Formsite.htm
Creation and dissolution forms are available for the spectrum of business entities. An application for trademark registration is also here. The format is Adobe Acrobat, and you may download the reader.

The Commerce Department's Division of Occupational and Professional Licensing posts applications for twenty-five licenses (including alternative dispute resolution provider) at **http://www.commerce.state.ut.us/dopl/wp-app.htm**. License and registration forms from the Division of Securities are at **http://www.commerce.state.ut.us/securit/forms.htm**.

State of Vermont Office of the Secretary of State
Business Registry Forms Index
http://www.sec.state.vt.us/tutor/dobiz/dobizdoc.htm
Articles of incorporation, organization, amendment, and dissolution are online for corporations, nonprofits, LLCs, LLPs, and limited partnerships. Change of registered agent and trademark registration forms comprise most of the rest of the archive. Some of the forms are available in WordPerfect, but many are only in HTML, which you will have to print directly from your screen.

The Office's Election Division posts lobbying and campaign finance report forms at **http://www.sec.state.vt.us/**.

Virginia State Corporation Commission
http://www.state.va.us/scc/division/clk/corp.htm
The forms for each type of business entity (corporation, limited or general partnership, LLC, and LLP) are posted along with the respective fee schedules. Formats are PDF or Word 6.0; the Adobe Acrobat Reader is available from each form's download page. Although the site discloses UCC filing fees, no financing statements or other UCC forms are online.

Washington Corporations Forms
http://www.secstate.wa.gov/corps/forms.htm
This small archive contains little more than a few formation or amendment documents for corporations and LLCs, registration forms for foreign versions of the same, and trademark registrations or renewals. All are PDF, and the Adobe Acrobat Reader is available.

For the Master Application required for business licenses and registrations, go to **http://www.wa.gov/dol/forms/700028.htm**. UCC-1, 3, and 4 forms are at **http://www.wa.gov/dol/bpd/uccfront.htm**. The Securities Division of the Department of Financial Institutions posts forms for securities registration and exemption, broker-dealer and investment advisor licensing, complaints, and business opportunity and franchise filings at **http://www.wa.gov/dfi/securities/forms.html**.

West Virginia Forms & Fees
http://www.state.wv.us/sos/corp/startup.htm
Near the middle of an excellent primer on starting a business is a chart of downloadable forms and their filing fees. Because of the start-up emphasis, all the forms on this page are geared to launching a new entity, whether a corporation, limited partnership, LLC, or voluntary association. For a handful of amendment forms, select Making Changes. Select Trademarks for a form to register or renew a trademark. The format is PDF, and the reader is available from each page.

The Secretary of State's Charitable Organizations Division posts registration forms for charities and professional fund raisers at **http://www.state.wv.us/sos/charity/registration.htm**.

Wisconsin Department of Financial Institutions
http://www.wdfi.org/corporations/
Click on the Corporations or UCC buttons to download forms in PDF (and also Adobe Acrobat Reader, if you need it). The corporate offerings are cradle-to-grave forms for business and nonstock corporations, cooperative associations, limited partnerships, LLCs, and LLPs, both domestic and foreign. The UCC section posts UCC-1, 3, and 4 statements. The format is PDF, and the reader is available. Financial institution and licensed financial services applications are at **http://www.wdfi.org/forms/default.htm**.

Wyoming Secretary of State
http://soswy.state.wy.us/corporat/corporat.htm
This index organizes forms by category, in PDF or WordPerfect. The gamut of creation, amendment, and termination forms are available for LLCs, limited partnerships, nonprofit corporations, profit corporations, LLPs, statutory close corporations, statutory trusts, trade names, and trademarks. The Adobe Acrobat Reader is available for download.

State Tax Forms

Every single state tax agency in the country maintains some degree of an online presence. Most of them make the full range of their forms, applications, and reports available for download. You can find any of the agencies from the first page in this section. The second site covers sales and use tax. Once you locate the link to your jurisdiction from either site, bookmark it.

Federation of Tax Administrators Links to Other Sources
http://www.taxadmin.org/fta/link/link.html
As figure 8.3 shows, this page starts with a map divided into four sections: Western, Midwestern, Northeastern, and Southeastern states. Click on a section and you

get more than a list of links; you get a succinct but loaded description of what's available from each state. In some, more than one taxing authority is online; California, for example, has two, the franchise tax board and board of equalization. You can jump from a description directly to that state's site.

The subpages with the descriptions have graphics for each state they list and, as a result, may take quite a while to load at slower modem speeds. An alternative is the Quick Access link, which brings up a chart of all online state tax offices, including two that don't strictly fit the category, Puerto Rico and New York City.

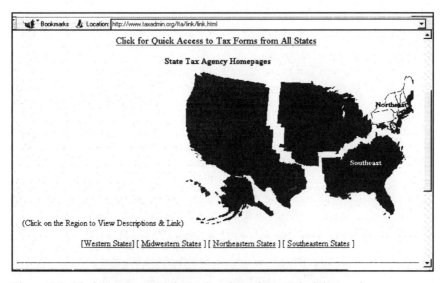

Figure 8.3: Find your state on the Federation of Tax Administrator's map.

Multistate Tax Commission State Sales/Use Tax Registration Forms
http://www.mtc.gov/txpyrsvs/actualpage.htm
From this chart you can jump to the sales or use tax sites of forty-seven states. (Alaska, Delaware, and Montana are missing.)

General State & Common Law Forms

For good measure I've thrown in a couple of places where you can pick up a variety of common documents. Think of these sites as electronic form books. I wouldn't use any of the downloads without pretty heavy reworking, but that's no different from the way I treat forms from a physical library, either. When you need a guide to get a project started, these sites might prove helpful.

FindLaw: Forms
http://forms.findlaw.com/
I would launch any search for a form from FindLaw's extensive index. FindLaw's own collection (at **http://forms.findlaw.com**) covers federal and state forms and "Tech Deals: Internet Contracts." Under the latter heading appear actual contracts from the spectrum of business deals involving technology companies, the identities of which are stated next to each link. The remainder of the index points to other form collections, forms on particular issues, and government forms. Each entry under the other headings discloses the sponsor of the linked site; most of the listings detail the contents as well.

The 'Lectric Law Library's Business Forms
http://www.lectlaw.com/formb.htm
The general business forms run from assignments and bills of sale to generic articles of incorporation, bylaws, minutes, and shareholders' agreements, employment agreements, joint ventures, and partnerships. Real estate forms are not merely the usual, but include rental management agreements, easements, and rent collection notices. In the general section are living wills adapted for six different states, powers of attorney, custody and prenuptial agreements, and lots of trusts and wills. The 'Lectric Law Library's Business Forms home page is shown in figure 8.4.

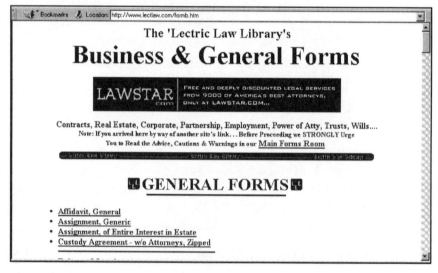

Figure 8.4: From the virtual stacks in the 'Lectric Law Library.

Legaldocs
http://www.legaldocs.com/
USA Law Publication's site has two self-explanatory categories. Under FREE DOCS is a smattering of miscellaneous documents, such as living wills, a promis-

sory note, insurance claims, a hunting lease, a car bill of sale, and a child care authorization. Everything else runs from $3.50 to $27.75, covering wills, trusts, sales and service agreements, employment and partnership agreements, leases, and business and real estate forms.

Quickform Contracts
http://www.quickforms.com/
This document assembly system walks you through online drafting of a variety of contracts related to computers, the Internet, and a few general business relationships–from a corporate electronic communications policy and employment agreements to software licensing, maintenance and marketing contracts. The system delivers the final document by e-mail after you enter into a license agreement and pay $19.95 by encrypted credit card.

Forms are just the beginning of the practical help you can get online from and about the government. Would your work be easier if you could follow congressional floor debate? How about accessing State Department travel advisories? Or getting your hands on an opponent's SEC filings? The Internet teems with answers, from statistics and publications to agency interpretation of statutes and regulations. Tools for mining this treasure trove are as close as the next page.

9
Locating Other Federal Resources

Do you need a statute's legislative history? Would you like to follow a bill that will affect a client? Or track a case being argued before the Supreme Court? How about accessing securities filings, State Department travel advisories, or copyright or trademark registrations?

You can have all the benefits of an office inside the Beltway, without having to deal with the traffic and the politicos. The Web teems with information about all three branches of the federal government. All the branches and most of the agencies have official sites, and general unofficial resources abound, as well. This is one area, in fact, where the Internet actually beats a regular law library. It would never occur to you to look in a book for some of the federally related resources you can find online. Filings, statistics, and even real-time broadcasts of proceedings are there for the having—or rather, for the clicking. You'd better get used to this new rule of thumb: If you need something that even remotely involves the federal government, look for it online, first.

This chapter begins with branch and agency sites. After that, I'll point you to some motherlodes of general federal government information.

Judicial Branch

Listen to recordings of oral arguments and announcements of opinions in major constitutional cases at the Oyez Project, **http://oyez.at.nwu.edu/oyez.html**, a multimedia work in progress spearheaded by Northwestern University Professor Jerry Goldman. You'll need RealAudio, which you can download from the site. The recordings are under the heading Cases. You can search the archive by case title, citation, subject, and date. You may also take a video tour of the Supreme Court building. Viewing the panoramic images requires QuickTime, which you may download from the site. The Justices heading leads to a searchable database with court-related resumes of the justices, starting with John Jay.

For the Supreme Court's official site, **http://www.supremecourtus.gov**, turn to chapter 7, "Locating Court Information & Rules."

> *To run a query through all federal government Websites at once, sign up for usgovsearch at **http://usgovsearch.com**. It's under the auspices of the meta-search engine Northern Light, which we'll look at in chapter 16, "General Research Resources." Public, school, and Federal Depository Libraries have free access to the service. Individual passes run $5-$250 for a day, month, or year; institutional accounts are also available.*

Legislative Branch

Congress has several official sites on the Web. Although the House of Representatives and the Senate each maintain a page, your best research bet is going to be courtesy of the library they share. The Library of Congress provides a marvelous guide to the legislative history and activities of both houses, in the form of the whimsically named THOMAS.

A number of private Web pages monitor Congress, as well. After discussing the government sites, I'll take you to a few standouts—where you can watch live floor debate, locate a congressperson with dispatch, or peruse well-seasoned political commentary.

THOMAS
Legislative Information on the Internet
http://thomas.loc.gov/
Making federal legislative information freely available is the goal of this Library of Congress project, which is named for Thomas Jefferson. Everything you could possibly want to know about current or past congressional activity is here, in a way that does its namesake honor. THOMAS is concise, helpful, and easy to navigate.

This is the premier site for federal legislative history and an excellent gateway to a spectrum of federal resources. A query box directly under the title (see figure 9.1) allows you to search the text of bills in the current Congress by number, word, or phrase. There are many other means of access, however. The heart of the site appears under the three major headings that dominate the top page.

The Legislation heading gives five avenues of approach. Bill Summary and Status allows browsing bills and amendments by public and private laws, vetoed bills, and sponsors. Search options in this section include keyword, subject, bill or amendment number, stage in legislative process, date, sponsor, or committee. The

Congress (1989-1990), searchable by word, phrase, or number. Major Legislation highlights significant bills and amendments from 1995 on; this area is browsable by topic, number, popular title, and by bills enacted into law. Besides posting browsable lists of public laws and vetoed bills, this portion is searchable in just about any way you could imagine: keyword/phrase, number, topic, stage in the legislative process, sponsors, and committee. Public Laws by Law Number indexes the legislation of the 93rd Congress through the present. Roll Call Votes charts the votes of each house from the 101st Congress on. For the Senate, this feature begins with the first session (1989), while the House tallies start with the second session (1990).

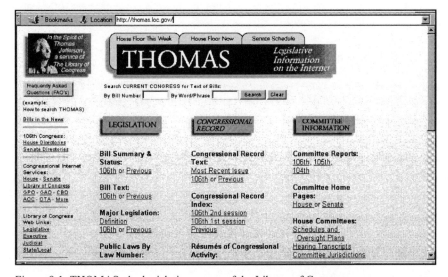

Figure 9.1: THOMAS, the legislative server of the Library of Congress.

Under the *Congressional Record* heading are links to the full text of the daily editions for the current and two prior Congresses. Routes for accessing the issues are many. You may search by keyword or congressperson's name. You may browse the issues by date and section or via the publication's index, which is arranged by member name and topic. You may also browse a topical index, which you enter by typing a keyword. To dragnet for discussions of anti-trust policies, for example, you would type "anti-trust" in the query box, click on that phrase when it comes up in the index, then scroll through a list of links to *Congressional Record* articles in which the word appears.

The Committee Information heading links to a database with the full text of all committee reports of the current and previous Congresses that were published by the Government Printing Office, searchable by keyword, report and bill number, and committee, and browsable sequentially. Other links under this heading jump to home pages of current congressional committees, hearings schedules of commit-

the Government Printing Office, searchable by keyword, report and bill number, and committee, and browsable sequentially. Other links under this heading jump to home pages of current congressional committees, hearings schedules of committees in both houses, and House committee hearing transcripts.

THOMAS relegates other information to smaller, less obvious links in the margins. Tabs at the top of the page lead to information about the House and Senate schedules. Along the left margin, links lead to House and Senate directories and Web pages, as well as to sites for the Library of Congress, the Government Printing Office, the General Accounting Office, and other congressional support agencies. The federal resources alone make THOMAS valuable to me, even though legislative history or tracking has never been important to my practice. If they are to yours, THOMAS definitely deserves a place on your bookmark list.

House of Representatives
http://www.house.gov/
At this site you'll find up-to-the-day status reports on bills and floor actions, floor and committee schedules, and Websites of members and committees. The page links to the searchable U.S. Code at the Office of Law Revision Counsel's page.

Senate
http://www.senate.gov/
Much the same calendar, status, and contact information is available as on the House page. The Senate page, however, allows keyword searches of its database and spotlights both its history and its art collection.

Congress Today
C-SPAN Online
http://congress.nw.dc.us/c-span/
The same outfit that brings Congress to cable television sends live audio and video coverage of selected congressional events across the Internet. From the Video and Audio link, check the broadcast schedules for C-SPAN, C-SPAN2, C-SPAN Radio and the network's two Internet programs—and then watch or listen to what's currently on the air. This section contains archived broadcasts and lets you download RealPlayer, the plug-in application necessary to play the multimedia files. C-SPAN and congressional schedules are also in the Guide to Programs. The site offers a searchable congressional directory and library of roll call votes, as well as an e-mail form for writing to senators and representatives.

Congressional Directories
http://www.lib.umich.edu/libhome/Documents.center/congdir.html
The University of Michigan Documents Center maintains directories of Congresses from the 103rd on, including e-mail addresses, committee assignments, and Websites.

> *If you need something more in-depth, immediate, or extensive than the materials discussed in this section, subscribe to Congressional Quarterly's On Congress at **http://www.oncongress.cq.com/**. This legislative tracking service offers a variety of features that subscribers may tailor to their needs and interests, such as alerts or vote analysis.*

Contacting the Congress
http://www.visi.com/juan/congress/
This site offers a quick way to locate a congressperson. Click on any part of a U.S. map to bring up contact information for the public servants in that region.

Roll Call Online
http://www.rollcall.com/
This is the online presence of a newspaper that has been covering Capitol Hill since 1955. Besides news scoops, commentaries, and policy briefings, it's brimming with such useful tidbits as a searchable directory of committee assignments for both houses.

Executive Branch

The Executive Branch is more than the president, and it's the "more than" part that will be of most use for online research. It's not that you can't find the people at the top; the White House, its primary occupant, and his right-hand man do have homes on the Web (and beautiful homes they are, fit for the pages of a magazine). But think of how often the president plays a direct role in the outcome of any research question. He hasn't yet for me, in twenty years of research. If he has for you, you'll have to admit the times have been few. The business of one Cabinet department or another, however, is more likely to have an immediate impact on the affairs of our clients. As table 9.1 demonstrates, the entire Cabinet is online.

Welcome to the White House
http://www.whitehouse.gov/WH/Welcome.html
This is a high-gloss affair, crafted more for public relations and citizen education than for technical research. The database of White House documents, press releases, and policy statements will be helpful, though, if you're watching which way the winds of national law are blowing.

Other parts of the Executive Branch, in contrast, maintain an online presence bordering on information overload. Every single Cabinet department has a page, each distinctive in design, but all laid out with great clarity. Clickable icons and hyperlinks lead to frequently asked questions (FAQs), statistical databases, reports, and pages for the agencies under each department's jurisdiction. Table 9.1 gives

and pages for the agencies under each department's jurisdiction. Table 9.1 gives all the addresses in one compact list. The next section will single out pages for agencies of more frequent interest to the legal profession.

Table 9.1: Cabinet Websites

Department	URL
Agriculture	http://www.usda.gov
Commerce	http://www.doc.gov/
Defense	http://www.defenselink.mil/
Education	http://www.ed.gov/
Energy	http://www.doe.gov/
Health & Human Services	http://www.os.dhhs.gov/
Housing & Urban Development	http://www.hud.gov/
Interior	http://www.doi.gov/
Justice	http://www.usdoj.gov/
Labor	http://www.dol.gov/
State	http://www.state.gov/
Treasury	http://www.ustreas.gov/
Transportation	http://www.dot.gov/
Veterans Affairs	http://www.va.gov/

Agencies & Commissions

Agencies take several different approaches to being online. Some focus on explaining their mission and procedures. Others post a wealth of technical or historical information. A few, like the Securities and Exchange Commission, actually permit access to documents that have been filed with it.

Below is a listing of agency pages that are likely to come in handy for lawyers. (All Department of Justice division listings appear alphabetically under that department.) If you need to find an agency that is not mentioned, try one of these two methods. If you know the Cabinet department that oversees the agency, pull up the department's page and look for a link. Otherwise, run a search for the agency.

Copyright Office
http://lcweb.loc.gov/copyright/
Chapter 8, "Locating Government Forms," introduced this site as a mecca for downloadable forms (see figure 9.2). The Library of Congress has filled it with a wealth of background material, as well. Anything the Copyright Office would send by mail it has put on the site, such as circulars explaining copyright basics and each type of registration, mandatory deposit requirements, and form letters on recurring topics. The site also addresses pending legislation, international copyright, and

service provider. In all, it's an excellent primer on federal copyright law.

Figure 9.2: The U.S. Copyright Office.

From this page you can search Copyright Office records through the Library of Congress Information System (LOCIS). LOCIS covers copyright registrations only from 1978, but my experience has been that coverage is not complete. On none of my visits over the past five years has LOCIS turned up a complete list of my personal copyright registrations. If you want to give LOCIS a try, you'll need a Telnet application, which will link your computer directly into the Library of Congress records. You'll don't actually have to launch Telnet, however. The page contains two hyperlinks that will do that for you. If neither works (I've never encountered any problems with them), look for connecting address just below them, which you should enter onto your Telnet screen after starting the application.

> To comb though copyright registrations more reliably, you'll have to ante up for a fee-based service, such as CCH-Trademark Research Corporation, at **http://www.cch-trc.com/**, which researches both copyrights and trademarks.

Read the LOCIS Users Guide (links to it are clear) before launching a search; in fact, it wouldn't hurt to print out the page for reference. The help menus, once you are in LOCIS, are abbreviated and it's hard to figure out which commands to enter to retrieve the information you want.

Antitrust Division, Department of Justice
http://www.usdoj.gov/atr/index.html
In addition to speeches and phone numbers, the Antitrust Division posts its guidelines for evaluating various commercial activities, including health care and mergers. (Look for them under Public Documents.) The Division also archives, by name, opinions in civil and criminal cases it has prosecuted since 1994. Selected appellate briefs are available. Other resources include business review letters since 1993 and cooperation agreements with Australia, Canada, Germany, and the European communities. The site links to other antitrust offices and organizations in this country and abroad.

Civil Division, Department of Justice
http://www.usdoj.gov/civil/home.html
Filings in a few, current major cases are the main research reason to visit this sparse site. As of this writing, they involved tobacco regulations, health care fraud, and agriculture program discrimination.

Civil Rights Division, Department of Justice
http://www.usdoj.gov/crt/crt-home.html
A handful of complaints, briefs, and consent decrees are the point of interest here, along with links to separate pages for each section in the Division.

Criminal Division, Department of Justice
http://www.usdoj.gov/criminal/criminal-home.html
Look under Publications and Documents for the Division's guidelines for searching and seizing computers, as well as papers on intellectual property prosecution and telemarketing fraud. The Public Services link leads to subpages for a variety of sections and programs, such as the Child Exploitation and Obscenity Section, Inter Agency Fugitive Lookout, and Gambling Device Registration.

Immigration & Naturalization Service, Department of Justice
http://www.ins.usdoj.gov/graphics/index.htm
In addition to agency forms, this extremely clearly laid out site contains a detailed guide to immigration law and policy. The Laws, Regulations and Guides link provides the governing statute and public laws that have amended it, regulations, interpretations, agency publications, and some Board of Immigration Appeals decisions.

Equal Employment Opportunity Commission
http://www.eeoc.gov/
The EEOC takes a public information approach, with how-to information targeted at both the employee and employer. Scroll down the page for laws enforced, regulations, and the agency's compliance manual.

Federal Communication Commission
http://www.fcc.gov/

This searchable site was spotlighted in chapter 8, "Locating Government Forms," but has other features worth your attention. Scroll down the top page (it's longer than it initially looks) to get the lay of the land. Noteworthy links include headlines of latest developments at the Commission and hot topics such as the V-chip and broadband Internet access. (A number warrant their own pages, under Major Initiatives.) Besides posting its weekly calendar, and open meeting agendas, the FCC broadcasts selected events live over the Internet; listening to a broadcast will require RealPlayer, which you can download free from the site. Look under Resources for a form to comment on proposed rules or file a complaint against a broadcaster.

The page also gives two means of access to the Daily Digest, an FCC publication containing synopses of orders, news releases, speeches, and titles of public notices. It shows up on the page by 1:30 p.m. Eastern Time, where it remains archived; it's also available by e-mail subscription, for which you can sign up on the page.

Figure 9.3: The Federal Trade Commission site.

Federal Trade Commission
http://www.ftc.gov/

At first glance this page (see figure 9.3) looks like it's geared to consumer and business education. Take a closer peek though—useful nuggets are scattered throughout this site. The Commission's Rules of Practice are available in Word-Perfect and PDFs, under the link to Legal Framework. Downloadable guides on antitrust issues include policy statements on health care and 1992 horizontal merger guidelines. Hart-Scott-Rodino Act premerger notification and report forms are available (in PDF format), as are also instructions and filing fee information. Even the Consumer Protection and Business Guidance sections are filled with handy FTC publications well worth printing out and passing on to clients.

Internal Revenue Service
http://www.irs.ustreas.gov/

Of all the agencies in the government, who would have guessed that the best sense of humor would come out of the tax man? This page has the perky personality of a faux 1950s greeting card. It's clear, easy to navigate, and clever as can be, delivering even technical tidings with a virtual wink.

Chapter 8, "Locating Government Forms," tipped you off to the wealth of forms and publications here. On top of them, the site explains an array of personal and business tax questions (including the thorny employee versus independent contractor problem). It gives step-by-step instructions for obtaining tax exempt status and maintains a searchable database of organizations that have qualified for it. The site archives (and provides summaries of) tax regulations issued since August 1, 1995; it also has a browsable list of proposed regulations, to which you can file comments directly from the page. And if you can't figure out where something is from the word links and icons, a search engine will find it for you.

National Labor Relations Board
http://www.nlrb.gov/

Look under Weekly Summary for current and back issues of the NRLB's weekly release of decisions and orders. (Each summary links to the decision's full text.) Searchable slip opinions are posted in PDF format under the link Decisions; older decisions (beginning with Vol. 312) are in text, HTML, and PDF formats. Case-handling manuals are also on the site, along with public notices, statutes, and regulations.

Patent and Trademark Office
http://www.uspto.gov/

The PTO has filled its Website to the brim with useful details, starting with changes in fees, legislation, and practice before the office. The Office has uploaded five critical publications in their entirety: both the patent and trademark manuals of Examining Procedure; the Trademark Trial and Appeal Board Manual of Procedure; the alphabetical index, identified by International Class, known as the Trademark Acceptable Goods and Services Identification Manual; and a roster of attorneys and agents registered to practice before the PTO. All are available from the Patent and Trademark Depository Library Program page, but take some looking to locate. From the top page, choose Libraries-PTDLs in the left column; scroll to

Publications, then click Printed or Microform Materials. The patent and trademark subpages also contain links to their respective documents.

The patent subpage contains a variety of guides for specific patent types, the Classification Index, classification definitions, legislation, and regulations. Look there, too, for the Patent Cooperation Treaty Legal Office, from which you can download international patent applications in PDF format. (Don't forget the flurry of domestic downloadable forms, covered in chapter 8, "Locating Government Forms.")

The PTO site also has one feature that makes up for a monthly Internet access charge several times over: free access to two searchable patent databases. In the main one, The U.S. Patent Bibliographic Database, you can find front page information from patents issued from January 1, 1976, to the present. The basic search engine supports Boolean operators, will look for two key terms in specified fields, and allows limiting searches to the year of issue. The advanced search will analyze a complicated search request, using much the same format as Westlaw or LEXIS. (Help is there for the clicking.) You can also search by patent number. For other searchable patent databases, see chapter 11, "Researching by Topic."

Besides forms, fees schedules, and manuals, the trademark subpage has three noteworthy features. The Trademark Electronic Application System (TEAS) facilitates filing applications over the Internet. The Trademark Application and Registration Retrieval System provides information from the PTO's internal database about pending or registered marks. The serial or registration number is necessary to retrieve information. The site also allows searching the PTO's trademark database by mark, registration or serial number, or keywords with Boolean constraints. Be sure to check the date of the latest data entry, because the database lags behind that date by about two months. The upshot is that the database is not up-to-the-minute and, depending on when you consult it, can miss as much as the past four months of filings and registrations. For the latest information, the site refers to fee-based trademark search libraries (in Arlington, VA, Sunnyvale, CA, and Houston, TX) and the Official Gazette, which discloses marks that have been registered or published for opposition.

Securities and Exchange Commission
http://www.sec.gov/
No mere public relations or citizens' educational tool, the SEC's site is loaded with prime practical material, and all of it is searchable. It includes proposed and final agency rules, as well as the SEC's own interpretation of its governing statutes and regulations. Investor Assistance posts a myriad of documents, links, directories, and publications geared to avoiding being taken by securities fraud—now including a complaint form for online filing. A Q&A guide to raising capital legally, perfect for client education, is under Small Business, along with forms for public and exempt stock offerings. The Enforcement Division link serves up orders, initial administrative law judge opinions, commission opinions in contested proceedings,

announcements of trading suspensions, and other alerts. Figure 9.4 shows the top page.

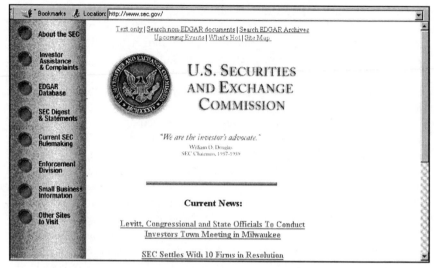

Figure 9.4: The SEC home page (prior to a planned site redesign.)

One particularly valuable feature is the Electronic Data Gathering, Analysis, and Retrieval system, called EDGAR for short. EDGAR allows online retrieval of electronic public filings since 1994. Except for hardship cases and submissions to regional offices, public domestic corporations have been required to make certain filings via EDGAR since May 6, 1996. Exactly what is and is not required to be filed is technical enough to make your vision blur. Among the required are Form 10K or 10KSB annual reports, as well as third-party filings such as tender offers and Schedule D. Many companies, including foreign, make voluntary filings of a number of nonmandatory documents, such as Forms 3, 4, 5, 13F, and 144. Whatever is in the database is up to the minute; postings go up within twenty-four hours of filing. The agency is currently restructuring the database, a process that will organize data by year and by registrant.

EDGAR is helpful to an extreme, with explanatory files and a multifaceted search engine. It allows searching the archives by keyword, accessing common forms by company name, and a half dozen or so special purpose searches, focusing on such aspects as prospectuses, ownership filings, or analysis of forms filed in the previous week.

The Other Sites to Visit page is worth a hearty nod, as well. It connects to sites of market regulators like the North American Securities Administrators Association, an array of stock exchanges and clearing agencies (such as NASD, NYSE, the Chicago, Pacific, and Philadelphia exchanges), educational institutions, and professional organizations.

United States Sentencing Commission
http://www.ussc.gov/
The 1994, 1995, 1997, and 1998 Sentencing Guidelines Manuals are online, along with enacted and proposed amendments.

Small Business Administration
http://www.sbaonline.sba.gov/
If you handle general business matters, do your entrepreneur clients a favor and send them to this page. It's unlikely that you will find anything you need (unless you're launching a side business, of course), but it's almost a certainty they will. This site teems with contact information and explanations of the SBA's start-up, development, and financing services. If it's anything, it's thorough, to an extent that counteracts the general wisdom of government offices giving citizens the run-around.

The site provides everything you need to know about getting SBA loans, procurement assistance, or grants, including the application forms themselves. It stockpiles downloadable shareware programs for financing, marketing, or managing a business. The site maintains browsable databases of online business cards and property for sale through the SBA, both of which are cataloged geographically. PRO-Net is a searchable database of small, disadvantaged, 8(a), and women-owned businesses, designed to facilitate procurement and subcontracting. The icing on the cake is more than 3,000 business-related links (under Outside Resources) on topics such as financing, home businesses, marketing, patents, tax, and trade shows.

> The Webgator, *http://www.inil.com/users/dguss/wgator.htm*, has pointers for obtaining military records, including links to specific divisions and squadrons.

General Federal Resources

Don't worry about keeping track of which issues are in a particular agency's bailiwick. You don't necessarily have to attack a federal research problem through an official government site. A specialized searchable index or search engine may provide an easy and efficient approach, especially when a question spans the jurisdiction of several bodies. (It's also a quick way to locate an agency or commission.) Here are a few stable and reliable starting points.

DocLaw Web
http://www.washlaw.edu/doclaw/doclawnew.html
Washburn University School of Law maintains this gateway to federal materials online. Besides offering access through a search engine, it organizes links in three

ways: in a subject index, an agency index (look for it in the pull-down menu) and a clickable organizational chart of the government. The subject index lists more than thirty topics (such as Banks & Banking, Criminal Justice, and Immigration); under each one, DocLaw divides the relevant resources into governmental, non-governmental, primary law, reference sources, and research guides. The agency index consists of an alphabetical chart with links to each agency's home page, a list of its publications online, and its location on DocLaw's organizational chart. The organizational chart has several levels; the top one covers the branches and departments, while agencies spill over into two successive charts. Clicking on a name leads to the appropriate Web home page, if one exists; if an agency is not online, pressing its name will bring you back to its spot on the chart.

The Federal Web Locator
http://www.infoctr.edu/fwl/
This is one of the essential bookmarks recommended in chapter 4, "Setting Up Your Online Library." If a federal government office has a Website, you should be able to jump to it from here. Links are divided into Latest Additions, Quick Jumps (which are abbreviations arranged by branch and category), and a list of Web servers, by full name, also arranged by branch and category.

FedStats
http://www.fedstats.gov/
Here's where the Federal Interagency Council on Statistical Policy stockpiles data generated by seventy agencies. FedStats gives multiple means of attack on this mass of information. For starters, FedStats has a browsable alphabetical list of topics, an engine for searching the database by keyword and a regional breakdown of statistics by agency. Follow the Fast Facts link for the latest economic and social indicators (presented in "Briefing Rooms") and the Statistical Abstract of the United States.

FedWorld Information Network
http://www.fedworld.gov/
Odds are you've never heard of the National Technical Information Service if you're outside the Beltway—and you've never visited this site. The NTIS (a Commerce Department agency, by the way) launched this project in 1992, during the Dark Ages of the Web. Since then it's built the page into a comprehensive clearinghouse of government and business information. FedWorld hosts twenty databases, which are updated daily, and provides links to many, many others.

Pull-down menus at the top of the page allow you to search or browse the network or a selected site. On your first visit, pull down the browsing menu to get a feel for the breadth of the holdings, from Clean Air and Davis-Bacon Act databases to Supreme Court decisions to the U.S. Customs Service. It's worth taking the time to go to and scan the first option, "About FedWorld," which gives a succinct and helpful introduction to the site. Back on the top page, below the pull-down menus, are the descriptions of the databases (and links to them), set out in a somewhat random order.

As part of its information repackaging, FedWorld acts as a gateway to 100 government bulletin boards, accessible through Telnet via a link directly from the site. Not only are the dial-up instructions fool-proof, but FedWorld actually gives a phone number for technical questions. (Getting to speak to a human is a rarity on the Web, which you'll come to appreciate the moment you hit a glitch, whether it's a connection that's down, a bad link, or a typo.) It also lists the bulletin boards, along with a description of their coverage. From these you can download an avalanche of files, ranging from information on the Americans With Disabilities Act, FDA policies, job opportunities, Superfund data, and tax forms.

Unless you cut your teeth on bulletin boards—which eliminates most of us relative newcomers to the technology—you'll probably feel more comfortable downloading files from FedWorld's enormous FTP library (currently more than 10,000 documents). That page supports a rudimentary keyword search, which can be limited to a directory selected from an extensive browsable list. (It runs from the Federal Aviation Agency to Nuclear Regulatory Commission public petitions files to the Treasury's electronic library.)

FindLaw Federal Government Resources
http://www.findlaw.com/10fedgov/index.html
FindLaw's top page should already be on your bookmark list. From this subpage you can enter keywords and search all of FindLaw or a federal site selected from a pop-up menu. You can also browse a list of indexes on the Web. They're not arranged in any discernible order (much less alphabetically), but the list is short and does give helpful descriptions of what's in each index.

GovBot Database of Government Web Sites
http://ciir2.cs.umass.edu/Govbot/
With only a couple of graphical interfaces on the page, the site may look bare bones. But as usual, the adage applies about not judging by appearances. The Center for Intelligent Information Retrieval (a University of Massachusetts project) has harnessed more than one million federal government Web pages. You can direct a query to a document's text, title, or URL. Search tips at the bottom of the page are simple but effective.

Government Documents at Yale
http://www.library.yale.edu/govdocs/gdchome.html
Government information resources are grouped into federal, state, local, international, and other; under each heading the page offers clickable search choices in language refreshingly close to normal English. You can peruse the U.S. government information by agency or subject, or you can scan a two-column list and

select options such as declassified documents, legislative information, standards and specifications, technical reports, or treaties.

Government Information Xchange
http://www.info.gov/
A graphical interface box allows exploring such topics as passport and visa information, Social Security and Medicare, federal telephone directories, and the Government Information Locator Service. Click on the top banner to reach a federal directory, the site's search engine, or links to state, local, and foreign resources.

GPO Access Database List
http://www.access.gpo.gov/su_docs/db2.html
Here the Government Printing Office offers free access to publications, including the *Congressional Record*, the Federal Register, bills, Supreme Court decisions, and federal agency files. The top page consists of a browsable index of links, sporadically in alphabetical order. Unless you spot a link to a database of interest, start with the link "Search across multiple databases." This will get you to descriptions of the databases, methods of accessing them, and a simple search engine. From either this page or the top page, the specialized search links connect to separately searchable databases, such as the Federal Register, GAO reports, Government Information Locator Services records, and Commerce Business Daily. Each search page contains instructions so detailed that they take you by the hand.

Hieros Gamos
http://www.hg.org/hg.html
Take the United States link under All Governments. Hieros Gamos links to the GPO Access for searching government records and also piggybacks on a number of legal and general interest search engines. Besides government news and federal statutes and regulations, the site provides a randomly ordered index to such sites as the Congressional Quarterly, the U.S. Business Advisor, and FinanceNet.

Infomine
http://lib-www.ucr.edu/search/ucr_govsearch.html
This is the government collection in an enormous scholarly database maintained by the University of California campuses and Stanford University. You can search the site by subject, keyword, or title, or go to the table of contents and click on a letter to see the subjects and files under it. (For example, press C to bring up everything associated with California.) The What's New link shows everything that's been added in the past twenty days. Infomine is an excellent source for scientific and technical information; it also pulls together state and international government sites, as well as federal.

U.S. Business Advisor—Agencies & Gateways
http://www.business.gov/busadv/onestop.cfm
This is a source of federal government information and services that affect businesses. Three graphical interface boxes take you to agency home and business pages, as well as a spectrum of gateways. The column of links cover every aspect of starting and running a business that is addressed by the federal government, including federal legislation and regulations, tax issues, workplace safety and benefits, and international trade concerns. Press the Search icon to access the engine for this site, as well as for FedWorld, the GPO Congressional and executive databases, the Government Information Xchange, and health, safety, and environmental regulations.

University of Michigan Documents Center
Federal Government Resources on the Web
http://www.lib.umich.edu/libhome/Documents.center/federal.html
The Congressional Directories section of this page came up earlier in the chapter, but the main site is well worth attention. In fact, this is an optimal starting point for any type of federal research. Navigating is a breeze, thanks to an easy-to-read chart of subheadings ranging from a directory of agencies to budget, executive orders, and historic documents. Each subheading takes you to a list of links that gives site descriptions in key points, so you have a good idea of what you'll find before jumping off into the Web. We'll come back to the Documents Center a time or two in later chapters, because it's also an outstanding source for state, local, and international governments.

If an issue has federal aspect, you can now find what Congress has to say on the subject. What's more, you know how to pinpoint even the most obscure federal agency's stance on the matter. But what if a problem is closer to home?

Several of the general starting points in this chapter—Infomine, Government Documents at Yale, and the University of Michigan Documents Center—will lead you just as easily to state and local government resources. Cities and counties all over the country have joined state governments on the Infobahn, and the only rhyme or reason, so far, is that somebody somewhere on a staff had enough interest in computers to make it happen. The next chapter explores the range of state and local presences online.

10
Locating Other State & Local Resources

Every state government has an official welcoming site. Don't let a public-relations-heavy top page make you dismiss its usefulness. While a message from the governor or splashy tourist tips may not have much impact on legal research, surprisingly handy information is tucked away in most state pages. Just as with the federal government, a wide array of state-level departments and agencies is accessible online. Many of them post public hearing calendars and announce changes in their procedures or governing legislation. A number even allow electronic searching of documents filed for public record, some by subscription, others for free. Business opportunities, natural resources, and registering to run for public office are other common topics, as are a few we've already explored. chapter 6, "Locating Statutes & Regulations," featured sites with political and legislative information, while chapter 8, "Locating Government Forms," pointed out ones that post government publications.

Reaching Individual States

Besides referring to the list below, here are two tricks for locating state government information on your own. If you are visiting a legislature site or downloading forms from a state government page—in other words, any of the state addresses in chapters 6 and 8—you can use it as a springboard to any official information that you might need for that jurisdiction. Each should have a link back to the state's top page, which should then give a clear picture of the resources under it. Or remember this short-cut: type **www.state.pc.us**, with pc being the state's two letter postal code. For example, find California by typing **http://www.state.ca.us**. (One exception is Washington, which has moved to **http://access.wa.gov/**.) A similar trick works for most Secretary of State pages. To reach those, try **http://www.sos.state.pc.us**.

Finding Public Records

If you're looking for public records information, whether in a specific state or nationwide, try one of these resources. Pacific Information Resources Search Systems, **http://www.pac-info.com/**, links to more than 1,200 free searchable databases, organized geographically. The scope varies by jurisdiction, but can include sex offenders lists, campaign finance reports, court filings, and property or tax records.

To approach by subject or search need, visit the Webgator, **http://www.inil.com/users/dguss/wgator.htm**. The headings at this index include searchable corporate and UCC databases, criminal history inquiries, departments of corrections and parole boards, hunting and fishing license agencies, motor vehicle offices, and other state government records.

Vital Records Information at **http://www.vitalrec.com/** points to sources of birth, marriage, or death certificates and divorce decrees anywhere in the United States and its territories. The site, which is geared to genealogy, spells out fees, contact information, and procedures for each office and links to Websites, where available.

What you will find at each state site will vary. Expect links to the governor's office, legislature, agencies, and judiciary (the last of which may range from a central judicial site for the state to an index of individual court sites). Many state agencies simply post paragraph after paragraph explaining services or setting out phone numbers and addresses. Some pages give much more information, and not just lottery numbers, road conditions, and kids' links.

The extent of the resources, however, is not always evident from the welcoming page. While state sites do not use a common system of indexing, there is usually an intuitive connection between a heading and the resources that lurk under it. Category names such as Business, Commerce, Economic Development, or Government are fruitful for exploration. Fortunately, search engines and agency indexes are a growing trend among these sites. In this section I've singled out the most pertinent features of each state's site.

Alabama Information Network
http://www.state.al.us/

From the top page (shown in figure 10.1) you can jump directly to the sites for the Attorney General, Secretary of State, courts, legislature, Treasury and Comptroller. Navigational tools include a Quick List of all state government Websites and a search engine for all executive branch sites. Unless you need only contact information, don't bother with the search tool for state agency information online. The

Secretary of State allows online searching of its corporations, elections, notary public, and UCC records. The Oil and Gas Board maintains searchable well file, production, and engineering databases.

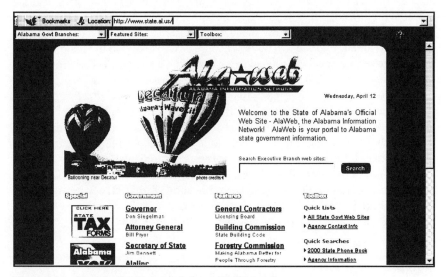

Figure 10.1: Alaweb, the Alabama Information Network.

State of Alaska Online
http://www.state.ak.us/

For a listing of state resources in some twenty categories, take the Departments link. From here you can reach both the court system and departmental pages. A number of agencies have uploaded public records to their sites. Under the Department of Revenue, the Alcoholic Beverage Control Board posts a master list of all liquor licenses, while the Child Support Enforcement Division discloses payment information upon entry of a member number. The Division of Banking, Securities and Corporations (part of the Department of Community and Economic Development) gives online access to its searchable database of domestic and foreign corporate records and reserved or registered business names. The Online Public Notice feature allows searching active and archived public notices by category, department, location, publication date, and title.

Use the Business button from the welcoming page to view a list of agencies and other online resources pertaining to business. The Communities link leads to an index of cities and local services online. If the welcoming or index pages load too slowly for you (as they did for me), select the Text Only option to eliminate the graphics.

Arizona
http://www.state.az.us/

Pull-down menus, a search engine, and a handful of hyperlinked headings are the means of access to Arizona's streamlined site. For counties and cities, use the respective pull-down menus. To find an agency site, look for the appropriate heading in the Services pull-down menu, use the search engine, or take the Branches of Government hyperlink. The first approach will take you to an alphabetical index of government offices related to the topic you've selected. The Branches of Government link will get you to the same place, with a stopover at a page explaining the executive, legislative, and judicial branches.

Public records available for online inspection include the Banking Department's list of licensed companies and the Secretary of State's searchable databases of UCC filings, lobbyists, notaries public, and registered telephone solicitors. The Department of Liquor Licenses and Control posts a searchable database of licenses, as well as tables of all pending and special event licenses. The Corporation Commission's Corporations Division offers a subscription service, the State of Arizona Public Access System (STARPAS), for online access to its database of corporations, LLCs, limited partnerships, trademarks, and trade names.

Arkansas
http://www.state.ar.us/

There are several avenues for locating pertinent information at this high-gloss site. Before using the search engine, try the Arkansas Government link. This leads to an online directory of government offices, organized by branch (departments and agencies are at the bottom of the page), and a scroll-down menu for jumping directly to specific categories of resources. Most are self-explanatory. Selecting Licenses & Permits will take you to an alphabetical list of issuing agencies, but the inclusion of a name does not mean that it has a Website. (A surprising number of them do not.) Some of the agencies under this heading, such as the Board of Architects and the Board of Registration for Professional Engineers and Land Surveyors, maintain searchable databases of their license roster. For a clear picture of which agencies are actually online (and to what extent), consult the Online Services & Citizens FAQ. Scroll down the page for a listing of searchable databases maintained by agencies.

Another approach is the Business & Employment button, which brings up an index of resources grouped by category (such as business, commerce, financing, labor, manufacturing, and standards). The Securities Department site includes orders, legal opinions, no action letters, and a searchable database of licensed or chartered financial institutions. At the Secretary of State's page, you may search databases of banks and insurance, home builders, incorporations, trademarks, cooperatives, home inspectors, and notaries public. The Secretary of State now accepts online incorporation filings from account holders with the Information Network of Arkansas.

Press the Community & Civic Info button for pointers to city, county, library, and police, sheriff, and fire department Websites. County information may also be accessed by moving your cursor over a clickable map of the state.

California
http://www.ca.gov/
The Golden State's well-designed, searchable site packs in the data, from historical and cultural facts to emergency relief instructions, under twenty main headings. Follow the Business link to reach related agencies and programs: For licensing information, visit the Trade and Commerce Agency site. Complaint forms for securities and financial services transactions are available at the Department of Corporations' site. Besides the forms discussed in chapter 8, Secretary of State's Business Programs Division offers online searchable databases of corporate, limited partnership and limited liability company (LLC) records and claim filings by successors-in-interest to deceased celebrities.

The Government section leads to legislature, court, county, and city pages. The California Courts page is also under the Legal heading. For a browsable index of agencies, subjects, and servers, take the Search & Indexes in the bar at the bottom of the home page.

Colorado
http://www.state.co.us/
Colorado's page covers the spectrum of information, from history and tourism to education and government sectors. The site has separate browsable indexes for agencies, subjects, and permits and licenses. Agency, legislative, court, city, county, and special district pages are under Government; city, county, and special district pages also appear under Community.

Within the Government heading, look under Elected Officials for the Secretary of State's Website. From there, go to Commercial Recordings for the online, searchable databases of UCC debtors and of fair campaign contributions and expenditures. The Department of State also offers direct electronic access to corporate, UCC, and Campaign Reform Act filings, by subscription. The basic rate (currently $550 annually) allows use in unlimited 15-minute increments; unlimited use plans, at higher rates, are also available. Look for information at **http://www.sos.state.co.us/diracces.html**.

From the state's main page, the Business Information link leads to an index of state agencies that deal with business, labor, and employment, as well as some economic resources and chamber of commerce pages. Also on the top page are income tax forms, which may be filed online, and a state government telephone directory.

State of Connecticut ConneCT
http://www.state.ct.us/

A few simple buttons organize Connecticut's extensive, searchable Web resources, which appear in figure 10.2. Under State Government, buttons lead to Web pages for the executive, judicial, legislative branches. A browsable alphabetical index of agency Websites is under Agencies/Organizations. To search corporate and UCC filings, follow links to Concord On-Line on the Secretary of State's page. The Towns/Cities button leads to links to municipal Websites, and local government directories, as well as statistical and regional resources and databases. Select the A to Z button (back on the top page) for an uncommonly detailed alphabetical subject index of the site's information.

Figure 10.2: ConneCT is the state of Connecticut's online home.

One novel feature that begs to be emulated is the Connecticut License Information Center (CLIC), which you reach by pressing the Licenses/Permits button on the welcoming page. By entering a keyword in the query box you can pull up requirements, explanations, and downloadable forms for most any license or permit issued by the state. The page also lists licenses alphabetically and by agency, and permits online verification of the status of health care or environmental health professional licenses.

The Connecticut Economic Resource Center offers information from two business start-up services otherwise available by phone. One is the Business Resource Index, a searchable database of state, federal, and local resources and programs (including license and permit requirements). The Center also gives online access to the browsable Access International database of private and public resources for companies interested in international trade. To find the CERC, press the Start Smart button on CLIC—or select it from the agency index that comes up after you select the Commerce button on the welcoming page.

Delaware
http://www.state.de.us/
Delaware annotates each top page heading with a pithy description of its resources. An pop-up menu of departments, agencies, boards, and commissions is under Delaware Government. Look for the state assembly and the Supreme and Family Courts under It's the Law. Business and Economy is one route to the site's business resources. (The top page's Quick Information Links include a jump to an incorporating guide, as well.) Besides how-to guides, these include the Division of Corporations' newsletter *The Corporate Edge*, which you may read online or download in PDF format. Local Government leads to town, city, and county links, which are few. A downside of the site is the paucity of public records databases; on the positive side, it does have a search engine.

District of Columbia
http://www.washingtondc.gov/
Follow the links under Government to reach a scroll-down menu of the district's services and agencies. Select Business Services for descriptions of agencies that provide business resources. This page isn't hyperlinked to their Websites; if you want to know whether an agency has a home page (few do), return to the Services & Agencies page and highlight the appropriate name in the menu box. The site has a search engine.

Florida Government Information Locator Service
http://www.dos.state.fl.us/fgils/index.html
The Department of State, State Library of Florida, is responsible for this simple but efficient (and searchable) gateway to Florida resources. Move your cursor onto one of the eight buttons to see an index of the topics to which it leads. Press Government for the legislature, courts, clerks of county courts, agencies, boards, commissions, cities, counties, municipal codes, police and sheriff departments, local tax collectors, and special districts. Both the agency and the boards and commissions listing pages will tell you that you may preview a site by pressing Information Resources. Do not bother with this tactic. It will only take you a page of links, arranged in a hierarchy without meaningful elaboration. Instead, it's quicker merely to load the agency, board or commission page.

To search records for corporations, general and limited liability partnerships, trademarks, UCC filings, federal liens, and fictitious names, use the Secretary of State's Sunbiz utility, which provides digital images of the actual documents on file. (Sunbiz also accepts corporate, general and limited partnership, LLC, and UCC filings online; this aspect of the service requires applying for an account and making a deposit of at least $300.) The Department of Business and Professional Regulation has searchable databases of its licensees and Alcohol Beverage and Tobacco delinquent invoices and activity lists. Other public records are available in complete files, rather than searchable databases. Visit the Comptroller's Division of Securities and Finance to download zipped files of finance, funeral and cemetery, securities, and money transmitter licensees. The Banking Division posts lists of all state-chartered banks, credit unions, and trusts; this site also links to search engines for retrieving financial data about banks, savings and loans, and credit unions.

The Business button on the top page is a starting point for related agency sites. Take the Professional Licensing link to see a comprehensive listing of issuing agencies. From here you can access search engines for license information about health care professionals and insurance agents.

Georgia Online Network
http://www.state.ga.us/
This well laid-out site groups its offerings under clear, simple headings and a handful of buttons. Links to legislative, judicial, and constitutional office sites are on the state page under Government, along with a pull-down menu of agencies, authorities, commissions, and councils. Need information on child support enforcement? Look for the link under the Department of Human Resources. Go to the Secretary of State's section to verify the status or registered agent of business entities, to check on a professional's record in more than thirty license examining board databases, or determine whether a charity is registered. The Local Government page has graphical interface boxes of links to city and county Websites.

Business & Economic Development links include information on small and minority business services, the central procurement bid registry, monthly Banking & Finance Department bulletins affecting financial institutions, and an economic development financing packet for businesses in the state. The Legal heading encompasses Websites for a variety of agencies (but not the legislature or courts) and jumps to the Georgia code and regulations. To reach legislative sites, press the button for the current session on the welcoming page.

Hawaii State Government
http://www.hawaii.gov/
Press Executive Branch for a hyperlinked list of offices and agencies, most of which use their Websites to describe their functions. Under Legal are links to the Attorney General's page, a few commissions, the judiciary, and a number of AG opinion letters. Agriculture, Labor, and Procurement Office rules dominate the Rulings & Regulations link. Take Permits & Licensing for a handful of links to issuing agencies, such as the Department of Transportation and Real Estate Commission. A few departments offer search engines on their pages, but the site is not searchable as a whole.

Access Idaho
http://www.state.id.us/
An agency index, topical index, and search engine aid navigation of Idaho's site. For an index of agencies that affect business, press Commerce on the top page; for courts and judicial agencies, take Judicial/Legal. Links to city and county Websites are under Other Links.

The pages uniformly take the approach of passing on information (often in detailed, step-by-step guides) and, at most, forms, rather than offering online access to public records. Download a PDF file of the guide Starting a Business in Idaho from the Department of Commerce's Business Services pages. The individual board pages under the Bureau of Occupational Licenses anticipate online searching of their licensee databases, but the search engines are not yet in place.

Illinois
http://www.state.il.us/
Illinois takes a succinct approach. Each heading on the welcoming page leads to a concise but descriptive index of associated resources, from which you can make informed choices about further surfing destinations. (The Legislature, Judiciary, and Agency headings explain and contain links to pages for the respective governmental bodies.) The cluster of links at the bottom of the welcoming page give information even more efficiently. When you place your cursor over a title, a description of its contents appears below the cluster. Two helpful features are a search engine and a site map, which appear near or at the bottom of each page. The respect for visitors' time continues under the Business Services link, which augments a query box with a list of most frequently requested items, such as the First Stop Business Information Center and business forms.

Besides cataloging helpful links to business development resources, the Secretary of State Illinois Gateway site, **http://www.sos.state.il.us/home.html**, allows online searching of corporate name availability. Follow Find It! links to the Illinois Government Information site, where you can search a database of documents from all state government agencies.

Access Indiana Information Network
http://www.state.in.us/
Using retro-futuristic design, the welcoming page emulates a spaceship portal looking out onto the universe. The site's major headings are arranged around the portal, but you can also navigate by using the search engine or consulting the site map. Under Local are hyperlinked icons for city, town, county, and county court sites. Press State for the legislature, courts, and an alphabetical index of agencies, boards and commissions. The Secretary of State's Business Services Online feature allows you to search for business entity names, check name availability, and obtain Certificates of Existence or Authorization (which you may print straight from the

site). Go to Campaign Finance Online to search the office's campaign finance records.

Other searchable databases are available if you subscribe to Access Indiana's premium services. These include Bureau of Motor Vehicle records, Health Professions Bureau licenses, the Department of Health's certified nurses aide registry, the Department of Natural Resources water well database (and online water permit filing) and the General Assembly's BillWatch program, which sends e-mail of changes in bills you are monitoring. A subscription is $50 a year and includes up to ten accounts.

State of Iowa
http://www.state.ia.us/
Under the Agencies & Resources button, Iowa has organized its offerings into fifteen major groups, each of which is further divided into government and nongovernment pages. (City, county, and local pages are accessible here.) Select Business for an alphabetical list of agencies such as the Departments of Commerce or Revenue and Finance, as well as examining boards and the Business License Information Center. The Center, which is still being developed, has a search engine for retrieving information about required permits, licenses, certifications, and registrations by business activity. Many other agencies maintain searchable public records databases. The Department of Commerce's Division of Banking and the Professional Licensing Division each offer one for its licensees. To check on the status of a physician's license, use the Board Medical Examiners' DocFinder. The Real Estate Commission posts rosters of its licensees, alphabetically and by county. Search corporate, notary, and UCC records at the Secretary of State's page.

Other subheadings of the Agencies & Resources index are well worth exploring. State Legal Resources will bring up an index of offices and agencies with a legal or judicial bent (some of which are also on the Business index). For one master list of state resources, select State Government. To round out the many means of access, Iowa's page has both a search engine and a site map.

Information Network of Kansas
http://www.state.ks.us/
A searchable database of foundations registered in the state is free. In addition, the Information Network of Kansas offers online access to an array of legal, banking, and industry-specific business applications; you must first, however, subscribe to the Information Network's premium service, which goes for an annual base rate of $50.00. Per minute connection fees are waived for subscribers who use INK via the Internet, but some services entail additional statutory or transaction fees.

Kentucky
http://www.state.ky.us/
Kentucky uses a horse-racing theme for its welcoming page, including an animated graphic of horses leaving the starting gate and an audio clip of the familiar trumpet

tune "Call to the Post." To begin surfing the law-related portions of the site, press the graphic of the capitol building. State government Web resources—by agency name and by topic—appear in a browsable alphabetical index; a button at the top of the page allows viewing the resources by organization, divided into the three branches and constitutional offices, as well. (A search engine is also available to speed navigation.) Click the Online Forms and Services icon to visit one concise directory of forms and services that are available throughout the site. Some documents, such as vital statistics records, require payment by credit card, while downloadable forms from the Secretary of State and a few other agencies are free.

Go to the Secretary of State's site to check business entity name availability or search its records for corporate status, registered agent and address, officers, assumed names, or LLC members or managers. A searchable database of UCC filings is also available.

Kentucky's welcoming page has direct links to a few helpful resources. Economic Development/Business leads to the Cabinet for Economic Development's extensive site, which includes an online business start-up guide. Choose One-Stop Business Licensing to search for license requirements and take links related to forming and financing a business. The general links, in the Special Interest column, contains a jump directly to the site of the Tobacco Settlement Trust Corporation.

INFO Louisiana
http://www.state.la.us/
The stark top page contains only a few headings, but they're self-explanatory and to the point. Take State Departments to see indexes of executive branch departments, boards and commissions, state agencies, and frequently asked questions or requested services (such as business, health and hospital licenses, corporations, and tax forms). Much of what you'll find consists of contact information and explanations of procedures. An exception is the Secretary of State Commercial Division Corporations Section, which has a search engine for its database of corporation information, registered agents, trademarks, and individual names. Use the Local Governments link to access indexes of municipal and parish Websites.

Maine
http://www.state.me.us/
State agencies and quasi-independent agencies rate separate headings on the welcoming page, below links to the legislature, governor, and judiciary. Find agencies by name or by program. (The latter index is sparsely populated and includes categories such as lemon law or victim compensation.) You can search a database of corporate names from the Bureau of Corporation's page under the Secretary of State. Don't leave the welcoming page without scrolling down to the bottom, which has a host of business-related links. Look for local Websites under Maine Cities Online.

Maryland Electronic Capitol
http://www.mec.state.md.us/mec/

Maryland uses the standard URL—**www.state.md.us**—as a referral page for the state's two major online resources. The first is the Electronic Capital, at the address given above. This simple, searchable page includes links to sites for the legislature, judiciary, agencies, cities, and towns. You can reach searchable databases of registered trademarks and charitable organizations from the Secretary of State's page (under State Agencies, Boards, and Commissions). From the same starting point, go to the Division of State Documents for information on subscribing to either Contract Weekly Online, a listing of government bids, awards, and notices, or the Maryland Information and Retrieval System, computer-searchable databases of statutes and regulations. Do not overlook the Department of Business and Economic Development, which spearheads the remarkably information-packed Maryland Business Information Network. This allows you to search corporate records (including nonprofit) by organization name, industry, keyword, and characteristics such as location of headquarters or nature of ownership. Look under Business Directory for this service. Licensing, permit, tax, and other start-up resources are under Regulatory Information.

The second major online resource is a public information network called Sailor, **http://www.sailor.lib.md.us/**. Sailor is both an intranet connecting Maryland libraries, agencies, and schools, and a searchable online information resource. Under Maryland Information it maintains an alphabetical index of Websites in the state. Legal Resources is an umbrella for regional law collections, state and municipal codes, and state and federal courts and statutes. Look for county and city home pages under Local Government, while State Government provides pointers to the executive office, Attorney General, judicial branch, federal delegation, and searchable online databases, such as the Charitable Organizations Division database and the Department of Assessments and Taxation Real Property System.

Commonwealth of Massachusetts
http://www.state.ma.us/

Massachusetts's novel page design divides its resources by a variety of viewpoints and needs: agency subjects, publications, and finding tools; site updates; and the category "Get things done," which encompasses downloadable forms and financial transactions that may be done online. The Secretary of Commonwealth divisions use their pages (at **http://www.magnet.state.ma.us/sec/index.htm**) to explain their offices' functions and give consumer information. Direct Access, a subscription service of the Corporations Division provides public information about business entities (corporations, limited partnerships, LLCs, and limited liability partnerships), as well as tax and child support liens and Uniform Commercial Code filings. The annual subscription fee is currently $149, with a 40-cents per minute charge for usage.

Office of the Governor, State of Michigan
http://www.state.mi.us/migov/MichiganGovernor.htm
The standard URL (www.state.mi.us) leads to a simple index of links—and a pointer to this newer, slick starting point, courtesy of the governor's office. Use Government Branches as the entryway to executive, legislative, and judicial Websites, or begin with State Agencies to find their pages. The Corporation Division of the Corporations, Securities and Land Development Bureau has put its corporations, limited partnership, and LLC database online, but access is availably only through fee-based services such as LEXIS-NEXIS and Information America. The site has a search tool.

Minnesota Government Information and Services
http://www.state.mn.us/
The meatiest information at the Minnesota site appears on pages for the legislature, the courts, and the Secretary of State, which have been discussed in chapter 6, "Locating Statutes & Regulations," chapter 7, "Locating Court Information & Rules," and chapter 8, "Locating Government Forms." Otherwise, the links to agencies and departments lead primarily to text explaining each governmental entity. Three features warrant special attention, however. To get an idea of the site's resources, browse the topical index on the search engine page. By following links to the Consumer Protection Office, you can run keyword searches of a database of charities registered with the Attorney General. The local government page indexes Websites of cities, counties, townships, and special districts.

Mississippi inter@active
http://www.state.ms.us/its/msportal.nsf?Open
Mississippi organizes its Website with seven headings, a search engine, and a topic index. Press the Government button for a variety of options, such as city, county, federal, judicial, legislative, and elected official pages; to reach the agency index from here, select State, then Name. Use Business to jump to a short hierarchical index of economic development or professional licensing agencies, chambers of commerce, agriculture, industry and employment resources, and a handful of legal pages (the Attorney General, Secretary of State, Supreme Court, and the Mississippi Lawyers World Wide Web Domain). The site has a search engine.

Missouri
http://www.state.mo.us/
In addition to a search engine and a welcoming page full of links to frequently requested information, Missouri offers pull-down menus for the three branches of government, as well as the state departments. Go to the Secretary of State's site (under Executive Branch) for the latest edition of the state blue book, a searchable database of business registration records, election night reports (for several years worth of balloting), and the One Stop Shop for Business start-up guide. The

Department of Economic Development posts downloadable licensee rosters, in PDF format, of some twenty-five occupations regulated by the Professional Registration Division.

Montana Online
http://www.mt.gov/

The welcoming page breaks each major heading into single word or phrase topics. With a glance you can see that agency, legislative, and professional licensing resources are all under Government. Look under Local Communities for city and county Web pages.

The Secretary of State has a searchable database of UCC filings, but access requires a user name and password. (Contact the office directly for information on registering; the site does not give particulars.) The Division of Professional & Occupational Licensing accepts e-mail requests for license verifications. The One-Stop Business Licensing site is a clearinghouse of requirements and forms for business licenses from a variety of agencies. Because it is a pilot project, though, its focus is limited, currently covering only grocery and convenience stores and gas stations.

A novel approach to grouping resources is the Virtual Human Services Pavilion, which is set up as if agency offices were behind doors around a rotunda. (An introduction explains the graph-heavy interface, and a virtual assistant icon appears on each page.) When you make a selection from on a button bar, the rotunda view displays the "doors" in that section. Run the cursor over a door to see a description of its resources. Only the Department of Justice Website is under Justice. Commerce brings up the Commerce Department, its Professional & Occupational Licensing division, Economic Development and Travel Montana. All of these sites may also be reached through the more straightforward approach of taking links off Montana Online's welcoming page—which is the way to go if you have a slow modem or processor (or low tolerance for graphics). Another caveat: once you enter the pavilion, a frame with its pop-up menu and virtual assistant icon will stay on the screen if you return to Montana Online's home page.

Nebraska
http://www.state.ne.us/

State Government links appear in a cluster of blue buttons halfway down the welcoming page. Click Agencies to see a browsable index of state agencies with Internet sites, which include the Energy and Film offices, state and community colleges, and the Workers' Compensation Court. The Secretary of State has a novel feature: posting the names and contact information for state-licensed collection agencies, debt management services, and polygraph and voice stress examiners. (The names and license numbers of private detectives and agencies are also available.) It also offers a subscription service, Nebrask@ Online, for access to online databases of public filings—business entity, UCC, drivers license, sales and use tax, and vehicle title, lien and registration records. A subscription includes the right to make certain filings (such as UCC) online. Subscription information packets are available on e-mail request. Nebraska's top page appears in figure 10.3.

Figure 10.3: Nebrask@ Online.

Nevada
http://www.state.nv.us/
State agencies, boards and commissions, and regulatory agencies each rate their own link on the welcoming page, which leads to an alphabetical index. Links to the executive, legislative, and judicial branch sites are under Elected Officials; look here for the Secretary of State's page. Take the Doing Business link for a short list of agencies involved in business development. If you have difficulty locating a resource, consult the State Index, which lists all governmental offices and indicates which have a Web presence.

You can search the Commercial Recordings Division's corporations database (by name, registered agent, or officer) from the Secretary of State's site, which helpfully posts the date through which the data is current. A veritable library of division publications are downloadable from the Department of Business & Industry's site. The Business Information Network has guides to business start-up and license requirements, as well as pointers to finance and incentive programs. Attorney General opinions are posted by year on that office's page, which is searchable.

WEBSTER: The New Hampshire State Government Online
http://www.state.nh.us/
New Hampshire's efficient top page offers several means of access to its resources. In addition to a subject index and search engine, links lead to directories of state

departments, a list of agencies that are online, statutes and regulations, resources for health and human services, economic development or tax questions, and legislative, court, and local government pages. Searchable databases include the Treasury Department's abandoned property records and two of the Office of Business and Economic Development, an inventory of available industrial property and a vendor matching program for locating manufacturers in the state.

New Jersey
http://www.state.nj.us/
Locate agencies through the Departments listing, Services index, or the search engine. The welcoming page offers direct links to legislative, judicial, municipal and county sites, as well as resources geared to business, technology, or taxes. Scroll down the top page for jumps to news releases and programs such as Business Gateway Services and a searchable database of unclaimed property.

A Division of Revenue project, the Business Gateway is a one-stop site for registering and recording a business (including required forms). Follow links to Corporate and Business Information and Reporting Services to search the registered business entity database, which is being updated to include UCC filings. The service requires registration and imposes a fee for status reports, but does permit browsing at no charge.

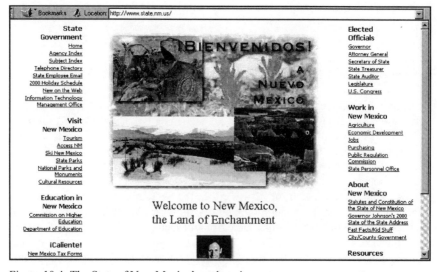

Figure 10.4: The State of New Mexico's welcoming page.

¡Bienvenidos! a Neuvo Mexico
http://www.state.nm.us/
Links to state government and elected officials' sites flank the top of New Mexico's welcoming page, shown in figure 10.4. From here you can proceed directly

to the Attorney General, Secretary of State, Treasurer, or legislature, or browse indexes of government agencies or subjects. Tax forms, online return filing, motor vehicle registration, and the Property Tax Division are toward the bottom of the page, under ¡Caliente! For city and county government links, look under About New Mexico.

To search the state's corporate records by entity or director name, use the inquiry form at the Public Regulation Commission page. The Secretary of State's site permits online searches of its UCC filings database. The office's Bureau of Elections offers downloadable PDF files of its indexes of lobbyists, represented organizations, and political committees. The Regulation and Licensing Department's boards and commissions all make their governing law and regulations available from their respective sites.

New York
http://www.state.ny.us/
Two routes lead to the alphabetical index to state agency pages: the Government Agencies button, or the Citizens' Access to Government link, both of which also point to federal and local (county and city) government sites. Look under "State, Department of" for applications, governing law, and training and exam schedules for numerous licensed businesses, such as notaries public, real estate, pet cemeteries, security guards, and a range of personal care and grooming services. The index includes the State Assembly, Senate, Office of the Comptroller, and Department of Taxation and Finance, but—as of this writing—no links to judicial sites. The index is the sole point of navigation for now; there is neither a search engine nor a site map.

North Carolina
http://www.state.nc.us/
The NC Agency button on the welcoming page is only one way to reach state government Websites. Two other buttons on the page lead to annotated indexes. The agency index under the Public Info link has a welcome flair that eliminates much of the usual "where do I begin?" guesswork; each entry gives a thumbnail description of the business of the office at hand. The same is true of the index under Business Info. Most of the subjects listed Business Info, including athlete agent, notaries public, and trademarks, have a FAQ with all the ins and outs of the subject. The Business License Information Office has a treasure trove of resources, such as a start-up checklist, tax information, licensing requirements, guides to incorporating or choosing a structure, and links to related state and federal sites. From the Secretary of State's top page you can search databases of corporate names and UCC filings; the name database is also accessible from the Business Info index.

North Dakota
http://discovernd.com/government/
Agency, judicial, and legislative links share the welcoming page with links to local

government sites and Vital Records (from which birth, death, and marriage certificates are available for purchase online).

Rosters of state chartered banks and licensed money brokers and collection agencies are online at the Department of Banking and Financial Institutions' site. The Secretary of State has a browsable index of registered lobbyists at the Administrative/Licensing Division page; a searchable database of corporate records was under construction as of this writing.

State of Ohio
http://www.state.oh.us/
On this neatly designed site (see figure 10.5), executive, judicial, and legislative links stand alongside citizen resources and a query box for the search engine. In the citizen information column, look under Popular Resources for city and county Websites, the searchable unclaimed funds database, tax forms and electronic return filing, and a listing of board site search engines for verifying professional licenses. Visit the Secretary of State's site to search the entire corporations database (which includes all registered business entities, fictitious names, and trademarks), as well as its UCC filings and campaign finance reports.

Figure 10.5: The State of Ohio's Web page.

Welcome to Oklahoma
http://www.state.ok.us/
An agency directory appears on Oklahoma's welcoming page, which also provides links (under Business) directly to licensing data, the Department of Commerce, and the Secretary of State.

Occupational licensing requirements are available from the Employment Security Commission, while the Department of Commerce provides a browsable, frames-based index of business license requirements by issuing agency and type of activity. The Attorney General sponsors a searchable legal research system, which features statutes, regulations, court and agency decisions, and AG opinions. The Banking Department offers listings of all the banks, credit unions, trust companies, and other institutions it regulates.

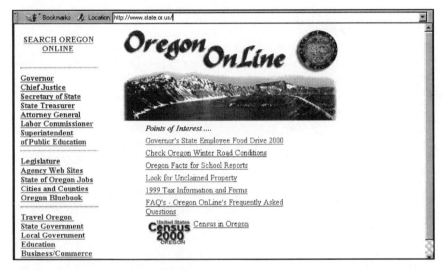

Figure 10.6: The State of Oregon, online.

Oregon OnLine
http://www.state.or.us/
Although many of the links on the top page of this searchable site (shown in figure 10.6) lead to alphabetical indexes, the ones in the uppermost section go directly to major offices, such as the Secretary of State, State Treasurer, and Attorney General. The Agency Web Sites link will take you to an alphabetical index of agency names, a few of which are tagged with short descriptions. (The state court home page is under Judicial Department.) Many of the agency sites focus on explaining their mission and services. Some, such as licensing boards and the Secretary of State, also provide guides to filing documents with the office and in many instances supply the forms as well.

On the Secretary of State's page, press Corporation Division to reach an index of services and databases. Take the Uniform Commercial Code (UCC) link to search filing records by lien number or debtor name. The UCC index page also gives filing tips, including the top ten reasons that the division rejects filings. The Notary Public link leads to uncommonly extensive information on the topic, including an online edition of the state notary guide and guidelines for obtaining and renewing a commission. The Business Registry supplies background information on assumed names and forming various business organizations; though the database is not yet currently online, the Registry has plans to put it up by late 2000 at the earliest.

The state's welcoming page also serves as a starting point for locating local government Websites.

Pennsylvania
http://www.state.pa.us/

To view the government resources, press the button to enter the site. (Take the text only option, if you do not want to deal with frames.) On the index page the comes up, four major sections will be of most interest. Look under the Government Connection for city and county links; the PA State Government link in this section leads to a hierarchical index of Websites organized by branch.

The Department of State offers a searchable database of registered charitable organizations, which you can jump to directly from the main Pennsylvania index. (Look for Charitable Information under the Special Links column.) Other resources include the department's Athletic Commission roster of registered athletic agents. Lists of chartered banks, credit unions, savings associations, and trust companies are at the Department of Banking in PDF format. The Securities Commission has an online research request form to obtain data from its records of registered broker-dealers, investment advisers, and representatives. The same commission has instituted an electronic filing program, which may still be accepting only investment company and unit investment trust initial filings.

Under Doing Business in PA (on the main state index page), press Professional Licensure Boards to browse hyperlinks to business and health-related boards, which post their procedures, forms, and governing regulations (but not their licensee rosters). Follow the Business Resource Network links to reach a searchable database of available business real estate, as well as guides to environmental permits. From the same heading, visit SourceNet for a searchable trade lead, sales lead, and supplier matching service.

Rhode Island On-Line Public Information Kiosk
http://www.state.ri.us/

The top page of this site, which is maintained by the Office of the Secretary of State, abounds with valuable and useful resources. The search engine will target legislation in four different years, in addition to searching either the site or bill tracking pages. Links lead directly to the General Assembly, laws, an index of departments and agencies, and several services of the Secretary of State. Take Corporations to search the notary database or download the latest incorporation filings, by week. (They're in a format called DBF, for which the site provides neither an explanation nor a reader.) Visit the Office of Public Information for legislative tracking and databases of lobbyists.

South Carolina On-Line
http://www.state.sc.us/
Under the Government heading are direct links to pages for the legislature, judiciary, elected officials, agencies, boards and commissions, cities, and counties. The Secretary of State's site is still under development, but the Department of Commerce has taken advantage of a Web presence with searchable databases of available industrial real estate, computer services, and state industries. They're all part of SiteSCope, at the Team South Carolina page. Downloadable rosters of suspended or revoked insurers are available from the Department of Insurance, which also offers an array of license and report forms in PDF format.

From the state's welcoming page you can subscribe to a free e-mail legislative tracking service. The Government Organizations subheading leads to associations that support a specific office or project, such as the Government Finance Officers Association.

South Dakota
http://www.state.sd.us/
In addition to a search engine and pull-down menu of agencies, this site offers two helpful navigational aids. How to Get It Done leads to an alphabetical index of possible transactions with government agencies. The list covers many topics of interest to lawyers and their clients, with securities, tax, and business start-up information and how-tos for filing banking or occupational license applications and administrative appeals. The top page's Government Info button brings up an alphabetical list of offices, agencies, and programs, augmented by direct jumps to the legislature and online forms and publications. These include Attorney General opinions since 1989, which have their own search engine.

From the top page you can go directly to DakotaCast Portal, South Dakota Public Broadcasting's live audio coverage of state House of Representative and Senate proceedings.

Tennessee
http://www.state.tn.us
Tennessee's navigational tools—an index of services, a search engine, and a site map—are a welcome combination. The resources most likely to interest attorneys appear under the Government link, which is a comprehensive gateway to the executive, legislative, and judicial branches of Tennessee government. Each department, commission, and board in the executive branch index provides a description of its services and mission, as an introduction to its own site. At least one has uploaded its filings. Two types of public records are accessible through the

Department of Commerce and Insurance page: listings of licensees in more than thirteen state-regulated professions (which are available in downloadable files) and searchable databases of more than fifty types of licensees.

Look for the Treasurer, Comptroller, and Secretary of State pages under the legislative branch. The Secretary of State's division pages are heavy on filing guides and brochures. Watch the page for the addition of a searchable online corporate database. The government page is also a springboard to county and city Websites.

Texas
http://www.state.tx.us

Navigational aids at this efficiently designed site include a site map and a pull-down menu of general items of interest, from which you may jump to pages for the legislature, laws, and licensing information, among others. The Search link is not a site-specific engine, but brings up a selection of engines for searching the Web. To comb through the agency pages, use the Texas Records and Information Locator (TRAIL) service at **http://www.tsl.state.tx.us/trail/**.

Each heading on the welcoming page contains keywords of the resources under it. Look under Communities for links to county, city, and special district Websites. Criminal Justice & Law umbrellas all the state courts, as well as the legislature and statutes, Attorney General, Department of Criminal Justice, Department of Public Safety, and Juvenile Probation Commission. A browsable index of agencies and commissions appears under Government. Many maximize the utility of a Web presence by providing public records that draw heavy phone traffic. Searchable databases of public records are especially prevalent at this site. Among them are the Department of Economic Development's economic development and financial assistance resources (both under Business Resources); the DPS convictions records and sex offender registrations (under Criminal Justice & Law); the franchise tax account status of corporations and LCCs (at the Office of the Comptroller); and the Railroad Commission's ACTI Texas Oil and Gas Production records from 1993-1999. Other public records are uploaded in full or in zipped formats; the Alcoholic Beverage Commission, for example, posts expired, canceled, or suspended permits, statewide mixed beverage tax receipts, and the credit law delinquent list. A few agencies (such as the ABC and the Department of Licensing & Regulation) sponsor free e-mail lists.

Following the trend of efficient information dissemination, the Secretary of State makes its filing guide available from its site. It has set up a fee-based Direct Access program for its database of corporate, limited partnership, LLC, assumed name, trademark and UCC filings. Instead of a subscription, the program requires a deposit, from which per-search charges are deducted. The office also accepts electronic filing of UCC forms.

Welcome to Utah!
http://www.state.ut.us/
This searchable site divides its government resources into citizen and business services, as well as the three branches and agencies. If you're not sure where to head with a business research question, try the Business Services link first; it brings up a quick list of agencies that regulate or handle business activities.

Run business entity, name availability, and UCC filing searches at the Commerce Department's Division of Corporations and Commercial Code. The Division of Real Estate offers its licensee databases in downloadable files.

Welcome to the State of Vermont
http://www.cit.state.vt.us/
Don't be misled by the Government link—it leads to an index of federal and non-Vermont state resources. For Vermont agencies, scroll down the welcoming page. About one screen down is an alphabetical index of executive, judicial, and legislative branch sites, with agency and department pages leading the pack.

With searchable databases galore, the Secretary of State's site makes it easy for you to stay at your computer. Under Elections you can search general and primary election results, and lobbyists' names, reported gifts, and employers. From the Corporations page you can find business name reservations and foreign corporation registrations; obtain the officers, registered agents, and addresses of registered corporations; determine the owner of a registered trademark or trade name; and search the UCC filings by debtor or keyword. The Professional Regulation page offers a licensing name finder (as well as self-extracting files of licensees in each profession), while notary public listings are under Archives.

Virginia Information Providers Network
http://www.state.va.us/
Under the State Government heading are links to the executive, legislative, and judicial branches, the code and constitution, agencies, online forms, federal and local resources, and military sites. You can also reach agencies by browsing the alphabetical list under State Websites. Another alternative is using the Business & Professional link, where agencies are grouped by category as AgNet, BankNet, CommerceNet, HealthNet, InsuranceNet, and LegalNet. Each "Net" index page ends with links to search engines for bills and resolutions, the code, and the Administrative Code.

The Corporation Commission's postings include a business registration guide in PDF (with a link for downloading the Adobe Acrobat Reader) and an explanation of Direct Access, through which subscribers may obtain information from the filings database. The commission broadcasts some of its hearings online, which require the Windows Media Player.

The Division of Securities and Retail Franchising offers a variety of forms relating to securities and advisor registration, franchising, and trademarks.

Access Washington
http://access.wa.gov/

When you select a heading on Washington's slick, smartly designed welcoming page, a black box of subtopics appears beside your choice. The Business and Government headings are the most reliably useful to lawyers.

From the Business heading you can go directly to significant online services. The Department of Licensing's Licensing Management Information System supplies a customized licensing guide to federal, state, county, and city requirements. There is also a searchable database of business records from the Department of Revenue. Take the Starting a Business subheading to jump to environmental permit information (including forms), the Business Assistance Center's state business resource directory, or the Secretary of State's Corporations Division, where you can search registration information for corporations, limited partnerships, LLCs, and LLPs. The Secretary of State also maintains a searchable database of registered charitable organizations, which you may access directly from the office's page.

Look under the Government heading for subject and agency indexes and links to courts, laws, elected officials, the legislature, and local government. The subject index is helpful for detailing services provided by state agencies. The State Department of Financial Institutions Securities Division, for example, offers a searchable database of securities, franchise, and business opportunity registration, exemption, and notification filings; broker-dealer and investment advisor filings are slated for addition. Local government links include cities, counties, ports, public libraries, and service districts.

State of West Virginia
http://www.state.wv.us/

Scroll to the bottom of the welcoming page for direct links to a variety of agencies services, such as a searchable database of unclaimed property, business registration, tax and worker's compensation forms, and order forms for birth and death certificates.

The Secretary of State Charitable Organizations Division posts browsable alphabetical indexes, updated monthly, of registered charitable organizations and professional fund raisers. The Corporations Division accepts e-mail requests for good standing and other corporation information. They're free for one or two companies; requests for three or more require prepayment of a $5 search fee and $0.50 per company.

State of Wisconsin Information Server
http://badger.state.wi.us/

Buttons on the welcoming page lead to indexes or pages for state agencies, the legislature, court system, and local governments. Though Wisconsin does provide links to all of its state agencies, many of those pages merely explain services and provide news briefs, rather than allowing significant interaction. The Department of Commerce, for example, provides extensive advice for starting, expanding, and financing a business, with program contact phone numbers and related Websites. The Department of Financial Institutions is the notable exception; not only does it provide an array of downloadable forms (which are referenced in the Department of Commerce's guides), but it also sends out news by e-mail. The state's legal notice database is searchable; reach it through the subject index or http://www.mostonmadison.com/legals/.

The Local Government heading leads to an extensive index of counties, cities, towns, villages, and other local sites (including a handful of police and fire departments).

Welcome to Wyoming
http://www.state.wy.us/
The government page has pull-down menus with links to state, city, county, and federal resources. From here you may jump to pages for the legislature, the courts, and elected officials or follow links to state agencies, which are listed in an index. In addition to trademark and business entity forms, the Secretary of State offers a searchable database of corporate, LLC, partnership, and sole proprietorship records. State securities forms are available from the secretary's Securities Division, while the Oil and Gas Conservation Commission permits downloading of well records and locations.

Comprehensive State Sites

When you need to feel free to jump from state to state, visit one of the following comprehensive sites.

FindLaw State Law Resources
http://www.findlaw.com/11stategov/index.html
It's hard to top the comprehensiveness of this index. You can use LawCrawler to search any state government site, or browse FindLaw's alphabetical listing to access any state's online resources. A hodge-podge of links at the bottom of the main state page runs from legal mailing lists to case law search engines to drafts of uniform and model laws. Each state's page jumps directly to the Attorney General's Office, Secretary of State, an agency index, business-related agencies, the legislature, judicial sites, and official business forms.

Library of Congress State and Local Governments
http://lcweb.loc.gov/global/state/stategov.html
If you want only one state and local resource site, this one is right behind FindLaw. For starters, the Library of Congress has done you the trouble of amassing about

a dozen links to meta-indexes covering a spectrum of state information, from statutes to cities to councils and conferences of governments. It will also take you to state maps and the main pages of every single state.

ABA LAWLink Legal Research Jumpstation
U.S. State and Local Government Sites
http://www.abanet.org/lawlink/states.html

The American Bar Association has assembled an alphabetical index of state and local government pages. All the states are represented by at least one site. Under some, the occasional city shows up, too (such as Cambridge, Massachusetts, Hanover, New Hampshire, and Salem, Oregon).

Hieros Gamos
http://www.hg.org/hg.html

Click State under All Governments. Beneath the index of state and territory pages lurk some unusual resources, starting with uniform laws, by topic. The Great Lakes Commission, South Atlantic Fishery Management Council, and other regional regulatory agencies follow. There is also an avalanche of local government associations, along the lines of the National Association of Regulatory Utility Commissioners, the National League of Cities, and Women Executives in State Government. At the base is a list of miscellaneous sites, including state-based think tanks, state rural development councils, and an online Lotto information service.

Internet Prospector
http://www.internet-prospector.org/secstate.html

This scroll-down index has several attractive features. At the top, it provides links to online corporate databases in twenty states, charities databases in eleven states, the IRS database of tax-exempt nonprofits, and a national directory of charity regulators maintained by Maryland. The primary draw, though, is the extensiveness of the individual state listings. For each state, the Internet Prospector posts URLs, phone numbers, and e-mail addresses, where available, for the main government page, the Secretary of State, and the corporations division.

NASIRE State Search
http://www.nasire.org/statesearch/

For research questions that involve more than one state, try the topical clearinghouse at the National Association of State Information Resource Executives site. It breaks resources into more than thirty categories, such as disabilities agencies, older adult services, and regulation and licensing. The site has a search engine.

Piper Resources State & Local Government on the Internet
http://www.piperinfo.com/state/index.cfm

Each state page in this alphabetical index contains direct links to specific state, county, and city offices. Multistate sites, federal resources, and national organizations (such as the National League of Cities) are at the bottom of the top index.

Local Information

A growing number of city and county governments are online. The scope of their resources vary from contact information and calendars to municipal codes to downloadable applications. (The site for Harris County, Texas, at **http://www.co.harris.tx.us/**, is exemplary in the latter regard.)

The catch is locating the pages. Some of them are indexed on state government pages. The section at the top of the chapter, "Reaching Individual States," pointed out sites with this feature. If your home base wasn't among them, as always, do not assume that it's not online yet.

For counties, a worthwhile starting point is the links index at National Association of Counties home page, **http://www.naco.org/**. Under the U.S. Counties link is a pop-menu for searching county sites by state. Select your state, press Submit Query, and scan the list of hyperlinks that appear.

For cities, use the Public Technology, Inc. links at **http://pti.nw.dc.us/**. They will require you to choose a region of the country and then a state, before an index of local government Websites appears. The National City Government Resource Center at **http://www.geocities.com/CapitolHill/1389/** has links to state capitol home pages.

If all else fails—run a search.

You've got all the basics down by now. Knowing how to find cases, statutes, forms, and government offices has given you the tools to locate anything online you might think of as relevant. Looking for a specific item is just one approach to research, though. You're ready to tackle the other major avenue: researching by topic. The next chapter spotlights specialized sites that will make that job all the easier.

11
Researching by Topic

One of the beauties of the Web is how it fosters focused attention on the most minute of subjects. No matter how obscure or specialized a topic may be, somebody somewhere has taken enough interest to build a Web page around it.

What does this characteristic have to do with legal research? Quite a bit. The benefit to you is direct. All across the Web sites have sprung up concentrating on specific areas of practice and issues of law. Some specialize in an aspect of a topic, while others offer a comprehensive overview. Both types can be of enormous help when you're doing a research dragnet on an issue.

Here's how: often, when you're researching a question, you want to know all the law that shapes the answer, regardless of whether the form is a case or a statute or a regulation. Whenever I'm in that mode, I'll cast my net out far and wide, pulling in articles in law reviews, journals, treatises, and the A.L.R. series—even the antiquated Corpus Juris Secundum and the much (often, rightly) maligned American Jurisprudence and Texas Jurisprudence series. Anything that might shed light becomes relevant, in the early stages especially, when I don't want to rule out anything.

Jumping around like that is significantly easier on the Web. When I take this approach online, the topic-focused sites have already done a lot of the legwork for me. I can coattail on the work of another researcher who has gone to the bother of hunting down and bundling pertinent resources together. I don't have to ponder what treatise to thumb through next; I can just follow one link to another. In the process, I invariably come across something for which I would have never thought of looking.

That's one of the advantages of doing research online rather than in a traditional library—serendipitous discoveries that expand your concept of what's possible. There's another big one, too (besides ease, efficiency, and alacrity, of course): timeliness. You don't have to wait for the next edition of a journal or advance sheets or pocket parts to arrive in the mail. Web pages, particularly the ones associated with large organizations, are updated as frequently as daily. Many of these make a point to follow litigation in progress or other ongoing developments that affect, determine, or create law. As a result, you can generally find the absolute latest breaking news, ruling, regulation, commentary, you name it, on the topic at hand.

How to Approach Topic Research

When you're ready to attack a research problem online, look for your topic in the Quick Reference List in the next section. If your subject is not there, don't automatically launch a search. Instead, before you run a topic through a search engine, try this technique first. No matter what the subject, online topical research by topic should always include a pass through one (or more) of three compilation sites. I could have listed these pages under every almost single topic heading in the Quick Reference List below; instead I'm giving this blanket advice—in every instance, check at least one of these sites out. Each is wide-ranging enough to have something remotely relevant to many a research problem. If nothing else, they ought to point you in some directions you may not have considered.

FindLaw Legal Subjects
http://www.findlaw.com/01topics/index.html
This searchable index demonstrates its worthiness as an essential bookmark once again, with nearly forty topic headings that pretty much bracket the practice of law. Subjects you'll find here and not in the other two include entertainment and sports law, international trade, litigation, and Indian law.

Laws of All Jurisdictions (Arranged by Subject)
Internet Law Library
http://www.infoctr.edu/ill/90.htm
The alphabetical index on this page covers laws of all jurisdictions on topics ranging from agriculture to war. I won't promise that the resources under any one topic are exhaustive, but they're certainly extensive, including state and federal statutes, regulations, and even some caselaw and the occasional foreign statute or decree. chapter 13, "Law Libraries Online," will explore all of the holdings of the Internet Law Library, which began as a project of the House of Representatives.

Legal Material Organized by Topic
http://www.law.cornell.edu/topical.html
Another worthwhile introductory spot is this list maintained by Cornell University's Legal Information Institute. Eighteen broad categories each contain a half dozen or more subtopics, which in turn lead to compilations of source material (statutes and cases) and Web pages on the issue. To access the same information,

you can also browse an alphabetical list of topics or search the index by keyword. What are you likely to find here? Once again, just about anything. The index encompasses commercial transactions; business formation; real and intellectual property; tax; administrative, constitutional, criminal, employment, and family law; torts; procedure; public benefits; international matters; ethics; and jurisprudence.

Special Subjects

Head directly to one of the comprehensive sites listed above for any of the following topics, which do not appear in the Quick Reference List:

Agriculture	Disability
Admiralty	Health
Antitrust	Immigration
Aviation	Labor
Banking & Commercial	Sports
Business Organizations	Transportation
Constitutional	

For subjects that come under the jurisdiction of a government agency, be sure to check out that office's Website for research starting points, as well. To find it, look back in chapter 9, "Locating Other Federal Resources," and chapter 10, "Locating Other State & Local Resources."

Quick Reference List

This chapter's Quick Reference List spotlights a few carefully selected sites for a variety of topics. The choices are not exhaustive by any means; they are merely good, solid, helpful springboards that should help—and inspire—you to develop your own list.

Alternative Dispute Resolution

Mediation and other forms of alternative dispute resolution (ADR) have certainly caught fire in the legal profession, so it's no surprise that ADR-focused organizations and sites are springing up on the Web.

Alternative Dispute Resolution Materials
http://www.law.cornell.edu/topics/adr.html
Cornell University's Legal Information Institute posts the arbitration title of the U.S. Code, state ADR statutes, and the Uniform State Arbitration Act. The page also links to sites for the American Arbitration Association, university programs, and international ADR resources.

CPR Institute for Dispute Resolution
http://www.cpradr.org/
This is the home base of a nonprofit alliance of corporations and law firms dedicated to integrating ADR into mainstream legal practice. A feature helpful to nonmembers is the section of practice tools (look under Procedures and Clauses), which include arbitration rules, mini-trial procedure, commentary, and both the European and North American versions of dispute resolution contract clauses.

> *Cybersettle, **http://www.cybersettle.com**, has come up with truly alternative dispute resolution: It compares confidential offers and demands submitted by parties who have registered at the site and, if the numbers fall within an agreed range, automatically settles the dispute. The service, which is available twenty-four hours a day, takes a sliding-scale fee only if a settlement is reached.*

Animal Rights

The Rutgers University School of Law Animal Rights Center has corralled cases, statutes, and regulations on a variety of domestic animal and wildlife issues at **http://www.animal-law.org/index.html**. Most of the commentary comes in the form of media coverage; the site specializes in source materials, such as pleadings, briefs, and orders from recent litigation involving contraception, hunter harassment, and animal sacrifice. The Animal Rights Center also tracks state anti-cruelty and product disparagement statutes, as well as federal legislation and regulations on animal welfare and wild and free-roaming horses and burros.

Bankruptcy

Up-to-the-minute news on pending litigation is a common feature of bankruptcy compilation sites.

ABI World
http://www.abiworld.org/
The American Bankruptcy Institute (see figure 11.1) provides a searchable database of selected bankruptcy opinions, analyses, and synopses, as well as access to court and clerks' directories, an index of foreign bankruptcy laws online, and the latest case and legislative headlines.

Figure 11.1: The top page of ABI World. *Reprinted with permission from the American Bankruptcy Institute.*

Bankruptcy Online
http://www.fedfil.com/bankruptcy/
This is a news service of the Federal Filings division of Dow Jones, Inc. From here you can track the status of major pending cases, catch summaries of the day's key bankruptcy news, a nd subscribe to the Daily Bankruptcy Review. Even if you're not interested in litigation in progress, the site is worth visiting for its long list of bankruptcy links.

InterNet Bankruptcy Library—Worldwide Troubled Company Resources
http://bankrupt.com/
The top page contains only a short index, but it ties together helpful information. The main attraction is a huge, scroll-down index of U.S. and international bankruptcy and insolvency source materials online. The site's features also include a directory of bankruptcy clerks and short list of discussion groups and mailing lists.

13 Network
http://www.13network.com
At this site participating Chapter 13 trustees make case information available to registered users who have obtained an ID and password. Neither is necessary to view the list of participants, who are categorized by state.

Criminal Law

Criminal Justice Links
http://www.criminology.fsu.edu/cj.html
The Florida State University School of Criminology and Criminal Justice has constructed an index of progressively narrower indexes. If you've got a slow connection speed, you may want to turn off your graphics feature for this site (unless you enjoy watching a spindly animated spider scurry across the screen). You'll have to scroll through the top level to get the big picture, which encompasses about every imaginable aspect of criminal law. Federal agencies, international sources, police resources, civil liberties, and juvenile, pornography, and punishment issues are a sampling of the headings. You can also reach related newsgroups and electronic journals.

If you prefer pointing and clicking, surf the site by using the hyperlinked Criminal Justice System Processing Flowchart; as you run the cursor over the chart, it will show which stages in the process (for example, arrest) have subpages at the site. No matter what the means of access, each subpage is staggeringly long, with links to agencies, task forces, papers, commentaries, programs, councils, bulletins, and, of course, courts, cases, and statutes.

Criminal Law Links
http://dpa.state.ky.us/~rwheeler/
The Kentucky Department of Public Advocacy maintains this defense-oriented list. Links are particularly extensive for federal primary materials and death penalty, medical, and statistical resources. State primary materials almost exclusively concern Kentucky.

Capital Defense Weekly
http://www.coramnobis.com/CDW/index.html
This page, formerly known as A Capital Defender's Toolbox, archives a free e-mail newsletter concerning death penalty cases, legislation, and news. The site also posts trial manuals, motions, and briefs from cases all over the country. Resources you can jump to from each page include the Capital Defense Network, Death Penalty Information Center, and Southern Methodist University's *Death Penalty News*.

National Criminal Justice Reference Service
http://ncjrs.aspensys.com/
This comprehensive site is the collaboration of seven offices of the Justice Department. The organization is streamlined to an extreme. Most of the headings (such as corrections, courts, crime prevention, law enforcement, or juvenile justice) lead to a brief subindex that consists of documents, Websites, and occasionally listservs, calendars, and press releases. Clicking on a subindex entry brings up an index of links, which are particularly strong on agencies and commissions. The document links are heavy on downloadable articles and papers. To stay current with new additions to the site, regularly visit the New This Week link or subscribe to JUSTINFO, a free e-mail newsletter.

Ethics

It's a required course in law school, and not a subject that attorneys usually think much about—until their own (or an opponent's) come into question. Here are two Websites that set out the rules of the game; the second also applies them to the online world.

American Legal Ethics Library
http://wwwsecure.law.cornell.edu/ethics/
Cornell's Legal Information Institute has compiled ethics rules, codes (including judicial), and opinions by state and by topic. Lawyer-written narratives are included for the eleven states with the largest attorney populations; others are in preparation.

Legalethics.com
http://www.legalethics.com/index.law
This searchable site addresses the unique issues raised by the Internet and its technology. In addition to a comprehensive collection of state regulations, Rules of Professional Conduct, and ethics opinions, the resources include links to organizations and Web resources concerned with ethics in a variety of disciplines. The site sponsors WebEthics, a discussion forum of ethical issues that arise in attorneys' use of the Internet.

Estate Planning, Probate, & Elder Law

An expansive gateway to estate planning and elder law is the Estate Planning Links Web Site, **http://www.estateplanninglinks.com**. The searchable site covers probate, family limited partnerships, charitable and living trusts, valuation issues, insurance, business continuity planning, IRAs, government benefits, and more.

Attorney Dennis Kennedy founded the page in 1995; it is now being maintained by Dennis Toman at Booth Harrington Johns & Toman, LLP in Greensboro, North Carolina.

Family Law

ABA Section of Family Law
http://www.abanet.org/family/home.html
What you want is in the middle of the listings for committees, meetings, and publications: links to other family law sites of interest (under Family Law Links). A preponderance deals with issues concerning children—such as custody, support, abuse, and rights.

Counsel Quest Family Law
http://www.counselquest.com/z-family.htm
This lengthy scrollable index divides into Web resources, journals and articles, and legal studies and education. Besides child welfare statutes from the U.S. Code and selected state laws, the resources include a variety of state sanctioned and private pages on divorce, custody, and violence. Among the magazines and newsletters toward the bottom of the page is an outline on community property from a bar review course.

Divorce-Without-War
http://www.divorce-without-war.com/
The purpose of this site, and this organization, is promoting peaceful and mediated divorces. The utility to attorneys is the page of links to the divorce statutes of every state. The next time a relative in another state puts you on the spot for advice about divorce laws you've never read, you can look them up here.

The 'Lectric Law Library's Lawcopedia on Family Law
http://www.lectlaw.com/tfam.html
This site posts articles with rudimentary information about divorce, child support, and alimony. Its real usefulness would kick in if you have a case with an off-the-wall wrinkle. Curious about the problems of second wives, or online affairs as grounds for divorce, or a lesbian mother fighting a murderer father for custody? All these topics come straight from the Lawcopedia's document list, and not the tabloids (though some probably appeared in those, too). A nice feature is disclosing the size of each file, so you know what you're getting into before you click.

> *For the basics of the general practice spectrum, consult Nolo Press' Legal Encyclopedia at **http://www.nolo.com/**. Because Nolo Press has made a name for itself by explaining legal concepts and procedures in straightforward language, this site is equally helpful to laymen and lawyers alike. Topics include small business, real estate, consumer and debt issues, personal injury, tax problems, estate planning, and employment.*

Intellectual Property

Under this heading I've grouped sites about copyright, entertainment, patents, and trademarks. Even though each topic is substantial enough to warrant an individual heading, they appear here together because of the number of sites that mingle them. I'll begin with six examples of compilation pages, then proceed to sites focusing on specific topics. I've listed the sites in each group alphabetically.

Franklin Pierce Law Center Intellectual Property Mall
http://www.ipmall.fplc.edu/
Bypass the kudos for the site and the school, which dominate the top page; what you want are the IP Pointer Box and the Tools and Strategies Corner. Nestled in the dark box with small type size, the IP Pointer Box has a compact grouping of Internet resources on all aspects of intellectual property law, including computer, multimedia, and technology transfer. The well-stocked pages under each heading have browsable (but not searchable) alphabetical indexes; the only short cut to scrolling down the list is clicking a letter in the alphabet at the top, which will propel you to that part of the index. In the Tools and Strategies Corner, Franklin Pierce Law Center librarian and assistant clinical professor Jon Cavicchi stockpiles student papers setting out the law and online resources for a variety of specialized issues. (The 1999 papers examined pharmaceutical search tools and chemical patent searches, among other topics.)

Kuester Law Technology Law Resources
http://www.kuesterlaw.com/
If you prefer simplicity, try this streamlined site, maintained by Georgia attorney Jeffrey R. Kuester. A tiny, tidy index in the left margin takes you to equally neatly organized indexes of resources. Look under Tech Law for the text of topic-related cases, statutes, and federal bills. IP Resources cover general and software patents, copyrights, trademark and Internet domain name resources, periodicals, and miscellaneous resources.

Oppedahl & Larson LLP Intellectual Property Law Web Server
http://www.patents.com/index.sht
This page covers all forms of intellectual property, even trade secrets, computer law, and Web law. Its New York law firm sponsors have laid out general information on all the topics in question-and-answer format, generously interspersed with links to source materials. The order of listing of the IP resources may be haphazard, but I encourage browsing them. They lead to a panoply of FAQs, university servers and associations, and even surprises such as Canadian and Swedish patent pages.

World Intellectual Property Organization
http://www.wipo.org/
This Geneva-based organization offers English, French, and Spanish versions of its page, which is a compact source of treaties and information about protecting rights internationally. A guide and application form are available for international registrations under the Patent Cooperation Treaty.

> *If your clients are concerned about infringement of their intellectual property on the Internet, look into hiring a commercial service to safeguard their interests. ImageLock.com,* ***http://www.imagelock.com****, tracks occurrences of text, logos, images, and sound clips in Web pages and collects ownership information about infringing sites. Monitoring and enforcement services are available from TradeName.com,* ***http://www.tradename.com****, and CyberGuards,* ***http://www.cyberguards.com****. CyberGuards also offers digital watermarking, as does Digimarc Corporation,* ***http://www.digimarc.com****. First Use,* ***http://www.firstuse.com****, maintains an online registry that places a dated digital fingerprint on files (including images and textual reports).*

Copyright

For copyright law, don't forget the U.S. Copyright Office, which was covered in both chapter 8, "Locating Government Forms," and chapter 9, "Locating Other Federal Resources." (That address again: **http://lcweb.loc.gov/copyright/**.) The following sites will get you to other practical help—and substantive law—on the issue.

Copyright Clearance Center Online
http://www.copyright.com/
This is the home base of a collective licensing system that provides, for a fee, authorizations and permissions for use of copyright works. The collection of online

copyright resources has two particularly useful features: listings of reproduction rights organizations in other countries (such as the UK's Copyright Licensing Agency) and a bevy of licensing and public interest organizations, from ASCAP and the Software Publishers Association to the Electronic Frontier Foundation.

Copyright & Fair Use
http://fairuse.stanford.edu:80/
The Stanford University Libraries allow searching of this site by keyword or descriptive phrase (see figure 11.2). You can also browse an index of primary materials, such as statutes, cases, regulations, and treaties; current legislation and litigation, including multimedia topics; other Internet sites; and pages that provide an overview of copyright law.

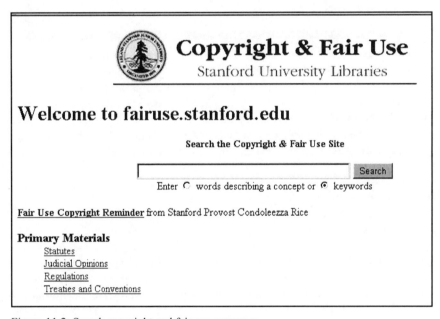

Figure 11.2: Search copyright and fair use resources.

Entertainment

Entertainment law is one more umbrella practice area, melding contract law with at least copyright, and often with several other aspects of intellectual property, as well. Here are two sites that approach the wide-ranging topic from a practical angle.

What Is the Capitol of Cyberia?

Combine the spectrum of intellectual property specialties and the world of computers, throw in a Molotov cocktail of First Amendment rights and libel issues, and what you get is the exploding area of cyberlaw. The CyBarrister Page at **http://www.ssbb.com/cybarr.html** provides solid explanations of problems peculiar to Internet and computer use, including digital defamation, links liability, privacy, and considerations for Web publishers. Ironically, this site will not send you flying off into the ether; everything connects back to one page or another authored by the site's sponsor, the New York law firm of Satterlee Stephens Burke & Burke LLP. Another article-heavy site on the topic is emerging under the auspices of the Cyberlaw Institute at **http://www.cli.org/**.

Entertainment Law Resources for Film, TV and Multimedia Producers
http://www.marklitwak.com/
Although pitched at industry professionals, attorney Mark Litwak's site offers contract and negotiation checklists with a level of detail that would be welcomed by deal makers of all kinds, including attorneys. Specific topics include film distribution, electronic publishing agreements, registering multimedia copyrights, and protecting film investors. The site offers a free e-mail newsletter.

Lawgirl.com
http://www.lawgirl.com/lawgirl.shtml
Entertainment lawyer Jodi L. Sax demystifies the practicalities of her field in several ways. She has written a detailed primer on copyright and constructed a step-by-step guide to registration for the spectrum of works, from traditional types to multimedia, computer programs, and font design. Sax sponsors (and participates in) bulletin boards dedicated to intellectual property and music law. Her posted interviews with entertainment industry professionals tend toward the alternative, but the legal information on the site applies to any entertainment field. This site also offers a free e-mail newsletter.

Patents and Trademarks

Patents and trademarks are the final major components of the intellectual property field. When researching either, don't forget the U.S. Patent and Trademark Office's page (with searchable database of patent registrations) at **http://www.uspto.gov/**. Several business and academic pages flesh out the assistance available online on both topics. We'll look at patent pages first and finish with trademarks.

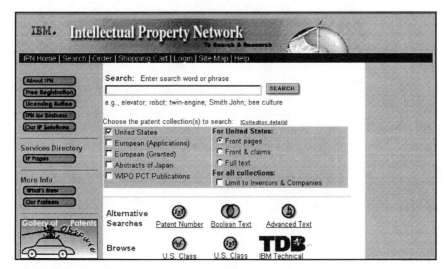

Figure 11.3. The IBM Intellectual Property Network.

IBM Intellectual Property Server
http://patent.womplex.ibm.com/
Formerly known as the IBM Patent Server, this site (shown in figure 11.3) maintains an emphasis on searchable patent databases. IBM's internal researchers developed this server for their own use, so it should come as no surprise that the scope is impressive. The U.S. database covers patent descriptions and images from 1974 on, as well as some descriptions dating back to 1971. Foreign records, which use bibliographic text, consist of European patent applications (with full images, since 1979) and registrations (with full images, since 1980), abstracts of Japanese applications (with representative images, since October 1976), and Patent Cooperation Treaty documents (since 1990, with full document images since 1998). You can search by descriptive word or patent number, or enter an identifier such as inventor, assignee, title, claims or agent in the Advanced Text Search form. The search results report how many patents matched the request and displays the most relevant, which you can read in detail or order (for a fee) by fax or mail.

When you have a moment to spare, stroll through the Gallery of Obscure Patents. It's not a static display, but changes periodically, to reflect new nominations made by visitors. (If you come across an odd patent on the server, press Nominate to bring it to the editors' attention.)

European Patent Office
http://www.epo.co.at/index.htm
The search engines available here access a variety of patent filings (United Kingdom, European, Patent Cooperation Treaty/World International Property Organi-

zation, worldwide, and Japanese) in English, French, and German. Nineteen European countries have separate engines in their national languages. Among the other searchable databases are EPO boards of appeals decisions and European patent attorneys and conventions. A toolbox for applicants provides EPO and PCT patent application forms and filing fees, examination guidelines, and European Patent Convention regulations.

Internet Patent News
http://www.bustpatents.com/
Source Translation and Optimization has replaced its pioneering patent searching tools with a site devoted to disseminating legal, economic, and statistical information about patents. Articles address topics such as biotechnology, software, and Internet patents (and their problems) and the costs of patent licensing or litigation. Click the site index to view a valuable collection of patent-related links, which are succinctly but clearly labeled. The site offers a free, near-daily e-mail newsletter called the Internet Patent News Service.

Yale University Engineering and Applied Science Library
http://www.library.yale.edu/scilib/engineer/patent.html
This page is a collection of searchable patent databases (including IBM's), as well as searchable pages containing technical standards information. Other patent resources include the British, European, and Japanese patent offices.

> *The legal translation firm InterLingua.com posts a free, searchable database of patent and trademark infringement cases (called Who's Suing Whom?) on the Litigation Support page at* **http://www.interlingua.com.**

All About Trademarks
http://www.ggmark.com/
The D.C. law firm of Gregory H. Guillot, Chartered, has compiled an exhaustive outline of federal, state, international, and general trademark resources. In addition to linking to federal statutes and agency sites, the page points to every single state's trademark laws and international laws, rules, and treaties (some in full text, in English; others in abstract). The firm recommends attorneys or agents in nearly seventy countries, lists online trademark search and support services, and points to online journals and organizations that address trademark issues.

Trademarks & Unfair Competition
http://www.law.wayne.edu/litman/classes/tm/trademark.htm
Wayne State University Law School professor Jessica Litman posts this concise outline of online trademark materials as a reference guide for her students. It is a

quick and handy springboard for practicing lawyers as well. Besides basic federal and agency resources, from here you can reach recent opinions, pending federal legislation, a mailing list, a sampler of disputes involving Websites, and a wealth of links addressing the interplay of trademarks and domain names.

> *The DomainMagistrate,* ***http://www.domainmagistrate.com****, is an assistance center for domain name disputes. Besides listing agencies that resolve disputes, the site provides the Uniform Domain Name Dispute Resolution Policy and Rules that have been adopted by the Internet Corporation for Assigned Names and Numbers (ICANN). To track the progress of disputes that are already under way, visit ICANN's site at* ***http://www.icann.org/udrp/proceedings-list.htm****.*

IP Commercial Search Services

Dialog Select offers an all-round intellectual property records search service. DialogIP, **http://www.dialogselect.com/ip/index.html**, gives user access to U.S. copyright filings, as well as U.S. and foreign trademarks and patents. You may retrieve documents for a per-item charge or subscribe for member access.

Micro-Patent, **http://www.micropat.com/trademarkwebindex.html**, offers online access to patent and trademark filings. Patent searches include U.S. records from 1964, worldwide front page information (from the U.S., Japan, European Patent Office, and Patent Cooperation Treaty), and full text of U.S., EPO, and PCT documents. The trademark options cover pending applications, active registrations dating back to 1884, and more than fifteen years of inactive registrations. Subscriptions are available on a daily and annual basis.

Thomson & Thomson, **http://www.thomson-thomson.com/**, has an online service with multiple features called SAEGIS. The trademark searches cover federal, state, Canadian, and thirteen European databases. It's also possible to search the four most recent issues of the U.S. Patent and Trademark Office *Official Gazette*. Other services screen Websites or domain names for occurrences of a proposed trademark. Pricing varies by service.

> *A compendium of class action resources—including pending legislation and summaries of issues currently in litigation—are at* ***http://www.classactionlitigation.com****. Webmaster and attorney Timothy E. Eble has also posted his federal class action procedure manual with checklists and forms.*

Medical/Personal Injury

Legal Resources
http://www.howardnations.com/#resources
Houston attorney Howard L. Nations has gathered resources that would be helpful to any case with medical considerations. From here you can search publications, access reference materials and government research databases, and obtain background information on physicians and pharmaceuticals. An informative description accompanies each link. Another page at the site provides equally valuable links to sites addressing brain injuries.

Personal Injury Law on the Web
http://www.vanderbilt.edu/Law/library/webguide/persinj.html
Vanderbilt University's Alyne Queener Massey Law Library has compiled federal agency sites, listservs, and legal, insurance, and medical practice resources.

The Med Engine!
http://www.themedengine.com/index.htm
Use this as a medical reference source. This index links to medical dictionaries, libraries, institutes, and organizations (both national and state).

Medical World Search
http://www.mwsearch.com/
The natural language search engine here looks only at selected major medical Websites that meet stringent screening criteria, including usefulness to medical professionals in a clinical practice.

The National Library of Medicine
http://www.nlm.nih.gov/
The National Library of Medicine has developed a free database of abstracts from some 4,300 biomedical journals, called Medline. You may search it here, or look through databases of clinical research studies, health organizations, and toxicology, among others. To search the National Institutes of Health's directory of more than 4,000 federal and private medical studies, go to **http://clinicaltrials.gov**.

> *To verify whether a physician is board certified, use the American Board of Medical Specialties' free service at **http://certifieddoctor.org/verify.html**. DocFinder, **http://www.docboard.org**, provides licensing information for health professionals in seventeen states.*

Oil & Gas

Rigmatch, **http://www.rigmatch.com/websearch.html**, has indexed more than 1,000 oil and gas Websites for its search engine, which will locate information about companies or drilling activity. A related engine searches more than 70,000 drilling permits in the Gulf Coast area since 1994.

Property

The Realty Engine! at **http://www.therealtyengine.com/index.htm** will give you bank rates and loan information, help calculate mortgage payments and qualification, and direct you to banks, lenders, property listing services, construction businesses, realtors' associations, and government agencies. Under Office Resources it shoots you to libraries of real estate forms and shareware.

Securities

This practice area is hardly esoteric, or static, for that matter. The very nature of the beast is enmeshed in an industry and market that changes every day. The first site below keeps up with all the major players, while the second tracks securities litigation.

Figure 11.4: SEC LAW.com tackles the financial industry.

SEC LAW.com
http://www.seclaw.com/
This searchable financial market site (see figure 11.4 on the preceding page) uses five information centers to organize its extensive resources, which run from federal and state law to market statistics. It has the polish of major corporate backing, but it's the work of one person, New York attorney Mark J. Astarita. Under each heading—arbitration, corporate finance, brokers, investors, and law and compliance—you'll find relevant articles, links, and an archive of all documents that have been posted since the site's inception. Each information center and the top page have links to the site's search engine, EDGAR (Electronic Data Gathering, Analysis, and Retrieval) searches, and pertinent laws, rules, regulations, and decisions.

Stanford Securities Class Action Clearinghouse
http://securities.stanford.edu/
The Robert Crown Law Library at Stanford Law School maintains this searchable archive of complaints, motions, opinions, settlement memoranda, and other filings in securities class action suits. The database consists of more than 2,000 documents filed since the effective date of the 1995 Private Securities Litigation Reform Act. Register at the site for free e-mail notification of litigation developments.

Tax

Tax considerations shape the structuring of businesses and deals and affect planning decisions in many areas of life. Here are four comprehensive tax sites that have pulled together resources that speak to all of them. After discussing these sites, I'll point out a more specialized resource.

Tax and Accounting Sites Directory
http://www.taxsites.com/
One concise index breaks online tax resources down into such categories as federal, state and local, or international law; forms and publications; software; and tax updates. Equally concise descriptions accompany the links under each heading, many of which lead to Big Five research or advice pages. The design makes locating resources easy and painless, two characteristics not usually associated with taxes. Accounting professor Dennis Schmidt of the University of Northern Iowa maintains the site.

Tax Master
http://vls.law.vill.edu/prof/maule/taxmaster/taxhome.htm
Supervised by professor James Edward Maule of Villanova University. This site is most valuable for its Gateways listings, which rank and describe search engines,

indexes, and encyclopedic collections of articles, forms, and advice. The Tax Master has also compiled state and foreign tax resources, sites for downloading federal tax forms, and programs for calculating estate taxes. Under Orphans, it files topics often ignored by comprehensive resources, such as tax history, legislative voting records, arguments for and against a flat tax, and information about discussion groups. You can go from the index page directly to Websites of the National Network of Estate Planning Attorneys and other tax organizations.

Essential Links to Taxes
http://www.el.com/elinks/taxes/
This scrollable list of links is a mix of legal and accounting practice aids and consumer-oriented resources. Large accounting firm and tax organization Websites appear on the list, which also covers federal, state, and international issues, news, newsgroups and mailing lists, and other collections of tax links.

Tax Resources
http://www.taxresources.com/
You can get much more here than just state and federal tax laws and forms. The site provides information (including rates and forms) about tax systems abroad, not to mention numerous resources for social security tax, software, treaties, newsgroups, and mailing lists. What Happened? takes you to daily and weekly publications and other timely updates, including IRS quarterly interest rates. The same link also explains, with clear examples, running searches for tax bills, treaties, and protocols using the GPO Access resource.

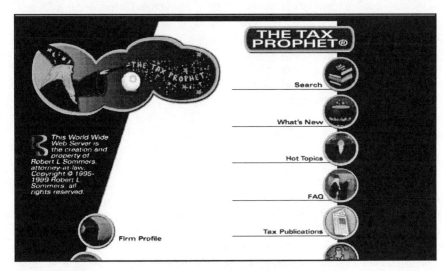

Figure 11.5: The Tax Prophet demystifies the Internal Revenue Code.

The Tax Prophet
http://www.taxprophet.com

Shown in figure 11.5 (on the preceding page), this site is a good resource for specialized issues, such as U.S. tax considerations for nonresident foreign nationals. San Francisco attorney Robert L. Sommers posts ongoing, frequently updated commentary about tax scams involving trusts or victimizing charities. His Hot Topics column addresses current court rulings, IRS policy, or tax strategies. Interactive aids include a flow chart for determining whether someone is an employee or independent contractor.

Commercial Tax Sites

Even if you don't need a subscription tax library, visit RIA Tax to get the latest Applicable Federal Rates (AFRs). The online product is the Checkpoint 3.0 system for researching federal, state, and international tax law, which includes pension and estate planning aids, as well as e-mail alerts. Preview a demo at **http://www.riatax.com/**.

BNA Tax Management Portfolios on the Web, **http://www.bna.com/tmweb/**, adds analysis of specific tax areas (income, estates, gifts and trusts, and foreign income) to an online library of the tax code, regulations, and IRS rulings, procedures, announcements, and publications. A 30-day trial subscription is available; contact BNA directly for pricing information.

CCH Internet Tax Research NetWork, **http://tax.cch.com/**, allows subscribers to mix and match CCH state and federal products and create an online tax library of their own choosing. The online service provides archival information, which is not available with CCH's CD-ROMs. The pricing for annual subscriptions varies according to the scope of libraries selected.

TaxLibrary.com, **http://www.taxlibrary.com/TaxLibrary/HomePage.nsf**, offers online access to the Internal Revenue Code and regulations, as well as IRS rulings, procedures, announcements, notices, and publications. Owned by Tax Analysts, the library includes reference tables for tax calculations, a weekly magazine, and articles from content providers Harcourt Brace Professional Publishing and Pro2Net. Subscription plans are by month, ninety days, and year.

As you can see, a well-stocked starting point or two can quickly send topic research into high gear. Many of the resources in this chapter serve up everything you need on a platter—statutory and case law, practice pointers, access to public filings, commentary, and organizations immersed in the subject. They are the virtual equivalent of specialized stacks in a law library. For a look at full-fledged libraries, turn to chapter 13, "Law Libraries Online." Another focused reference section, international law resources, follows in the next chapter.

12
International Law Resources

Up to now, all the sites we've visited have been based in North America. Hosts of online international law resources, however, are all over the map. To be sure, foreign statutes and treaties can be found on several U.S.-based pages, just as in larger academic libraries. Yet information about the laws, organizations, and governments of other countries also appears on Web pages emanating from all over the globe. This area is where online research really becomes fun, if you think about it: without leaving your desk, you can tap into a computer database, several time zones away, on a completely different continent, whether you can speak the language of the people who put it together or not. In this chapter, we'll pick up two different types of international resources: comprehensive pages, which cover legal materials from all over the globe, and sites that focus on a country or region.

> The State Department posts the requirements for obtaining service of process on parties in some thirty countries at **http://travel.state.gov/judicial_assistance.html**.

Comprehensive Resources

Most legal systems are on the Web in some form, whether through official government sites (parliaments and ministries are especially prevalent) or privately maintained pages. The type of information available varies wildly depending on the country. The more globally involved it is, the more likely at least a portion of its laws are online.

You can find some level of constitutions, statutes, and cases at most of the online law libraries listed in the next chapter, "Law Libraries Online." Those collections are an excellent point of departure for research in this area. Canadian

collections are an excellent point of departure for research in this area. Canadian and United Kingdom resources are particularly prevalent in the U.S. holdings, but don't let that bounty spoil you. The pickings are significantly slimmer with countries in areas such as Africa and Eastern Europe. Don't be lulled into complacency by the presence of English on a linking page—original source materials will be in their original language, whatever it may be.

With those caveats in mind, here are a few other places to dig.

Jurweb
http://www.uni-bayreuth.de/students/jurweb/jurweb-home-engl.html

Though the rest of the sites in this section will be discussed alphabetically, Jurweb ranks at the top of the list because of its inclusiveness. Based largely at the University of Bayreuth in Germany, it strives to catalog primary materials for the entire globe. The scope varies wildly (Antarctica, for example, has only treaties), but some type of material is available for some 57 countries in Africa, 51 in Asia, 44 in Europe, 35 in the Americas, and 15 in and around Australia. Headings are in both German and English.

> *WorldSkip,* ***http://www.worldskip.com****, supplies government, currency, and economic information, news, weather for selected cities, and tourism links for every country on the planet.*

ASIL Guide to Electronic Resources for International Law
http://www.asil.org/resource/home.htm

This guide, maintained by the American Society for International Law, takes a topical, rather than geographical, approach. It addresses criminal, environmental, private (including sale of goods and commercial arbitration), and economic law, human rights, the United Nations, treaties, and mailing lists, newsgroups, and networks. The resources, which appear under the subheadings in each topic's outline, are weighted toward the comprehensive, rather than country-specific sites.

Cornell Legal Research Encyclopedia
http://www.lawschool.cornell.edu/library/encyclopedia/

A project of the Cornell Law Library (rather than the Legal Information Institute), this site groups international resources by country, topic, and organization. Some form of primary legal materials (which may be only a constitution) are accessible for some thirty-five nations via the country index. A more wide-ranging starting point is Charlotte Bynum's annotated Foreign and International Law Sources on the Internet; look for the link to it above the country index. This guide divides foreign law sites into global; national government and court collections; Africa; Asia and the Pacific Rim; Europe (including former Eastern bloc countries); the

Middle East; and the Western Hemisphere. Each heading leads to a list of supporting links, arranged by country and accompanied by one-sentence descriptions of what each resource contains and, when necessary, including tips for use. Topical sites focus on specific areas of law, such as bankruptcy, environment, and international trade. The site also provides pointers to U.S. government sources for international information, supranational organizations, and mailing lists on international issues.

The International button on the Legal Research Encyclopedia's home page leads directly to two sections of the guide: the topical law index and links to supernational organizations.

Embassy Row

> The searchable Electronic Embassy at **http://www.embassy.org/** is an excellent springboard for foreign commerce, culture, and travel information—perfect for getting ready for an international business trip. The catalog gives contact information for every embassy in Washington, D.C.; more importantly, it links to their Websites when they exist, whether based in D.C. or from an outpost in another country. The range of information at the embassy sites is wildly inconsistent. Gone are the days when the Republic of Georgia's London base posted e-mail addresses of expatriate Georgians and the entire online population of Tblisi, but all kinds of unexpected and useful information still turns up on these sites. Finland's strikingly glitzy page, for example, provides daily news, travel facts, and a newsletter, while the Republic of Azerbaijan presents position papers, UN resolutions, and a downloadable True Type font in the country's native language. Do not let preconceptions about a particular country stop you from looking; details that an embassy found interesting enough to put on a Website may well be helpful to you.

FindLaw International Law
http://www.findlaw.com/01topics/24international/index.html
This essential bookmark comes through in spades, as always, this time with an index of primary materials, publications, mailing lists, and individual country pages. It also has a line-up of international organization Websites.

ForInt-Law
http://www.washlaw.edu/forint/forintmain.html
Although Washburn University's library site will be featured in chapter 13, "Law Libraries Online," the foreign resources warrant special mention. The individual country pages cover more than primary legal materials by including such aids as

official government, legislative or court sites, general information resources, and local law firms and faculties. The site's index, too, encompasses more than individual countries. Specific legal topics, journals, international organizations, and mailing list archives are among its listings. You can access a simple keyword search form from the top page or the individual country pages.

Global Legal Information Network
http://lcweb2.loc.gov/law/GLINv1/GLIN.html
This Library of Congress project is a searchable database of recent laws (full text and abstracted into English) from nearly fifty countries. To use the search engine, take the link for nonmembers; members are part of a country team. The search form requires you to select a country and input terms from the GLIN thesaurus. You can also limit results by date of legislation. To view resources and links by country, press the Law On-Line button and scroll through the alphabetical index, which covers an exponentially greater number of nations.

Figure 12.1: The World Government Resources frame at Hieros Gamos.

Hieros Gamos
http://www.hg.org/hg.html
This site, shown in figure 12.1, is a one-stop springboard to a slew of resources for each country. The World Governments frame boasts the heroic title "All Countries of the World." Select the first letter of a country to reach an alphabetical list of nations, under the even more heroic title "Every Country and Government on Earth." Next to each name you'll see a sequence of words or abbreviations identifying sources of material (such as Yahoo!, Library of Congress, or individual

country collections). Government, the first in each sequence, leads to HG's index for the country, which gives the official languages (and its official name). This index may include links to ministries, government institutions, and political parties. HG's border stays in place when you jump to links, so you can move back and forth (by hitting the Back button) from link to link. If you're looking for more than laws, Hieros Gamos is an efficient means of access.

Northwestern University Library Government Publications International Information
http://www.library.nwu.edu/govpub/resource/internat/
Current legislative information is available here for a few nations, but finding it takes some digging under the extensive Foreign Government Links, which are arranged by country. This searchable index is weighted toward links to government offices, which can be anything from a parliament to a minister of finance to a central bank.

> *Ixquick,* ***http://www.ixquick.com/***, *has search engines for sites in French, German, Italian, Spanish, and Portuguese.*

United Nations
http:// www.un.org
Besides calendars of conferences and meetings and wide-ranging general information, the United Nations's searchable official site covers a couple of discrete areas of international law—trade, marine, and justice. The International Trade law link contains conventions, model laws, and working documents on topics such as electronic commerce, contracts, and insolvency. Under Law of the Sea, read the text of the Law of the Sea Convention and access sites for related institutions. The International Law section warehouses summaries of judgments and advisory opinions of the International Court of Justice. The page for the International Criminal Tribunal for the Former Yugoslavia contains indictments, transcripts, and judgments from trials and appeals. The tribunal's governing statute and rules of procedure, evidence, and detention are also browsable. Similar information is available for the International Criminal Tribunal for Rwanda, which has uploaded its governing statute, rules, and directives, as well as indictments, decisions, and case summaries. The UN's Documentation Research Guide explains and links to its courts and legal bodies. (It will also point you to an International Law Pathfinder, which is not an online research source but a list of UN publications for sale on specific topics.) Online access to the UN treaty collection is available by monthly or annual subscription.

http://www.polisci.umn.edu/information/parliaments/index.html
This index is nothing but links to national parliaments, from the Andorran to the Uruguayan Poder Legislativo. What you get with each depends, of course, on the country; in most cases that information includes how the body works and who its members are. As always, not all sites are in English. The page, maintained by the Political Science Department of the University of Minnesota, also links to international parliamentary institutions like the European Parliament and the North Atlantic Assembly.

> *The Tax and Accounting Sites Directory points to tax resources for some ninety countries at* ***http://www.taxsites.com/international.html***.

Inter-Parliamentary Union
http://www.ipu.org/english/home.htm
An international organization of parliaments maintains this site, which has two particularly useful features: an alphabetical list of links to national parliament Websites, and a searchable database (PARLIT) of books and articles discussing parliamentary law and practice. The engine's definable parameters include the country, the parliamentary body, subject, author, type of periodical, date, and language of publication.

Regional Sites

For some countries more research options exist than the comprehensive sites we've just visited. Many academic and commercial pages specialize geographically. These tend to contain a wide variety of materials and links for the focus countries. In the sites below you'll find a wealth of information pertaining to Australia, Canada, China, Europe, Latin America, and the United Kingdom.

Australasian Legal Information Institute
http://www.austlii.edu.au/
This site, shown in figure 12.2, contains searchable full text databases of most Australian legislation and court decisions, which you can browse by geographical indexes. It's maintained by the law faculties of the University of Technology, Sydney, and the University of New South Wales.

Canada: LexUM
http://www.droit.umontreal.ca/en/index.html
Legal resources of Canada and Quebec are the focus of this bilingual site maintained by the Faculty of Law of the University of Montreal. Primary materials

Figure 12.2: The query box and country index of the Australasian Legal Information Institute.

include federal and provincial statutes, the Quebec Civil Code, decisions of the Human Rights Tribunal, and searchable Supreme Court decisions since 1989. A wide selection of statutory and judicial materials are under the Law Library heading, which also umbrellas links to legislatures, government agencies, publications, attorneys, societies, and journals.

Osgoode Hall Law School Canada Law
http://www.yorku.ca/faculty/osgoode/offline/ucplain.htm
Beginning with short columns of options, such as governments, statutes, journals, and decisions, this well-organized, searchable page requires a little more scrolling than the University of Montreal's. It also offers links on law by topics, such as aboriginal, criminal, and family, and includes newsgroups, mailing lists, and links to other Canadian law collections.

Canada: American Law Sources On-Line
http://www.lawsource.com/also/
ALSO's Canada holdings are a one-stop compendium of legal practice aids for both the country and its states. National resources include the Supreme Court and Federal Court decision databases at LexUM, recent bills, statutes and most codified laws, regulations, court rules, and links to home pages of courts, bar associations, and government departments. The state resource pages are set up for the same scope of information, but their actual contents depend on what is online for the particular state.

ALSO has Mexican practice aids as well, but the few primary materials that are available are in Spanish.

> *Yahoo!* at ***http://www.yahoo.com/*** *has country-specific editions for eight European and nine Pacific Rim nations, as well as for Canada, Mexico, Argentina, and Brazil.*

China: Asia Law & Practice
http://www.lawmoney.com/homepage/default.asp
LawMoney.com's China Law Reference Service should be online now with a searchable bilingual database of the laws of the People's Republic of China since 1979. (Subscriptions are initially running $2,700 a year.) The page allows access at no charge to archives of bulletins on tax, intellectual property, and business law issues, as well as an Asian legal directory.

Internet Chinese Legal Research Center
http://ls.wustl.edu/Chinalaw
Wei Luo, associate law librarian at the Washington University School of Law library, has compiled legal and news resources and research guides for China, Taiwan, and Hong Kong.

European Laws and Legal Systems
http://www.jura.uni-sb.de/english/euro.html
Sprechen Sie Deutsch? It doesn't matter with this project of the University of Saarland (in Saarbrücken, Germany), which has compiled government and legal sources for all members of the European Union, as well as fourteen nearby countries. Link descriptions indicate when a resource is in a language other than English. Constitutions are prevalent; statutes are available for Austria.

EUROPA
http://europa.eu.int/index-en.htm
The European Union posts its treaties, legislation, and caselaw on the English language page of its Web server, EUROPA. Official Euro rates and home pages for a host of Union institutions are also reachable from the top page.

Guide to European Databases
http://www.llrx.com/features/europe4.htm
Written by NYU School of Law reference librarian Mirela Roznovschi, the LLRX evaluates search engines, suggests search techniques, and explains the scope of European databases online, for both countries and topics. The countries included in the November 1999 update (check to see if there's a later one) are Austria, Belarus, Belgium, Croatia, Denmark, England, Estonia, France, Germany, Greece, Hungary, Italy, Kyrgyz Republic, Latvia, The Netherlands, Norway, Poland, Romania, Russia, Spain, Sweden, Switzerland, Ukraine, and Uzbekistan.

> *If you have a reading understanding of Spanish, visit Derecho.org,*
> ***http://www.derecho.org/**, a searchable legal research site covering Spain, Puerto Rico, and Central and South America.*

Latin American Information Center
http://www.lanic.utexas.edu/la/region/government/
For a spectrum of information about governments in Central or South America or the Caribbean, surf the University of Texas's Latin American Information Center (see figure 12.3). The information is arranged in a list, by country, linking to various ministries and organizations. In the case of some, such as Argentina, it includes municipal information, as well. If you want details that aren't strictly legal, take the link back to LANIC's top page, where you can access a particular country by name or region. The site's topic index includes such matters as government, human rights, and immigration. There is also a search engine.

Figure 12.3: LANIC has Latin America covered.

Russia: Garant Legal System
http://garant.park.ru/eng
Russian legislation, judicial procedures, and some recent Constitutional Court decisions are in this searchable, English-language database. The index structure is not always self-evident; look for legislation covering courts under Cases.

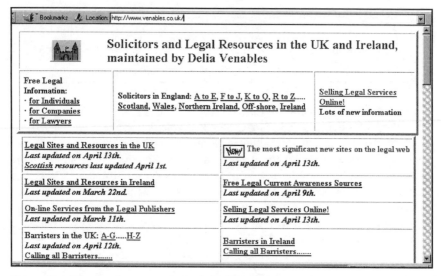

Figure 12.4: The portal to resources in the United Kingdom and Ireland.

Portal to Legal Resources in the UK and Ireland
http:// www.venables.co.uk/

This gateway (shown in figure 12.4) is a jam-packed collection of links to the spectrum of United Kingdom and Irish legal resources. Primary and secondary materials are divided geographically, by area of practice, and by legal publishers with online services, whether by subscription or at no charge. Legislative links are buried in the topic index, under Legislation and Parliaments. The site has rosters of solicitors and barristers in the United Kingdom and Ireland, and links to a variety of legal periodicals. The force behind the page is British computer consultant Delia Venables.

With international resources under your belt, you've become acquainted with the techniques and types of Web tools necessary to do legal research online. If you've been bookmarking along the way, you've made significant inroads into setting up your personal online law library. A look at real-world and electronic libraries is next on the agenda.

13
Law Libraries Online

Out in the real world, law libraries crop up in several predictable places. They're an integral part of law schools. Outside academia, they're attached to firms, corporations, organizations, and government departments. The situation is much the same online. Virtual law libraries are the arm of many a law school, whether as part of an existing physical library or, in a few instances, a separate Internet project altogether. Some come under the aegis of the government; still others are freestanding collections, with no affiliations except to the Web. In this chapter, we'll look at examples of all the forms of law libraries online.

A Catalog of Catalogs

To see if your alma mater is on the Net, consult FindLaw's browsable list of Law Schools A-Z at **http://lawschools.findlaw.com/**. This page provides direct links to the Web pages of schools and libraries. The list also gives links to electronic versions of card catalogs, where available. In some cases, these catalogs do not appear on Web pages; instead, libraries store them in databases accessible by Telnet connections. The list points out when a link requires Telnet and discloses any special code that is required to gain entry.

An Aside about Card Catalogs

Thumbing through worn index cards in wooden drawers has always been part of the research process. Increasingly, it's fading into history. More and more libraries are moving the entries on all those cards into electronic databases. No longer do you have to wait for the person in front of you to finish with the drawer containing the part of the alphabet you want. The electronic card catalogs are accessible from terminals all over the library and in many cases all over the Web, usually via Telnet.

Before you get carried away by the thrill of the technology, stop and think about the underlying purpose of those card catalogs. They tell what's on the shelves, and where. While it may be intriguing to track down the call number for a book in a library a couple of states away, that number is not going to do you much practical good if you can't actually get your hands on the book it designates (unless your research is esoteric enough to warrant requesting the book through interlibrary loan). Searching through the card catalog of a nearby law library makes sense; if you find a helpful treatise, you can send someone over to plough through it. In the case of libraries at a distance, though, it's just an academic exercise—and probably a waste of time.

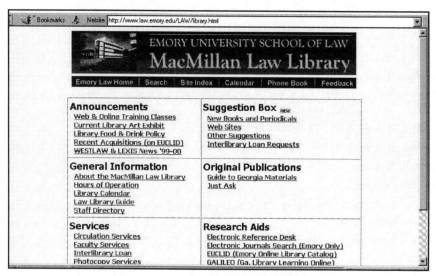

Figure 13.1: Emory University offers the best of both worlds.

Physical Libraries with a Virtual Presence

Most law school libraries have established some sort of presence on the ether. Many remain focused on their physical existence, with descriptions of the paper-and-ink collection and services, statements of hours, directions, and the like. A number, though, have developed substantial Internet tools, as well—and not just the big guys, either. The Web is providing a means for schools that have been in the background to establish a weighty national presence. As chapter 5, "Locating Caselaw," pointed out, a number of libraries serve as the official online repositories for the opinions of specific courts.

Here are some individual library pages that give a range of what's out there. (I've left out examples of schools that just post narrative information about physical library resources.) Put allegiances aside—try out a few and see which match your style.

Emory University School of Law
http://www.law.emory.edu/LAW/library.html
As figure 13.1 shows, Emory's site deftly spans the physical and virtual worlds. All the pertinent details are there for the Hugh F. MacMillan Law Library, such as floor maps, hours, rules, and a description of services. Its Web services begin with the Electronic Reference Desk, a searchable and browsable index of law by country or subject, career information, firms, schools, and more. Under the desk's Reference Materials heading, you'll find legal and nonlegal research starting points, while the Entertainment & Culture heading teems with extracurricular fun. The U.S. Federal Courts Finder gives two clicking options for accessing opinions: a hyperlinked map of the country and an index of the Supreme Court and circuits underneath. To students, faculty, and staff, the library offers a catalog and database gateway called EUCLID (Emory University Computing and Library Information Delivery System).

Georgetown University Legal Explorer
http://www.ll.georgetown.edu/
The Edward Bennett Williams Library's Website (see figure 13.2) is a meaty starting point for all types of research and searchable at that. Besides explaining the

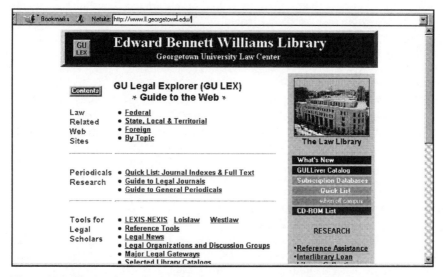

Figure 13.2: The legal resources page of Georgetown University's Legal Explorer.

physical setup, it divides its virtual resources into law, other, and those restricted to school use; it also gives Web access to the card catalog, GULLiver. Legal resources are split into primary law, subject, reference tools, publications, organizations and groups, and comprehensive research sites, which it calls gateways. The Other Internet Sources link is a handy catchall of reference and news pages, geographically based information, and sites on a spectrum of subjects, from arts to travel and recreation.

Indiana University School of Law
http://www.law.indiana.edu:80/
Here's a another good example of a site that consolidates the physical and virtual. Basic information about the physical library includes a textual user's guide for the tangible collection. The first bridge between the 3-D and virtual worlds consists of online renewal of library materials and Telnet access to the card catalog (which is explained in rare and exceedingly clear detail). An Internet Resources link on the main library page gets you to legal and general resources, search engines, and materials targeted to librarians or students.

Go back to the top page for the virtual fireworks. Indiana maintains the law section of the World Wide Web Virtual Library, a massive project of an international industry consortium. Run a keyword search, or browse legal information by organization type (law firms, government servers) or topic. This library also links to a number of comprehensive search engines and starting points.

The University of Chicago
http://www.lib.uchicago.edu/e/law/home.html
The D'Angelo Law Library takes a clear and simple approach by summing up all of its information, real-world and virtual, in a handful of headings. Most are self-explanatory, such as the links to the library's card catalog (which is searchable online), law journals, and nonlegal journals. The Databases page is a gateway to research services that require registration or subscription. Research Guides is the home of Law Lists, the definitive compilation of legal mailing lists. Internet Links compile starting points for the spectrum of legal research topics. Search engines are not in that category, but under Reference, along with encyclopedias, dictionaries, style and citation manuals, and law-related directories. Don't overlook the fine print at the bottom of the library's main page. Catch of the Day spotlights new developments in useful research sites, while Frolic & Detour leads to the librarians' personal pages, which reflect diverse literary and pop culture interests.

University of Michigan Law School
http://www.law.umich.edu/library/
Two features are of interest on this succinct page. Under Electronic Resources is an index of the research databases to which the site links. The page notes which are available only to users within the University of Michigan network. If you are close

enough geographically that searching the card catalog makes sense, press the link to the Lexcalibur. This action will automatically launch your Telnet application and connect to the catalog.

Northwestern University School of Law
http://www.law.nwu.edu/lawlibrary/
The Pritzker Legal Research Center puts its index of resources in an exceptionally clear layout. Besides disclosing basic information about the physical library, it offers four categories of online resources. The basic ones are NucatWeb (the online catalog of the Northwestern University libraries), a variety of search engines, and the subscription services LegalTrac, LEXIS-NEXIS, and Westlaw. Legal material headings include international, government, subject listings, law libraries online, news, and research guides. This page also allows access to a number of electronic law journals, the main library's databases, and, for subscribers, the Current Index to Legal Periodicals.

WashLaw WEB
Washburn University Law Library
http://www.washlaw.edu/
Washburn University Law Library offers an avalanche of research and practical resources, from law school information to zip code directories, arranged in a four-column index. If the tiny print makes your head swim, focus on four of the site's major attractions: Full Text Searches, Reference-Legal (RefLaw), Search State Law Full-Text (StateLaw), and Documents (DocLaw Web).

From the Full Text Search page you can research just about everything but international topics: federal and state legislation, cases, court rules, and administrative law, not to mention full text of law journals. If you prefer using an index, surf over to RefLaw, the Virtual Law Library Reference Desk. StateLaw offers full text searching of state laws and browsable indexes for searching by state or by categories such as judicial or legislative information. It also links to a number of specialty search engines and sites containing information that collate common state information, such as tax rates, governors' associations, and model statutes. DocLaw organizes federal Internet resources by subject and by organizational charts that illustrate which agency is under which department; it also posts a handy chart linking to home pages and downloadable forms sites of federal agencies.

Other notable features of WashLaw Web include links to legal dictionaries, contact information on- and offline for law libraries across the country, and Continuing Legal Education requirements for every state.

Lillian Goldman Library at Yale Law School
http://www.yale.edu/law/library/
From here you may search the online catalogs at the law library (MORRIS) and the university library (ORBIS). The site details research databases available through the school, almost all of which require a password. The Internet resources point to

comprehensive starting points (FindLaw, Hieros Gamos, and the like), associations, federal and state law and government, foreign sites, and card catalogs at other libraries. The legal article and periodical resources listed are available only to the Yale community.

Two special Yale databases are under the wide-ranging general reference links. Look under Historical Documents for the Avalon Project, a database of historical documents in the fields of law, diplomacy, economics, history, and politics, and hyperlinked to supporting documents to which they refer. The documents are segregated by century and listed alphabetically by author and title, from the Code of Hammurabi and Athenian Constitution to the 1992 European Parliament Resolution on the situation in Tibet. Amid the extensive Human Rights Organizations & Documents links is Project DIANA, a searchable database of documents pertaining to international human rights. (The University of Cincinnati College of Law, University of Minnesota Human Rights Library, and Bora Laskin Law Library at the University of Toronto also maintain sites for DIANA, which stands for Direct Information Access Network Association.)

Virtual Libraries, Academic Style

Several of the most helpful online libraries are special projects of their sponsoring law schools. Some focus on a narrow topic, such as the Franklin Pierce Law Center Intellectual Property Mall, which we strolled through in chapter 11, "Researching by Topic." Of the comprehensive ones, Cornell's are the two that you will encounter most often.

Cornell Law School Legal Information Institute
http://www.law.cornell.edu/
This research project of the Cornell Law School has popped up frequently in earlier chapters, and no wonder—it stockpiles decisions of the Supreme Court and New York Court of Appeals, federal laws and regulations, state statutes and cases (where available), foreign and international resources, and online materials by topic. It's a single springboard to many avenues of attack. It also has a directory of academic e-mail addresses and a handful of links for locating other professionals online. The site is set up as an index, which means you click on headings and subheadings until you run out of options. (See figure 13.4.)

This is not the law school's library, however. That collection maintains a page at **http:// www.lawschool.cornell.edu/lawlibrary/default.html**. The library page contains a helpful online Legal Research Encyclopedia, which subdivides the entirety of legal research into four major headings: subject, countries, United States, and international. As you proceed deeper into a topic, the resources range from links to primers (particularly in the international section) to descriptions of what you can find in the stacks at Cornell.

Figure 13.4: Cornell's Legal Information Institute.

Virtual Libraries beyond the Ivory Tower

As in the real world, law libraries without any academic association exist on the Net. Here are three well-stocked collections, one with governmental roots and two from private commerce.

Internet Law Library
http://www.lectlaw.com/inll/1.htm
http://www.infoctr.edu/ill/
The Internet Law Library began as a project of the House of Representatives. When the House disbanded the site in 1999, it offered copies of the collection to other Web hosts. As a result, the library is available in a number of places online. The two URLs listed above are merely a sampling of locations at which it appears. All retain the original format, and the only difference among them is the address. The top page is a simple column of headings setting out the contents of the collection: federal laws, by source and agency; state and territorial laws; laws of other nations; treaties and international law; all jurisdictions' laws arranged by subject; law library catalogs; professional directories; and law book reviews and publishers. Click on one to browse an index of subheadings. Pressing Laws of Other Nations, for example, brings up an alphabetical list of countries. Picking a country gets its flag and links to whatever the library has regarding it relevant treaties; in the case of Azerbaijan, for example, it has a treaty (in Kurdish and French) and UN,

Commerce, and State Department documents, whereas Chile's page contains the constitution and statutes.

LawLinks.com
http://www.lawlinks.com/
This site maintains a comprehensive list of subject headings. Each entry in the Legal Subject Index contains introductory and in-depth articles, selected cases, and links to statutes and codes. Besides the research fundamentals of cases and legislation, this site has compiled resources related to personal injury, ADR, treaties, and downloadable forms for litigation as well as business transactions. Since it's a browsable index, all you have to do is scan and click, then scan again.

The 'Lectric Law Library's Rotunda
http://www.lectlaw.com/rotu.html
Here's a site with a sense of humor—or should I say, an attitude? Playing with the concept of a physical library, the 'Lectric Law Library sets up its subdivisions as rooms and lounges. The roster takes up the top page, and you wander down a virtual hallway by clicking. The Business Law Lounge spotlights issues relating to starting and running an enterprise, including tax and employee considerations, while both the News Room and Periodicals Room stockpile the expected. Enter the Reference Room for materials by area of practice and links to search engines and starting points. Articles on hot issues (and difficult clients) abound in the Legal Professional Lounge, which has specialized reading rooms for lawyers, judges, and paralegals. The Lay People's Law Lounge addresses legal issues that come up in ordinary life. The Rubber Room, on the other hand, is a cornucopia of the sort of stuff that gets faxed and forwarded every day—more lawyer jokes than you ever wanted to know existed, much less hear, courtroom bloopers, supposedly true news briefs, weird statutes, and parody pleadings. (Boomer lawyers: Ian Frazier's parody opinion *Wile E. Coyote v. Acme Company* is here—uncredited.) To round things out, this library has a FAQ (in the Inner Sanctum) and a guided tour, which sneaks a lot of real (and helpful) information in with all the sarcasm. The tone isn't the only thing that separates this library from its online colleagues. Not just a compilation of links, most of its materials actually appear on its pages, in compressed format for downloading.

Many law library pages function quite well as comprehensive starting points. After visiting the ones in this chapter—and any others that you stumble upon—see if you don't end up adding one or two to your personal essential bookmarks.

Speaking of which, we still haven't tied down a major component of your online library. Plenty of them come across your desk with regularity; in chapter 14, "Journals, Periodicals, & Legal News," we'll take a look at publications available in electronic form.

14
Journals, Periodicals, & Legal News

Periodicals are a mainstay of a legal practice. Academic and professional journals, digests of opinions, and even newspapers provide ways of keeping up with current events that affect the law, our clients, and our profession. It's no surprise, then, that you can get easy electronic access to numerous familiar sources—and many new ones. We'll look at the online offerings in this order: law reviews, professional journals, e-mail periodicals, legal newspapers, and regional publications.

Law Reviews

This area is still in the growth and expansion stage. While a large number of law reviews are online, their presence is, for the most part, limited to conveying details about the publication, the staff, and the contents of the current issue. (One example: *Harvard Law Review* at **http://www.harvardlawreview.org/**.) Their Web pages function as information packets and not as electronic versions of the printed pages. A few of these student-run organizations have tested the virtual waters by uploading abstracts of their contents, while others post their issues in full, along with explicit copyright statements. Because the situation is in such a state of flux, this section will give examples of various approaches and starting points for locating journals, rather than attempting an exhaustive survey.

Abstractly Speaking

When law reviews started going up on the Web, most of the ones that posted any content at all merely offered abstracts, or summaries, rather than the full text of issues. Even the publications that did include abstracts rarely offered them for every single item in an issue. It was not unusual to find abstracts limited to articles (which are generally written by professors), with student-written work largely ignored. While incomplete abstracting is still prevalent, it is now more likely to include student work.

An example of a partial approach to abstracts is *Michigan Law Review* at **http://www.law.umich.edu/pubs/journals/mlr/**. It posts paragraph-length synopses of selected items; scan the table of contents for hyperlinks to determine what has been abstracted. *Stanford Law Review* takes a similar tact. Beginning with Volume 50, this publication posts abstracts of selected articles, notes, and book reviews at **http://www.stanford.edu/group/lawreview/**. Neither site offers a search engine (the lack of which is a common situation at law journal pages).

Full Text

The leader in this arena is one of the rare online-only journals, the *Richmond Journal of Law and Technology* at **http://www.urich.edu/~jolt/**, which began in April 1995. Its focus is, appropriately, the impact of technology on the law. The site, shown in Figure 14.1, takes full advantage of its Web-based existence by adding a twist to each article, book review, note, and comment. Click "View Related Browsing" under any entry and you will be taken to a list of sites that provide further information on the topic.

Figure 14.1: The Richmond Journal of Law and Technology publishes only online.

Among the full text pioneers is the *American University Law Review* at **http://www.wcl.american.edu/pub/journals/lawrev/aulrhome.htm.** Clicking on a title in the table of contents—which looks remarkably like a printed page—brings up the article, comment, or note. Beginning with Volume 47 (October 1997), the site displays the introduction to each article or comment issue and makes the entire document available in PDF.

Another pioneer from the print world is *Florida State University Law Review* at http:// **www.law.fsu.edu/journals/lawreview/index.html**. It provides the contents of issues from 1995-98 in hypertext (which you can read on the page) and PDF; some of the earlier ones also include abstracts.

A number of leading law reviews have jumped midstream into full text posting. The *University of Chicago Law Review* launched its site with only the table of contents, beginning with the 1994 volume. With the Spring 1999 issue, the site (at **http://student-www.uchicago.edu/orgs/lawreview/**) switched to up-loading the full text. *Columbia Law Review*, at **http://www.columbialawreview.org**, instituted the same change with Volume 97. Beginning with the December 1998 issue, *New York University Law Review* now posts the full text at **http://www.nyu.edu/pages/lawreview/**. For earlier editions, only article abstracts are posted.

Professional Journals

Numerous professional organizations post excerpts from their journals on their Websites. The heavyweight of them all is the American Bar Association, the various sections and subgroups of which put out a small village of publications. Some of these give out only a dry table of contents, but several tip their hand more fully.

A miniature of the current cover—and links to the text of featured stories, trends, and news—appear at the *American Bar Association Journal*'s main page, **http://www.abanet.org/journal/home.html**. To see which other periodicals are online, jump to the ABA home page, **http:// www.abanet.org/**. Browse the index of ABA entities under Sections/Divisions/Forums, select a name, and then scan its top page for a journal reference. This method is best if you have an entity and publication in mind. If you don't, it will be more quick and efficient to start instead at the ABA portion of the University of Southern California Law School and Law Library list at **http://www.usc.edu/dept/law-lib/legal/journals.html**. (This list names actual journals, rather than the entities that sponsor them.)

ABA publications cover the scope of legal and practice issues, and many make significant portions of their articles available online to nonmembers. The General Practice, Solo and Small Firm Section, for example, posts full text excerpts from its eponymous quarterly at **http://www.abanet.org/genpractice/magazine/magazine.html**. The Law Practice Management Section—a hotbed of Internet savvy practitioners—uploads most of its current issue at **http://4.21.247.201/default.asp**.

For journals of state bar associations and other professional organizations, refer to the discussion of organization home pages in chapter 15, "Locating Lawyers & Other Helpful People." In the case of any association, directions to the associated journal page should be easy to locate from the index or site map, if not the top page.

Fee-based Subscriptions

The prevalence of free services on the Internet make it easy to lose sight of the fact that some periodicals still charge subscription fees. Here is one periodical that takes that old-fashioned approach while covering the forward-looking intersection of law and the Web. The *Internet Lawyer* at **http:// www.internetlawyer.com/** uses print and Web space to explore the Net's practical relation to the legal profession. Don't be misled by the How to Subscribe link under TIL Online; the periodical itself is not an online newsletter, as the name implies, but a monthly print magazine that is delivered by snail mail for $129 a year. A sample is free for the asking. Selected articles are posted in full at the site, which also allows you to dispatch a question to TIL's Internet Guru and browse some answers to previous queries.

Reviews & Journals: Where to Find Them

Although you certainly may run a search query to locate law reviews and journals, there's really no need when several indexes have bounteous options listed in one place.

There are three main reasons to use FindLaw's Academic Journal Page, **http:// lawschools.findlaw.com/journals/index.html**. First and foremost, it has an engine that will search the full text of all the academic journals on the Web. This is enormously useful, because search engines are still a rarity among law review sites. FindLaw's search function sidesteps the inconvenience of jumping from one law review site to another and browsing through tables of contents at each site. Second, FindLaw sends out journal abstracts, as they're released, by e-mail; sign up at the page for this free service.

The third reason is the index of journals itself. The index's primary utility is determining quickly whether a particular publication is online in any form. The page is set up to disclose each publication's approach as well, since it does tag entries with "full text" or "abstract," where appropriate. Theoretically, this tagging should tell you at a glance how a particular journal couches its online contents, without the bother of loading a journal's page in your browser. The benefit would be greater, however, if updating were more frequent. This page has not consistently kept up with changes in journal sites, with the result that a journal may now have more online than the tag indicates. Trust a tag if it says "full text." Journals that are marked as "abstract" may well include full text by now, while the absence of a tag no longer guarantees that the site is devoid of print content.

For journal descriptions as well as names, try the University of Southern California Law School and Law Library's Legal Journals on the Web at **http://www.usc.edu/dept/law-lib/legal/journals.html**. This series of alphabetical lists separates entries by type (general, commercial, or foreign law; topic-specific; ABA publications; general interest and computing; and review or e-journal locating services). Its holdings include academic journals from the United States, Australia, Canada, and the UK, and a handful of publications and newsletters by bar associations and professional organizations. Codes indicate whether a site has full text, abstracts, or a table of contents. This site discloses when the page was most recently updated, a helpful fact in determining the reliability of the codes.

Tarlton Law Library of the University of Texas School of Law has compiled a formidable list of links (with no descriptive information other than the journal and sponsor name) on its Law Journals and Periodicals page at **http://tarlton.law.utexas.edu/hook-em/journal/journal.htm**.

Periodicals by E-Mail

You don't always have to surf the Web to get legal periodicals. Just like the subscriptions that show up on your desk, a whole breed of them will come straight to your e-mail box. These are, as a general rule, the work of commercial enterprises, law firms, and attorneys with an exceptional bent for technology. Not just cut-and-dried statements of the law, many capitalize on (if not focus on) the electronic media, such as by including hyperlinks to referenced sites.

I've come across many by serendipity, usually when my eye falls on a blurb on an associated Website. A central source for electronic publications is Newsletter Access at **http:// www.newsletteraccess.com/**, which provides information about more than 500 law-related publications. To find one, browse the legal index or search the site. All the search results give are titles, but if you click one, you'll get a page with subscription information. Keep in mind that this database includes print publications without online counterparts.

The Internet Lawyer Legal Newsstand posts a list of newsletters and online periodicals, with brief descriptions, at **http://www.internetlawyer.com/news.htm**. Many, but by no means all, have a technological bent; appellate law, bankruptcy, and other normal areas of practice are also represented.

To whet your appetite, here are a few special interest newsletters.

Cyberlaw: The Internet & Beyond

For a free monthly newsletter on legal issues concerning computer technology, fill out the subscription form at CyberLaw, **http://www.cyberlaw.com/**. More policy-oriented than ILPN, the substance runs toward provocative, in-depth think pieces. Cyber-publisher and attorney Jonathan Rosenoer also reports on computer-related legal news in CyberLex, which is posted at the site.

Each business day, GigaLaw.com dispatches the latest headlines involving the intersection of law and technology. Subscribe for the free newsletter at **http://www.gigalaw.com**.

Internet Research Resources
Two free newsletters (both mentioned in chapter 4's Essential Bookmarks) ship out lists of law-related Internet resources. In the weekly LLRXBuzz, Tara spotlights new sites, changes at old favorites, and other developments. Most are law-oriented, but the mix always includes more general resources that could be useful to attorneys. Subscribe and read back issues at **http://www.llrx.com**.

The ABA's Site-tation focuses on law-related sites that may or may not be new, but have recently caught the reviewers' eyes. The frequency began as weekly, but has been only once or twice a month since late 1999. Sign up at **http://mail.abanet.org/archive/site-tation.html**.

> *If you are a BNA subscriber or interested in trying out one of its services, visit BNA's Web reference library of its publications **http://web.bna.com/**. Access to each product is by subscription. Limited free trials are available.*

Tax
The IRS sends out two free electronic newsletters. The Digital Dispatch discusses IRS announcements, new tax forms and publications, and Website additions. IRS Local News Net tailors its content to the recipient's geographic area. Information about both periodicals appears on the Tax Information for Business Page at **http://www.irs.ustreas.gov/prod/bus_info/**.

Legal News

Online legal news sources offer up-to-the-day reports on any number of subjects affecting or involving the profession—trials and appeals, legislative and administrative battles and developments, deal-making, IPOs, even personalities and scandals. This section will divide legal news sources into general, special interest (or topical), and regional.

General Legal News Sources

FindLaw Legal News
http://legalnews.findlaw.com/
Scan the latest headlines at FindLaw Legal News, a constantly updated page that divides stories into legal practice areas (i.e., Supreme Court, business litigation, intellectual property, telecommunications). For sports and entertainment law news, return to FindLaw's top page (type **www.findlaw.com** or press the left-most link in the top button bar) and take the appropriate links under the heading Legal News. In the same column are insider reviews of legal TV shows. For an index of other legal publications, do not select Legal News (which will take you to the headline page), but the heading News & Reference.

Law.com
http://www.law.com
This site is striving to be the ultimate legal news source online. It has merged with Law News Network, which was the umbrella site for a host of American Lawyer Media publications. Those periodicals, along with major newspapers, provide much of the journalistic content.

The top page of the site itself is splashed with synopses of significant stories and links to the articles in full. The state sites supply local legal headlines, case summaries, and practice guides, as well as national news briefs. (Nine of the state sites are successors to American Lawyer Media newspaper pages, which will be discussed individually in the next section.) Articles and resources target three other audiences: law students, business people and lawyers, and the general public.

Finding resources beyond these obvious ones requires persistence and a willingness to snoop. Though the addition of a search engine is welcome, the site map shows only the major headings (which are already evident from the top page) and not extent of the content, which is the point behind most site maps. Go to the Legal Professionals "channel" for such other features as IPO Watch, a weekly report about law firms handling public offerings, and the Law Biz, which has lawyer and firm profiles and lively features on marketing, management, verdicts, settlements, and deals. Registration (which is free) is required to view some portions of the site and sign up for the daily e-mail newswire.

Separate subscriptions (at $108 each) are necessary to access the Practice Centers, which cover technology, employment, intellectual property, litigation, and corporate law. Each practice area offers breaking legal news, developments in case law and excerpts from Practising Law Institute treatises, as well as weekly e-mail updates. Free thirty-day trial subscriptions are available.

The American Lawyer
http://www.americanlawyer.com/
From the home page for this weekly print magazine you can view the table of contents of the current issue, as well as selected stories, in full, from the current and

recent issues. When you click a hyperlink to a story, you will be taken to its spot in the Law News Network archives.

The National Law Journal
http://www.nlj.com/

At this site, which is shown in figure 14.2, nonsubscribers can read (and search) legal news, columns, editorials, the previous week's decisions, verdicts and settlement, and other staples of the *National Law Journal*. Excerpts from its affiliate *Corporate Counsel Magazine* are posted at **http://www.nlj.com/ corporatecounsel.html**. This site is now affiliated with Law.com.

Figure 14.2: The *National Law Journal* online. *This originally appeared at http:// www.nlj.com and is reprinted with permission © 2000 NLP IP Company.*

Lawyers Weekly USA
http://www.lawyersweekly.com/

This national newspaper, which is geared to small firm practice, fills its opening page (see figure 14.3) with summaries of breaking legal news, verdicts, and practice-oriented features. To view a story in full, look for a parenthetical at the end of the summary. If the parenthetical says "free" or refers to another news source, such as Reuters or the Associate Press, the story is accessible regardless of whether you subscribe to the paper. The site does let you try it out first before making an investment; a free trial subscription includes three issues of the paper and access to the site archives. Chapter 5, "Locating Caselaw," spotlighted one subscription benefit of this site: an e-mail alert service announcing important court decisions. Whether you subscribe or not, you may jump from this site to pages for *Lawyers Weekly*'s seven state publications, which will be discussed in the next section.

Figure 14.3: The headlines of the day at *Lawyers Weekly*.

Court TV Online
http://www.courttv.com/
In addition to posting its broadcast schedule, Court TV uses its searchable site for coverage of high-profile lawsuits, prosecutions, and arrests. Resources include legal news involving celebrities (such as wills, divorces, and crimes by or against them) and state-by-state links to the country's most wanted criminals.

Special Interest Publications

The Web houses publications on every imaginable aspect of the law or a legal practice. Here are some examples. Many more appear under specific topics in FindLaw's Library Subject Outline at **http://findlaw.com/01topics/index.html**.

Legislative News
The Hill, a print newspaper covering the congressional beat, uploads its current cover stories in full at **http://www.hillnews.com/**.

Caselaw Developments

Visit the Lawletter at **http://www.nlrg.com/lawlet/lawlet.htm** for discussions of recent court decisions in a variety of areas of practice, as well as archives of past issues. The National Legal Research Group's monthly newsletter is also available by snail mail, for the astonishingly long free trial period of one year.

To keep up to date on judicial law in your jurisdiction, nothing requires less effort from you than subscribing to an e-mail opinion notification service. For the ones covering your jurisdiction, refer back to chapter 5, "Locating Caselaw."

Financial

Top legal financial news stories, often with an international scope, are digested on the legal industries subpage of Dow Jones's site, which is published by the *Wall Street Journal* at **http://dowjones.wsj.com/i/law/law-main.cgi**. Each digest contains a link to the article in full. In the far left column, links also lead to articles about court rulings (under Deals) and to an index of law firm Websites. The page also conducts readers' polls and links to special reports in the WSJ and a legal forum for discussing current issues.

International Business

For worldwide legal news with a financial focus, visit LawMoney.com, **http://www.lawmoney.com/homepage/default.asp**. The News Centre covers litigation, law firm news, and changes of law throughout the world. Deal Watch looks at the firms behind the largest mergers and acquisitions, capital markets, and joint ventures. Four print periodicals—*International Financial Law Review*, *Managing Intellectual Property*, *International Tax Review*, and *World Business Law*—are available here three months after publication. Free registration is required to access the site, which includes archives that may be searched geographically as well as by keyword. Among other valuable research aids are Asia Law & Practice, which offers headline news, bulletins on regulations, and bilingual, searchable laws from the People's Republic of China, and Expert Guides, which spotlight attorneys in specific international practice areas. Watch the site for a new publication, an International Internet Law Review covering international business and e-commerce.

Tax

Tax Analysts Online, **http://www.tax.org/**, posts the day's tax news and features discussing breaking federal, state, and international tax issues.

RIA offers current excerpts from a variety of its print publications at **http://www.riatax.com/**. Look for the hottest topics from its weekly periodicals under News Items. Feature articles from its monthlies (such as the Journal of Taxation, Practical Tax Strategies, or Estate Planning) are also available.

Technology
The Law & Politics section of ZDNet News covers the latest technology litigation and prosecutions at **http://www.zdnet.com/zdnn/law/**. The site is searchable and links to ZDNet News' sections on business, computing, investing, and the Internet.

The print magazine *Law Office Computing* offers free help with technology decisions at **http://www.lawofficecomputing.com/**. It has archived more than 300 legal technology product reviews from the magazine, which you may search by keyword or browse by category (document assembly, for example, or speech recognition software.)

The biweekly Web journal LLRX (formerly Law Library Resource Exchange), **http://www.llrx.com/**, looks at research, management, legislation, and technology issues from a legal perspective. It's an excellent source for the latest Internet research tools and pending legislation affecting electronic affairs, as well as in-depth evaluations of commercial services.

GigaLaw.com, **http://www.gigalaw.com**, publishes articles on a wide range of legal topics, geared to both Internet professionals and high-tech lawyers. It offers two free newsletters, a daily digest of breaking technology news with a legal bent, and a weekly announcement of new articles.

Associate Life
"The Rodent," a saucy underground newsletter for law firm associates, is part of the members-only legal job database EmplawyerNet, at **http://www.emplawyernet.com/**. The private portion of the database includes an "Ask a Rodent" service, for trying to make sense of aspects of firm life that don't. The publicly accessible Run with the Rodent page lets nonmembers look at past pearls of wisdom from the varmint.

Regional Publications

On the Web and off, some publications target attorneys, issues, and news in a specific jurisdiction. Despite the focus, local ownership is becoming an increasingly rare phenomenon. Two national conglomerates have emerged as the heavy hitters in the area of regional publications: American Lawyer Media and Lawyers Weekly, each of which owns a cluster of state newspapers. The sites in each publication family offer similar features, require subscriptions for the more valuable services, and often follow a common layout. Because the similarities cross so many state boundaries, this section will group affiliated sites together, rather than listing newspapers by state.

American Lawyer Media/Law.com Affiliates
The American Lawyer Media sites vary in content, because they did not all spring full-grown from one corporate template. Instead, many originated with independent

local periodicals, some of which American Lawyer has since purchased. As a result, services and features have not been uniform, though all of them have adopted the Law.com site look. Some site names may have changed as a result of the Law.com redesign.

Cal Law at **http://www.Callaw.com/** splashes its public top page with headlines of court and legislative developments in the state and the Ninth Circuit. Subscriptions are free for a 30-day trial basis (or to subscribers of *The Recorder*), but otherwise $144 a year. Nonsubscribers have access to hard-hitting features about law firms, associate salary and satisfaction surveys, and the site's first-rate collection of court links, which include county rules sites, Supreme Court orders, opinions and oral argument calendars, judicial profiles, and court directories. Subscribers get daily opinions, a news and case e-mail alert, and concurrent subscriptions to *The Recorder* and *California Law Week*.

DeLAWnet, **http://209.92.232.821**, makes top statewide news stories available to all visitors. A subscription is necessary to view most of the site's resources, which include court calendars, judicial and attorney profiles, and Delaware digests. (Although the subscribers-only index lists a number of courts, the site does not disclose the nature of the databases—i.e., whether they include access to the latest opinions.) The cost is $39.95 a month, discounted to $19.95 for subscribers to *Delaware Law Weekly* or the *Delaware Corporate Reporter*. Firm rates are available, as is a thirty-day trial.

The District of Columbia paper *Legal Times* makes its online home at **http://www5.law.com/dc/**. The site offers more than articles from the paper, though those are exceptional for linking to related court decisions and other related materials. Other important features include daily news updates and summaries of the most recent decisions of the Supreme Court, D.C. and Federal Circuit Courts, and the D.C. Court of Appeals—which are searchable by area of law or keyword. Access does not require a paid subscription to either the site or the newspaper, but visitors must register to read case summaries.

South Florida's business and financial news is the focus of FloridaBiz.com, **http://www.floridabiz.com/**, the online home of the print newspaper the *Daily Business Review*. The site archives articles on legal business, technology reports, and practice focus since August 1999, which are freely searchable by keyword.

Georgia's *Fulton County Daily Report* is online at **http://www.dailyreportonline.com/**. The site features daily news and opinion briefs, searchable court calendars and legal notices, a directory of judges and courts, and an e-mail alert service for appellate opinions and court calendars. Recent news and the classifieds are freely accessible; all other features require a subscription. An annual site subscription costs $275 ($60 for *Daily Report* subscribers), and a 30-day trial is available.

The day's top stories dominate the home page of *New Jersey Law Journal*, **http:// www5.law.com/nj/index.shtml/**. The New Jersey courts section umbrellas both court calendars and summaries of recent decisions, linked to their full text.

The articles archives (which begin November 1, 1999) are freely searchable by keyword. An e-mail or fax alert service is available that summarizes state, federal, and administrative decisions.

Substantial portions of the *New York Law Journal* are freely available online at http:// www.nylj.com/. These include top legal stories, features targeted at young or solo lawyers, courts' and judges' rules, and decisions of interest in New York state and federal courts.

Content from *The Legal Intelligencer* and *Pennsylvania Law Weekly* is available at Law.com's Pennsylvania site, **http://www.law.com/pa**, formerly known as PaLawNet. The site archives articles from both print publications, along with a database specializing in settlements and verdicts. The main attraction, though, is immediate access to decisions from a variety of courts in the state (Supreme through Commonwealth, with slip opinions also available from a handful of county courts of common pleas), as well as the Eastern District of Pennsylvania, the Third Circuit, and the U.S. Supreme Court. It also has legislative news, profiles of judges and lawyers (for checking up on your adversaries), and a pocket guide to local practice. Much of the site is accessible only to registered subscribers. A 30-day trial is available.

TexLaw has also given up its name with the Law.com site redesign and now resides at **http://law.com/tx/**. It gives all visitors headlined opinions and articles, a "super-site" of state bar-approved CLE programs, five regional directories of—and a newsletter about—expert witnesses, contact information for state and federal courts and agencies, and IPO Watch, which reports on the law firms handling public offerings. Subscribers also get the full text and summaries of recent appeals decisions, a daily e-mail alert summarizing the latest opinions, and articles from the *Texas Lawyer*. Subscriptions cost $249 for a year (or $60 for *Texas Lawyer* subscribers); a free thirty-day trial is available.

Midwestern Publications

At **http://www.lawbulletin.com/**, Law Bulletin Publishing Company posts one timely article from three of its print offerings, the *Chicago Daily Law Bulletin*, *Chicago Lawyer*, and *Illinois Real Estate Journal*. Each periodical's online home (including subscription information) is accessible from this URL. Cover stories from the company's biweekly *Minnesota Real Estate Journal* are online at **http://www.mrej.com/**.

Lawyers Weekly

Lawyers Weekly not only has a massive Website, which was discussed in the general legal news section, but it has put its seven state papers online as well, spotlighting Massachusetts, Michigan, Missouri, North Carolina, Ohio, Rhode Island, and Virginia law. The top page of each displays summaries and articles on stand-out rulings and legislative moves; the full text of selected feature articles is also accessible from *Lawyers Weekly*'s home. The state paper sites link to resources and cases in the jurisdiction, as well. (Chapter 5, "Locating Caselaw," spotlighted the opinion archives at each *Lawyers Weekly* state paper site.) You can subscribe electronically to the print publications from their sites. A subscription includes access to the nonpublic features of the Website, such as the articles archive, daily e-mail alerts of new decisions, and, in some states, Supreme Court dockets. The top page of each paper's site contains clear, easy-to-find links to every other *Lawyers Weekly* publication. Use table 14.1 to go directly to the publication site for your jurisdiction.

Table 14.1: *Lawyers Weekly* Newspaper Sites

Publication	URL
Massachusetts	http://www.masslaw.com/
Michigan	http://www.michlaw.com/
Missouri	http://www.missourilaw.com/
North Carolina	http://www.nclawyersweekly.com/
Ohio	http://www.ohiolawyersweekly.com/
Rhode Island	http://www.rilawyersweekly.com/
Virginia	http://www.virginialaw.com/

After a couple of virtual skims through the publications we've just explored, you'll settle on a few for regular sampling. Staying current with the real world is necessary for keeping up with the profession, and it's certainly efficient (and even fun) to do it online.

The Internet facilitates another way of gaining perspective. The next chapter discusses how to locate colleagues, experts, and even friends and family online.

15
Locating Lawyers & Other Helpful People

When I was an associate at a law firm, I took for granted being able to walk a few steps out my door, stick my head in someone else's office, and launch into a conversation. Though at times those visits were just to shoot the breeze, they often involved a good deal of brainstorming, too.

My experience was not unusual. Bouncing ideas off colleagues is one of the time-honored traditions of the legal profession. Put a couple of lawyers in a room and sooner or later (even, I'm ashamed to admit, at a party), they will end up talking business. Invariably, somebody will bring up a problem he's working on, and everyone within earshot will throw in his or her two cents' worth. We can't help it. Lawyers love to give advice, but even more, we love to show off what we know, especially around each other.

The dynamic is a great resource. Since everybody sees things from a slightly different perspective, discussing questions with other lawyers can broaden or shift your take on a subject. Sometimes they know the answer outright; other times they merely point you in a direction, intentionally or not. Even casual comments can catalyze you into recognizing problems or solutions that hadn't occurred to you before. And every once in a while, the people you're talking to agree with your conclusion.

Stumpers do arise, though. It does happen that you come across a question nobody in your office has dealt with (even if they won't admit it!). And what about people who work alone, as I do? Flipping through the Rolodex and trying to corner colleagues on the phone is the usual response.

Make that: the low-tech response. And what's the high-tech? Logging on, of course. Thanks to the Internet, you can help yourself to the know-how and experience of attorneys all over the country—all over the world, in fact. You can find colleagues to hire or refer matters to in other jurisdictions. You can locate expert witnesses, court reporters, document management services, and anybody else you want, even a long-lost pal from junior high. In this chapter, I'll show you where and how to accomplish all of these tasks.

You Have the Technology

The tools to pull off all these marvels are already at your fingertips. Mailing lists, Website forums, and newsgroups are the avenues to kicking questions around with other attorneys, while three different types of Web pages are useful for finding people.

- Bar associations and other organizations are the first valuable source of leads.
- Specialized online directories put you in touch with listings of attorneys and other service providers.
- General directories will give contact information—an e-mail, street, or mailing address, and sometimes all three—for just about anybody.

I'll examine these resources one at a time, starting with mailing lists.

Mailing Lists

Set aside your notion of what the term means when paper and postage are involved. Online mailing lists have a completely different set of definitions, rules, and workings.

An electronic mailing list is a group of people who exchange messages, by e-mail, on a specific, narrow topic. With easily more than 70,000 lists online, the topic can be anything: evidence, practicing law in a particular jurisdiction, TV shows, popular performers, homebrewing—anything.

When a member has something to say, he doesn't actually send a message to every single person on the list. Messages go instead to the list's e-mail address, from which it is then distributed, either manually or automatically, to everyone who has subscribed to the list (including the original sender).

Technically messages are supposed to be relevant to the topic of the list. If the list has a moderator, messages must be relevant for anyone to see them besides the owner of the list, who has total say over what gets distributed. As a general rule list members pose or answer questions, discuss and react to each other's comments, and pass on interesting news or URLs. On lists without a moderator, off-the-subject comments do slip in, like jokes and chain letters and even personal news, as members get to know each other. As a courtesy, the subject heading should reveal when a post is heading off course, so that uninterested members may delete it without bothering to read it. Still, the level of relevancy stays high on many lists, especially the law-related ones. And if a member crosses the line with inappropriate or abusive posts, the owner has the power to remove him (if social Darwinism doesn't force him out first).

Mailing lists are by subscription. Some are restricted access and require authorization to join. (An example would be an organization that distributes a list only to its members.) Regardless of the type of list, the subscription process is the same. You subscribe by sending an e-mail message containing specified language in either the subject line or the body of the message. Each of the sites mentioned in "Where the Lists Are" below will give you the magic language for its lists. Unlike a magazine subscription, you can quit a mailing list, without penalty, at any time, by sending the appropriate unsubscribe message.

Some lists offer the alternative of subscribing to a digest, which will send you one large message, usually daily or weekly, containing all the posts since the last digest. If you're more interested in monitoring a particular topic than commenting on it, this option may save you some time. It will definitely save you aggravation if the list you are joining is active. The first time you find 250 messages from one source waiting in your mailbox, your interest in staying on the list that sent them will come up for immediate reevaluation. Granted, a deluge this extreme has happened to me only with hobbyists' lists (and you'd better believe I jumped ship, each time it happened). Most of the professional ones I subscribe to have fewer than twenty messages a day, and some don't even have that many in a month. Legal lists do tend to be less troublesome than others, because the members use them as a professional resource—which means they usually don't bother posting irrelevant chatter.

One problem that legal lists aren't immune to is the occasional mechanical glitch. You may get multiple copies of the same message. You may send an unsubscribe message and continue receiving mail from the list for days. And you will, without fail, receive one cry for help after another from people having trouble getting off the list.

The cause is not human error—at least, not usually, and rarely on the part of the list owner. Although there is always a person somewhere in charge, most mailing lists are actually managed by a computer program called a listserver. A listserver is an automated process for adding people to the list, taking them off, and distributing messages. When you send a message to a listserver, keep in mind that you are talking to a computer program. A program understands only what it's been told to recognize. If you use language that differs from the canon in the slightest—by as little as a letter—a listserver will not process your request. Instead it will return your e-mail and say it didn't understand.

A listserver comes in three main varieties: Listserv, Majordomo, and, less commonly, Listproc. The only critical difference among them, from the subscriber's perspective, is the language you have to use to send them commands. Fortunately, it is not necessary to memorize the syntax differences. Website directories of mailing lists will spell out the exact language for subscribing to each list. All you have to do is follow the instructions. In many cases, that means entering your name in a box and pressing a button, because subscription boxes are increasingly being offered as an alternative to signing up by e-mail.

Be sure to turn off your mail signature before you send a command to a list-server. If you don't, the signature file may confuse the program.

> *If you're going offline for any length of time (but definitely a week or longer), consider unsubscribing from active lists before you go, then signing up again when you come back. Otherwise, there'll be more than mounds of letters and magazines waiting on your desk; there may be hundreds of posts in your e-mail box as well. If your system is set up to send an automatic reply that you are out of the office, unsubscribing is a must; if you don't, you could alienate the entire list, because it will receive that reply every single time someone posts.*
>
> *Also, unsubscribe from all your lists if your e-mail address changes, then sign up again using the new address.*

Where the Lists Are

Finding general interest mailing lists can be tricky, because there is no central posting place. When it comes to law-related lists, though, the situation is different—and how. Many law sites amass addresses and subscription instructions for all sorts of legal lists. A few of these pages take an encyclopedic approach. I'll explore some of these in a moment. Others spotlight lists that are associated, either because they cover related topics or come from the same organization as the page. Two examples of this type are Tennessee Criminal Law's searchable stockpile of criminal-law related lists at **http://www.tncrimlaw.com/crimlist.html** and Cyberspace Law's index at **http://www.jmls.edu/cyber/discuss.html**.

While you're wading through mailing list options, let me single out three that may get buried. Each specializes in legal resources on the Internet. The reason for the excitement? They're the ultimate low-maintenance research tool. If you'd like to keep abreast of online developments without having to look for them yourself, these will drop them right into your mailbox; all you have to do is read. (The first two are singled out as Essential Bookmarks in chapter 4, "Setting Up Your Online Library.")

LLRXBuzz is Tara's weekly look at the latest developments in sites and resources of interest to lawyers. Most address legal research, but a few involve peripheral topics that might be useful. Subscribe and read back issues at **http://www.llrx.com**. The ABA's Site-tation is another announcement-only list, which passes on URLs that the compiler chose to spotlight. (Frequency varies.) The scheme works for me—in every issue I find many sites worth a look, and several I end up keeping. (Subscribe through your browser by using the form at **http://mail.abanet.org/archive/site-tation.html**.) The third must-have is Net-Lawyers, a moderated, participatory list that discusses Internet resources and issues. (To subscribe, send a message to listserv@peach.ease.lsoft.compton. The body of your message should contain only the words: subscribe net-lawyers [your name].)

> *Do not trash subscription confirmations. These will tell you everything you need to know about posting messages, unsubscribing, and getting in touch with the list administrator. In every case, they will give you two key e-mail addresses. One you will use to send messages to all the other people on the list; the other is for subscribe, unsubscribe, and help commands. Save these confirmations. If you don't, you may well end up posting one of those annoying "How do I get off this list?" messages. If your mail reader allows it, set up a special mailbox for each list you join, and put the subscription confirmation there.*
>
> *And speaking of mailboxes, here's another tip: If your reader has a filters feature, you can tell it to send all incoming messages from the list directly into its special mailbox. That way they will all be in one compact place, when you take the time to read them.*

Law Lists
http://www.lib.uchicago.edu/~llou/lawlists/info.html
If you haven't stopped by this mother of all list sites yet—as recommended in chapter 4, "Setting Up Your Online Library"—go! The University of Chicago database is enormous and, fortunately, searchable. Enter a word or two describing an area of your practice, and the engine will spit out all the related lists. Two more fun facts about the database: it includes announcement-only lists and journals, and it's available in Spanish (entirely) and French (partially). On top of that, the site has clear instructions, and the searchable portion of the database is continuously updated. (For the browsable section, the site discloses when it was last updated.) If you'd rather approach Law Lists' database by scanning a list of practice areas, use Hieros Gamos's topical index at **http://www.hg.org/listservs.html**.

LawGuru
http://www.lawguru.com/subscribe/listtool.html
Overwhelmed by choices? LawGuru has combed through the multitudes and singled out more than 600 lists (not just legal, but also about art, business, computers, humor, music, news, and other topics)—and devised a mailing list manager

that will sign you up for multiple lists at once. Figure 15.1 shows some of the lists available through the manager. This site is run by the California firm of Eslamboly & Barlavi.

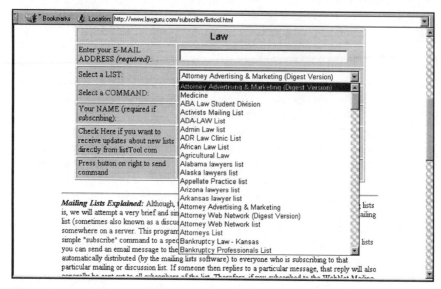

Figure 15.1: LawGuru.com's legal mailing list manager.

What if you want a list that's not focused on a legal issue? The need may well come up in your practice. Mailing lists can be useful for background research—if you want to learn about a specific industry, say, or make of a car, or some other arcane but real-life subject. (Too, the day may come when a personal interest sets you thinking about subscribing to a list of fellow afficionados.)

To find lists on all sorts of topics, try LISZT's directory of more than 90,000 lists at **http://www.liszt.com**. It's searchable by keyword and has a browsable topic list, too. Another option is CataList, **http://www.lsoft.com/lists/listref.html**, which catalogs the more than 33,000 public listservs.

Getting Answers without Posting Questions

Do you have a question you're thinking of posting to a list? You may not be the first person who's posed it. Many mailing lists archive their posts and sometimes a question-and-answer document called FAQ (frequently asked questions). The answer to your question may be waiting for you there.

Granted, this is a hit-or-miss proposition. Not all mailing lists have archives, but many of the legal ones do. Some of them are archived on the Web, which means you can get to them with your browser and not bother with sending letter-perfect commands.

The first place to look is the subscription confirmation message. It may tell you whether—and where—the list is archived. If it doesn't give a URL, that's not the end of the story. The next thing to do is to look at the information about the list on Law Lists. If a Web archive exists, Law Lists ought to mention it and give the URL. Another place to look is Washburn University School of Law Library's archive, which appears on the Web Law Lists and Discussion Groups page at **http://www.washlaw.edu/listserv.html**. Or you could post a message to the list asking whether an archive exists and where it is.

Before I talk about the specifics of communicating with people on the Internet (at the end of the chapter, starting with the section on Netiquette), let's look at the other avenues for linking up with people online.

> *If unwanted solicitations start flooding your e-mail box, use your mail reader's filter function to keep these annoyances out of your sight. I set my filters up to trash all messages from senders whose names contain the domain name or the entire address of repeat offenders. (Certain domains are notorious; you'll develop a list all too quickly.) You'll need to set up a filter for each name or address. The inconvenience of setting up filters is minor compared to the aggravation of deleting unwanted message after message. The filter function can also help you organize mail that you do want, by the way. If you want to keep all your messages on a specific topic in one folder, program a filter to move them automatically for you.*

Web or Discussion Forums

Web forums used to be few and far between. They are increasingly common at sites that package themselves as an online community or meeting place. The term is used for a Web page that posts messages discussing specific topics. Sometimes this type of site goes by the name of message board or bulletin board. I haven't found a freestanding one yet; in the legal field, at least, most Web forums are associated with special interest sites, and all the discussion topics are related to that interest. They work simply. Click on a topic heading, and you'll usually get an index of the messages and a form that lets you post, as well.

An example is the WebEthics discussion forum on Legalethics.com's page at **http:// www.legalethics.com/webethics.htm,** The form for posting to the WebEthics forum appears in figure 15.2.

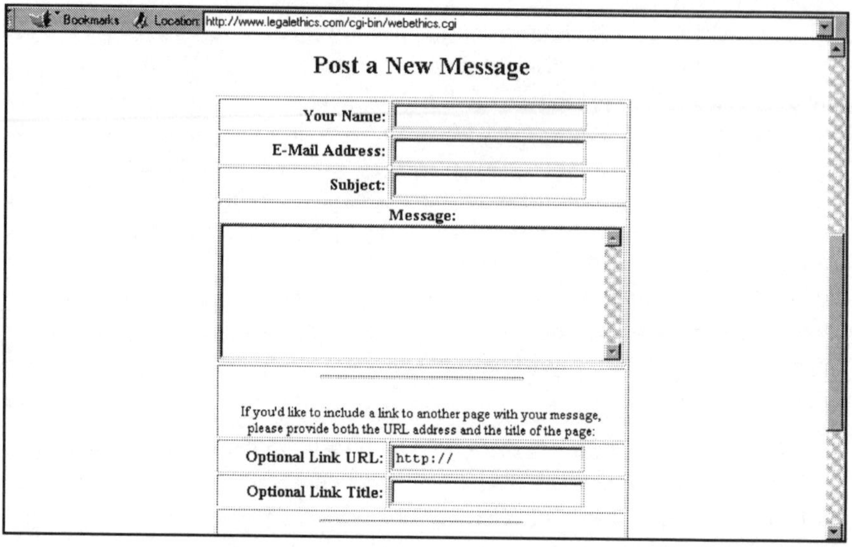

Figure 15.2: Use this form to post a new message to the WebEthics discussion forum.

Two sites with forums on a variety of legal topics are FindLaw and Pro2Net. FindLaw's Legal Minds, **http://www.legalminds.org/,** breaks its message boards into such categories as legal subjects, geographic areas, research, technology, and careers. Each category encompasses a number of narrower topics; in each instance, the page discloses the number of posts and indicates how many are new.

Newcomer Pro2Net, **http://legal.pro2net.com/,** a hub for online legal, accounting, human resources, and financial services communities, launched its legal forums at the beginning of 2000 with seven topics: anti-trust, contracts, government regulation, international law juries, legal software, and private practice. In addition to a search engine, this site has the welcome practice of posting excerpts from selected messages (usually requests for advice or information), which give a preview of the level of discussion in the forums. Early indications are that the level is both serious and intelligent.

Newsgroups

Newsgroups are message discussion groups that live in a free-for-all region of the Internet called Usenet. In a sense, they work like mailing lists. Individuals post messages (called articles, in this context) asking questions, making comments or replying to previous posts. The messages don't go to mailboxes, though; you have to use a newsreader program to view them. (Go back to chapter 2, "Introduction to the Basic Tools," for a refresher on using the newsreader function of the browser.) Postings do not stay online indefinitely, but are automatically cleared out periodically, usually after a week.

Tens of thousands of these groups exist, each organized around a single topic. Very few have anything to do with law. (Hold that thought.) As with a mailing list, you have to subscribe to read newsgroups. None require permission to join. (Hold that thought, too.) Some are moderated, however, which means that all articles go to the moderator, who decides which get posted in the group. Whether you can subscribe to a particular list depends on your Internet service provider and the capacity of your newsreader program. Since the numbers have mushroomed, some providers channel only a selected portion of Usenet as part of their basic service. Getting access to all of the groups (or the "full news feed") usually requires a request (though not necessarily any extra cost), not to mention a newsreader that can handle the full feed.

But don't knock yourself out on Usenet's account. Having introduced you to them, I'll be honest: newsgroups have limited usefulness in legal research. First off, there just aren't that many of them. Check out the pickings for yourself. The Legal Domain Network at **http://www.kentlaw.edu/lawnet/lawnet.html** will give you access to law-related regions of Usenet. It's read-only, so you can't post, but you can always subscribe through your newsreader if you find a group you like.

The real problem, though, is the nature of the beast. Newsgroups are a hotbed of free-flowing expression—sometimes obsessive; frequently misguided or misinformed; often impassioned, to the point of ranting; and occasionally abusive, argumentative, and offensive. Are these qualities you look for in a legal resource? My point exactly. Which is not to say you won't ever find helpful information in newsgroups. Just keep in mind that a good portion of the articles will be opinion, and not fact. Of the others, a discouraging percentage will be commercial solicitations that have nothing to do with the topic. This brings up another discouraging fact of Usenet life: if you post to a newsgroup, the e-mail address in your article becomes public knowledge—where it will be picked up by a never-ending stream of bulk e-mailers.

> *To ward off bulk e-mailers, slightly alter the reply to-address in your newsreader settings, such as by replacing "@" with "[at]." This will effectively vaporize mail sent to an address picked up from the header from one of your newsgroup posts. Put the same altered address in your signature, to get around any spider or other automated program that searches entire messages for e-mail addresses. So that people who have actually read your post will be able to reply to it, put an explanation in your signature explaining how to correct the address as disclosed.*

The problem of irrelevant ranting does go away with moderated lists, such as misc.legal.moderated. Still, there is no guarantee that posts are coming from people who work in or are familiar with the legal field. A lot seek answers to personal problems; it's not uncommon to come across post after post wanting advice on filing for divorce or bankruptcy.

One type of newsgroup sidesteps all these problems: ones with the prefix "clari." This is short for Clarinet, a news distribution service. No matter what the rest of the name is, you can rely on two comforting constants with a clari newsgroup: The contents will consist only of articles posted by that organization, not by readers (and definitely not by spammers—about which more in the Netiquette section), and the contents will consist only of news reports (unless it's a humor group, of course). A few law-related Clarinet groups you may want to sample are clari.news.usa.law, clari.news.usa.law.supreme and clari.usa.law. If your newsreader doesn't recognize Clarinet names, check with your Internet service provider about getting a full news feed.

To be fair, I'll grant newsgroups one other area of potential help in our field: fast access to information on time-sensitive subjects. There's a way to get it without dealing with all the posts: search a group's archives. The best known newsgroup archive is Deja.com, formerly know as Deja News. Its Power Search feature, at **http://www.deja.com/home_ps.shtml**, supports Boolean searching and a number of other refinements; on top of this, it's self-explanatory and extremely easy to navigate. You can also search the Legal Domain Network, to limit the field to legal sites.

The Big Ear's Listening

Here's an odd hybrid resource: The Big Ear at **http://barratry.law.cornell.edu:5123/notify/buzz.html** tracks a hodgepodge of legal mailing lists and newsgroups, extracts messages that refer to legal resources on the Web, then links to both the message and the resource. Listings go off after a week. The top of the page discloses what the Ear is currently listening to.

Professional Associations on the Web

Professional associations, national and state, are using the Web as a point of contact with their members. These sites are more than repositories of information about membership, CLE, and bar programs and meetings; they teem with data, resources, and leads that have great value to you, whether or not you're a member yourself. If you're trying to figure out what to do with a problem that is outside your jurisdiction—or your ken—these sites can put you in touch with organizations and people who may be helpful.

A great starting place for finding help is the ABA Network, the American Bar Association's home on the Web at **http://www.abanet.org/**. Scour the subpages of the ABA's various sections, committees, task forces, and other entities (more than 2,200). Then read articles from the *ABA Journal* and other books and publications. A visit to the Discussion Groups Catalog is a must; from it you can join mailing lists on a spectrum of topics. Closed groups require ABA membership, but the open ones do not, and there are many of them. The Network also links to Websites for national, international, state, and local bar associations at **http://www.abanet.org/lawlink/associations.html**. Because it is one long list, organized geographically, the ABA site will show you at a glance the scope of organizations that are online.

> The ABA's Section of Legal Education and Admissions posts law licensing requirements for each state at **http://www.abanet.org/legaled/baradmissions/bar.html**.

If all you want is a URL for a specific group, head for FindLaw's simple index at **http://www.findlaw.com/06associations/index.html**. National, state, local, international, and specialty bar associations are all there, for the clicking. What are you likely to find? Anything from the Federal Bar Association (**http://www.fedbar.org/**) to the National Asian Pacific American Bar Association (**http://www.napaba.org/index.html**) to the Lawyer Pilots Bar Association (**http://www.lpba.org/**)—and a multitude of special interest organizations, like the American Civil Liberties Union (**http://www.aclu.org/**), and utility industry groups. (Plug in to the full range of them at The Utility Connection, **http://www.utilityconnection.com/**.) Of the official state bars, all but New Jersey are online, too. Most of these pages have membership guidelines and requirements, lists of seminars and meetings, and, usually, information and links on all sorts of topics (including legislation in progress) related to the focus of the association. Some offer online CLE programs as well.

Online Directories

Sometimes you want to locate a specific person. It doesn't matter whether you're looking for a lawyer who handles divorces in Pennsylvania, or a court reporter in San Francisco, or even a long-lost law school buddy in you're not sure what city.

Odds are you can track them down online. Two main types of resources will help you do this. The first is the equivalent of a professional directory; the second is like a phone book. Both will give you some way to reach the people you're seeking—at least a phone number and address, and often e-mail and home page contact information, as well.

Attorneys

When you go into a library to look up an attorney, what book do you open? You can engage in the same automatic behavior on the Web. Martindale-Hubbell is online, here with the Lawyer Locator at **http://www.martindale.com/locator/home.html**. Martindale-Hubbell's listings and ratings of more than 900,000 lawyers and firms worldwide are searchable by name, firm, location, area of practice, and a number of other parameters. The Locator's database includes corporate law departments, U.S. government agency staffs, and law school faculties. The site also hosts firm and lawyer Web pages.

If you prefer West's Legal Directory, there's no need to change allegiance. West's listings are online, too, at **http://www.lawoffice.com/**. The online Legal Directory has streamlined its search options since it moved to the consumer-oriented LawOffice.com. The primary query boxes require selecting an area of practice ("all categories" is one) and a city or territory. It's also possible to find a lawyer in the directory by law school, firm size, keywords, government agency, or corporation. This site also hosts firm home pages.

Experts, Consultants, & Support Services

You don't have to look far for online directories of expert witnesses, consultants, and support services of all kinds. One caveat: The appearance of a name in a directory or index is not necessarily a recommendation. Many online directories contain paid listings, much like Yellow Pages. It's always prudent to look into how listings got into any directory you consult.

FindLaw, **http://www.findlaw.com/13experts/index.html**, groups experts and consultants into nearly a dozen browsable indexes. Directories lead the list, which also includes alternative dispute resolution resources; recruiters; expert witnesses; incorporation, intellectual property, economics, or management services; litigation support; and real estate. FindLaw does not limit listings to the United States, so this is a good place to come if you need an expert in (or familiar with) another country. There is no indication that anyone has paid to be in FindLaw's index; it would be contrary to the rest of the site's set-up if anyone has.

Hieros Gamos at **http://www.hg.org/ex_sel.html#exm** is exceptional in many ways. The scope is the first. Once again, Hieros Gamos has among the most toys on the block. Unlike many expert directories, it will search for an organization by name. It has categorized the database with mind-boggling specificity, from accident reconstruction to zippers. It also splits offerings into expert listings (businesses that regularly advertise in publications) and a searchable self-listing database. This is noteworthy for two reasons: the experts had to provide credentials but did not necessarily pay to be included. (Basic contact information is free, while posting credentials triggers a fee.)

The entire National Directory of Expert Witnesses, which Claims Providers of America has published for thirty-five years, is available free of charge at **http://www.claims.com/**. The database contains more than 1,200 experts in some 400 technical, medical, and scientific fields. The database is searchable by keyword, category, or expert/company name.

The membership database of the National Registry of Experts is freely searchable at **http://www.expert-registry.com/**. An unusual feature is providing statistics about each expert's experience, such as number of times in arbitration, mediation, or trial, types of cases, and the percentage split between plaintiff's and defense work.

Consolidated Consultants Company maintains a freely searchable database of medical and technical consultants—and their curriculum vitae—at **http://www.freereferral.com/**. Requirements for inclusion in the listings include litigation experience and availability for both plaintiff's and defense work.

It's hard to beat the ease of use of the Noble Group's advertising directory at **http://www.experts.com/**. You can search the database of experts, consultants, and speakers (and links to their home pages) by a combination of name, topic, location, and even zip codes. Don't limit inquiries to strictly legal matters; this database includes consultants on art, investments, and, of all things, weddings.

> To survey directories of experts or association pages on the Web for yourself, browse through the one-page index at ***http://www.nocall.org/experts.htm***.

The Expert Pages at **http:/expertpages.com/** indexes its encyclopedic listings by topic; to get to them, just click on a heading. When you reach a subheading, you will be asked to select a state from either a list or a map. Because the site allows experts to list themselves under more than their home state, don't be surprised if a geographical approach gives more than you expect. Press "Texas," for example, and then "chemists," and a long list of out-of-staters will dominate the resulting contact information. Experts who have chosen to list themselves under every state appear under the National Experts heading.

For more than expert witnesses, an option are the directories at ExpertFind, **http://www.expertfind.com/directory/**, which contain listings for business, financial, and computer consultants, mediators, private investigators, speakers, dentists, and mental health professionals. Membership is required for inclusion in the listings, but not for browsing them. According to the site information, the experts listed in the database were invited to join.

Lawinfo.com's Legal Industry Directory at **http://lawinfo.com/** will get you to lawyers, expert witnesses, and an array of support businesses (court reporters, process servers, paralegals, and so on). The search query boxes for each type of business allow you to specify a category, state, or company name. The page doesn't reveal the size of the database, though, and while there are a large number of listings, they do seem to be scattered all over the country.

Many referral services use their Web pages merely to advertise their presence and services. TASA, Technical Advisory Service for Attorneys, does not post its directory online. Instead, it provides a scroll-down menu showing representative areas of expertise (more than 7,800 are in the directory). TASA's home page is at **http://www.tasanet.com/**. Similarly, the research agency LexPert, which provides law professors for project work, merely explains its services at **http://www.lexpertresearch.com/**.

> *Do you have a document that nobody in the office can read? Maybe someone online can do it for you. Translation Services on the Web at **http:// hake.com/languages.htm** lists nearly 600 translators, who can make sense of everything from Afrikaans to Vietnamese. (Eastern European and Asian languages are heavily represented.) InterLingua, **http://www.interlingua.com**, which uses only advanced-degree experts, specializes in legal, business, science, and technology translations from all major Asian, European, and Latin American languages.*

A part-subscription, part-free database is the Expert Witness Network at **http://witness.net/**. (Ninety-nine dollars nets unlimited access for a year; pay-as-you-go use is $25 a day.) If you do a lot of litigation, particularly personal injury, this service is worth investigating. A subscription gives substantially more than contact information; it includes CVs (currently around 2,000), a library of articles, and an online discussion forum. There is no charge to search or browse EWN's index of expert witness home pages, which contains logos and descriptive annotations as well as links.

A membership service with unusual expert witness resources is IDEX, **http://www.idex.com/**, which targets the insurance defense bar. Although members can use IDEX to hire an expert witness—the searchable index lists more than 50,000—the site offers multiple avenues for investigating (and perhaps discrediting) an opponent's witness. IDEX maintains a database of professionals who have faced disciplinary action, as well as trial and deposition transcripts from nearly 600,000 lawsuits that involved expert witness testimony. It will search for articles by or mentioning a witness, or research scientific or medical literature. In addition to a membership fee (currently $375), there is a separate charge for each service, although some are free if no results are produced.

Friends, Family, & Other Folk

What if a nostalgic TV special reminds you of a long-lost friend from junior high and you find yourself wondering where he is? The Internet can help you out. You can find out where he lives, what his address and phone number are (if they're published), and if he's online.

People-finding sites have exploded all over the Web. Many of them use search forms into which you enter first and last names, cities, countries, and sometimes domains. It's also common to offer the option of registering your own data (not always for a charge).

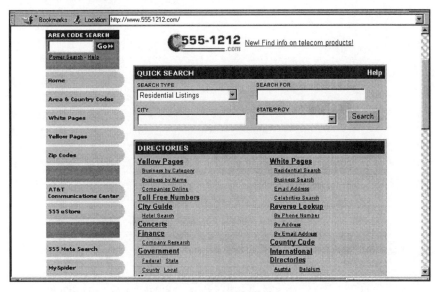

Figure 15.3: Reverse look-up options at www.555-1212.com.

555-1212
http://www.555-1212.com
A simple option is using the same number as long distance directory assistance. The Website with exactly that address (shown in figure 15.3) offers a good deal more than phone numbers and street addresses, though. Area, country, and postal zip codes, e-mail addresses, and business fax numbers are among the resources you

can tap into here. The reverse look-up options will search for the name behind a phone number or street or e-mail address. Although none of the Web phone directories are completely current with phone company listings, a colleague has located people through this site that better-known Switchboard didn't turn up.

Switchboard
http://www.switchboard.com/
This licensee of InfoUSA lets you find individuals and businesses online by using names, cities, states, and organizational affiliations; it will also search for businesses by distance from a location. Type in as much as you know of a name and location, and the search results will give matching names, mailing addresses, and e-mail addresses, when available. If you wish to remove your own listing, follow the modify option under Find a Person. You will need to log in to the site to complete the request. A clear explanation of the procedure appears under Policies, which has an inconspicuous link under the cluster of banner ads at the bottom of the top page.

Infospace
http://www.infospace.com/
This huge site harnesses Yellow Pages, white pages, state and federal government listings, and information from Canada, the UK, and a number of northern European countries. (It also links to a variety of foreign Web directories, organized by continent.) After searching by name and location, you can dial the resulting phone number just by clicking, if you have a touch-tone phone. Infospace will also give e-mail addresses, door-to-door directions to businesses, and fax and toll-free numbers. The reverse look-up page will let you find the name behind residential and business phone numbers, as well as residential and e-mail addresses.

Who Rang?

Curious about a mystery phone number? Try running it through an online criss-cross directory. A residential phone number is enough to retrieve a name and address from InfoUSA.com, which stockpiles white pages nationwide at **http://infousa.com**. (You can also search by name and/or location to get a phone number.) AT&T's reverse directory, AnyWho, is at **http://www.anywho.com/telq.html**; this site also has a directory for 800 numbers. And don't forget the multiple options at InfoSpace's reverse look-up page, **http://www.infospace. com /info/reverse.htm**, which will also investigate residential and e-mail addresses, as well as business phone numbers.

Yahoo! People Search
http://people.yahoo.com/
Use this site to locate a phone number or an e-mail address. Advanced options are available for e-mail searches, which you can refine by domain, former e-mail address, and name of high school, college, or company.

Internet Address Finder
http://www.iaf.net/
Want to know who's behind an e-mail address? Run it through the Internet Address Finder. While you can search by a person's name, organization, or domain, this site will also take an e-mail address and report the account holder's name and physical address, if it's available. (If you don't want your information to be disclosed, take advantage of the Remove Listing feature.) The Finder is also available in Dutch, French, German, Italian, and Portuguese.

Locating & Investigating People Online

A few commercial services offer online access to public records, at a price.

CDB Infotek
http://www.cdb.com/public/
CDB Infotek provides access to more than 1,600 databases of local, state, and national public records. It has set up its databases to address a range of investigations, from finding people or businesses, identifying and verifying their assets, to looking into insurance claims. A series of tools are geared toward pretrial preparation, including obtaining comprehensive reports on an individual or a business. Subscribers may access the databases online or by using custom software; extensive training and support are available. Pricing information is not on the site, but sent on request.

KnowX
http://knowx.com
KnowX sells access to public records from the databases of Information America. Its services include locating people, businesses, or their assets and checking backgrounds, professional licenses, or business name availability. A staggering array of information is available in single databases, such as air- and watercraft ownership, bankruptcy, real property, litigation, assumed name, corporate officers, death, divorce, and military records. Single-state searches of many of the databases are free. Rather than a subscription or set-up fee, KnowX uses both a per-search and a per-record basis for charges, which vary by database.

Merlin Information Services
http://www.merlindata.com/
Merlin grew from a Southern California skip-tracing service to a CD-ROM publisher of public records. Now on the Internet (and based in Montana), it has expanded from a California focus to national investigations. It boasts numerous online databases: a national bankruptcy index; social security number or name and address search; people, residence, or business locators; and judgments, tax lien, and real property records. California public record searches include liquor licenses, corporations, partnerships, Uniform Commercial Code, professional licenses, fictitious business names, Superior Civil Court index, and Los Angeles Municipal Criminal records. Pricing varies; a flat rate subscription is available for national database access. Another site feature is the Ultimate Weapon, a massive, searchable database of California public records, national bankruptcy and residence information, and more. It costs nothing to sign up for an account or run a search with the Ultimate Weapon, but looking at records requires a deposit of at least $100.

1-800-U.S. Search
http://1800ussearch.com/
This publicly traded company offers an array of investigative services. In addition to locating people and performing background checks, it will screen potential employees, research assets, comb court, tax lien, and vital statistics records, and investigate contractors and professionals. The site requires registration and submitting a variety of forms to certify business use and comply with any applicable Federal Fair Credit Act reporting requirements. People locating and a few other "instant" searches—death, bankruptcy, court records, civil judgments—are available for personal use, without the certifications, for a minimal fee.

Communicating Online

You've outfitted yourself with mailing list subscriptions, maybe a newsgroup or two, and e-mail addresses for people you'd like to contact. It's time for a few more new concepts. Communicating with people online, no matter what the means, is not like talking to someone face-to-face or even writing a letter. Before you jump into the fray of a list or a newsgroup or shoot off e-mail, it's prudent to become acquainted with some special ground rules, as well as some guidelines for clear communication.

A Few Words About Netiquette

Special ground rules have developed for communication online. These are loosely called Netiquette, and they make up a code of behavior followed by all honorable Web surfers. Violate it and you'll mark yourself as a neophyte (a "newbie") or a jerk.

This code serves several purposes. It's a way of compensating for the subtext that's present in other forms of communication. Remember that you'll be exchanging words with people who cannot see your expressions, hear your tone of voice, or see the pressure and style of your handwriting. The potential for misunderstandings is enormous, and that leads to another reason for Netiquette. This loose set of rules encourages civil behavior in an arena swarming with anarchy. And it works, believe me. The group mind is quick to jump on infractions and put pressure on offenders.

One more thing—Netiquette holds true all across the Net—in mailing lists, private e-mail, newsgroups, and messages to Websites.

As for what's permissible on a particular list, the subscription confirmation may give an idea. Some will outright ban profanity and personal attacks. Others will hint just by their tone. Assume that courtesy and professional behavior will be expected on any law-related list.

It all boils down to being polite. You won't go wrong following a few specific rules of thumb, though.

Get the Lay of the Land First

When you walk into a group of people for the first time, don't you sit back and observe for a while? Watching the interaction helps you get a handle on the group, who the members are, how they interact, and what sort of behavior is accepted or appropriate. It's an advisable approach to take with mailing lists and newsgroups. Read some posts to get an idea of what goes on before you jump in with a message. The beauty of the Internet is that no one will ever know you're watching. The term for this, by the way, is *lurking*.

Do Unto Others

Before you press the Send key, it doesn't hurt to ask yourself: would I want to receive this? If you have any doubts, rethink your message.

Avoid Commercial Posts

Do not send messages advertising products or services, especially not your own. Instead, ask first whether anyone on the list is interested, or invite inquiries by private e-mail. This is a good idea even if a mailing list specifically permits advertising—which legal lists will not, as a rule.

Post Off-Topic with Caution

It doesn't hurt to take the same approach with anything that veers off topic. Even if you're sure it'll delight the rest of the list, ask first.

One category of posts you can eliminate altogether: those urgent messages that announce dire or heart-wrenching news and implore you to forward them to as many people as possible. (Just about every virus warning is by definition in this category. So is anything that claims any major corporation will award money for each person who receives the message.) A lot of these are outright wrong, while others have picked up distortions along the way. If one interests you enough to consider passing it on, investigate it first. If it says that more information is on a Website, visit the URL. Also, see if the message is on the list of commonly circulating hoaxes compiled on the Department of Energy's Computer Incident Advisory Capability Internet Hoaxes page at **http://ciac.llnl.gov/ciac/ CIACHoaxes.html**. Even if the message checks out, don't send it to a law list. You'll be doing your colleagues—and your reputation—a favor.

> **Flaming Spam?**
>
> It's not something you'll want to taste, but you may indulge in it without knowing. Each word is part of the peculiar jargon that Web surfers have adopted. To *flame* is to make abusive, insulting, nasty statements to or about someone. *Spam* is a message, usually unsolicited and commercial, distributed by mass mailing—like the multilevel marketing ads you trash from your mailbox every morning. Both words do double duty as noun or verb, and the second generally leads to the first. (Spam, and ye shall be flamed.) You do not want to deploy either, except to describe someone else's behavior.

Tips for Clear Communication

The absence of facial and vocal expressions fosters misunderstandings. Going overboard to make yourself clear helps. So do these concepts.

Be Concise
You don't have time to type tomes, and don't presume your recipients have time to read them, either. Get to the point, fast.

Don't Shout
How can you shout if no one can hear you? Easily—and probably unknowingly. Online, typing in all capitals, LIKE THIS, is called *shouting*. Emphasizing something isn't the problem; it's the way you go about it. Surrounding a word with asterisks like *this* is one acceptable convention. Sandwiching the word with _lines_ is another.

Be Precise
No matter what the recipient—a list, a group, or a person—use a clear, specific subject line when writing a message. On lists and groups, your message will more

quickly get the attention of people who might be able or inclined to help. In private correspondence, the practice is a courtesy that respects the recipient's time. "Need tax accountant in Florida," for example, is a more effective subject line than "Accountants" or "Help!"

In the message itself, try to put what you want in one introductory sentence—whether it's a referral to a business transactions attorney in Oregon or details about a new software program. People commonly scan postings (you will soon, too) and glaze over ones with subjects that aren't immediately self-evident. If you've already looked for an answer, mention that. If someone referred you to the recipient, mention that as well.

If you post to a list or group and want responses to come back directly to you, rather than to all of creation, specifically ask for reply by private e-mail.

Be Polite

I always thank people in advance when I post a question to a list or newsgroup. If someone goes to the trouble of responding to a post or a direct e-mail request, thank them.

Understand the Abbreviations

To eliminate time-consuming typing, the Internet has spawned a host of symbolic shortcuts for recurring phrases and reactions. Table 15.1 contains common acronyms that you'll encounter.

Table 15.1: Common E-Mail Acronyms

Acronym	Meaning
BTW	By the way
IMHO	In my humble opinion
LOL	Laughing out loud
ROFL	Rolling on the floor laughing

Other abbreviations involve visuals, rather than letters. Emoticons aren't common parlance in professional communications, but you'll run in to them sooner or later somewhere online. These are typed characters arranged in groups—usually sideways faces—to convey emotion. They give the reader an idea of how serious you were about what you just said. They can tone down a statement that could otherwise be interpreted as flaming; they also go a long way to show when you're being sarcastic or flip or wry, or just plain kidding. Silly as they are, they do lessen the potential for trouble and misinterpretation.

Table 15.2 shows a few common emoticons. If smiley faces aren't your style, you could simply type <g> for grin.

Table 15.2: Common Emoticons

Emoticon	Meaning
:-> or :-)	Smile
:-/	Half smile
;-) or ;->	Winking smile
:-(	Frown

Strictly legal questions aren't the only ones that come up in a day's work. The last chapter recommends resources for general research and reference.

16
General Research Resources

Verbal spice can mean the difference between a dry brief and one that makes its points come alive. A number of things can do the trick—uncommon word choices, a dead-on quote, or little-known background details, to name a few. The World Wide Web is a 24-hour library for reference resources that will give you all of these, and more. This chapter will recommend general search engines, as well as online equivalents of reference desks and encyclopedias, all of which will help you get the facts straight. We'll line up a few dictionaries, too, for spell-checker-defying words and foreign language texts. We'll end with a survey of general news and information sources online, from newspapers to broadcast networks.

> *To keep up with the latest sites and tools for the spectrum of research, subscribe to Tara's free weekly ResearchBuzz. (This version has minimal overlap with LLRXBuzz, the legal resource update she compiles for LLRX.com.) Sign up at* ***http://www.researchbuzz.com****, where you can also search the newsletter's archives.*

General Search Tools

The first section singles out some of the most powerful (as opposed to high-visibility) general resources. These sites aren't really useful for legal research of any complexity. General engines (and indexes, for that matter) are not the most efficient avenues for that task. They are quite handy, however, for locating facts and compiling background information. They may also help with matters incidental to your work, such as booking a flight or checking weather conditions at a destination.

All of the following offer two levels of searching: the very basic (just typing in a phrase) and varying types of advanced (which may restrict such parameters as the type of database, type of document, or date of the document). All engines recognize Boolean operators of some kind; if this information is not right next to the query form, a hyperlink to "tips" or "advanced" should take you to it. Instructions, as a rule, are simple and idiot-proof. Designed to read at a glance, they tell you what to do in language that is as concise as most legal documents are not.

Searchable Indexes

Yahoo!
http://www.yahoo.com/
Yahoo! is probably the single best known site on the Web. Everybody goes there, so everybody wants to be listed on it. As a consequence, this searchable subject index is humongous, which makes it a good place to look for sites of organizations, companies, and businesses, among other things. The first level alone is so wide-ranging that it takes up two screens. (A portion of it appears in figure 16.1.) It also has companion pages focusing on children, a few U.S. cities, and more than twenty countries (Canada, France, Germany, Japan, and the United Kingdom among them). Head here when you're unsure where else to begin, because its info pages are a veritable encyclopedia of all the ins, outs, whys, wherefores, how-tos, and you-name-its of the Web.

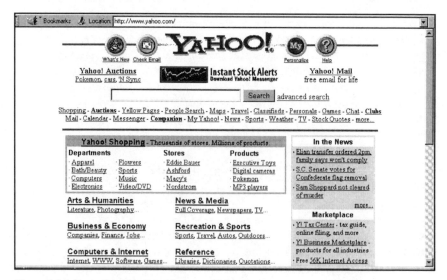

Figure 16.1: Part of the top-level index at Yahoo!

Open Directory Project
http://dmoz.org
This uncluttered, searchable subject index is decidedly low-profile, compared to Yahoo! Its goal is outpace even Yahoo! by compiling the most comprehensive directory of the Web. To keep up with the growth and address changes of sites, this database is maintained by an army of expert volunteer editors, each of whom has responsibility for a narrow category, of which there are nearly 250,000. The top level subject headings run the gamut from art, science, and computers to games, sports, and recreation.

Search Engines

Google
http://www.google.com
The pioneering full-text search engine Google promises rapid, ranked results that match your search query, without the chaff that other engines frequently pick up. The results display cuts out frustration further by excerpting the matching text, with search terms highlighted, so you can judge the nature of a page before loading it. To proceed directly to the highest ranked result, press the "I'm Feeling Lucky" button. This is especially useful when your query consists of a company name or other commonly searched phrase. Google now offers a searchable subject index, too, based on the dmoz.org directory discussed in the previous paragraph.

FAST Search All the Web, All the Time
http://www.ussc.alltheweb.com/
Lightning speed is also a benefit of the FAST Web Crawler. (Running Kathy's name through it turned up 157 results in 0.0774 seconds; Tara's yielded 784 in .1051 seconds.) FAST has set up its database to avoid duplication of pages and has cataloged more than 300 million documents. The advance search options allow filtering by specific words, domains, and more than thirty languages.

Northern Light
http://www.northernlight.com
To heighten the relevancy of search results, Northern Light organizes them by categories, which it calls Custom Folders. The technique allows you to choose the categories that are relevant to your query and bypass unrelated results. Some of the material, Special Collection Documents, comes from publications and requires purchasing. Northern Light would be an excellent resource for obtaining news articles on a specific topic or from specific periodicals. The Search Alert function will send you periodic e-mail notices of new sites on topics you specify; the service is free, but requires registration. Use Business Search for locating industry-related Web pages (including company reports). The Investext Search combs through investment research reports; the Stock Quotes function pulls up the latest information by stock symbol.

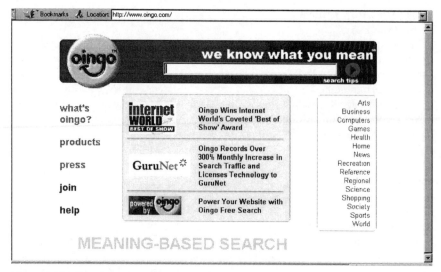

Figure 16.2: Search by a word's meaning at Oingo.

Oingo
http://www.oingo.com
This streamlined engine takes keyword searching to its most useful extreme. Instead of merely looking for the characters in your text, Oingo uses the meaning of the words in your query to locate documents. The process, called meaning-based searching, compares a query against the site's unique lexicon, then generates drop-down menus of possible meanings, from which you select the one to search. The technique cuts out the flood of irrelevant sites that pad search results at many other engines. Oingo's top page appears in figure 16.2.

> *To verify (or discredit) testimony about light conditions, enter a date in the U.S. Naval Observatory's calculator at* **http://aa.usno.navy.mil/AA/data/docs/RS_OneDay.html** *and it will give the time of sunrise, sunset, moonrise, moonset, and twilight, as well as the moon phase.*

Reference Tools

Reference Indexes

The following indexes will lead you to a spectrum of reference resources, from the general to the arcane.

RefDesk
http://www.refdesk.com/
This may well be the most inclusive, comprehensive reference site on the Web. (See figure 16.3.) The jam-packed, but tidy array of links covers every imaginable topic and resource—search engines, reference tools, subject indexes, newspapers, advise sites, exchange rates, chemical element tables, dictionaries, almanacs, people locators, calendars, measurements, geography, translators, even current time on the atomic clock are all accessible from the top page. It also offers query boxes for searching Britannica, *Webster's Dictionary*, *Roget's Thesaurus*, stock quotes, the weather, or AP/Reuters headlines.

Figure 16.3: Some of the resources available at RefDesk.

Research-It!
http://www.iTools.com/research-it/research-it.html
Here you'll find one simple search form after another for virtual dictionaries, biographical data, currency converters, stock tickers, maps, and more. Want the meaning of a foreign word? The translator function goes to and from most European and Slavic languages, as well as Greek, Latin, Chinese, and Japanese. Other language tools include a thesaurus or three, *Bartlett's Quotations*, and engines that will identify a word's language or generate acronyms for it. Research-It! can also track FedEx and UPS packages. From Research-It you can also grab maps, lookup telephone area codes, and browse the CIA Factbook.

Virtual Reference Desk
http://thorplus.lib.purdue.edu/reference/index.html
There's no truth in advertising problem with this feature of the libraries of Purdue University. It's filled with a range of materials similar to a book library. Dictionaries are plentiful, running from Webster's to technical and scientific ones to a translator engine; the foreign language dictionaries include uncommon choices like Estonian, Japanese, and Russian. Check the Maps and Travel Information section for currency exchange rates; look under Science Data for the Periodic Table of Elements and weights and measures conversion tables. Time and Date will get you monthly and yearly calendars, as well as time and date data for different time zones. Looking for government information? Click on "Selected Government Documents" to locate Federal items such as the Code of Federal Regulations and the latest census data. You can also find the IBM Patent Server and the White House home page. (The thorough description of the government links here comes in handy; when you're looking for general federal information, the endless listings on some of the federal clearinghouse sites can be intimidating.)

Internet Public Library Ready Reference Collection
http://www.ipl.org:80/ref/RR/
This collection has pinpointed online reference sources according to their ease of use, quality and quantity of information, frequency of updating, and authoritativeness. The wide-ranging selection of general aids includes almanacs, census data, dictionaries, encyclopedias, genealogical and geographical information, and news. It links to a multi-faceted calendar page, a searchable nonprofit directory, a dictionary of weights and measures, financial calculators, and a currency converter. This site also does double duty as a bit of an encyclopedia: Back on the main page, a variety of reference sources are available on the arts, business, computers, medicine, law, and science, social science, technology, and arts and entertainment.

dictionary.com
http://www.dictionary.com/
One big order of language guides, coming up! Besides the 1913 version of Webster's (with two keyword search forms), you can access several dictionaries of computing, Internet, and hacker's lingo here. In a more traditional vein, you can consult Strunk and White's *Elements of Style*, *Bartlett's Quotations*, and *Roget's Thesaurus*. Read The King's English to reacquaint yourself with utterly proper communication. From dictionary.com you can access 800 on-line dictionaries in 150 languages including The Wordsmyth SAT Dictionary, the 1893 Christian Common Law Institute Dictionary, and alternative dictionaries.

> *Need to calculate something? With more than 10,000, Calculators On-Line probably has some types you may not even realize exist. This bonanza of links to free applications covers car pricing, mortgages, child support, damage awards, title insurance, and many, many scientific and domestic subjects. Browse the index at **http://www-sci.lib.uci.edu/HSG/RefCalculators.html.***

Encyclopedias

For background information, try these encyclopedic sites.

Information Please Dictionary and Encyclopedia
http://www.infoplease.com
Information Please is a full-spectrum reference site with an Almanac, dictionary, and encyclopedia. There's also a browsable subject index that encompasses a wide range of items, including Sports, Business and Economy, Society, and World Information.

Funk & Wagnalls
http://www.funkandwagnalls.com/
Register for free access to the entire Funk & Wagnalls unabridged twenty-nine-volume encyclopedia (complete with multimedia), *Webster's College Dictionary*, and Reuters World News Service, which is updated hourly. You can search these resources separately or all at once.

The World Wide Web Virtual Library
http://www.vlib.org/
This catalog of sites functions much like an online encyclopedia, though it's not one, strictly speaking. It has topical headings on every imaginable subject—AIDS, international security, micro-credit, nonprofit organizations, technology transfer, and even brewing, roadkill, and wine. Each one leads to a full-scale collection of pertinent resources, maintained by differing institutions in association with the WWW Virtual Library.

Encyclopaedia Britannica
http://www.britannica.com/
All thirty-two volumes—plus special Internet editions—of this old standby are now free online, supported by ads. When you search britannica.com you're also searching through the encyclopedia itself, a hand-picked set of Websites, related maga-

zine articles, and books relevant to your topics. That's a lot of ground to cover with one little search.

Dictionaries

The following sites have collected a wide range of dictionaries, from foreign language to the strictly technical.

Dictionaries
http://www-math.uni-paderborn.de/dictionaries/Dictionaries.html
This German site has a variety of dictionaries pairing English with a foreign language. English-German databases are extensive; other available languages include most European tongues, Chinese, Indonesian, Czech, and Halaka. Besides a handful of thesauruses and hacker's dictionaries, the page has rhyming dictionaries (in Swedish, even), Aussie slang, etymology, technical tomes (including an international legal dictionary), and the Unofficial Smiley Dictionary, which decodes the emoticons that pepper e-mail.

OneLook Dictionaries
http://www.onelook.com/
This may be the easiest searchable dictionary online. It's certainly one of the largest, with 2,989,470 words in 593 dictionaries indexed at this writing. (It may not be the *Oxford English Dictionary*, but for a free online resource, it's close enough.) Enter a word in the search form, and OneLook will run it through more than 120 dictionaries at once. Click Browse Dictionaries at the bottom of the page to see the reference works that OneLook uses. You can also select a dictionary from the list and go directly to it. Databases likely to include legal terms are at the top of the stack, under Business Dictionaries. Clicking on More Dictionaries will give you additional sources (such as American Sign Language), and tools to improve your word power.

> The *Oxford English Dictionary* has finally come online, at **http://www.oed.com/**. Access is by annual subscription ($550 for an individual). Network licenses for unlimited users start at $795.

A Web of On-Line Dictionaries
http://www.yourdictionary.com/
Here you will find links to literally dozens of dictionaries in dozens of languages, including specialized dictionaries in English (Agriculture, Chemistry, Botany,

Computing), pointers to other dictionary indexes, and links to other word references like thesauruses and acronym dictionaries. This is an extensive and fast-loading resource.

Wordbot
http://www.wordbot.com/
Wordbot is a robot assistant that looks up translations, definitions, synonyms, and antonyms of words in Web pages. This is a handy tool for getting the gist of a foreign statute. Wordbot treats every single word as a link. To access Wordbot, you have to indicate whether your browser supports JavaScript with frames and/or multiple windows. Once in Wordbot, you select a dictionary database (French to English, for example) and enter the URL of the document that contains the words you want to look up. When the document has loaded, click on any word to get its meaning (or translation). Don't worry about being overwhelmed; Wordbot contains extensive explanations for using it.

Thesauruses

When a word is on the tip of your tongue, consult one of these thesauruses.

Library of Congress Research Tools
http://lcweb.loc.gov/rr/tools.html
Under Thesauri, the Library of Congress has two potentially useful to the legal profession. The Legislative Indexing Vocabulary consists of legislative and public policy subject terms used to index acts of Congress, while the Global Information Network contains retrieval terms used for indexing legislation from around the world. Both databases are searchable.

Roget's Internet Thesaurus
http://www.thesaurus.com/
This one's easy as pie. Enter your word in the search box and press OK. Click on any of the results to get its definition. This site also includes a categorical outline, a "Word of the Day," and a translator to translate text or Web pages.

Literary Reference

Whether you need to add flair to a brief or merely settle an argument (in your own mind or with a colleague), the Internet may once again come to the rescue. Web sites abound with the full text of many a great work of literature. Here are a few useful stockpiles.

Project Bartleby
http://www.bartleby.com/

Calling all English majors and literary buffs—has Columbia University got something for you. The cornerstone of its Project Bartleby is *Bartlett's Quotations*, linked to by several sites already mentioned in this chapter. Herman Melville's *Bartleby the Scrivener* is there, of course, but this searchable database contains much more: *The Odyssey*, F. Scott Fitzgerald's *This Side of Paradise*, Thomas Paine's *Common Sense*, Mary Wollstonecraft's *Vindication of the Rights of Woman*, and verses by the likes of Dickinson, Eliot, Frost, Hopkins, Keats, Sassoon, Wilde, Wordsworth, and Yeats. BartlebyVerse has indexes to American and English Poetry 1250-1989, searchable chronologically, by author, title or first line. The reference section includes the *Columbia Encyclopedia*, *American Heritage Dictionary of the English Language* and *Book of English Usage*, *Simpson's Contemporary Quotations*, and *Roget's II: The New Thesaurus*. Presidential addresses are also on the site, along with the 1922 edition of *Emily Post's Etiquette* and the precursor to the *Fanny Farmer Cookbook*.

Project Gutenberg
http://www.gutenberg.org/

Believe it or not, this project has been around for more than twenty-five years. Its philosophy has always been to make books and other texts as widely available as possible electronically. To ensure this, Project Gutenberg uses what it calls "plain vanilla" ASCII for all of its files, so that they are readable by 99 per cent of software and hardware. The goal is having 10,000 books online by 2001; plans are also in the works for becoming a repository of works in the public domain. The library falls into light literature (such as fables and Lewis Carroll), heavy literature (including the Bible and major novels), and reference texts. "Etexts" are indexed by author or title; you can also find them with a search engine.

The Complete Works of William Shakespeare
http://tech-two.mit.edu/Shakespeare/

Shakespeare gave the legal profession one of its most repeated jibes: "The first thing we do, let's kill all the lawyers." If you're like me and can't keep straight which Henry play the line came from, this site provides the answer, and more. The bards works are divided into four categories: comedy, history, tragedy, and poetry. You can search any or all of them by keyword (which is how you'd pull up a quote), or select a work by name and read it scene by scene. (The quote source is *Henry VI, Part 2*, by the way.)

> *Can't get enough Shakespeare? The Electronic Literature Foundation presents his plays and sonnets at **http://www.theplays.org/**. The Internet Public Library shelves his complete works, with lots of links, at **http://www.ipl.org/reading/shakespeare/shakespeare.html**.*

The Online Books Page
http://digital.library.upenn.edu/books/
More than 10,000 significant English language texts are in this database, which is both searchable and browsable by author, title, or serials. The page contains a subject index and new book listing, as well as special exhibits featuring banned books or books celebrating women authors. Other features include a foreign language archive and special categories, such as dissertations, historical, and religion. This site is a convenient jumping point to many other online repositories (some in other countries and languages); look for a list of links at the bottom of the top page.

News & Information Sources

Where do you get your news? Newspapers, magazines, TV, and radio, right? You're not going to have to change your behavior much to keep up with current events by surfing the Web. Lots of familiar media faces have quite a noticeable Net presence.

You'll find hundreds of thousands of news sources on the Web. If you want more than the highlights listed below, browse the listings in the media directories at **http://www.newsdirectory.com/** or **http://www.News365.com/**. If you're looking for headlines rather than lists of publications and organizations, try a headline aggregator like Moreover, **http://w.moreover.com/**, Yahoo! News, **http://dailynews.yahoo.com/**, or NewsLinx, **http://www.newslinx.com/**.

Court TV Law Center
http://www.courttv.com/trials/
The News section of this glossy site offers virtual immersion in high profile litigation. You can view video highlights of Court TV broadcasts (which requires an MPEG player, downloadable from the site), or read pleadings, depositions, and transcripts from recent key trials. The page also posts legal news from the cable channel's affiliate publications. Look at On the Air for the TV broadcast schedule.

AJR's Newslink
http://www.newslink.org/
Talk about efficient—you can access thousands of magazines, broadcasters, and news services from this one site, which is a collaboration between the *American Journalism Review* and an online research and consulting firm. Yet don't be afraid that the bounty will overwhelm you. Its design gives you a couple of easy routes to the goodies. You can search article archives by keyword, or look at indexes by type of news source, which are then organized by such characteristics as topic or region of coverage. The site also includes links to journalism forums and specialized journalistic discussions.

ABC News
http://abcnews.go.com/
This site is laid out like a splashy magazine and allows you to get your news quickly or in depth. You can eyeball headlines on the top page, or click any to read the full story, which comes full of links to related articles. Go to News Now for pithy summaries of even more major stories (each of which you can read in full, of course). As in a newspaper, there are sections of news, as well, such as world, business, science, and local. With a RealAudio player, you can listen to radio news, too. This site also features videos and an interactive calculator. While you're there, you might as well check the prices of your favorite stock or funds.

CNN Interactive
http://www.cnn.com/
This site follows much the same set-up as ABC's page. One difference is the front-page index of top stories by category, including health, politics, and weather. The Video Vault accents a recent story with QuickTime movie clips, CNNMobile provides news and information for those of you surfing on mobile phones, and Desktop Headlines runs current headlines through a small window on your desktop.

National Public Radio
http://www.npr.org/
NPR updates its site multiple times daily. With RealAudio, you can listen to news broadcasts on the hour. You can also play current shows and archived segments of a number of NPR programs, such as All Things Considered and Morning Edition. This site also links to local NPR stations, some with on the air broadcasting.

World News Connection
http://wnc.fedworld.gov/
This subscriber-based service of the U.S. government facilitates monitoring foreign news sources. It offers full text and summaries of newspaper and magazine articles, TV and radio broadcasts, and nonclassified technical reports from all over the world, translated into English, where necessary, and organized by region. There are six subscription plans for the single user, ranging from $25.00 to $1,000.00 in price. Network pricing is also available.

Newspapers

Have your morning news and coffee at your computer.

Newspapers Online!
http://www.newspapers.com/
Want to see if a paper's online? This index is the place to do it. It's nothing but a clearinghouse of links, organized by geography and focus (such as business,

religious, or college). For the geographic divisions (which are U.S. and non), select a region by clicking on a map or highlighting its name in the nearby pop-up menu.

The New York Times on the Web
http://www.nytimes.com/
You can browse or search the day's edition here at no charge. Register for a subscriber name and password to enter for the first time. Though searching the archives is free, retrieving or printing an article costs $2.50.

The Los Angeles Times
http://www.latimes.com/
The West Coast's newspaper giant channels the day's news into pull-down menus that fine-tune your destination as narrowly as traffic reports or the AP sports wire. What's more, the site is searchable. Register for free to access a Hunter service that retrieves news fitting up to ten selected topics. Searchable archives and a crossword puzzle feature are available as well for a fee.

The Washington Post
http://www.washingtonpost.com/
The Post's daily edition is free for the browsing, but site use is subject to a member agreement. The front page has current market information (including time of posting) from the Dow Jones, Standard & Poor's 500, and NASDAQ. You can search the archives and receive any article published less than two weeks ago, both free of charge. There is a fee for any article more than two weeks old.

The Wall Street Journal Interactive Edition
http://interactive.wsj.com/home
The Journal gives you two weeks to try out its online version for free. Otherwise subscriptions are $59 a year ($29 for print subscribers). It offers plenty of reasons to spring for the added expense: a 14-day searchable archive, an index to market data, a sports section, and lots of audio and multimedia to make the information more interesting than on newsprint. Additional incentives include 24-hour-a-day updates and Barron's Online.

All the components of your personal online law library are in place now. You've assembled a collection of cases, statutes, regulations, and forms. You've set up your mailbox for receiving correspondence and subscribed to a few mailing lists and electronic newsletters. You've stocked a reading room with periodicals and set up a general reference shelf, as well.

These resources are only the beginning. As you use them, you will discover more and more reasons to log on for your work. (Some are in the appendixes, which suggest alternate starting points and online sources for CLE information, job hunting, office management, and general amusement.) Much like our body of law, the Internet is a continuously evolving organism. There's no end in sight for the possibilities it offers for learning, exchanging information, and linking with people, courts, and organizations.

Glossary

Article. A message posted to a newsgroup.

Bookmark. A URL and Web page name saved by a browser; the act of saving a URL and Web page name in a browser. Bookmarking allows you to retrieve a Web page without retyping the URL.

Boolean operators. Symbols used to define the parameters of a database search. Named for George Boole, the father of symbolic logic, Boolean operators tell a search program to look for (or exclude) documents containing specified occurrences of words or word combinations. Examples of Boolean operators are AND, OR, NOT, IF, THEN, and EXCEPT. See chapter 4, "Setting Up Your Online Library."

Browser. A program, such as Microsoft Internet Explorer or Netscape Navigator, that displays documents from the World Wide Web.

Cookie. A statement of the information that a Website detects about your computer, such as the identity of your Internet service provider and of the provider's computer you're being routed through, your browser type, and your location. It may include a password and user name or other identifying details. A cookie is placed onto your computer by the Website and may be read by the same site on later visits.

Downloading. Taking information off the Internet by saving a file to disk or printing it.

EDGAR. The Securities Exchange Commission's Electronic Data Gathering, Analysis, and Retrieval system of electronic public filings.

Emoticons. Groups of typed characters, usually shaped like sideways faces, created from punctuation marks to convey emotion. See table 15.2 in chapter 15, "Locating Lawyers & Other Helpful People," for examples of commonly used emoticons.

FAQ. A list of frequently asked questions (and answers) on a specific topic.

Firewall. A configuration that protects data on a network of computers from outside access or interference.

Flame. To make abusive, insulting, nasty statements to or about someone in an online communication.

FTP. File Transfer Protocol; a means of moving files back and forth between individual computers and online archives.

GIF. Graphics Interchange Format; a type of graphic file.

Gopher. A simple, menu-based means of posting files to the Internet, now rarely used; named after the mascot of the University of Minnesota, where it was developed.

Helper application. An application that a browser launches to read a specific type of file (usually multimedia).

Hierarchical index. A Website that organizes links into multilevel categories and lists, often alphabetical.

Home page (see also: *Web page*). A site on the World Wide Web that displays text and graphics in a browser.

HTML. HyperText Markup Language; codes used to indicate to a browser how to display the text and graphics of Web pages.

http. HyperText Transfer Protocol; the beginning of a Website's URL; indicates that the URL contains a document coded in hypertext.

Java. A programming language, developed by Sun Microsystems, that creates moving text and other effects on Web pages. A Java *applet* is an application that uses Java language to transmit information between your computer and the server. Although they produce somewhat similar effects, Java differs from JavaScript, which is proprietary to Microsoft.

Link. Highlighted text in a Web page that contains an embedded URL and that, when clicked, causes the browser to load the referenced page; also used to refer to the referenced or target page.

Listproc. A type of listserver.

Listserv. A type of listserver.

Listserver. A program that administers a mailing list. A listserver adds and removes subscribers, distributes posts, and manages the formatting and archiving of messages.

Lurking. Reading a newsgroup or mailing list without posting messages.

Mailing list. A group of people who exchange messages, by e-mail, on a specific, narrow topic. Messages on a mailing list are sent to a central address from which they are distributed, usually by automation, to all list subscribers.

Mail Reader. An application for sending and receiving e-mail.

Majordomo. A type of listserver.

Netiquette. The uncodified rules of behavior on the Internet.

Newsgroup. An online discussion forum dedicated to a topic, usually indicated by the group's name; found in a portion of the Net called Usenet.

Newsreader. An application for reading and posting to newsgroups.

PCL. Hewlett Packard Printer Control Language.

PDF. Portable Document Format; a file type used by the Adobe Acrobat Reader.

Plug-in. An application that is added to a browser to enable interpreting, viewing, or playing a specific file type (usually multimedia).
Posting (see also: *uploading*). Moving a copy of a file from your computer onto a site on the Internet.
Push technology. A program that brings Websites and information from Websites automatically to your computer.
RTF. Rich Text Format, a document type read by most word processors.
Search engine. A program that combs a database for occurrences of keywords.
Shouting. In e-mail, typing in all capitals, LIKE THIS.
Signature. Information (such as name, e-mail address, home page URL, etc.) that a mail reader has been programmed to add at the end of outgoing e-mail.
Spam. A message, usually unsolicited and commercial, sent to multiple recipients.
Streaming audio. A sound file that plays as it downloads.
Streaming video. A video file that plays as it downloads.
Surfing. The process of going from page to page on the Web.
Telnet. An application that links your computer to the files of a remote computer, such as a library card catalog.
Thread. A series of messages in a newsgroup or mailing list addressing the same topic, often indicated by the subject line.
Uploading (see also: *posting*). Moving a copy of a file from your computer onto a site on the Internet.
URL. Uniform Resource Locator; the Internet address of a Web, FTP, or Gopher site.
Virus. A bug embedded in an executable program or macro, which corrupts data or applications when the program or macro runs.
Web page (see also: *home page*). A site on the World Wide Web that is displayed in a browser. Also called *Website*.
ZIP. The format of a compressed file, which must be decompressed or "unzipped" to be read or run.

Appendix A
Where to Go When the Connection's Slow

Sometimes a favorite bookmark will let you down. A connection will take forever or be refused. Or you'll access the home page, click on a link, and play a round of computer Solitaire in less time than it takes to bring up the document you're after.

Fortunately, your options aren't limited. It's not like when you're in the library and every single last copy of the book you want is missing from the shelf. If a legal resource is accessible through one Web page, odds are it's also somewhere else online. So if you hit a traffic jam, don't wait it out. When one part of the Web is running slow as molasses, go someplace else. This appendix will outfit you with more starting points for legal and general research, then point out some places just for fun.

Legal Reference Rooms

Besides the starting points and academic law libraries mentioned in the book, here are some alternative sites for legal resources.

All Law
http://www.alllaw.com/
This is a hierarchical index, without a search engine, that groups links under such topics as attorney or bar associations, court reporters, expert witnesses, federal or state courts, legal placement, and state links (which include a good number of municipal codes).

Attorney's Toolbox
http://www.mother.com/~randy/tools.html
Attorney Randy Singer has compiled an index of links to substantive law pages, citation guides, legal forms and dictionaries, job sites, search engines, and people

directories. The layout is practiced-oriented, grouping resources under discovery matters, researching the law of a case, preparing for trial, and discovery or employment matters.

CataLaw
http://www.CataLaw.com/
This is a searchable meta-index of more than 100 catalogs from the United States, Canada, Australia, Germany, Israel, Italy, New Zealand, Sweden, and the United Kingdom. Pull-down menus allow narrowing a search to specific topics or regions.

Counsel Quest
http://www.counselquest.com/
This browsable index (now part of the burgeoning Law.com empire) organizes its materials in the expected broad categories and a few surprising ones, such as archaic laws and humor. Scroll partway down the page for quick access to federal cases, statutes, and agencies, as well as state decisions and legislation. Searchnet (under Legal Research) provides a meta-index of search forms for major engines, people finders, and newsgroup databases.

Counsel Quest offers a unique tool called the Remote Briefcase. If your browser supports JavaScript (as versions 4.0 and above of both Netscape and Internet Explorer do), the Remote Briefcase makes it quicker to go back and forth between pages while you surf. The application keeps two pages running at once; you see them only one at a time, but you can switch between them almost instantaneously (instead of waiting for them to reload).

Emory Law Library Electronic Reference Desk
http://www.law.emory.edu/LAW/refdesk/toc.html
Representative headings of this searchable site are law by country or subject, search engines, career information, journals and periodicals, law firms and lawyers, law schools and education, and reference materials.

The Internet Lawyer Law Library
http://www.internetlawyer.com/start.htm
This is a browsable index that requires extensive scrolling. Headings include general search engines, federal court and legislative sites, and international resources.

Internet Legal Resource Guide
http://www.ilrg.com/
Here you can search federal and state caselaw and jump to federal government Websites. IRLG also offers indexes of state business forms and statutes and of state and federal tax forms, law school rankings and course outlines, and links to Websites of the 250 largest U.S. law firms.

Internet Tools for Attorneys
http://www.netlawtools.com/
Take the Research link for sources of primary materials, legal directories, search engines, and mailing lists.

Jurisline
http://www.jurisline.com
This emerging site offers federal and state case law, the U.S. and New York codes, and access to the SEC's EDGAR database. Check the scope of coverage before searching caselaw here. Supreme Court cases, for example, run only from 1956 to 1999. Registration (which is free) is required to download material.

Jurist
http://www.jurist.law.pitt.edu
Hosted by the University of Pittsburgh School of Law, this education-oriented network offers annotated subject guides edited by tech-savvy law professors. Each guide spotlights related news, books, journal articles, resource pages, legislation, mailing lists, and superior Websites. The reference desk accepts research questions by e-mail.

Katsuey's Legal Gateway
www.katsuey.com
The name may be lighthearted—it comes from the site founder's cat—but the scope of resources targets the serious professional. The category index includes some twenty areas of practice, with particularly extensive (and practical) medical and real estate pointers. Each category's links range from association Websites to pertinent articles to government resources.

LawGuru
http://www.lawguru.com/
Chapter 15, "Locating Lawyers & Other Helpful People," singled out this site's legal list manager. The Legal Research Page links to more than 400 resources and search engines, which you select from a drop-down menu. The Multiple Resource Legal Reference section allows searching a variety of resources individually or simultaneously. (Free registration is required for access.) The Weird Laws link highlights some ill-conceived statutes in the United States and abroad, courtesy of dumblaws.com.

LegalEthics.com
http://www.legalethics.com/index.law
The Practicing Attorney's Home Page has merged with the ethics resources at this page, the Web forum at which received mention in chapter 15, "Locating Lawyers & Other Helpful People." Use pull-down menus to reach indexes of state and federal pages, links to court directories, and a wealth of resources by area of practice.

The Legal Omnibus
http://www.ili.org/Omnibus.html
This index divides its links into development and trade resources (including banks and agencies), public and private international law, general international and U.S. resources (mostly federal and comprehensive), electronic commerce, law and economics, and reference tools.

The Law Engine!
http://www.thelawengine.com/index.htm
Once the site loads and you scroll down a screen, the voluminous headings of this index appear in an easy-to-read chart. Besides the usual federal and state legal categories, there are links to news organizations, dictionaries, law enforcement pages, litigation aids, forms, and many California sites. This is affiliated with the Med Engine! and the Realty Engine! mentioned in chapter 11, "Researching by Topic."

Milbank, Tweed, Hadley & McCloy LLP
http://www.milbank.com/library/ library.html
This firm library site offers a good compendium of links for banking, bankruptcy, corporations, environmental law, intellectual property, litigation, public utilities, securities, tax, telecommunications, transportation finance, and trusts and estates.

Professional City/Esquire Heights
http://www.professionalcity.com
Professional City targets specific industries by grouping prescreened resources in "neighborhoods." The legal one, Esquire Heights, contains an index of area of practice, research aids, and office resources. Research assistance is available, for a fee, through the Cybrarian.

State Jurisdictions

The following sites have a concentration of resources for a particular jurisdiction.

Arizona: Arizona Lawyer's Guide to the Internet
http://www.azstarnet.com/~frey/
This site provides extensive federal and Arizona links, with an emphasis on state and local agencies, records, and publications.

California: NAPALAW
http://www.napalaw.com
Attorney Stephen J. Thomas posts California real estate forms and links to brokers and other professionals. Law Lite spotlights legal and real estate humor.

Florida Law Online
http://www.gate.net/~wyman/flo.html
Attorney James Wyman has rounded up links to Florida opinions, rules, forms, statutes, legislation, government sites, journals, and directories.

Georgia Legal Research Links
http://library.law.mercer.edu/galaw.html
The Walter F. George School of Law at Mercer University sponsors an index of legislation, ordinances, caselaw, state and local government Websites, law schools and libraries, and legal organizations.

Iowa Law
http://www.uiowa.edu/~lawlib/iowalaw.html
The University of Iowa Law Library points to caselaw, legislative and administrative materials, government Websites, law schools, and journals.

The Maine Lawyers' Network
http://www.mainelaw.net/
This site links to statutes, opinions of federal courts in the states, government pages, agency rules, and libraries.

Michigan: ICLE Online Partnership
http://www.icle.org/partners/
Michigan's Institute for Continuing Education sponsors this subscription service, which offers more than 1,100 forms for business, family law, probate and estate planning, and real estate.

Law and Politics in Nevada
http://www.nevadaindex.com/
Supreme court opinions, court rules, legislation, and state and local government sites are among the links here.

New Jersey Law Network
http://www.njlawnet.com/
This extensive site has statutes, caselaw, rules, government sites, resources by topic, mailing lists, and links to legal sites in New York and Pennsylvania.

Oklahoma: Marshall K. Dyer, Attorney At Law
http://www.emitech.com/dyer/
This site provides federal and Oklahoma legal resources, including the Tulsa County Courthouse Personnel Directory.

Pennsylvania Legal Research Web Sites
http://www.mathcs.duq.edu/~raod/
Dittakavi Rao, associate director of the Duquesne University Center for Legal Information, has stockpiled links to comprehensive Pennsylvania legal sites, schools, journals, libraries, caselaw, court sites and rules, legislation, government agencies, bar associations, county and city pages, and public records.

Rhode Island Law Links
http://www.snesl.edu/rilaw.htm
The Southern New England School of Law has compiled government and general legal resources for the state.

South Carolina Legal Resources
http://www.law.sc.edu/refdessc.htm
The University of South Carolina School of Law links to the three branches of state government (including caselaw and statutes) and miscellaneous resources.

Texas Legal Research Index
http://brandtlaw.com/lydia/table.html
Lawyer Lydia M.V. Brandt's outline is a survey course in Texas legal research issues. She covers citation practice (including writ history), "Shepardizing," tracking session laws, and the statutory revision program. Click Internet Sites: Legal Research for her index of online resources.

Virginia Law Resource Center
http://www.us-law.com/
Attorney James Gray Norman, Jr., has gathered links to caselaw, legislation, regulations, Attorney General opinions, law schools, CLE, and comprehensive Virginia legal research sources.

West Virginia: WV Legal Research
http://www.wvbar.org/technet/index.htm
This state bar index covers the code, court rules, Supreme Court and legal ethics opinions, agency regulations and decisions, and legal forms.

General Reference Tools

One of these general sites might suit your fancy more than the better-known resources in the main book.

All-in-One Search Page
http://www.allonesearch.com/
As the name says, from this one site you can run searches through a multitude of engines (more than 500), software libraries, directories, publications, Internet tools, technical reports, desk references, and more.

Dogpile
http://www.dogpile.com/
This multisearch engine fetches results successively from eleven search engines. Results are instantaneous and appear in the order of the engines' responses.

Find-It!
http://www.itools.com/find-it/
A companion to Research-It!, which was mentioned in chapter 16, "General Research Resources," this will search the Web, software libraries, Deja News, and a people locator database.

go2net Metacrawler
http://www.metacrawler.com/index.html
This engine sends one query simultaneously to a number of major search engines and combines the results.

Search.com
http://www.search.com/
In addition to major tools such as Alta Vista and Infoseek, here you can access a number of specialty search engines on such topics as automotive, computing, entertainment, health, shopping, sports, and travel.

W3 Search Engines
http://cuiwww.unige.ch/meta-index.html
Wide-ranging and eclectic, this meta-index of search engines links to all the major general ones, as well as country-specific databases, people-finders, FAQs, software databases, publications, and more. The site is a service of Centre Universitaire d' Informatique of the University of Geneva.

Fun & Games

You know what they say about all work and no play.

Anagram Insanity
http://www.anagramfun.com/
Scramble your name (or an opponent's).

Dumb Laws
http://www.dumblaws.com/
Marvel at ill-conceived laws from the United States and other countries. The only downside (besides encouraging work avoidance) is the absence of citations. For a look at the depths of human stupidity, visit the companion site Dumb Criminal Acts, **http://www.dumbcriminalacts.com/**.

ExLawyer.com
http://www.exlawyer.com
We've all heard lawyer jokes, but what about ex-lawyer jokes? This site is full of them, as written by Jack Thomas, who quit law for stand-up comedy.

Guide to Wacky Court Cases
http://members.aol.com/schwenkler/wcc/index.htm
Every lawyer's run into nut cases, but rarely as extreme as the ones behind the opinions here. The site includes the legendary (but real) class action suit against Satan and his staff. Citations are included.

The Internet Oracle
http://www.cs.indiana.edu/~oracle/
Got a problem? Want insight into one of life's mysteries? Consult the omniscient Internet Oracle and you'll get a response by e-mail. So what if its utterances are rarely useful? They are usually amusing, sometimes so side-splitting as to trigger a scene in front of your computer. In return, the Oracle may require you to perform a small service—writing its response to a question someone else poses. Periodically the Priesthood of the Oracle culls through the assembled questions and answers and posts its favorite pairs to the Oracle's mailing list and newsgroup, **rec.humor.oracle**.

Magic 8-Ball
http://ofb.net/8ball/
It mystified us all when we were kids. I've kept one on my office desk, and now you can have one on your desktop. If the 8-Ball emulator leaves you unsatisfied, peruse its catalog and ratings of other 8-Ball sites across the Web.

Shakespearean Insult Generator
http://alabanza.com/kabacoff/Inter-Links/cgi-bin/bard.pl
Each time it loads, this site spits out barbs from the Bard.

Shark Talk
http://www.nolo.com/sharktalk/sharktalk.html
It's a game like Hangman, with a couple of twists (and animation). All the answers are legal terms, and when you get a letter wrong, a shark swims up and attacks a stick figure in an inner tube. Nolo Press is the sponsor.

The Smoking Gun
http://www.thesmokinggun.com/
The foibles of public figures and institutions come to light in this stockpile of authentic pleadings and government documents. The archives teem with ridiculous contract provisions, regulatory slaps on the wrist, unbelievable FBI file excerpts (don't miss Groucho Marx's), and pleading allegations that put tabloid headlines to shame.

Tilt
http://www.concentric.net/~Outlawyr/tilt/tilt.html
Not the usual lawyer's monthly, this online magazine features sometimes lyrical, always offbeat vignettes into the realities of law school and practice. How real? One of the running column topics is frustration.

Wills on the Web
http://www.ca-probate.com/wills.htm
The bequests of twentieth-century celebrities (sports, glamour, political, and rock 'n' roll figures) and ordinary people from 1293-on fill this site.

The World's Greatest Law Review Article
http://www.kohnmusic.com/articles/lawrev.html
Law professor Andrew L. McClurg takes footnotes to their logical extreme in what must also be the world's shortest law review article.

Appendix B
Taking Care of Business

Without logging off, you can rack up Continuing Legal Education credits, amass law office technology tips, and look for a job. Here is a smorgasbord of Internet sites for just that.

Continuing Legal Education

Some of the following Internet sites offer online courses for credit, some allow online registration for real-world seminars, and some merely post schedules.

Before registering for an online course, be sure to read the site's system requirements. These commonly include a multimedia plug-in (such as RealAudio) and a sound card, both of which are necessary to play recorded speeches. To review plug-ins, flip back to chapter 3, "Making the Most of Your Browser."

ABA-CLE
http://www.abanet.org/cle/home.html
The American Bar Association's CLE Now! program allows you to play broadcasts of courses from your desktop, at your convenience and at no charge. The files require a frames-enabled browser (which the latest versions of Internet Explorer and Netscape Navigator are), the RealAudio Player, a sound card and speakers, and at least a 28.8K modem connection. Also on the top page is the schedule of the ABA's formal programs, which include online courses, national institutes, satellite seminars, and teleconferences. The site describes courses available by phone (the ABA-CLE On Demand program) and compiles the CLE requirements of the states in which it is mandatory.

All Law Continuing Legal Education
http://www.alllaw.com/schools_and_education/cle/
This index points to some forty CLE programs, many of which are state-specific.

CLE Online.com
http://www.cleonline.com
Courses at this site count for credit in at least California, Colorado, Florida, New York, Texas, Vermont, and, to a limited extent, Tennessee. The programs consist of written materials, RealAudio files (in some instances), and forums in which the moderator and participants post and answer questions. This differs from the usual in-person CLE course in that registrants have access to materials for a month and may come and go as they please.

Hieros Gamos: Legal Education and CLE
http://www.hg.org/hg.html
Below links to organizations that provide CLE is a listing of online sources. Among them are HG's free audio seminars, which require the RealPlayer.

Internet Legal Research Guide
http://www.ilrg.com/cle_ref.html
Here's an index to Websites of about twenty-five CLE institutes and resources. The content of the linked pages varies. Not all offer CLE online; some post only schedules and descriptions of video or audio products.

LegalSeminars.com
http://www.legalseminars.com
Law.com's online CLE programs have previously received credit in twenty states: Arizona, California, Colorado, Connecticut, Florida, Kentucky, Missouri, Montana, Nevada, New Hampshire, New Mexico, New York, North Dakota, Oregon, Tennessee, Texas, Vermont, Washington, West Virginia, and Wyoming. E-mail the site to verify current accreditation before enrolling. Courses costs less than $100 each; a premium subscription ($229) allows entry to all courses for a year. Tuition assistance is available, with special consideration given to public interest and government lawyers, as well as recently admitted solo practitioners.

National Practice Institute
http://www.npilaw.com/schedule.html
The Institute's schedule of live CLE programs across the nation is here. The site accepts online registration.

Practising Law Institute's cle-net
http://www.cle-net.edu/
PLI's online audio and video courses are accredited in California, Colorado, Florida, Kentucky, Missouri, Montana, New Hampshire, New Mexico, New York, Tennessee, Texas, Utah, Virginia, Washington, and West Virginia. RealAudio and Shockwave are required. For cost information, follow links to a course's registration page.

Seminars and Continuing Legal Education
http://www.washlaw.edu/postlaw/seminars.htm
Need to check on a state's CLE requirements? The Washburn University School of Law Library posts them on WashLawWeb, along with links to national organizations and institutes. The search engine locates courses by city, subject, or date.

Law Office Technology

Here are some springboards for bringing the law office into the computer age.

ABA Technology Center
http://www.abanet.org/tech/home.html
This page links to all the tech-related sites among the American Bar Association's pages. Besides the Science & Technology Section, Computer & Technology Division, and Macintosh Computer Interest Group, you will find the Law Practice Management Newsletter and the Legal Technology Resource Center, which offers legal software samplers on CD-ROM, information packets (called InfoPacs) about categories of software on the market, and referrals to other legal technology sites.

Law Office Computing Online
http://www.lawofficecomputing.com/
Use the Product Locator to access reviews from *Law Office Computing*.

The Law Office Software List for the Macintosh Computer
http://www.mother.com/~randy/index.html
Attorney Randy B. Singer has compiled a scrollable index (it's long!) of Mac software for every imaginable aspect of law practice. Office administration tools include packages for time, billing, and accounting; document assembly, imaging, management, or redlining; and forms creation. There's a huge variety of software for practice areas, too, such as bankruptcy, family law, estate planning, intellectual property, litigation, and real estate.

Lawyerware Legal Technology Tools
http://www.lawyerware.com/
The site is a directory of software and other technology products that address the spectrum of office needs, such as time or case management, file recovery, word processing and document assembly, and forms for specific practice areas. Free trial versions are available for many of the featured applications.

LLRX.com
http://llrx.com
This online publication provides extensive, thoroughly documented reviews of new office management and Web-based products.

Get a Job

Whether you're interested in a firm, corporate, teaching, or nontraditional position, the following sites are full of leads.

The Counsel Network
http://www.thecounselnetwork.com/
This Canadian recruiting firm (with affiliates all over the United States and the globe) offers newsletters, pointers and forms for resume drafting, and a searchable database of positions it is looking to fill.

eAttorney
http://198.5.146.10/
This online placement agency offers its services to law students and attorneys interested in lateral moves. It provides a secure recruiting system for employers and law school placement offices.

EmplawyerNet
http://www.emplawyernet.com/
This service takes the opposite approach from real-world placement agencies: employers post openings for free, while job seekers pay a monthly membership fee to see the job listings. Benefits include access to more than 6,000 job postings, e-mail notifications, and the cheeky column "The Rodent," which is a mouthpiece for disgruntled associates. A database of merely 600 jobs is available with basic membership, which is free.

Jurist
http://www.jurist.law.pitt.edu
The University of Pittsburgh's legal education network lists job openings, fellowships, and other opportunities for law professors, in the United States, Australia, Canada, and the United Kingdom.

Lawyers Weekly Jobs
http://www.lawyersweeklyjobs.com/
The national newspaper offers a searchable database of jobs for lawyers, paralegals, and legal secretaries all over the country.

The Legal Employment Search Site
http://www.legalemploy.com/
St. Louis attorney Gregory J. Hickel has compiled legal employment sites, law school placement offices, and general employment resources.

Major, Hagen & Africa
http://www.mhasearch.com/
The prominent search firm posts domestic and international job openings, which are searchable by location, minimum or maximum experience requirements, practice area, keyword, or in-house/law firm.

Wet Feet.com
http://www.wetfeet.com
Law is only one of the fields covered by this broad-based job resource, which offers resume pointers and city profiles that focus on livability factors. Because of the expansive focus, the site is a particularly valuable stop for anyone interested in doing something other than working for a firm or legal department. For ideas, read The Insider's Guide to Alternative Legal Careers (in the Law section under the Industries tab) and the feature "Life Beyond the Firm," which profiles lawyers who've leapt into public service or Internet jobs.

Index

abbreviations, common e-mail, 291
ABC News, 304
Access Indiana Information Network, 199-200
address: e-mail and street, finding, 285; Internet protocol, 17; not working, what to do, 41, 147; reverse lookup, 286; Web page, 10
Administrative Office of the U.S. Courts: Appellate Bulletin Board System, 51, 55, 107, 110; bankruptcy forms, 132, 148; Directory of Electronic Public Access Services, 107; U.S. Party/Case Index, 108; Website, 107
admiralty law resources, 221
Adobe Acrobat Reader, 23; download sites, 23, 54, 59, 93, 94, 99, 108, 109, 110, 112, 113, 115, 137, 140, 148, 149, 151, 152, 153, 154, 155, 156, 157, 158, 159, 161, 162, 163, 164, 166, 167, 168, 213
Agriculture, Department of, U.S., 178
agriculture law resources, 221
Air Force, U.S., Court of Criminal Appeals: opinions, 48, 59; FLITE Supreme Court database, 49
AJR's Newslink, 303
Alabama Information Network, 192, 193
Alabama Legal Information Center: Alabama appellate opinions, 60; Eleventh Circuit opinions, 55
Alabama, State of: Administrative Office of Courts, 132; appellate court opinions, 60-61; Attorney General opinions, 132; Attorney General Website, 192; bills, code, and constitution, 88; Comptroller, 192; courts, 192; legislature, 192; official home page, 192-193; Oil and Gas Board forms, 153; Oil and Gas Board Website, 193; Real Estate Commission forms, 153; Secretary of State filings, searchable, 193; Secretary of State forms, 152-153; Secretary of State Website, 152-153, 192-193; session laws and statutes, 88; Supreme Court opinions, 60-61; Treasury, 192; Unified Judicial System Website, 132; well file, production, and engineering databases, searchable, 193
Alaska Legal Resource Center, 6, 112
Alaska, State of: Alcoholic Beverage Control Board forms, 153; Alcoholic Beverage Control Board Website, 193; Appellate Courts Case Management System, 133; bills and constitution, 88; Child Support Enforcement Division, 193; Court of Appeals opinions, 61, 133; Court System Website, 132-133; Division of Banking, Securities & Corporations forms, 153; Division of Banking, Securities & Corporations Website, 193; official home page, 193; statutes, 88, 133; Supreme Court opinions, 61, 133
All Law, 311, 321
alternative dispute resolution (ADR) resources, 221-222, 256, 283
American Bankruptcy Institute (ABI World), 223
American Bar Association: CLE Now!, 321; Computer & Technology Division, 323; discussion groups catalog, 280; General Practice, Solo and Small Firm Section, 259; *Journal*, 259; Law Practice Management Section, 259; LAWlink (Legal Research Jumpstation), 39, 216; Science & Technology Section, 323; Section of Family Law, 226; Site-tation, 39, 262, 274-275; state law license requirements, catalog of, 281; Technology Center, 323; Website, 280
American Board of Medical Specialties, 235
American Civil Liberties Union, 281

American Journalism Review, 303
American Law Sources On-Line (ALSO): Canadian resources, 245; Federal Register, 86; federal resources, 106; Mexican resources, 245; opinions, federal, 48; opinions, state, 60; statutes, federal, 84; statutes, state, 87; territories and protectorates, U.S., 79
American Lawyer, 263-264
American Lawyer Media: affiliates, 62, 64, 267-269; Law.com and, 263
American Legal Publishing, 101
American Samoa, 79
American Society for International Law, 240
American University Law Review, 258
Americans With Disabilities Act, 187
Anagram Insanity, 317
Anderson Publishing Company: Ohio codes, 96
Andorra, 244
animal rights, 222
Anonymizer.com, 8
antitrust law resources, 221. *See also* Justice, Department of, U.S.
AnyWho, 286
Appellate Voice Information System, 110
Archie, 15
Arizona Lawyer's Guide to the Internet, 314
Arizona, State of: Administrative Code, 89; bills, 89; corporate forms, 153; Court of Appeals opinions, 62, 133; insurance forms, 153; liquor license forms, 153; Liquor Licenses and Control, Department of, 194; Judicial Department, 133; official home page, 194; real estate licensing forms, 153; Secretary of State, 89, 194; Secretary of State filings, searchable, 194; statutes, 89; Supreme Court opinions, 61-62, 133
Arkansas, State of: banking forms, 154; Board of Architects, 194; Business Department forms, 153; code, 89, 133; Court of Appeals opinions, 62; Court of Appeals Website, 133; General Assembly, 89; Judiciary Website, 133; local resources, 195; official home page, 194-195; Secretary of State, 153, 194; Secretary of State filings, searchable, 194; Securities Department, 194; securities forms, 154; Supreme Court opinions, 62, 133; Supreme Court Website, 133
Armed Services Board of Contract Appeals opinions, 59

ASCAP, 229
Asia Law & Practice, 266
Astarita, Mark J., 236
attorneys, directories of, 282
Attorney's Toolbox, 311-312
Australasian Legal Information Institute, 244
Australia, 244, 312
Austria, 246
Avalon Project, 254
aviation law resources, 221
A.V.V., Inc.: Ohio Code, 96
Azerbaijan, Republic of, 241, 255

Backflip software, 25
banking and commercial law resources, 221
Bankruptcy Appellate Panel opinions, 48; Eighth Circuit, 54; Sixth Circuit, 53
Bankruptcy Code, U.S., 123, 125, 129
Bankruptcy Courts, U.S., 58; Alabama, Middle District Website, 111, 122; Alabama, Southern District opinions, 58, 122; Alabama, Southern District Website, 122; Alaska Website, 112, 123; Arizona Website, 123; California, Central District opinions, 58, 123; California, Central District Website, 123; California, Eastern District Website, 123; California, Northern District opinions, 58, 123; California, Northern District Website, 123; California, Southern District opinions, 58, 124; California, Southern District Website, 123-124; Colorado opinions, 58, 124; Colorado Website, 124; docket information, 106, 118, 122, 124, 126, 127, 128, 129, 130, 131, 132; Electronic Bankruptcy Noticing, 122, 123, 125, 127, 128, 129, 130, 131; Florida, Middle District Website, 124; Georgia, Middle District opinions, 125; Georgia, Middle and Northern District Websites, 125; Georgia, Southern District Website, 114, 125; Idaho opinions, 56; Idaho Website, 125; Illinois, Northern and Southern District Websites, 125; Illinois, Southern District opinions, 58, 125; Indiana, Northern District Website, 125-126; Iowa, Northern District opinions, 58, 126; Iowa, Northern District Website, 126; Kentucky, Eastern District opinions, 58, 126; Kentucky, Eastern and Western District Websites, 126; Kentucky, Western District opinions, 58, 126; Louisiana, Western District Website, 126; Maine Website, 126; Maryland opinions, 58, 126-127; Maryland

Website, 126-127: Massachusetts Website, 116, 127; Michigan, Western District Website, 117, 127; Minnesota opinions, 58, 127; Minnesota Website, 127; Missouri, Eastern District opinions, 58; Missouri, Eastern and Western District Websites, 118, 127; Nevada Website, 127; New Hampshire opinions, 58, 128; New Hampshire Website, 128; New Jersey opinions, 58, 128; New Jersey Website, 128; New Mexico opinions, 58, 128; New Mexico Website, 128; New York, Northern District opinions, 58, 128; New York, Northern and Southern District Websites, 128; North Carolina, Eastern District Website, 128; North Carolina, Middle District opinions and Website, 129; North Carolina, Western District opinions, 58; North Carolina, Western District Website, 129; North Dakota Website, 129; Ohio, Northern District Website, 129; opinions, list of courts posting online, 58; Pennsylvania, Eastern District opinions, 58, 129; Pennsylvania, Eastern and Middle District Websites, 129; Pennsylvania, Middle District opinions, 58; Rhode Island opinions, 58; Rhode Island Website, 129-130; South Carolina opinions, 58, 130; South Carolina Website, 130; South Dakota opinions, 58, 130; South Dakota Website, 120, 130; Tennessee, Eastern, Middle, and Western District Websites, 130; Texas, Northern District Website, 130; Texas, Southern District Website, 121, 131; Texas, Western District opinions, 58, 131; Texas, Western District Website, 131; U.S. Party/Case Index, 107; Utah opinions, 58; Utah Website, 131; Vermont opinions, 58, 131; Vermont Website, 131; Virginia, Eastern District opinions, 58, 131; Virginia, Eastern and Western District Websites, 131; Washington, Eastern District opinions and Website, 131; Washington, Western District Website, 132; Wisconsin, Eastern District local rules, 132; Wisconsin, Western District opinions, 132; Wisconsin, Western District Website, 122, 132; Wyoming opinions, 58, 132; Wyoming Website, 132
bankruptcy law resources: ABI World, 223; Dow Jones, Inc., 223; InterNet Bankruptcy Library, 223; I3 Network, 224

bar associations, 280-281; Colorado, 63; D.C., 63, 134; Michigan, 68; New Jersey, 281; Rhode Island, 74; South Dakota, 75; state, 281; Tennessee, 75; Wisconsin, 79, 122, 132, 146. *See also under specific bars*
Belarus, 246
Belgium, 246
Big Ear, The, 280
bisexual resources, 36
Bluebook, The. See Uniform System of Citation, A
BNA: Tax Management Portfolios on the Web, 238; Web reference library, 262
Book Publishing Company, 101
bookmark: creating, 11; management software, 25-28; organizing, 11-12, 33
Bookmarks, Essential, 29, 32-40, 45, 48, 186, 220, 241, 262, 274
Boolean logic, 4, 30; examples, 31
Boolean operators: defined, 31; recognized by FindLaw, 34; recognized by LawCrawler, 37; recognized by LawRunner, 38; use with U.S. Patent and Trademark Office databases, 183
Booth Harrington Johns & Toman, LLP: Estate Planning Links Web Site, 225-226
Bora Laskin Law Library: Project DIANA, 254
Botluk, Diana, 84
Brandt, Lydia M.V., 316
BriefServe.com, 49
broadcasts, online: Congress, 176; Eighth Judicial District of Texas oral arguments, 143; Federal Communications Commission, 181; Florida Supreme Court oral arguments, 134; Ohio Supreme Court hearings, 141; South Dakota legislature, 211; Virginia Corporation Commission, 213
browser: bookmark, 11; cookie, 7; downloading program in, 13; error messages, 41, 147; explained, 9-10; Lycos Neoplanet, 45; multimedia, built-in, 20; navigating, 10; Opera, 19, 45; saving pages in, 12; security, 21; software available, 19
Business Advisor, U.S., 188, international resources, 189
business guides: Connecticut, 196: Delaware, 197; Hieros Gamos, 35; Idaho, 199-201; Missouri, 203-204; North Carolina, 207; Oklahoma, 209; South Dakota, 211; Virginia, 213; Wisconsin, 215
business organization law resources, 221, 227
Bynum, Charlotte, 240

CacheX software, 28
calculators: child support, 133, 298; light conditions, 296; miscellaneous, 298
Calculators On-Line, 298
California, State of: agencies, 37; bills and codes, 89; Corporations, Department of, forms and Website, 195; Court of Appeals opinions, 62-63, 133; Court of Appeals Website, 133; judiciary Website, 195; local resources, 195; municipal codes, 100, 101; official home page, 37, 195; searchable databases, 195; Secretary of State filings, searchable, and Website, 195; Secretary of State forms, 154; Supreme Court opinions, 49, 62-63, 133; Supreme Court Website, 133; trial courts, 133
Cal Law, 268; California appellate court opinions, 62
Calvin House Ninth Circuit Appellate Counselor, 109
Canada, 244
Caribbean, the, 247
CataLaw, 312
CataList mailing list catalog, 276
Cavicchi, Jon, 227
CCH Internet Tax Research NetWork, 238
CDB Infotek, 287
Center for Information Law and Policy Federal Web Locator, 38-39, 186
Center for Intelligent Information Retrieval GovBot Database of Government Web Sites, 187
charities, registered, searchable databases of: Georgia, 198; Internet Prospector, 216; Kansas, 200; Maryland, 202; Minnesota, 203; Washington, 214
charters, financial institutions, searchable databases of: Arkansas, 194; Florida, 198; Iowa, 200
Chicago Daily Law Bulletin, 269
Chicago Lawyer, 269
Chicago-Kent College of Law, Illinois Institute of Technology: Center for Law and Computers, 54; Information Center, 39
child support calculator, 133, 298
child support guidelines: Alabama, 132; Arkansas, 133; Iowa, 136; Kansas, 136; New Jersey, 139
Chile, 256
China, 246, 266
Circuit Courts of Appeal, U.S.: D.C. Circuit opinions, 55-56, 110, 113; D.C. Circuit Website, 110; docket information, 51, 106, 108; Eighth Circuit BAP opinions, 54; Eighth Circuit opinions, 54, 109; Eighth Circuit Website, 109, 118, 126; Eleventh Circuit opinions, 55; Eleventh Circuit Website, 110, 125; Federal Circuit opinions, 56, 111; Federal Circuit Website, 111; Fifth Circuit opinions, 52-53, 108; Fifth Circuit Website, 108; First Circuit opinions, 51, 108; First Circuit Website, 108, 116; Fourth Circuit opinions, 52; Ninth Circuit Appellate Counselor, 109; Ninth Circuit Office of the Circuit Executive, 109; Ninth Circuit opinions, 54-55; Ninth Circuit Website, 109; opinions, nationwide, 48-56, 49, 80; rules, 106; Second Circuit opinions, 51, 64; Seventh Circuit library Website, 109; Seventh Circuit opinions, 54; Seventh Circuit Website, 108-109; Sixth Circuit opinions, 53-54, 68, 108; Sixth Circuit Website, 108; slip opinions, 51; Tenth Circuit opinions, 55; Tenth Circuit Website, 109-110; Third Circuit opinions, 52
citators: Shepard's Citations, 40, 48; West Group KeyCite Citation Research Service, 40
cities. *See* municipal codes; municipal Websites; *and specific states*
Claims Providers of America National Directory of Expert Witnesses, 283
class action resources: Classactionlitigation.com, 233; Stanford Securities Class Action Clearinghouse, 236
Classactionlitigation.com, 233
CLE Online.com, 322
Clean Air Act databases, 186
Cleaves Law Library: Maine Supreme Court opinions, 67
ClicknSearch software, 35
client confidentiality. *See* privacy
clipboard, 27
ClipMate software, 27
CNN: Interactive, 304; World Time Website, 24
Code of Federal Regulations (CFR), 37, 38, 84-86
Code, U.S., 84-85; Classification Tables, 84; search engines, 52, 84, 85, 176
Colorado, State of: Attorney General opinions, 134; Court of Appeals opinions, 63, 134; Judicial Branch Website, 134; local resources, 195; official home page, 195; Secretary of State filings, searchable, and Website, 195; Secretary of State forms, 154;

Index

State, Department of, 195; statutes, 89, 134; Supreme Court decisions, 63; Supreme Court opinions, 134
Columbia Law Review, 259
Commerce, Department of, U.S., 178, 186; Contract Law Division, Office of General Counsel, 59
commercial research services: Access Indiana Information Network, 200; Advanced Court Engineering (ACE) System (New Mexico), 118; Alabama Legal Information Center, 60; California appellate court opinions, 62, 63; caselaw, comprehensive, 80; China Law Reference Service, 246; Colorado Department of State databases, 195; comprehensive databases, 43, 45; copyrights, 233; Court Link, 106; Dialog Select, 233; Eleventh Circuit opinions, 55; Georgia appellate opinions, 64; Information America, 203; Information Network of Kansas, 91, 200; intellectual property, 233; Law.com, 263; LawResearch, 45; Legaldocs, 170-171; LEXIS-NEXIS, 40, 44, 48, 80, 101, 203; LexPert, 284; Loislaw.com, 44, 80, 101; Louisiana Legislative Subscriber System, 91; Maryland Contract Weekly Online, 202; Maryland Information and Retrieval System, 202; Massachusetts Direct Access, 202; MicroPatent, 233; Mississippi code, 93; Mississippi Lawyers World Wide Web Domain, 69, 138, 203; Nebrask@ Online, 204; New Jersey Corporate & Business Information & Reporting Services, 206; Ninth Circuit opinions, 55; On Congress, 177; opinions, 44, 50; patents, 233; pros and cons of using, 42, 43; public records searches, 287-288; RIA Tax, 238; Shepard's Citations, 40, 48; State of Arizona Public Access System, 194; statutes, state, 101-102; Supreme Court opinions, U.S., 50; TBALink, 75; Texas Direct Access, 212; 13 Network, 224; Thomson & Thomson, 233; trademarks, 233; United Nations treaty collection, 243; V., 44, 80; Virginia Direct Access, 213; West Group KeyCite Citation Research Service, 40; WestDoc, 80, 101; Westlaw, 44, 80, 102
commercial services: asset locating, 287-288; digital marking, 228; Expert Witness Network, 284; expert witnesses and consultants, 283-284; IDEX, 284-285; Inter-Lingua, 232, 285; investigation, business or personal, 287-288; legal support, 284; Technical Advisory Service for Attorneys, 284; Translation Services on the Web, 285; Web monitoring services, 228; World News Connection, 304
company information, locating, 40
Complete Works of William Shakespeare, 302
Computer Incident Advisory Capability Internet Hoaxes Website, 290
Congress, U.S.: bill tracking, 174, 177; committees, 175-177; directories of, 176, 177; roll call votes, 176; schedules, 176. *See also* House of Representatives, U.S.; Senate, U.S.
Congressional Quarterly, 188
Congressional Record, 36, 175, 188
Connecticut, State of: Access International database, 196-197; Banking, Department of, forms, 154; bills, 89; Business Resource Index, 196; Comptroller forms, 154-155; Concord On-Line, 196; Economic Resource Center, 196-197; Environmental Protection, Department of, forms, 154; General Assembly, 89; License Information Center, 196; local resources, 196; official home page, 196, 197; searchable databases, 196; Secretary of the State filings, searchable, 196; Secretary of the State forms, 154;statutes, 89; Superior and Supreme Court Websites, 134
Consolidated Consultants Company, 283
constitutional law resources, 221
Continuing Legal Education (CLE): Arkansas approved courses, 133; Michigan Institute of, 68; New York requirements, 140; online courses, 34, 35, 321, 322; requirements, 253; requirements, by state, 321
cookie, 7, -blocking software, 8
Copyright Clearance Center, 228-229
copyright law resources: Copyright & Fair Use Website, 229; Copyright Clearance Center, 228-229; Lawgirl.com, 230
Copyright Licensing Agency, U.K., 229
Copyright Office, U.S.: forms, 151-152; registrations, searchable, 179; Website, 178
Cornell Law School: Code, U.S. at, 102; Law Library Legal Research Encyclopedia, 240-241, 254; Law Library Website, 240-241; Legal Information Institute, 49-51, 52, 72, 81, 84, 85, 87, 107, 220- 221, 222, 225, 254
Corporate Counsel Magazine, 264

Index 331

corporate records, searchable databases: Alaska, 193; California, 195; Colorado, 195; Connecticut, 196; Florida, 197; Illinois, 199; Indiana, 199; Internet Prospector, 216; Iowa, 200; Kentucky, 201; Louisiana, 201; Maine, 201; Maryland, 202; Missouri, 203; Nevada, 205; New Jersey, 206; New Mexico, 207; North Carolina, 207; Ohio, 208; Pacific Information Resources Search System, 192; Texas, 212; Utah, 213; Vermont, 213; Washington, 214; Webgator, 192; Wyoming, 215
Counsel Network, 324
Counsel Quest, 312; Family Law, 226
county Websites, 215-217. *See also under specific states*
Court Link, 106
Court of Appeals for the Armed Forces: opinions, 48; Website, 111
Court of Appeals for Veterans Claims opinions, 48
Court of Federal Claims opinions, 48, 59
Court of International Trade, U.S. opinions, 48, 59
court reporters, 35, 284
court, supreme, state. *See under specific states*
Court, Supreme, U.S. *See* Supreme Court, U.S.
Court TV: Law Center, 303; Online, 265
courts, bankruptcy. *See* Bankruptcy Courts, U.S.
courts, district, state. *See under specific states*
courts, district, U.S. *See* District Courts, U.S.
courts, special. *See under specific courts*
Courts.Net, 105, 106
CPR Institute for Dispute Resolution, 222
criminal law resources: Capital Defense Weekly, 224; Florida State University School of Criminology & Criminal Justice, 224; Kentucky Department of Public Advocacy, 224; National Criminal Justice Reference Service, 225
Croatia, 246
C-SPAN Online, 176
Customs Service, U.S., 186
CyBarrister Page, The, 230
CyberGuards, 228
cyberlaw, 230, 261-262
CyberLaw, 261-262
Cyberlaw Institute, 230
Cybersettle.com, 222
Cyberspace Law Website, 274
Cybrarian, the, 314

Daily Business Review, 268
DakotaCast Portal, 211
Davis-Bacon Act databases, 186
Defense, Department of, 178
definitions: archive, 15; article, 14; browser, 9; clipboard, 27; cookie, 7; disk cache, 27; downloading, 5; e-mail, 13; edited search engine, 30; FAQ (frequently asked questions), 276; File Transfer Protocol (FTP), 15; flame, to, 290; Gopher, 16; helper application, 19; hierarchical index, 30; home page, 9; Hypertext Mark-up Language (HTML), 9; hypertext transfer protocol (http), 10; Internet, 1; link, 10; Listproc, 273; Listserv, 273; listserver, 273; mail reader, 13; mailing list, 14; Majordomo, 273; newsgroup, 14; newsreader, 14; plug-in, 19; posting, 5; search engine, 30; Shepardizing, 3; signature (sig), 13; snail mail, 13; source code, 9; spam, 290; subscribe, 14; surfing, 5; Telnet, 16; thread, 14; Uniform Resource Locator (URL), 10; uploading, 5; utility, 19; virus, 5; Web page, 9; Website, 9
Deja.com (formerly DejaNews), 280. *See also* newsgroups
Delaware Corporate Reporter, 268
Delaware Law Weekly, 268
Delaware, State of: assembly, 197; banking forms, 155; bills, 90; code, 89-90; Corporations, Division of, forms, 155; Corporations, Division of, Website, 197; Legislative Information System, 90; local resources, 197; lower courts, 197; official home page, 197; Register of Regulations, 90; Research, Division of, 89-90; securities forms, 155; Supreme Court opinions, 63, 134; Supreme Court Website, 134, 197
DeLAWnet, 268
Denmark, 246
Derecho.org, 247
Dialog Select, 233
dictionaries: Dictionaries Website, 300; dictionary.com, 298; OneLook Dictionaries, 300; *Oxford English Dictionary*, 300; Web of On-Line Dictionaries, 300-301; Wordbot, 301
Dictionaries Website, 300
dictionary.com, 298
digest, mailing list, 273
Digimarc Corporation, 228
directories: address, 285-287; attorneys, 282; e-

332 Index

mail, 285-287; expert witnesses and consultants, 282-285; legal support, 284; Martindale-Hubbell, 282; phone, 285-287; reverse lookup, 286, 287; West's Legal Directory, 282

disability law resources, 221. *See also* Equal Employment Opportunity Commission

discussion forums, 288-289, 292; abbreviations used in, 291; communication tips, 289-292; emoticons used in, 291; FindLaw Legal Minds, 278; how they work, 277-278; Pro2Net, 278; WebEthics, 225, 278

disk cache, 27

District Courts, U.S., 56-57; Alabama, Middle and Northern District Websites, 111; Alabama, Northern District opinions, 56; Alabama, Southern District Website, 112; Alaska opinions, 56; Alaska Website, 112; Arizona Website, 112; Arkansas, Eastern and Western District Websites, 112; California, Central District opinions, 56, 113; California, Central District Website, 112-113; California, Eastern, Northern, and Southern District Websites, 113; Colorado Website, 113; Connecticut opinions, 113; Connecticut Website, 113; D.C., opinions, 56, 113; D.C. Website, 113; docket information, 106, 111, 113, 114, 115, 117, 118, 119, 120, 121; Florida, Middle District Website, 113; Florida, Southern District Website, 114; Georgia, Middle District Website, 114; Georgia, Northern District Website, 114, 125; Georgia, Southern District Probation and Pretrial Services and Website, 114; Hawaii Website, 114; Idaho opinions, 56; Idaho Website, 114; Illinois, Central District opinions, 57, 114; Illinois, Central District Website, 114; Illinois, Northern District opinions, 57; Illinois, Northern and Southern District Websites, 115; Indiana, Northern and Southern District Websites, 115; Indiana, Southern District opinions, 57, 115; Iowa, Northern District opinions and Website, 115; Iowa, Southern District opinions, 57, 115; Iowa, Southern District Website, 115, 126; Kentucky, Western District opinions, 57, 116; Kentucky, Western District Website, 116, 126; Louisiana, Eastern, Middle, and Western District Websites, 116; Maine opinions, 57, 116; Maine Website, 116; Maryland opinions, 57, 116; Maryland Website, 116; Massachusetts opinions, 57; Massachusetts Website, 116; Michigan, Eastern and Western District opinions, 57; Michigan, Western District Website, 117; Mississippi, Northern District opinions, 57, 117; Mississippi, Northern and Southern District Websites, 117; Missouri, Eastern District Pretrial and Probation Services, 118; Missouri, Eastern District Website, 117-118; Missouri, Western District Website, 118; Nebraska Website, 118; New Jersey opinions, 57; New Mexico opinions, 57, 118; New Mexico Website, 118; New York, Eastern District opinions, 57, 118; New York, Eastern and Northern District Websites, 118; New York, Southern District opinions, 57; New York, Southern District Website, 118-119; North Carolina, Eastern, Middle, and Western District Websites, 119; North Carolina, Middle District opinions, 57, 119; North Dakota opinions, 57; North Dakota Website, 119; Ohio, Northern District Website, 119; opinions, list of courts posting online, 56-57; Oregon opinions, 57, 119; Oregon Website, 119; Pennsylvania, Eastern District opinions, 57, 119; Pennsylvania, Eastern District Website, 119; Pennsylvania, Middle District opinions and Website, 120; Pennsylvania, Western District Website, 120; Puerto Rico Website, 120; South Carolina opinions, 57, 120; South Carolina Website, 120; South Dakota Website, 120; South Dakota, opinions, 57; Texas, Eastern District opinions, 57, 120; Texas, Eastern District Website, 120; Texas, Northern District Website, 120-121; Texas, Southern District opinions, 57, 121; Texas, Southern and Western District Websites, 121; Texas, Western District opinions, 57; U.S. Party/Case Index, 107; Utah Website, 121; Virginia, Eastern District Website, 121; Washington, Eastern District opinions and Website, 121; Websites, 52; Wisconsin, Eastern District local rules, 122; Wisconsin, Eastern District Website, 121; Wisconsin, Western District opinions, Probation and Pretrial Services, and Website, 122; Wyoming Website, 122

District of Columbia: Banking and Financial Institutions, Office of, forms, 155; Business Regulation Administration forms, 155; code, 90; Court of Appeals opinions, 63,

Index 333

134; Court of Appeals Website, 134; official home page, 197; Superior Court, 134
Divorce-Without-War, 226
DocFinder, 235
docket information, online: Alabama, 132; Alabama, Northern District, 111; Alaska appellate, 133; Arkansas, Eastern District, 112; Connecticut, 134; Hawaii, 135; Idaho, District of, 114, 125; Indiana, Southern District, 115; Kansas district courts, 136; Minnesota, Bankruptcy Court, 127; Missouri, 139; Missouri, Western District, 118; Nevada, 139; New Jersey, Bankruptcy Court, 128; New Mexico, 139; New York, Southern District, Bankruptcy Court, 128; North Carolina, Western District, Bankruptcy Court, 129; Oklahoma, 141; Tennessee, Middle District, Bankruptcy Court, 130; Texas appellate, 142, 143; Virginia, Eastern District, Bankruptcy Court, 131; Virginia, Western District, Bankruptcy Court, 131; Washington state courts, 144; Wisconsin, 145
DocLaw Web, 185
document management services, 35
DomainMagistrate, 233
Dow Jones, Inc., 266; Bankruptcy Online, 223
downloading, 5, 148
Duquesne University Center for Legal Information: Pennsylvania Legal Research Web Sites, 316
Dyer, Marshall K., 315

eAttorney, 324
EDGAR, 35, 184, 236, 313
edited search engines, defined, 30
Education, Department of, U.S., 178
Edward Bennett Williams Library, 251-252; Legal Explorer, 251
elder law resources, 225
Electronic Embassy, 241
electronic filing systems: Arizona, District of, Bankruptcy Court, 123; Arizona incorporations, 194; Arkansas incorporations, 154; California, Southern District, 123; Colorado tax forms, 195; Federal Communications Commission, 148; Florida, Middle District, Bankruptcy Court, 124; Florida Secretary of State, 197; Georgia, Northern District, Bankruptcy Court, 125; Kansas district courts, 136; Kentucky, Western District, 116; Kentucky, Western District, Bankruptcy Court, 126; Missouri, Western District, 118; Nebrask@ Online, 205; New Mexico, District of, 118; New Mexico, District of, Bankruptcy Court, 128; New Mexico Supreme Court, 140; New York, Eastern District, 118; New York, Southern District, Bankruptcy Court, 128; North Carolina appellate courts, 140; Ohio, Northern District, 119; Oregon, District of, 119; Pennsylvania Securities Commission, 210; Texas UCC forms, 212; Texas, Western District, Bankruptcy Court, 131; Virginia, Eastern District, Bankruptcy Court, 131
Electronic Frontier Foundation, 229
Electronic Literature Foundation, 302
Electronic Reference Desk. *See* Emory University School of Law, Electronic Reference Desk
e-mail, 292; abbreviations, 291; addresses, finding, 285-287; addresses, reverse lookup, 287; communication tips, 288-292; emoticons used in, 291-292; hoaxes, 290; Netiquette, 288-289; unwanted, protection against, 7, 277, 279, 280. *See also* newsletters, e-mail
Emory University School of Law: Constitution, U.S., 85; Electronic Reference Desk, 312; Eleventh Circuit opinions, 55; Federal Circuit opinions, 56; First Circuit opinions, 51; Fourth Circuit opinions, 52; Hugh F. MacMillan Law Library, 51, 52, 54, 56, 251, 312; Sixth Circuit opinions, 54; state opinions, 60; statutes, state, 88; Tenth Circuit opinions, 55
emoticons, explained, 291-292
EmplawyerNet, 267, 324
employment: consultants, 35; resources, 324-325
encryption, 7
Encyclopaedia Britannica, 299-300
encyclopedias: Encyclopaedia Britannica, 299-300; Funk & Wagnalls, 299; Information Please Dictionary and Encyclopedia, 299; Nolo Press Legal Encyclopedia, 227; World Wide Web Virtual Library, 252, 299
Energy, Department of, 178; Computer Incident Advisory Capability Internet Hoaxes Website, 290
England, 246
entertainment law resources: Lawgirl.com, 230; Resources for Film, TV and Multimedia Producers, 230
Equal Employment Opportunity Commission,

180
error message. *See* browser
Eslamboly & Barlavi: LawGuru, 276
Essential Bookmarks, 29, 32-40, 45, 48, 186, 220, 241, 262, 274
estate planning, 225-226, 266; Nolo Press Legal Encyclopedia, 227
Estate Planning Links Web Site, 225-226
Estonia, 246
ethics resources, 225. *See also under specific courts*
EUROPA, 246
European Parliament, 244; Patent Office, 231-232, 233
EWAN, 16
ExLawyer.com, 318
Expert Pages, 283
Expert Witness Network, 284
expert witnesses, 35, 282-284
ExpertFind, 283

family law resources: ABA Section of, 226; Counsel Quest, 226; Divorce-Without-War, 226; 'Lectric Law Library's Lawcopedia, 226
FAQ (Frequently Asked Questions), 276
FAST Search All the Web, All the Time, 295
federal: agencies, 37, 38-39; agency and commission Websites, 38-39, 148-152, 178-182, 184-185; bills, 174; constitution, 85; legislation, pending, 36; legislative history, 84, 174, 176; opinions, 33-36, 38, 48-59, 74, 79, 80, 88; private laws, 174; public laws, 84, 85, 175; resources online, scope, 173; rules, 84, 112, 120, 125; statutes, 33-37, 39, 52, 83-85, 88, 101, 102; Websites, comprehensive, 38-39. *See also under specific agencies, commissions, courts, and primary materials*
Federal Bar Association, 281
Federal Communication Commission, 148-149, 181
Federal Interagency Council on Statistical Policy, FedStats, 186
Federal Register, 84-86, 188
Federal Rules: of Admiralty, 112; of Appellate Procedure, 106, 107, 109, 110, 113, 114; Bankruptcy Appellate Panel, 106, 109, 110, 112, 114, 123, 125, 127-130; of Bankruptcy Procedure, 106, 112, 114, 123, 125, 129; of Civil Procedure, 106, 107, 112, 113-115, 123, 126; of Criminal Procedure, 106, 107, 113-115; of Evidence, 106, 107, 114, 115. *See also* Supreme Court, U.S.; Tax Court, U.S.; *and specific appeals and trial courts*
Federal Trade Commission, 181-182
Federal Web Locator, 38, 39, 186
Federation of Tax Administrators, 168-169
FedStats, 186
FedWorld Information Network, 150-151, 186-187, 189; FLITE database, 49
FIEN Group nfoweb, 101
File Transfer Protocol (FTP), 15
FinanceNet, 188
financial consultants, 35
FindLaw, 33-34; academic journals, 260; bar associations, 281; California codes, 89; Circuit Courts of Appeals opinions, U.S., 51; Constitution, U.S., 85; D.C. Circuit opinions, 56; discussion forums, 278; Eighth Circuit opinions, 54; Eleventh Circuit opinions, 55; experts and consultants, 282; Federal Circuit opinions, 56; federal government resources, 187; Fifth Circuit opinions, 53; First Circuit opinions, 51; Florida appellate court opinions, 65; Florida Supreme Court opinions, 63; forms, 170; Fourth Circuit opinions, 52; Hawaii appellate opinions, 64; Idaho appellate opinions, 65; Indiana appellate opinions, international resources, 65, 241; Kansas appellate opinions, 66; Kentucky Supreme Court opinions, 66; Law Schools A-Z, 249; Legal News, 263; Library Subject Outline, 265; lower courts directory, nationwide, 146; Maine Supreme Court opinions, 67; Maryland appellate opinions, 67; Massachusetts appellate opinions, 67; Michigan appellate opinions, 68; Minnesota appellate opinions, 69; Missouri appellate decisions, 70; Montana Supreme Court opinions, 70; Nebraska appellate opinions, 70; Nevada Supreme Court opinions, 71; New Hampshire Supreme Court opinions, 71; New Mexico appellate opinions, 72; New York statutes, 95; Ninth Circuit opinions, 54; North Carolina appellate opinions, 73; Second Circuit opinions, 52; Seventh Circuit opinions, 54; Sixth Circuit opinions, 54; South Carolina Supreme Court opinions, 75; state opinions, 60; Supreme Court opinions, 48-49, 81; Tenth Circuit opinions, 55; Texas codes and statutes, 98; Third Circuit opinions, 52;

Index 335

topic research, 220; Utah appellate opinions, 76; Washington appellate opinions, 78
Finland, 241
First Use, 228
555-1212.com, 286-287
flame, to, defined, 290
Florida Law Online, 64, 315
Florida, State of: Banking Division, 198; banking forms, 156; bills, 90; Business and Professional Regulation, Department of, forms, 156; Business and Professional Regulation, Department of, Website, 198; Circuit and County Courts, 134; Comptroller's Office Division of Securities and Finance forms, 156; Comptroller's Office Division of Securities and Finance Website, 198; constitution, 90; Court of Appeals opinions, 64, 134; Court of Appeals Website, 134; Elections, Division of, forms, 156; Judicial Ethics Advisory Committee opinions, 134; legislature, 90, 197; licensing, health care and insurance, 198; local resources, 197; municipal codes, 100; official home page, 197-198; searchable databases, 197; Secretary of State filings, searchable, 197; State, Department of, forms, 155-156; State, Department of, Website, 197; statutes, 90; Sunbiz, 197; Supreme Court opinions, 63- 64, 134; Supreme Court Website, 134
Florida State University: *Law Review*, 259; School of Criminology and Criminal Justice, 224
FloridaBiz.com, 268
Folio Infobase: Delaware code, 90; Montana code, 93; New Jersey statutes, 94; New Mexico statutes, 95; Ohio codes, 96; South Carolina statutes, 97; Wisconsin code, 100
Food and Drug Administration policies, 187
Foreign and International Law Sources on the Internet, 240-241
ForInt-Law, 241
forms, bankruptcy, 107, 123-132, 148; collections of, 170-171; Copyright Office, U.S. 151-52; court, 54; federal agency, 148, 149, 151; Federal Communications Commission, 148-149; Federal Trade Commission, 181; Freddie Mac, 149; Immigration & Naturalization Service, 149, 156; Internal Revenue Service, 149-151; international patent applications, 183; LegalDocs,

170-171; National Labor Relations Board, 151; Patent and Trademark Office, U.S., 152; Quickform Contracts, 171; scope available online, 147; Securities Exchange Commission, 151; Small Business Administration, 185; Social Security Administration, 151; state agency, 152-169, 312; tax, 149-151, 156, 168-169, 195, 312; Veterans Ad ministration Forms, 152. *See also under specific courts and state agencies*
France, 246
Franklin Pierce Law Center Intellectual Property Mall, 254
Freddie Mac, 149
Free Agent newsreader, 14
Fulton County Daily Report, 268
Funk & Wagnalls, 299

gay resources, 36
General Accounting Office: reports, 188; Website, 176
General Code Publishers, 101
Georgetown University Law School: D.C. Circuit opinions, 55; Edward Bennett Williams Library, 251-252; Federal Circuit opinions, 51, 56
Georgia Legal Research Links, 315
Georgia, Republic of, 241
Georgia, State of: Banking and Finance Department forms, 156; Banking and Finance Department Website, 198; code, 90, 198; Court of Appeals opinions, 135; Environmental Facilities Authority forms, 156; legislature, 198; Merit System forms, 156; Natural Resources, Department of, forms, 156; official home page, 198; Revenue, Department of, forms, 156; Secretary of State filings, searchable, 198; Secretary of State forms, 156; Supreme Court opinions, 64, 135; Supreme Court Website, 135; Worker's Compensation, Board of, forms, 156
Georgia State University School of Law: Meta-Index for U.S. Legal Research, 35-36, 48-49
Germany, 246, 312
GIF file extension, 20, 148, 149
GigaLaw.com, 262, 267
Global Information Network, 301
Global Legal Information Network, 242
Goldman, Jerry, 173
Google search engine, 295
Gopher, 16
Gottstein, James B., Law Offices of: Alaska Le-

gal Resource Center Website, 61
GovBot Database of Government Web Sites, 187
Government Information Locator Service, 188
Government Information Xchange, 188-189
Government Printing Office, 189; committee reports, congressional, 175; Federal Regulations, Code of, 85, 86; GPO Access Database List, 188; Website, 176
government resources, state, 191-192. *See also under specific states*
government, U.S.: cabinet Websites, 178; executive branch Websites, 177-178; judicial branch Websites, 107-132, 173-174; legislative branch Websites, 174-176; White House Website, 177
governments, non-U.S.: embassies, 241; WorldSkip, 240
GPO Access: Database List, 188; public laws, 84
GPO gateways: Federal Register, 85; Federal Regulations, Code of, 85-86; Libraries of Purdue, 85; public laws, federal, 85; University of California, 85-86
graphics file types, 20, 149
Greece, 246
Guam, Supreme Court opinions, 79
Guide to European Databases, 246
Guide to Wacky Court Cases, 318
Guillot, Gregory H., 232

Harcourt Brace Professional Publishing, 238
Hart-Scott-Rodino Act, 182
Harvard Law Review, 257
Hawaii State Bar Association: Hawaii appellate opinions, 64
Hawaii, State of: Attorney General opinions, 198; Business Registration Division forms, 156; Court of Appeals opinions, 64, 135; financial institutions forms, 157; Judiciary Website, 135; official home page, 198; Real Estate Commission, 198; real estate licensing forms, 157; statutes, 90; Supreme Court Law Library, 64; Supreme Court opinions, 64, 135; Transportation, Department of, 198
headline aggregators, 303
headnotes, x, 3, 40, 43, 44, 47
Health and Human Services, Department of, 178
health law resources, 221
helper applications: explained, 19; where to find, 22
Hickel, Gregory J., 324

hierarchical indexes, defined, 30
Hieros Gamos, 34-35; CLE, 322; experts and consultants, 282-283; federal government resources, 188; international resources, 242; Law Lists index, 275; state government resources, 216
Hill, The, 265
hoaxes, e-mail, 290
home page, defined, 9
Hong Kong, 246
House of Representatives, U.S.: Code, U.S., at, 84-85; committees, 175; Internet Law Library, 220, 255, 256; Office of Law Revision Counsel, 84-85, 176; roll call votes, 175; Website, 174, 176
Housing and Urban Development, Department of, 178
Hricik, David, 6
Hugh F. MacMillan Law Library, 51, 52, 54, 56, 251, 312
humor, legal, 36, 312, 314, 318
Hungary, 246
HyperTerminal, 16
Hypertext Mark-up Language (HTML), 9
hypertext transfer protocol (http), 10

Idaho, State of: Bureau of Occupational Licenses forms, 157; Commerce, Department of, 199; constitution, 90; Court of Appeals opinions, 65, 135; Insurance, Department of, forms, 157; Judiciary Website, 135; official home page, 199; Oil and Gas Board forms, 157; Secretary of State forms, 157; statutes, 90; Supreme Court opinions, 65, 135
IDEX, 284-285
Illinois Court Reports, 65
Illinois Real Estate Journal, 269
Illinois, State of: Appellate Court opinions, 65; Business Services, Department of, forms, 157; corporate name availability, online searching, 199; First Stop Business Information Center, 199; Fourth Judicial Circuit Website, 135; Legislative Reference Bureau, 90; legislature, 199; municipal codes, 101; Nineteenth Judicial Circuit Website, 135; official home page, 199; public acts, 90; Reporter of Decisions, Office of the, 65; statutes, 90; Supreme Court opinions, 65
ImageLock.com, 228
Immigration & Naturalization Service, 149, 180
immigration law resources, 221. *See also* Immigration & Naturalization Service

Indiana University School of Law: Indiana appellate opinions, 65; Library, 252
Indiana, State of: Access Indiana Information Network, 66; code, 91; corporate name availability, online searching, 199; Court of Appeals opinions, 65- 66; Court of Appeals Website, 136; Insurance, Department of, forms, 157; legislature, 199; local resources, 199; municipal codes, 101; official home page, 199-200; Professional Licensing Agency forms, 157; searchable databases, 199-200; Secretary of State filings, searchable, 199; Secretary of State forms, 157; Supreme Court opinions, 65-66; Supreme Court Website, 136; Tax Court opinions, 66
Infomine, 188
Information America: Michigan business filings, 203
Information Network of Arkansas, 154, 194; searchable databases, 194
Information Network of Kansas, 200
Information Please Dictionary and Encyclopedia, 299
InfoSelect, 28
Infospace, 286
InfoUSA.com, 286
intellectual property resources: comprehensive, 227-228; copyright, 228, 230; Domain-Magistrate, 233; entertainment law, 230; Internet Corporation for Assigned Names and Numbers (ICANN), 233; patents, 230-232; trademarks, 230, 232, 233; Web monitoring services, 228. *See also* Copyright Office, U.S.; Library of Congress Information System; Patent and Trademark Office, U.S.
Interior, Department of, 178
Interlingua, 232
Internal Revenue Service, 149-151, 182, 262
international, comprehensive starting points, 37-38
International Financial Law Review, 266
international law resources: Africa, 240; Antarctica, 240; Argentina, 247; Asia, 240, 246; Australia, 240, 244, 312; Austria, 246; Azerbaijan, 255; bankruptcy, 223; Belarus, 246; Belgium, 246; Canada, 244-245, 312; Chile, 256; China, 266; Croatia, 246; Denmark, 246; England, 246, 248; Estonia, 246; Europe, 240, 246; European Patent Convention, 232; European Patent Office, 231-232; European Union, 246; France, 246; Germany, 246, 312; Greece, 246; Hungary, 246; Ireland, 248; Israel, 312; Italy, 246, 312; Kyrgyz Republic, 246; Latin America, 240, 247; Latvia, 246; Middle East, 241; Netherlands, The, 246; New Zealand, 312; Norway, 246; Pacific Rim, 240; Patent Cooperation Treaty, 152, 183, 228, 231; patents, 152, 183, 228, 231; Poland, 246; Romania, 246; Russia, 246, 247; service of process, 239; Spain, 246, 247; Sweden, 246, 312; Switzerland, 246; tax, 244; Ukraine, 246; United Kingdom, 248, 312; Uzbekistan, 246
International Tax Review, 266
Internet: explained, 1; scope of, 2
Internet Address Finder, 287
InterNet Bankruptcy Library, 223
Internet Chinese Legal Research Center, 246
Internet Corporation for Assigned Names and Numbers (ICANN), 233
Internet Explorer: adding favorites, 11; editing and organizing favorites, 12, 33; e-mailing pages in, 12-13; entering URL in, 10; navigating, 10; printing pages in, 13; reading saved files in, 12; saving files in, 12; viewing source code in, 9
Internet Law Library, 220, 255-256
Internet Lawyer Law Library, 312
Internet Lawyer, The, 260
Internet Legal Research Guide, 322
Internet Legal Resource Guide, 38, 312
Internet Oracle, The, 318
Internet Prospector, 216
Internet Public Library, 302-303
Internet Public Library Ready Reference Collection, 298
Internet Tools for Attorneys, 313
Inter-Parliamentary Union, 244
Iowa, State of: Banking, Division of, forms, 158; bills, 91; Business License Information Center, 200; codes, 91; Court of Appeals opinions, 66, 136; Court of Appeals Website, 136; General Assembly, 91; legislative history, 91; local resources, 200; official home page, 200; Real Estate Commission forms, 158; Secretary of State filings, searchable, 200; Secretary of State forms, 157-158; Secretary of State filings, searchable, 200; Supreme Court opinions, 66, 136; Supreme Court Website, 136
Israel, 312

Index

Italy, 246, 312

Java, disabling, 21
JavaScript, disabling, 21
jokes, lawyer, 36, 312, 314, 318
Journal of Taxation, 266
journals, professional, 259, 261
JPEG (JPG) file extension, 20
Judicial Panel on Multidistrict Litigation opinions, 48
JuriSearch: California appellate court opinions, 62-63; Ninth Circuit opinions, 55, 63; Supreme Court opinions, U.S., 63
Jurisline, 313
Jurist, 313, 324
Jurweb, 240
Justice, Department of, U.S.: Antitrust Division, 180; Civil Division, 180; Civil Rights Division, 180; Criminal Division, 180; Immigration & Naturalization Service, 149, 180; National Criminal Justice Reference Service, 225; Website, 178

Kansas, State of: bills, 91; Court of Appeals opinions, 66, 136; Court of Appeals Website, 136; Information Network, 91, 200; Judicial Branch Website, 136; legislative history, 91; lower courts, 136, 200; Real Estate Commission forms, 158; searchable databases, 200; Secretary of State forms, 158; session laws, 91; statutes, 91; Supreme Court opinions, 66, 136; Supreme Court Website, 136
Katsuey's Legal Gateway, 313
Kennedy, Dennis, 226
Kentucky, State of: Administrative Office of the Courts, 137; Alcoholic Beverage Control forms, 158; Cabinet for Economic Development, 201; Circuit Court Website, 137; Court of Justice Website, 136-137; Financial Institutions, Division of, forms, 158; Legislative Research Commission, 91; Occupations and Professions, Division for, forms, 158; One-Stop Business Licensing, 201; Public Advocacy, Department of, 224; public records, 201; Secretary of State filings, searchable, 201; Secretary of State forms, 158; statutes, 91; Supreme Court opinions, 66, 136; Supreme Court Website, 136; Tobacco Settlement Trust Corporation, 201
Key Numbers, x, 40, 43

KnowX, 287
Kuester, Jeffrey R., 227
Kuester Law Technology Law Resources, 227
Kyrgyz Republic, 246

Labor, Department of, U.S., 178
labor law resources, 221. *See also* Labor, Department of; National Labor Relations Board
Latin American Information Center (LANIC), 247
Latvia, 246
Law Bulletin Publishing Company, 267
Law Engine!, The, 314
Law Lists, 39, 275
Law News Network, 263
Law of the Sea Convention, 243
Law Office Computing, 267, 323
law reviews, 33-36, 257, 259-261
Law.com: affiliates, 62, 64, 264, 267-269; Counsel Quest, 312; LegalSeminars.com, 322; Website, 263
LawCrawler, 34, 56, 215
Lawgirl.com, 230
LawGuru: mailing list manager, 275-276; Website, 313
Lawinfo.com Legal Industry Directory, 284
Lawletter, The, 266
Law Library Resource Xchange. *See* LLRX
LawMoney.com, 266
LawOffice.com, 282
LawResearch, 45
LawRunner, 38
lawyer jokes, 36, 312, 314, 318
Lawyer Pilots Bar Association, 281
lawyers, directories of, 282
Lawyers Weekly: job database, 324; Massachusetts, 67, 270; Michigan, 68, 270; Missouri, 70, 270; North Carolina, 73, 270; Ohio, 73, 270; regional publications, 269-270; Rhode Island, 270; USA, 264; Virginia, 78; Website, 264
Lawyerware Legal Technology Tools, 323
'Lectric Law Library: family law Lawcopedia, 226; forms collection, 170
Legal Domain Network, 279-280; archives, 36
Legal Employment Search Site, The, 324
Legal Information Institute: American Legal Ethics Library, 225; Code, U.S., 84; Constitution, U.S., 85; constitutions, codes and statutes, state, 87; Circuit Courts of Appeals opinions, U.S., 52, 81; New York Court of Appeals opinions, 72; Project Hermes, 49,

Index 339

107; Supreme Court opinions, U.S., 49-50; topic research, 220-221; uniform laws, 87, 222; Website, 254
Legal Omnibus, The, 314
Legal Research Encyclopedia, 240-241
Legal Times, 268
LegalDocs, 170-171
LegalEthics.com, 225, 313
LegalSeminars.com, 322
lesbian resources, 36
Lexis Law Publishing: D.C. code, 90; Delaware code, 89-90; New Mexico statutes, 94-95; South Carolina statutes, 97; Tennessee code, 97
LEXIS-NEXIS: caselaw, comprehensive, 80; Michigan business filings, 203; scope, 44; Shepard's Citations, 40; Shepardizing with, 48; statutes, state, 101
LexPert, 284
LexUM Canadian resources, 244-245
libraries, law, 249-256; Alyne Queener Massey Law Library, 234; card catalogs, 249-250; Cleaves Law Library, 67; Cornell Law Library, 240, 254; Edward Bennett Williams Law Library, Georgetown Univ. Law Center, 55, 56, 251-252; Hugh F. Macmillan, Emory School of Law, 51, 52, 54, 56, 251, 312; Indiana University School of Law, 252; Internet Law Library, 255-256; LawLinks.com, 256; 'Lectric Law Library, 256; Lillian Goldman Library, Yale Law School, 253-254; New York University School of Law, 246; Northern California Association of, 106; Pritzker Legal Research Center, Northwestern University School of Law, 253; Robert Crown Law Library, Stanford Law School, 236; Social Law Library, 68; Tarlton Law Library, University of Texas School of Law, 108, 261; University of Iowa, 315; University of Kansas, 66; University of Southern California Law School, 259, 261; Washburn University School of Law, 66, 241, 253, 277, 323; Washington University School of Law, 246. *See also* Legal Information Institute
Library of Congress, 215, 242; Global Legal Information Network, 242; Information System (LOCIS), 179; Research Tools, 301; Thomas, 84, 85, 174-176; Website, 176
library, online law: components, 2; Essential Bookmarks, 29, 32-40, 45, 48, 186, 241, 262, 274; vs. fee-based computer database, 4
license, law, catalog of state requirements for, 281
licenses, financial institutions, searchable databases of: Arkansas, 194; Florida, 198;
licenses, liquor, searchable databases of: Alaska, 193; Arizona, 194; Indiana, 200; Texas, 212
licenses, professional, searchable databases of: American Board of Medical Specialties, 235; Arkansas, 194; Connecticut, 196; DocFinder, 235; Florida, 198; Georgia, 198; Idaho, 199; Iowa, 200; Missouri, 204; Ohio, 208; Tennessee, 212; Vermont, 213
Lillian Goldman Library, 253-254
link: broken, what to do, 41; defined, 10
Linux, Pretty Good Privacy for, 7
Listproc, 273. *See also* mailing lists
Listserv, 273. *See also* mailing lists
listserver, 273. *See also* mailing lists
LISZT mailing list catalog, 276
Litman, Jessica, 232
Litwak, Mark, 230
LLRX, 40, 267, 323; Guide to European Databases, 246
LLRXBuzz, 40, 262, 274
Loislaw.com: caselaw, comprehensive, 80; scope, 44; statutes, state, 101
Los Angeles Times, The, 305
Louisiana, State of: Administrative Code, 91; Clerks of Court, 137; codes, 91; constitution, 91; Legislative Subscriber System, 91; local resources, 201; lower court Websites, 137; official home page, 201; Secretary of State filings, searchable, 201; Secretary of State forms, 158-159; statutes, 91; Supreme Court opinions, 66-67; Supreme Court Website, 66, 137
Louis-Jacques, Lyonette, 39
Luo, Wei, 246

Macintosh: Computer Interest Group, ABA, 323; Consultant, 28; Law Office Software List for, the, 323; MacZilla, 22; Media Player, 24; multimedia, built-in, 20; Pretty Good Privacy for, 7; QuickTime, 22; RealPlayer, 23; URL Manager Pro, 26; Yet Another NewsWatcher, 14
MacZilla, 22
Magic 8-Ball, The, 318
mail reader, 13-14
mailing lists, 14, 272-274, 276, 292; abbrevia-

tions used in, 291; archives, finding and searching, 276-277; Big Ear tracking site, The, 280; CataList, 276; catalogs of, 39, 274-276; communication tips for, 289, 291-292; cyberlaw, 274; digest, 273; emoticons used in, 291; FAQ, 276; Fifth Circuit opinions, 53, 108; general interest, 276; Georgia appellate opinions, 64, 268; how they work, 272-274; Illinois appellate opinions, 65; Internet Oracle, The, 318; Law Lists, 39, 275; LawGuru, manager, 275-276; listserver, 273; Massachusetts appellate opinions, 67-68; Michigan appellate opinions, 68; Middle District (Pennsylvania) Bankruptcy Bar Association, 129; Missouri appellate opinions, 70; Netiquette, 288-289; Net-Lawyers, 275; New Hampshire Judicial Branch, 139; *New Jersey Law Journal*, 269; New York Court of Appeals opinions, 72; Ninth Circuit, 109; Ninth Circuit opinions, 55; North Carolina appellate opinions, 73; North Dakota Supreme Court opinions, 73, 141; opinions, 63; saving subscription confirmations, 275; Supreme Court opinions, U.S., 50; Tennessee appellate opinions, 75; Texas Alcoholic Beverage Commission, 212; Texas appellate opinions, 269; Texas Court of Appeals (Fifth District) opinions, 76, 143; Texas Department of Licensing & Regulation, 212; tracking site, 280; turning off signature for, 274; unsubscribing for vacation or e-mail address change, 274; using mailbox filters for, 275; Virginia appellate decisions, 78

Maine Lawyers' Network, 315

Maine, State of: constitution, 91; Financial Institutions Bureau forms, 159; Judicial Branch Website, 137; legislature, 201; local resources, 201; official home page, 201; Secretary of State filings, searchable, 201; Secretary of State forms, 159; session laws, 91; statutes, 91-92; Supreme Court opinions, 67, 137

Major, Hagen & Africa, 325

Majordomo, 273. *See also* mailing lists

Managing Intellectual Property Website, 266

marketing consultants, 35

Martin Law Offices: Pennsylvania statutes, 96

Maryland, State of: Attorney General, 202; bills, 92; corporate charter forms, 159; Court of Appeals opinions, 67, 137; Court of Special Appeals opinions, 67; General Assembly, 92; Judiciary Website, 116, 137; legislature, 202; local resources, 202; Maryland Business Information Network, 202; municipal codes, 202; official home page, 202; Sailor public information network, 202; searchable databases, 202; Secretary of State filings, searchable, 202; statutes, 92, 202; Supreme Court opinions, 137

Massachusetts, Commonwealth of: Consumer Protection Office, 203; Court of Appeals opinions, 67-68; Court of Appeals Website, 137; lower court Websites, 137; official home page, 202; Secretary of Commonwealth, 202; Secretary of Commonwealth forms, 159; session laws, 92; statutes, 92; Superior Court opinions, 68; Superior Court Website, 137; Supreme Court opinions, 67-68

Maule, James Edward, 236

McAfee: Guard Dog software, 8; VirusScan software, 21

McClurg, Andrew L., 319

McGuire, Colleen, 72

Med Engine!, The, 234

mediation resources, 221-222, 256, 283

medical law resources, 234-235, 313; Medical World Search, 234; MedLine, 234; National Library of Medicine, The, 234

Medical World Search, 234

MedLine, 234

Mercer University: Walter F. George School of Law, 315

Merlin Information Services, 288

Meta-Index for U.S. Legal Research, 35-36, 48-49

Mexico, 245

Michigan Institute of Continuing Legal Education: forms, 315; Michigan appellate opinions, 68

Michigan Law Review, 258

Michigan, State of: Clerk's Offices, 138; Corporation Division forms, 159; Corporations, Securities and Land Development Bureau, 203; Court of Appeals opinions, 68; Court of Appeals Website, 137-138; legislature, 203; official home page, 203; statutes, 92; Superior Court opinions, 68; Supreme Court Website, 137-138; Washtenaw County Court opinions, 69

Michigan Supreme Court Report, 137

Micro-Patent, 233
Milbank, Tweed, Hadley & McCloy LLP, 314
Minnesota Finance and Commerce Appellate Courts Division: opinions, 69
Minnesota Real Estate Journal, 269
Minnesota, State of: Administrative Hearings, Office of, opinions, 69; administrative rules, 93; Attorney General opinions, 69; Attorney General Website, 203; bills, 92; Court of Appeals opinions, 69, 138; courts, 203; legislature, 203; local resources, 203; official home page, 203; Revisor of Statutes, Office of, 93; searchable databases, 203; Secretary of State, 203; Secretary of State forms, 160; session laws, 92; State Court System Website, 138; statutes, 92-93; Superior Court opinions, 69; Supreme Court opinions, 138; Tax Court opinions, 69, 138; Tax Court Website, 138; Worker's Compensation Court opinions, 69
Mississippi Lawyers World Wide Web Domain, 203; Mississippi appellate decisions, 69
Mississippi, State of: Attorney General, 203; bills, 93; code, 93; Court of Appeals opinions, 69, 138; Court of Appeals Website, 138; legislature, 203; local resources, 203; official home page, 203; real estate appraiser forms, 160; Secretary of State, 93, 203; Supreme Court opinions, 69, 138; Supreme Court Website, 138, 203
Missouri, State of: CaseNet , 139; Circuit Courts Website, 138; Court of Appeals opinions, 70, 138; Court of Appeals Website, 138; Economic Development, Department of, 204; General Assembly, 93; licensing rosters, professional, 204; official home page, 203-204; Professional Registration Division, 204; Register, 93; Regulations, Code of , 93; Secretary of State filings, searchable, 203; Secretary of State forms, 160-161; statutes, 93; Supreme Court opinions, 70, 138; Supreme Court Website, 138
Montana, State of: bills, 93; code, 93; Commerce Department, 204; Economic Development, 204; Justice, Department of, 204; local resources, 204; master business license, 161; official home page, 204; One-Stop Business Licensing, 204; Professional & Occupational Licensing, Division of, forms, 161; Professional &

Occupational Licensing, Division of, Website, 204; Secretary of State filings, searchable, 204; Secretary of State forms, 161; State Law Library, 70; Supreme Court opinions, 70, 139; Virtual Human Services Pavilion, 204
Moreover.com, 303
movie files, 21-22
MPEG player, 303
Multistate Tax Commission, 169
Municipal Code Corporation, 100
municipal codes, 34, 87, 100-101; Alaska, 133; American Legal Publishing, 101; Book Publishing Company, 101; California, 100-101; Florida , 100; General Code Publishers, 101; Illinois, 101; Indiana, 101; New Jersey, 101; New York, 101; North Carolina, 100; Ohio, 101; Pennsylvania, 101; Texas, 100
municipal Websites, 215-217. *See also under specific states*
MySpider.com, 26

NAPALAW, 314
National Archives and Record Administration: Federal Regulations, Code of, 85-86
National Asian Pacific American Bar Association, 281
National Association of Counties, 217
National Association of State Information Resource Executives, 216
National Center for State Courts: lower courts directory, nationwide, 146
National City Government Resource Center, 217
National Directory of Expert Witnesses, 283
National Labor Relations Board, 151; opinions, 182
National Law Journal, 264
National League of Cities, 216
National Library of Medicine, 234
National Practice Institute, 322
National Public Radio, 304
National Registry of Experts, 283
National Technical Information Service FedWorld Information Network, 186-187
Nations, Howard, 234
Naval Observatory, U.S.: light conditions calculator, 296
Nebraska, State of: Administrative Code, 94; bills, 94; Court of Appeals opinions, 70; official home page, 204-205; Secretary of State filings, searchable, 204; Secretary of State forms, 161; Secretary of State Web-

site, 94; slip laws, 94; statutes, 94; Supreme Court opinions, 70; Workers' Compensation Court, 204
Net Lizard software, 45
Netiquette, 288-289
Netscape Navigator: adding bookmarks, 11; editing and organizing bookmarks, 12, 33; e-mailing pages in, 12; entering URL in, 10; mailboxes, Netscape Messenger, 13; navigating, 10; plug-ins and helper applications, new, 22; printing pages in, 13; reading saved files in, 12; saving files in, 12; viewing source code in, 9
Nevada, State of: Administrative Code, 94; Attorney General opinions, 205; Business & Industry, Department of, forms,162; Business & Industry, Department of, Website, 205; Business Information Network, 205; legislature, 205; Office of the Clerk, 71; official home page, 205; Register, 94; Secretary of State forms, 161; Secretary of State Website, 205; Securities Division forms, 161; statutes, 94, 127; Supreme Court opinions, 71
New Hampshire, State of: bills, 94; Business and Economic Development, Office of, 206; courts, 206; Judicial Branch Website, 139; legislature, 206; local resources, 206; official home page, 205; Real Estate Commission forms, 162; State, Department of, forms, 162; statutes, 94, 206; Supreme Court opinions, 71, 139; Treasury Department, 206
New Jersey Law Journal, 268
New Jersey Law Network, 315
New Jersey, State of: bills, 94; Court of Appeals opinions, 71; courts, 206; insurance forms, 162; Judiciary Website, 139; legislature, 94, 206; local resources, 206; municipal codes, 101; official home page, 206; Real Estate Commission forms, 162; Revenue, Division of, Business Gateway, 206; searchable databases, 206; State, Department of, forms, 162; statutes, 94; Supreme Court opinions, 71; Tax Court opinions, 71
New Mexico Technet: New Mexico appellate opinions, 72
New Mexico, State of: Administrative Code, 95; Attorney General, 207; bills, 94; codes, 94-95; Court of Appeals opinions, 72; Elections, Bureau of, 207; Financial Institutions Division forms, 163; Judiciary Website, 139-140; legislative concordances, 95; legislature, 207; local resources, 207; official home page, 206-207; Public Regulation Commission forms, 162; Real Estate Commission forms, 162; Regulation and Licensing Department forms, 162-163; Regulation and Licensing Department Website, 207; searchable databases, 207; Secretary of State filings, searchable, 207; Secretary of State forms, 162; Securities Division forms, 162; statutes, 94-95; Supreme Court opinions, 72, 139; Treasurer, 207
New York Law Journal, 269; Court of Appeals, Appellate Division, and Supreme Court opinions, 72
New York, State of: Appellate Division opinions, 49, 72; bills, 95; Comptroller, 207; Court of Appeals opinions, 49, 72, 140; Court of Claims opinions, 72; Housing Court decisions, 72; legislature, 207; local resources, 207; municipal codes, 101; official home page, 207; Secretary of State forms, 163; State Assembly, 95; statutes, 95; Supreme Court opinions, 72; Taxation and Finance, Department of, 207; Unified Court System Website, 140
New York Times on the Web, The, 305
New York University: School of Law, Guide to European Databases, 246; *Law Review*, 259
New Zealand, 312
news, broadcast, 303-304; financial, 266; headline, 303; international business, 266; legal, 262-270, 303; legislative, 177, 265; technology, 267. *See also* newsletters; newsletters, e-mail; periodicals, Web-based; *and specific publications*
newsgroups, 14, 278-280, 292; abbreviations used in, 291; archives, 280; Big Ear tracking site, The, 280; catalogs of, 39, 279; Clarinet, 280; communication tips for, 289, 291-292; emoticons used in, 291-292; Law Lists, 39; Netiquette, 288-289; rec.humor.oracle, 318; tracking site, 280
Newsletter Access, 261
newsletters: *Corporate Edge, The* (Delaware Division of Corporations), 197; *Death Penalty News*, 224; *Law Practice Management Newsletter*, 323; New York, Northern District Public Defender's Office, 118; *Rodent, The*, 267
newsletters, e-mail: Alabama Supreme Court de-

cisions, 60; Cal Law, 268; Daily Bankruptcy Review, 223; Digital Dispatch, 151, 262; GigaLaw.com, 262, 267; Internet Lawyer Legal Newsstand, 261; Internet Patent News Service, 232; IRS Local News Net, 151, 262; Lawgirl.com, 230; LLRXBuzz, 40, 262, 274; Local News Net, 262; National Criminal Justice Reference Service, 225; ResearchBuzz, 293; Site-tation, 39, 262, 274-275
NewsLinx, 303
newspapers: *Chicago Daily Law Bulletin*, 269; *Daily Business Review*, 268; *Delaware Corporate Reporter*, 268; *Delaware Law Weekly*, 268; *Fulton County Daily Report*, 268; *Hill, The*, 265; *Lawyers Weekly USA*, 264; *Legal Intelligencer, The*, 269; *Legal Times*, 268; *Los Angeles Times,* The, 305; *Massachusetts Lawyers Weekly*, 67, 269-270; *Michigan Lawyers Weekly*, 68, 269-270; *Missouri Lawyers Weekly*, 70, 269-270; *New Jersey Law Journal*, 268; *New York Law Journal*, 269; *New York Times* on the Web, The, 305; Newspapers Online!, 304-305; *North Carolina Lawyers Weekly*, 73, 269-270; *Ohio Lawyers Weekly*, 73, 269-270; *Pennsylvania Law Weekly*, 269; *Recorder, The*, 268; *Rhode Island Lawyers Weekly*, 269, 270; *Roll Call* Online, 177; *Texas Lawyer*, 269; *Virginia Lawyers Weekly*, 78, 269-270; *Wall Street Journal,* The, 266, 305; *Washington Post,* The, 305
Newspapers Online!, 304-305
newsreader, 14. *See also* newsgroups
Noble Group directory, 283
Nolo Press: Legal Encyclopedia, 227
Norman, Jr., James Gray, 316
North American Securities Administrators Association, 184
North Atlantic Assembly, 244
North Carolina, State of: Business Licensing Information Office, 163, 207; corporate name availability, online searching, 207; Court of Appeals opinions, 73, 140; Court of Appeals Website, 140; lower court Websites, 140; official home page, 207; Secretary of State filings, searchable, 207; Secretary of State forms, 163; session laws, 95; statutes, 95, 129; Supreme Court opinions, 73; Supreme Court Website, 140

North Dakota, State of: Attorney General's Licensing Section forms, 164; Banking and Financial Institutions, Department of, forms, 164; Banking and Financial Institutions, Department of, Website, 208; code, 95; courts, 207; legislature, 207; official home page, 95, 207; Secretary of State forms, 163-164; Secretary of State Website, 208; Securities Commissioner forms, 164; Supreme Court opinions, 73, 141; Supreme Court Website, 140-141; Vital Records, 208
Northern Light search engine, 174, 295
Northern Mariana Islands, Commonwealth of: Superior and Supreme Court opinions, 79
Northwestern University: Oyez Project, 173; School of Law, international library resources at, 243; School of Law, Pritzker Legal Research Center, 253
Norton: AntiVirus software, 21; Internet Security software, 8
noticing, e-mail: Illinois, Northern District, 115; Indiana General Assembly BillWatch, 200; Nebraska, District of, 118; New Mexico, Bankruptcy Court, 128; New Mexico, District of, 118; New York, Southern District, 119; North Dakota, 141; South Carolina legislation, 211; Texas, Fifth Court of Appeals, 143; Virginia, Eastern District Bankruptcy Court, 131. *See also* Bankruptcy Courts, U.S.

Ohio, State of: Administrative Code, 95; Administrative Services, Department of, 95; code, 95-96; Commerce Department forms, 164; Court of Appeals opinions, 141; courts, 208; General Assembly, 95; legislature, 208; licensing rosters, professional, 208; local resources, 208; municipal codes, 101; Secretary of State filings, searchable, 208; Secretary of State forms, 164; session laws, 95; Supreme Court opinions, 73-74, 141; Supreme Court Website, 141
oil and gas filing databases, searchable: Alabama, 192; Gulf Coast, 235; Texas, 212
Oingo search engine, 296
Oklahoma, State of: Attorney General opinions, 141, 209; Banking Department, 209; Commerce, Department of, 208; Court of Appeals opinions, 74, 141; Court of Criminal Appeals opinions, 74; Court of Criminal Appeals Website, 141; court rules, 74; Employment Security Commission, 209; offi-

cial home page, 208; Secretary of State forms, 164; Secretary of State Website, 208; Securities Commission, 165; statutes, 74, 96, 141, 209; Supreme Court Network, 48, 74, 96, 141; Supreme Court opinions, 74, 141; Supreme Court Website, 141

OmniForm Internet Filler software, 160

1-800-U.S. Search, 288

OneLook Dictionaries, 300

Oneview, 26

online research: by topic, 219-238; components of, 4; guides, 40; resources, scope of, 29-30; tutorials, 40; vs. fee-based computer database, 4; vs. library research, 3

Open Directory Project searchable index, 295

Opera browser, 19

opinions. *See under specific courts*

opinions, same day posting of: California appellate courts, 62; Eighth Circuit, 54; Eighth Circuit BAP, 54; Fifth Circuit, 52; First Circuit, 108; Florida Supreme Court, 64; Idaho appellate, 65; Indiana appellate, 66; Nebraska appellate, 70; Sixth Circuit, 53; Supreme Court, U.S., 50; Texas Court of Criminal Appeals, 76; Wisconsin, 145

Oppedahl & Larson LLP: Intellectual Property Law Web Server, 228

Oregon, State of: Attorney General, 209; bills, 96; Business and Economic Development, Office of, 209-210; Court of Appeals opinions, 74; courts Website, 209; Judicial Department Website, 141; legislature, 96; licensing board forms, 165; licensing, health care and insurance, 210; Secretary of State filings, searchable, 209; Secretary of State forms, 165; statutes, 96; Supreme Court opinions, 74; Tax Court opinions, 74; Treasurer, 209

Osgoode Hall Law School Canada Law Website, 245

Oxford English Dictionary, 300

Oyez Project, 173

PACER: access numbers, 111, 122; explained, 107, 111, 122; public access, 51; sites using, 108, 109, 110, 112, 113, 114, 115, 116, 118, 119, 120, 121, 122, 123, 124, 125, 126, 127, 128, 129, 130, 131, 132; Website, 107

PACERNet: explained, 111, 122; sites using, 121, 123, 126

Pacific Information Resources Search System, 192

PaLawNet, 269

Patent and Trademark Office, U.S.: forms, 152; registrations, searchable databases of, 183; Website, 182-183

Patent Bibliographic Database, U.S., 183

Patent Cooperation Treaty, 152, 183, 228, 231, 233

patent law resources: Franklin Pierce Law Center, 227; international, 228; Kuester Law Technology Law Resources, 227; Patent Cooperation Treaty, 152, 183, 228, 231; World Intellectual Property Organization, 228

patents: British, 232; European Patent Office, 231-232, 233; IBM Intellectual Property Server, 231; Internet Patent News, 232; Japanese, 231; pending litigation involving, 232

PCDEZIP decompression utility, 110

PCL file extension, 148

PDF file extension, 148

Pennsylvania, Commonwealth of: appellate opinions, 49; Athletic Commission, 210; Banking, Department of, 210; bills, 96; code, 96; Commonwealth Court opinions, 74; General Assembly, 96; Health, Department of, forms, 165; licensing, health care and insurance, 210; lower court Websites, 141-142; municipal codes, 101; official home page, 210; searchable databases, 210; Securities Commission forms, 165; Securities Commission Website, 210; State, Department of, forms, 165; State, Department of, Website, 210; statutes, 96; Superior Court opinions, 74; Superior Court Website, 141; Supreme Court opinions, 74; Supreme Court Website, 141

Pennsylvania Law Weekly, 269

Pennsylvania Legal Research Web Sites, 316

periodicals: law office management, 40; legal research, 40; legal technology, 40; tax, 266; *Tilt* magazine, 319. *See also* law reviews; news; newsletters; newsletters, e-mail; newspapers

personal injury law resources, 234-235, 256

phone numbers: finding, 285-286; reverse lookup, 286

Piper Resources, 216

PKUNZIP decompression utility, 148

Plug-In Plaza Website, 22

plug-ins: Adobe Acrobat Reader, 23; explained, 19; movie files, 22, 24; QuickTime, 22,

Index 345

124, 173, 304; RealAudio, 304, 322; Real-Player, 23, 176, 181, 322; Shockwave, 24, 322; where to find, 22; Windows Media Player, 24, 213
PNG file extension, 20
Poland, 246
Portal to Legal Resources in the UK and Ireland, 248
posting, 5
Powermarks software, 26
Practical Tax Strategies, 266
Practicing Attorney's Home Page, 313
Practising Law Institute, 322
Pretty Good Privacy encryption software, 7
Pritzker Legal Research Center, 253
privacy: e-mail, 6; and encryption, 7; on the Web, 7-8
private investigators, 35
probate law resources, 225. *See also* estate planning
process servers, 35
Professional City/Esquire Heights, 314
Project Bartleby, 302
Project DIANA, 254
Project Gutenberg, 302
Project Hermes, 49, 50, 107
property law resources, 235, 313
Pro2Net, 238; discussion forums, 278
PS file extension, 148
Public Technology, Inc, 217
Puerto Rico, 79
Purdue University: GPO Access, 85; Virtual Reference Desk, 298

Quebec LexUM, 244-245
query. *See* search query
Quickform Contracts, 171
QuickTime, 22, 124, 173, 304

RACER: explained, 111, 122; sites using, 120, 127, 131, 132
Rao, Dittakavi, 316
RealAudio, 23, 304, 322
RealPlayer, 23, 176, 181, 321, 322
Realty Engine!, The , 235
Recorder, The, 268
records: military, 185; public, search services, 287-288; public, searchable databases, 193-194, 287. *See also* corporate records, searchable databases of; *and specific courts and state agencies*
RefDesk, 297

reference indexes: dictionary.com, 298; Internet Public Library Ready Reference Collection, 298; RefDesk, 297; Research-It!, 297; Virtual Reference Desk, 298
reference sites, literary: Complete Works of William Shakespeare, 302; Electronic Literature Foundation, 302; Internet Public Library, 302; Online Books Page, 303; Project Bartleby, 302; Project Gutenberg, 302
research, online: components, 4; vs. fee-based computer database, 4; guides, 40; vs. library research, 3; resources, scope of, 29-30; by topic, 219-228, 231, 232, 234-238; tutorials, 40
ResearchBuzz, 293
Research-It!, 297, 317
research services. *See* commercial research services
Rhode Island Law Links, 316
Rhode Island, State of: bills, 210; corporate forms, 165-166; General Assembly, 96, 210; lower court Websites, 142; official home page, 210; probate forms, 166; public laws, 96; Secretary of State filings, searchable, 210; statutes, 96-97, 210; Superior Court opinions and Website, 142; Supreme Court opinions, 74, 142; Supreme Court Website, 142
RIA, 266
Rigmatch, 235
Roby v. Corporation of Lloyd's, 81
Rodent, The, 267
Roe v. Wade, 81
Roget's Internet Thesaurus, 301
Roll Call Online, 177
Romania, 246
Rosenoer, Jonathan, 261
Roznovschi, Mirela, 246
RTF file extension, 148
Russia, 246, 247
Rutgers University School of Law: Animal Rights Center, 222; New Jersey appellate opinions, 48, 71
Rwanda, International Criminal Tribunal of, 243
Rzesniowiecki, Linda, 72

Satterlee Stephens Burke & Burke LLP: CyBarrister, 230
saving: bookmarks, 11; newsgroup articles, 15; Web pages, 12
Sax, Jodi L., 230
Schmidt, Dennis, 236

search engines: All-in-One Search Page, 317; defined, 30; Deja.com, 280; Dogpile, 317; FAST Search All the Web, All the Time, 295; Find-It!, 317; foreign language, 243; general reference, 293-296; go2net Metacrawler, 317; Google, 295; how to use, 31-32; Ixquick, 243; LawCrawler, 37, 56; LawRunner, 38; legal, 37-38; for newsgroups, 280; Northern Light, 174, 295; Oingo, 296; Search.com, 317; usgovsearch, 174; W3 Search Engines, 317

search query: constructing, 4; for a case on point, a specific case, or subsequent citations, 47; phrasing tips, 31, 32, 47, 80-82, 102-103. *See also under specific search engines*

searchable indexes, 33-36; FindLaw, 33; general reference, 293-295; Hieros Gamos, 34-35; Open Directory Project, 295; Yahoo!, 242, 294; Yahoo! Law, 36

Seattle Public Library, 100

Securities Exchange Commission: EDGAR, 35, 184, 236, 313; forms, 183; Small Business Forms & Associated Regulations, 151; Website, 183-184

securities law resources: SEC LAW.com, 236; Stanford Securities Class Action Clearinghouse, 236. *See also* Securities and Exchange Commission; *and specific state agencies*

security. *See* browser; virus.

Senate, U.S.: committees, 175; Congressional Research Library, 85; roll call votes, 175; Website, 174, 176

Sentencing Commission, U. S., 185

services, commercial. *See* commercial services

services, commercial research. *See* commercial research services

SGML file extension, 148

Shakespeare, William: Complete Works of, 302

Shakespearean Insult Generator, 318

Shark Talk, 318

Shepardizing, defined, 3

Shepard's Citations, 40, 48

Shockwave, 24, 322

signature (sig): defined, 13; turning off when e-mailing listserver, 274

Singer, Randy B.: Attorney's Toolbox, 311-312; Law Office Software List for the Macintosh Computer, The, 323; state and federal law links, 88

Site-tation, 39, 262, 274-275

Small Business Administration: PRO-Net, 185; Website, 185

Smoking Gun, The, 319

Social Law Library: Massachusetts appellate opinions, 68

Social Security Administration, 151

software: ad- and cookie-blocking, 8; anti-virus, 21; bookmark management, 24-28; browser, 19; ClicknSearch, 35; clipboard management, 27; Corel WordPerfect viewer, 76; encryption, 8; Envoy viewer, 94; information management, 28; IP/TV, 136; MacZilla, 22; Media Player, 22; Microsoft Word Viewer, 59, 73, 141; MPEG player, 303; Net Lizard, 45; Netscape plug-ins and helper applications, 22; newsreader, 14; OmniForm Internet Filler, 160; OneForm, 158; Palm Pilot, 28; PaperPort Viewer, 130; PCDEZIP, 110; PKUNZIP, 98; Plug-In Plaza Website, 22; QuickTime, 22, 124, 173, 304; Remote Briefcase, 312; research sidekick, 45; Telnet, 16; TUCOWS Website, 22; Windows Media Player, 24, 213

Software Publishers Association, 229

Sokolski, Robert E., 72

Sommers, Robert L., 238

sound files, 20

source code, 9-10

Source Translation and Optimization, Internet Patent News, 232

South Carolina, State of: Administrative Law Judge Division opinions, 75; Administrative Law Judge Division Website, 142; Attorney General opinions, 211; code, 97; Commerce, Department of, 211; courts Website, 211; Judicial Website, 142; legislature, 211; local resources, 211; official home page, 211; Regulations, Code of, 97; searchable databases, 211; Supreme Court opinions, 75, 142

South Dakota, State of: agency forms, 166; corporate forms, 166; official home page, 211; statutes, 97; Supreme Court opinions, 75

Southern New England School of Law: Rhode Island Law Links, 316

Spain, 246

spam: defined, 290; protection, 7, 277, 279-280

sports law resources, 221

Stanford Law Review, 258

Stanford University: Infomine, 188; Law School, Robert Crown Law Library, 236; Libraries, 229

STARPAS (State of Arizona Public Access System), 194
starting points, comprehensive: Arizona law, 314; bar association Websites, 281; California law, 314; commercial, 43-45; court Websites, 105-106; federal government sites, 38; Florida law, 315; general legal research, 33-38, 311-314; general reference, 293-296, 298-300; Georgia law, 315; international law, 239-244; international resources, 187-188; Iowa law, 315; local government resources, 188-189, 217; Maine law, 315; Michigan law, 315; Nevada law, 315; New Jersey law, 315; news sources, 303; Oklahoma law, 315; opinions, 44, 106; opinions, state, 60; Pennsylvania law, 316; records, military, 185; records, public, 192; Rhode Island law, 316; South Carolina law, 316; state government resources, 187-188, 215-216; state government Websites, 215-216; state resources, 216; statutes, federal, 84-85; statutes, state, 86-88; Texas law, 316; topic research, 220-221, 227; U.S. government resources, 185-189; Virginia law, 316; West Virginia law, 316
state: agencies, 34, 152-169; caselaw, 34, 38, 47, 48, 60-80; courts, 34, 105-106, 132-146; home pages, 34, 37-38; opinions, 34, 38, 47, 48, 60-80; statutes, 34, 38, 83, 86-102. *See also under specific states*
State, Department of, U.S.: foreign service of process requirements, 239; Website, 178
Sterling Codifiers, 101
stock exchange Websites, 184
subscribing, 14
Superfund data, 187
Supreme Court, U.S.: Clerk's Automated Response System, 107; FLITE database, 49; opinion listserver, 50; opinions, 33-37, 48-50, 80, 107, 113, 186, 188, 313; opinions hyperlinked to constitution, 85; oral arguments, recordings of, 173; order lists, 50; Oyez Project, 173; rules, 106-107; Website, 50, 107, 174
surfing, 5; privacy concerns, 7
Sweden, 246, 312
Switchboard, 286
Switzerland, 246

Taiwan, 246
Tarlton Law Library: Fifth Circuit information, 108; Law Journals and Periodicals Website, 261
Tax Analysts: TaxLibrary.com, 238
Tax Analysts Online, 266
Tax and Accounting Sites Directory, 236, 244
Tax Court, U.S.: opinions, 48, 59; Rules of Practice and Procedure, 107
tax law resources: commercial research services, 238; general resources, 236-237; periodicals, 266. *See also* forms, tax; Internal Revenue Service; Tax Court, U.S.; Treasury, Department of, U.S.; *and specific states*
Tax Master, 236-237
Tax Prophet, The, 238
Technical Advisory Service for Attorneys, 284
technology, law office, 323
Telnet, 16, 179, 187; explained, 16-17
Tennessee Criminal Law Website, 274
Tennessee, State of: code, 97; Comptroller, 212; Court of Appeals opinions, 75, 142; Court of Criminal Appeals opinions, 75, 142; courts, 211; judicial ethics opinions, 142; legislature, 211; local resources, 212; official home page, 211; public and private acts, 97; Rules and Regulations, 97; searchable databases, 212; Secretary of State forms, 166; Secretary of State Website, 97, 212; Supreme Court opinions, 75, 142; Supreme Court Website, 142; Treasurer, 212; Workers Compensation Panel rulings, 75
Texas Lawyer, 269
Texas Legal Research Index, 316
Texas Records and Information Locator, 212
Texas, State of: Administrative Code, 98; Attorney General, 212; Banking, Department of, forms, 166; bills, 98; codes, 97-98, 142; Court of Appeals (Fifth District) opinions, 76, 82; Court of Criminal Appeals opinions, 76, 142-143; Court of Criminal Appeals Website, 143; Courts of Appeals Website, 143; courts Website, 212; Criminal Justice, Department of, 212; Harris County Website, 217; Judicial Ethics Advisory Committee opinions, 142; Judiciary Website, 142-143; Juvenile Probation Commission, 212; Legislative Subscriber System, 98; legislature, 212; local resources, 212; official home page, 212; Public Safety, Department of, 212; regulations, 142; searchable databases, 212; Secretary of State filings, searchable, 212; Secretary of State forms,

166; Securities Board forms, 166; statutes, 97-98, 142, 212; Supreme Court opinions, 75, 142, 143; Supreme Court Website, 143
TexLaw, 269
thesauruses, 301
13 Network, 224
THOMAS, 174-176; Code, U.S., 84; Congressional Record, 175; legislative history, federal, 174; public laws, 84, 85
Thomas, Jack, 318
Thomas, Stephen J., 314
Thomson & Thomson, 233
thread, 14
Tilt magazine, 319
Toman, Dennis, 226
Touro Law Center: Second Circuit opinions, 52
Trademark Application and Registration Retrieval System, 183
Trademark Electronic Application System, 183
trademarks: All About Trademarks, 232; pending litigation involving, 232; Trademarks & Unfair Competition outline, 232-233
TradeName.com, 228
translators, 35, 285
Transportation, Department of, U.S., 178
transportation law resources, 221. *See also* Transportation, Department of, U.S.
Treasury, Department of, U.S., 178
TUCOWS Website, 22, 26, 28
TXT file extension, 148

Ukraine, 246
Uniform Resource Locator (URL), 10; doesn't work, what to do when it, 41
Uniform System of Citation, A, 34, 48
United Kingdom, 312
United Nations, 240, 243
University of Bayreuth, Germany: Jurweb, 240
University of California: GPO Gate, 85-86; Infomine, 188
University of Chicago Law School: D'Angelo Law Library, 252; Law Lists, 39, 275, 277; *Law Review*, 59
University of Cincinnati College of Law: Project DIANA, 254
University of Florida Levin College of Law: Florida Supreme Court opinions, 63
University of Geneva: Centre Universitaire d' Informatique, 317
University of Michigan: federal and local government resources, 189; Documents Center, congressional directories in, 176; Law

School library, 252
University of Minnesota: Human Rights Library Project DIANA Website, 254; political science department, 244; Websites on National Parliaments Page, 244
University of Montreal: LexUM, 244
University of New South Wales: Australasian Legal Information Institute, 244
University of Northern Iowa: Tax and Accounting Sites Directory, 236
University of Pittsburgh: Jurist Website, 324; School of Law, 313
University of Saarland, Germany: European Laws and Legal Systems, 246
University of South Carolina School of Law: South Carolina Legal Resources, 316; South Carolina Supreme Court opinions, 75, 142
University of Southern California Law School and Law Library, 259, 261
University of Technology, Sydney: Australasian Legal Information Institute, 244
University of Texas: Latin American Information Center, 247; School of Law, Tarlton Law Library, 108, 261
University of Toronto: Bora Laskin Law Library, 254; Project DIANA, 254
UnMozify software, 28
uploading, 5
URL. *See* Uniform Resource Locator
URL Manager Pro software, 26
Uruguay, 244
USA Law Publication, Legaldocs, 170
Usenet, archives, legal, 36. *See also* newsgroups
usgovsearch, 174
USLawcenter: Pennsylvania, Middle District, Bankruptcy Court, 129
Utah, State of: Administrative Code, 98; bills, 98; code, 98; Commerce Department databases, searchable, 213; Commerce Department forms, 167; Court of Appeals opinions, 76, 144; Court of Appeals Website, 143-144; judicial ethics opinions, 144; legislature, 98; official home page, 213; Real Estate, Division of, 213; Supreme Court opinions, 76, 144; Supreme Court Website, 143-144
utilities, disk cache, 19, 27-28
Utility Connection, The, 281
Uzbekistan, 246

V.: caselaw, comprehensive, 80; scope, 44
Venables, Delia, 248
vendors, 35

Vermont, State of: Automated Library System, 144; bills, 98; code, 144; courts Website, 213; Environmental Board and Court opinions, 77; General Assembly, 98-99; Judiciary Website, 144; Labor Relations Board opinions, 77; legislature, 98, 213; Libraries, Department of, 76, 77, 144; official home page, 213; Secretary of State filings, searchable, 213; Secretary of State forms, 167; statutes, 98-99; Supreme Court opinions, 76-77, 144; workers compensation opinions, 77

Veterans Administration Forms, 152

Veterans Affairs, Department of, 178

Villanova University, School of Law: Third Circuit opinions, 52; Tax Master, 236-237

Virgin Islands, 79

Virginia Law Resource Center, 316

Virginia, State of: Administrative Code, 98, 213; bills, 99, 213; code, 98, 213; constitution, 213; Corporation Commission forms, 167; Corporation Commission Website, 213; Court of Appeals opinions, 77-78, 144; forms, 213; General Assembly, 98; Judicial Ethics Advisory Committee opinions, 144; Judicial System Website, 144, 213; legislature, 213; official home page, 213; Securities and Retail Franchising, Division of, 213; Supreme Court opinions, 77-78, 144; Workers Compensation Commission opinions, 144

Virtual Chase, The 40

Virtual Reference Desk, 298

virus: defined, 5; protection, 5, 21

Vital Records Information, 192

Wall Street Journal, The, 266, 305

Wallace, Jordan, Ratliff & Brandt, L.L.C.: Alabama Supreme Court decisions, 60-61

Washburn University School of Law: archive, law mailing list, 277; ForInt-Law, 241; Law Library, 253; StateLaw, 88; WashLaw Web, 55, 60, 62, 88, 185, 241-242, 253, 277, 323

Washington Post, The, 305

Washington, State of: Administrative Code, 99; bills and code, 99; Court of Appeals opinions, 78, 144; courts Website, 144, 214; Financial Institutions, State Department of, 214; judicial ethics opinions, 144; legislature, 214; local resources, 214; Master Application, 167; official home page, 214; Revenue, Department of, searchable database, 214; Secretary of State filings, searchable, 214; Secretary of State forms, 167; Securities Division forms, 167; statutes, 214; Supreme Court opinions, 78, 144

Washington University School of Law: Eighth Circuit opinions, 54; Internet Chinese Legal Research Center, 246

WashLaw Web:, archive, law mailing list, 277; Arkansas appellate court opinions, 62; CLE requirements, by state, 323; DocLaw Web, 185, 253; ForInt-Law, 241-242; RefLaw, 253; state opinions, 60; StateLaw, 88, 253; Tenth Circuit opinions, 55; Website, 253

watermarking, digital, services, 228

Wayne State University Law School: Trademarks & Unfair Competition outline, 232-233

Web of On-Line Dictionaries, 300-301

Web page: e-mailing, 12; defined, 9; not found, what to do, 41-42; printing, 13

Webgator, 185, 192

WebPACER: explained, 111, 122; sites using, 116, 117, 119-121, 123, 126, 127, 129, 130, 131

WebPrint for Java software, 132

WebRACER: explained, 111, 122; sites using, 128

WebSeries Viewer software, 144

Website: defined, 9; not found, what to do, 41, 42

Webspector software, 27

WebWasher software, 8

West Group: KeyCite Citation Research Service, 40; official pagination, 44, 48. *See also* WestDoc; Westlaw; West's Legal Directory

West Virginia, State of: bills and code, 99; Court of Claims opinions, 78; official home page, 214; searchable databases, 214; Secretary of State filings, searchable, 214; Secretary of State forms, 168; Supreme Court opinions, 78, 145; Supreme Court Website, 145

WestDoc: caselaw, comprehensive, 80; statutes, state, 101

Westlaw, 44; caselaw, comprehensive, 80; statutes, state, 102

West's Legal Directory, 282

Wile E. Coyote v. Acme Company, 256

Wills on the Web, 319

Wisconsin, State of: Administrative Code, 100; Circuit Courts Website, 145; code, 99-100; Commerce, Department of, 215; Court of Appeals opinions, 79, 145; Court of Appeals Website, 145; court rules, 146; courts

Website, 214; Employment Rela-tions Committee rulings, 79; Financial Institutions, Department of, forms, 168; Financial Institutions, Department of, Website, 215; Labor and Industry Review Commission rulings, 79; legislature, 214; local resources, 215; official home page, 214-215; Register, 100; searchable databases, 215; Supreme Court opinions, 78-79, 145; Supreme Court Website, 145
Wordbot, 301
World Business Law Website, 266
World Intellectual Property Organization, 228
World News Connection, 304
World Wide Web Virtual Library, 252, 299
World's Greatest Law Review Article, The, 319
WorldSkip, 240
Wyman, James, 64, 315
Wyoming, State of: bills, 100; courts Website, 215; forms, 215; Judiciary Website, 146; legislature, 215; local resources, 215; official home page, 215; Oil and Gas Conservation Commission, 215; Rules and Regulations, 100; Secretary of State filings, searchable, 215; Secretary of State forms, 168; Securities Division, 215; statutes, 100; Supreme Court opinions, 79, 146

XBM file extension, 20

Yahoo!, 242, 294; Law, 36; News, 303; People Search, 287
Yale Law School: Avalon Project, 254; Lillian Goldman Library, 253; Project DIANA, 254
Yale University, 232; government documents, 187; local government resources, 188
Yet Another NewsWatcher, 14
Yugoslavia, the former, International Criminal Tribunal of, 243

ZDNet News: Law & Politics, 267
ZIP file extension, 148

About the Authors

Kathy Biehl (www.fortunaworks.com) maintained a solo law practice for sixteen years before turning to full-time writing and research. She has written more than 500 articles on legal, Internet, and general interest topics for national, regional, and online publications. A member of the State Bar of Texas, she has taught legal research and writing at the University of Houston Law Center and business law at Rice University.

Tara Calishain is the co-author of *Official Netscape Guide to Internet Research* (2d ed.) and author or co-author of four other books. She is the owner of Copper-Sky Writing and Research (www.CopperSky.com).